T0259674

Web Programming
with Dart

Moises Belchin
Patricia Juberias

Apress®

Web Programming with Dart

ISBN-13 (pbk): 978-1-4842-0557-0

ISBN-13 (electronic): 978-1-4842-0556-3

Managing Director: Welmoed Spahr
Lead Editor: Ben Renow-Clarke
Technical Reviewer: Matthew Butler
Editorial Board: Steve Anglin, Mark Beckner, Gary Cornell, Louise Corrigan, Jim DeWolf, Jonathan Gennick, Robert Hutchinson, Michelle Lowman, James Markham, Matthew Moodie, Jeff Olson, Jeffrey Pepper, Douglas Pundick, Ben Renow-Clarke, Gwenan Spearing, Matt Wade, Steve Weiss
Coordinating Editor: Melissa Maldonado
Copy Editor: Lori Cavanaugh and April Rondeau
Compositor: SPi Global
Indexer: SPi Global
Artist: SPi Global
Cover Designer: Anna Ishchenko

Distributed to the book trade worldwide by Springer Science+Business Media New York, 233 Spring Street, 6th Floor, New York, NY 10013. Phone 1-800-SPRINGER, fax (201) 348-4505, e-mail orders-ny@springer-sbm.com, or visit www.springeronline.com. Apress Media, LLC is a California LLC and the sole member (owner) is Springer Science + Business Media Finance Inc (SSBM Finance Inc). SSBM Finance Inc is a Delaware corporation.

For information on translations, please e-mail rights@apress.com, or visit www.apress.com.

Apress and friends of ED books may be purchased in bulk for academic, corporate, or promotional use. eBook versions and licenses are also available for most titles. For more information, reference our Special Bulk Sales–eBook Licensing web page at www.apress.com/bulk-sales.

Any source code or other supplementary material referenced by the author in this text is available to readers at www.apress.com. For detailed information about how to locate your book's source code, go to www.apress.com/source-code/.

Contents at a Glance

Contents

About the Authors

Moises Belchin has worked with Dart from its inception in March 2011, is co-author of Aprende Dart, he contributes to Dart development and debugging, works with the community, and conducts seminars and developing www.blogdart.es, the first point of reference about Dart for Spanish developers.

Moises is a software engineer with 15 years of experience and thousands of lines of code under his belt; he's an expert in cloud computing solutions, big data, and web development.

Patricia Juberias loves new technologies and graphic design. She is a multimedia engineer, specializing in information architecture, responsive design, user interface, and user experience.

As a developer she has 10 years of experience with major programming languages and platforms, she has participated in numerous projects, is co-author of Aprende Dart, and collaborates in Dart spreading.

About the Technical Reviewer

Matthew Butler is an applications developer, focusing on web-based applications. He has over 14 years of experience in the industry in various roles. Matthew has contributed source code and documentation directly to Google's Dart programming language and has been active in the Dart community since 2012. He spends his evenings at home in Nova Scotia, Canada, with his wife Julie Ann and his boys Cody and Jaxon. You can contact him at www.google.com/+MatthewButler.

Acknowledgments

We would like to thank the many people who helped to make this book possible.

Moises and Patricia would like to thank his wife, her husband, pets and friends, for their very considerable patience during the evenings and weekends while we were working on this book.

We would like to thank Ben, our lead editor; Melissa for guiding us through the process of building this book; James, Matthew, Dhaneesh, Lori and April, for the edits, reviews, and the final magic touch.

Special thanks must go to Matthew Butler, our technical reviewer. We are indebted to him for his excellent, detailed reviewing of our work and the many helpful comments and suggestions he made that contributed decisively to the quality of this book.

Thanks are also due to the Dartlang development team for creating such a wonderful programming language.

Introduction

Welcome to *Web Programming with Dart*. Early, in our careers we came to recognize how our world would change thanks to the Internet and especially to web applications. Every device we use in our daily lives uses the Internet intensively. If we consider the different sizes and characteristics of devices and the different operating systems available, we understand the complexity of software application development.

Web applications can help us with that. You develop an application and deploy it through different devices and screen sizes, but to accomplish this task you need a programming language designed to understand the web development complexity and run in different platforms. The applications must be highly optimized and support numerous options: geo-localization, notifications, upload and play media files, or the interaction between users, among others. We can develop web applications with those functionalities but the only way to develop such complex applications is by using a high-level programming language specific to Web development with support for the latest web technologies.

In this book you will master Dart, with a progressive and dynamic learning approach. It is one of the most complete books on Dart written so far and provides the basics of developing web applications using Dart, an object-oriented and structured language that supports interfaces, large hierarchy of classes, and optional typing. You will see examples and even develop your first complete web application, step by step. You will learn how to integrate Dart with CSS3 and HTML 5, combine Web Services with Dart, use Dart on the server side, implement design patterns and create web components. The book had been written with consideration for programmers who want to learn this new programming language but also for web designers because Dart can interoperate perfectly with HTML5 and CSS3.

This book is oriented to developers and web designers who want to develop high-level web applications and are sick and tired of fighting with the creation of cross-platform web applications; for everyone who needs a new, yet familiar web programming language for modern web applications and really big projects; and for developers who need a typed language for a fast, secure, and easy development and debugging process.

In the book we will travel from the most basic to the most complex functions of this language but we will also cover all the tools available to get the most of Dart. With this book you will know the language, how the tools work, and you will see the core functions and libraries. We will show you the history behind Dart and how it came to us. We will develop some UI animation samples for web, work with web services, server-side Dart applications, and the new Polymer.dart library for the new HTML UI web component generation.

- We will take a broad tour, showing the Dart basic and advanced functionalities.

- You will learn the tools that come with Dart SDK and the main, most important libraries. Additionally you will work with the newest Polymer.dart library for web component creation.

- You will be able to develop your own command-line and server-side applications and, of course, web applications with Dart.

CHAPTER 1

■ ■ ■

Dart's Flightpath So Far

In this chapter we will introduce you the Dart programming language, including how Dart functions and what Dart is. We'll see what structured programming is and how we can take advantage of it using Dart.

Dart brings us great advantages for web development. We will see these advantages compared to JavaScript or jQuery on the client side as well as Dart's most interesting functionalities.

What is Dart?

Dart is an open-source, structured, and flexible programming language developed by Google, particularly oriented for web development, but not exclusively. This new programming language has arrived to make programmers lives easy, allowing them to develop more complex web applications with better maintenance and improved performance.

■ **Note**   Structured programming is a programming model aimed at improving the clarity and the quality of the code, cutting down development time, using subroutines and three basic structures: block structures, selection structures (if and switch), and looping structures (for and while loops).

Behind Dart are Lars Bak and Kasper Lund, two of the authors of the V8 JavaScript engine for Google Chrome. For that reason the performance and efficiency of the language were two factors that were very important at the moment of developing this language.

Gilad Bracha was also involved in the creation of Dart. Bracha is the author of Newspeak Programming Language, co-author of *Java Specifications* and the second edition of the *Java Virtual Machine Development*.

Dart is a class-based, object-oriented language with simple inheritance. Dart also supports interfaces, abstract classes, and optional typing.

Don't worry about all of those terms. We will see everything in depth step by step and you will enjoy all of those advantages in a very simple way.

We have commented that Dart is an alternative for web development, especially in the client side. Currently the trend is that, programmers try to develop most of the tasks in the client side allowing the server to be smaller and faster. Thus, with a very simple, lighter server it can manage more requests per second.

Despite what it seems Dart was not developed to replace JavaScript, however it was developed to offer an additional, modern option for web development with better performance and above all for big projects in which the maintenance process is complicated.

Dart has a C-style syntax, thereby to all programming languages that inherit from it. So, if you have previously worked with JavaScript, Java, PHP, C++, Objective C, or C#, you would be very happy because you now know Dart.

Dart is the best option for really big web projects with special importance in the client side. This programming language allows for better organization of the code and you can maintain your project more easily than with others programming languages, such as JavaScript.

Dart produces a very readable code and runs in mainstream browsers (you can compile your Dart code to JavaScript and run it in all of the modern web browsers).

Dart code runs over DartVM (Dart Virtual Machine), which is two times faster than JavaScript. As you can see in Figure 1-1, Dart code compiled to JavaScript is faster than native JavaScript code running on V8 engine for the Tracer test.

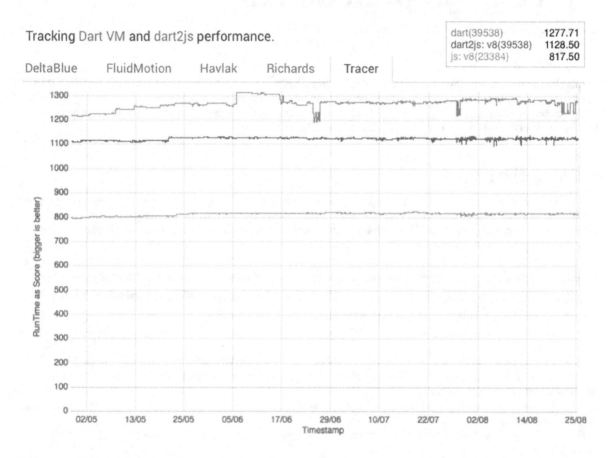

Figure 1-1. Dart VM, dart2js, and JavaScript V8 performance

■ **Note** You can learn more about Dart performance in https://www.dartlang.org/performance/

Advantages to Using Dart

One of the main advantages is its high performance. Currently, in some benchmarks, even running Dart code compiled to JavaScript is faster than JavaScript native code running on V8. Another advantage is its simplicity and clarity when you use it and most importantly when you have to learn it. Dart offers unimaginable possibilities when you need to develop and maintain big, complex applications.

Furthermore, Google Dart developers and the open-source community have created great documentation, including tutorials and samples. This is welcome when you need to start with a new programming language.

One great advantage is the ability to use a full IDE (Integrated Development Environment) just out of the box. This IDE is known as Dart Editor where you can find all the SDK, classes, and methods with their documentation, a very powerful debugger, and tools to compile and test your applications.

Dart Editor is not the only IDE you can use to work with Dart. Dart has official support for other editors like Intellij / Webstorm, Eclipse, or Sublime Text 2 and 3.

Asynchronous programming is one of the most powerful features of this new language. We will dive into this subject in coming chapters but for the moment we want to explain the basic idea of the asynchronous programming in Dart.

The asynchronous programming is made in Dart thanks to Future API, which allows you to run tasks and processes in the background without waiting to get the results of these processes. The results will come later and you'll be able to get those results and make other tasks, change the layout, or show information to the user.

We don't want to end this section without mentioning a very interesting and powerful advantage. You can use Dart to develop web applications, as we previously have said, but in addition, you can use Dart to develop command-line applications and server-side applications. You only need to have DartVM installed on your system to run your Dart applications. You can run your Dart apps on Mac, Windows, and Linux.

But not all aspects of Dart are advantages. Regardless of the documentation we have mentioned, you cannot find a lot of documentation as it applies to other programming languages like PHP or JavaScript. Dart is a very young programming language, having just reached its 1.0 stable version at the end of 2013. With the new releases 1.6 and 1.7 everything would be easier. Google and the community are making efforts to improve the Dart documentation and, we also hope to help meet the shortfalls of documentation and make the learning task easy and fun with this book.

Dart's Origins

The programming paradigm has changed a lot over the past few years. To start with the server was in charge of doing everything. When a user visits our web page (as shown in Figuserver makes database queries, makes access validatre Figure 1-2), the ion processes, builds the HTML document, and loads external resources as CSS, JavaScript scripts, images, and videos. This is happening in web applications developed with PHP, Python, JSP, or Ruby.

Figure 1-2. *Standard server-client requests scheme*

Every link you visit makes all the processes run again and finally displays an HTML document rendered by the client browser. This makes every request very expensive each time the client wants to view any resource on the server. Thinking how the web services have changed during last years, the emergence of new mobile devices and social networks, there are thousands of people trying to request something from our server.

We will have a serious problem trying to attempt all those requests. Our server won't be able to meet all the demands because every request uses a lot of time and resources. Can we do certain tasks on the client browser to allow our server to be lighter? Can we use the CPU, memory, and all the resources on the client to make certain processes?

New HTML, CSS, and JavaScript versions make it possible. Every time you browse through the Internet, access a web service, or login to your social network profile, the server sends to your browser several scripts that use your browser, your computer, and create jobs on your web browser. This makes server life easier. See Figure 1-3 to understand how the client applications make requests to the servers.

Figure 1-3. *New asynchronous server-client data requests*

These applications running on the client browser make asynchronous data requests, avoiding blocking the client, to the server. The client won't wait for the request to finish and the browser won't appear to stop responding while waiting for a blocking request. The client application could make several requests and they'll get the server information and with that information they can manipulate and change the web page showing or hiding different parts of the document. Thus we can simplify server requests and our server will take less time to complete its job, attending to more clients per second.

Thanks to these asynchronous data requests made with JavaScript and the HTML evolution we can develop a lot of process in the client side in a very simple way. We can forget old plugins like ActiveX, Java Applets, and Adobe Flash Player, because JavaScript is standard and supported by all the modern web browsers.

Imagine now an application like Gmail or Google Docs that can develop all the web user interfaces, manage all the requests, and all the events on the client web browser, that would be a very hard task to accomplish. The maintenance process of an application like Gmail would be hard and expensive even if you use JavaScript frameworks.

JavaScript was not designed for those purposes, as it is not robust enough and the code will be unreadable and obscure when you begin working with callbacks. Additional JavaScript suffers really big problems with memory management.

When they have to develop applications like Gmail, the Google developers end up asking if JavaScript was really the programming language for that purpose. They will try to find other alternatives like GWT. With GWT they acquire a more structured approach, but it had very poor performance for the web.

Dart was created in response as a programming language that combines both worlds as it has the dynamism of JavaScript with the power and structure of languages like C# or Java.

Dart will let you develop big, complex applications as you will do with Java, Python, or C#. In addition, with Dart you could develop small scripts to simplify the concrete tasks on your web pages as you can do with JavaScript.

Currently Dart can run on all the major, modern web browsers, but previously Dart code needed to be compiled to JavaScript (dart2js). In the near future Dart will run directly on our web browsers thanks to DartVM and we don't need to compile it in advance. Google Chrome plans to include DartVM so you can run your Dart applications on that browser with all the power and performance we have described.

Converting From Other Programming Languages

We have explained that Dart was designed with consideration for complex web applications, development and maintenance processes, and with special attention to its performance. In depth understanding of the language is the most important task in your TODO, which is why we wrote this book. However if you have previous experience with JavaScript or the jQuery JavaScript framework we would like to show you quickly some simple examples between JavaScript, jQuery, and Dart.

Dart Names are Simpler and More Structured

As you can see in Table 1-1 the names were simplified, more structured, and more consistent using `CamelCase` for capitalization.

Table 1-1. *Dart Vs JavaScript. The names*

JavaScript	Dart
HTMLElement	Element
ownerDocument	document
XMLHttpRequest	HttpRequest
CSSStyleSheet	CssStyleSheet

Searching for DOM Elements is Easier

With the advent of jQuery several JavaScript frameworks were inspired to query the DOM with CSS selectors (Dart does this too). The search DOM elements methods (Table 1-2), were cleaned up and it has only two methods compatible with the new HTML5 standard `querySelector()` and `querySelectorAll()`.

Table 1-2. *Dart vs. JavaScript and jQuery. DOM elements*

JavaScript	jQuery	Dart
getElementsById('id')	$('#id')	querySelector('#id')
getElementsByTagName('tag')	$('tag')	querySelectorAll('tag')
getElementsByName('name')	$('[name="name"]')	querySelectorAll('[name="name"]')
getElementsByName('name')	$('.class')	querySelectorAll('.class')

Dart Has Real Data Collections

Dart has different data types to represent data collections, `Lists`, `Maps`, and `Sets`.

In JavaScript, the data collections of DOM elements when you retrieve elements using, for example, `getElementsByTagName` are different from the built-in JavaScript Array type.

In Dart, this is easier and the methods that manipulate the DOM (for example, `children`, `nodes`, or using `querySelectorAll`) always return real data collections as Lists, Maps, or Sets. No matter what method you use you will always have built-in data collections.

Using `dart:html`, the Dart library to manipulate the DOM, when you retrieve a list of elements by tag name you will have this kind of structure `List<Element>`.

```
import dart:html
void main() {
  List<Element> my_divs = document.querySelectorAll('div');
}
```

As a result, several JavaScript methods have been cleaned up. For example, in JavaScript when you retrieve an element you have a lot of different methods to manage its attributes. As you can see in Table 1-3, with Dart you can work with the attributes of an element as you do with a regular `Map`, because Dart stores all the attributes in a `Map`.

Table 1-3. *Dart Vs JavaScript and jQuery. Real Data collections*

JavaScript	jQuery	Dart
elem.hasAttribute('name')	elem.attr('name')	elem.attributes.containsKey('name')
elem.getAttribute('name')	elem.attr('name')	elem.attributes['name']
elem.setAttribute('name', 'value')	elem.attr('name', 'value')	elem.attributes['name'] = 'value'
elem.removeAttribute('name')	elem.removeAttr('name')	elem.attributes.remove('name')

Constructors to Create New DOM Elements

If you want to create new DOM elements, in JavaScript (jQuery use the same method as well for performance) you can do it using `createElement()`. With Dart, because it's an object-oriented language, you can use a different constructor for each different DOM element (Table 1-4).

Table 1-4. *Dart vs. JavaScript and jQuery. New DOM elements*

JavaScript	jQuery	Dart
document.createElement('div')	$(document).add('div')	new DivElement()
	$(document).append('div')	new InputElement(type:'checkbox')

Dart Improves and Unifies the Events System

Events are the most important and useful to change, as you will find in Dart. The development team has changed how the events are bound with event handlers.

The DOM has two ways to work with events. The old one that binds one event handler with an element by setting one of the on properties of the element and the new one using `addEventListener()` and `removeEventListener()` that allows multiple listeners for the same event.

In Dart, things are simplified. All the on element properties are removed and it uses API `Stream` that provides a unified event model (Table 1-5).

Table 1-5. *Dart vs. JavaScript and jQuery. The events system*

JavaScript	jQuery	Dart
elem.addEventListener('click', (event) => print('click'), false);	$('#elem').on('click', function(event) {});	var eventListener = elem.onClick. listen((event) => print('click'));
elem.removeEventListener('click', listener);	$('#elem').off('click');	eventListener.cancel();

For each event type on the DOM, each element has a property to manage that event, such as `onClick`, `onMouseOver`, and `onBlur`.

Say Goodbye to Vendor Prefixes

When you are working in the client side, you know you need a widely standard application and you need it to work in all the web browsers. For that reason programmers usually work with frameworks that let them have standard problems fixed.

Working inside the browser you sometimes will find some methods have different names for each different browser and its rendered engine.

For instance, if you need to check if the browser supports IndexedDB you should ask for `window.indexedDB` or `window.mozIndexedDB` (Firefox browser) or `window.webkitIndexedDB` (Safari and Chrome) or `window.msIndexedDB` (Internet Explorer).

In Dart you won't find those options. There is only one standard way to call this method and check if indexedDB is supported in the client browser: you will only need to call `window.indexedDB`.

With this simplification we will write better, more readable code and are prone to errors. We will develop applications with multi-browser support without having a lot of checks to do.

Future-Based APIs

When you want to write asynchronous code using JavaScript you need to use AJAX and callback functions as the return result for your functions or use the callbacks as parameters for other functions. So, you will end up chaining functions. When you are working in a very complex and big project using this system produces unreadable code that is very prone to errors. The maintenance process would be unbearable.

Dart has incorporated `Future class` into its SDK. This class allows you to isolate in an object-oriented way asynchronous return results as built-in functions.

This is one of the major advantages of the language; everything is asynchronous in Dart. You will have to change the way you've been working but once you've done so you will never go back to the old callback hell.

`Future` API makes your code more readable, cleaner, and allows you to make asynchronous tasks in a very simple way.

If you had this kind of JavaScript code:

```
function showResult(xhr) {
  if (xhr.readyState==4 && xhr.status==200) {
    document.getElementById("result").innerHTML=xhr.responseText;
  }
}
function getResult() {
  var xhr = new XMLHttpRequest();
  xhr.onreadystatechange = showResult(xhr);
  xhr.open('GET', 'http://www.google.es', true);
  xhr.send();
}
```

Now with Dart your code looks like this.

```
void getResult() {
 HttpRequest.getString('http://www.google.es')
   .then((resp) => querySelector('result').setInnerHtml(resp));
}
```

Undoubtedly this is an amazing improvement that makes your job easy. As we mentioned the Future objects are used all the time in the Dart SDK; you will use them in your applications too, because Dart has been designed to be totally asynchronous.

Libraries

Dart has a great clean up and new organization regarding DOM libraries. Thanks to this new organization the library for managing DOM and HTML is lighter and simpler.

All the classes and methods for indexedDB, audio, web_sql, and svg have been taken from DOM basic library and new libraries have been created for each different purpose. Furthermore in these new libraries they have cleaned up names, deleting unnecessary and repetitive prefixes. Now each library has its own namespace making it much simpler and more efficient.

■ **Note**   A namespace is often used to refer to a collection of names that we have defined and all the names have unique identifiers.

Cross-Browser Consistency

We have already mentioned, in Dart all the vendor prefixes have been deleted, and all the libraries have been simplified and reorganized. Those changes allow us to have a simple code that runs all over the web browsers.

You don't need to add an additional framework to your projects, so you don't have an additional layer between your code and built-in language functions.

■ **Note**   Cross-Browser means web pages or applications that run and work in the same way in all the web browsers.

Cascaded DOM Construction

You will use this operator a lot. In the beginning Dart did not have this operator and it was included to simplify your daily job when you are working with DOM elements.

It's very common when working with HTML elements to decide to change several properties or attributes for one element. This kind of task produces big code blocks, repeating the same element name several times. Our code becomes illegible.

If you have to repeat the element name maybe ten times, instead of defining a very descriptive name for that element you will use a very shortened name, that will make our code less readable.

For instance, in JavaScript you will have this code.

```
var el = document.createElement("input");
el.setAttribute("id", "my_identifier");
el.setAttribute("type", "number");
el.setAttribute("value", "my_value");
el.setAttribute("name", "my_name");
```

With Dart you could set all the attributes at the same time and you could use more descriptive names for the element. Those advantages make your code more readable, auto-documented, and small.

```
var inputNumberOfChildren = new InputElement(type: 'number')
  ..id = 'my_identifier'
  ..value = '0'
  ..name='number_of_children';
```

Why Dart is Perfect for Web Development

We have various aspects we think make Dart the perfect platform for building web pages and web applications, including Asynchronous programming with Future API, cross-browser SDK, User experience, responsive design or mobile friendly, and the way you can control your applications and debug them from the start of your coding.

The asynchronous programming on web browsers arose a few years ago thanks to an Internet Explorer bug related to XMLHttpRequest object. This bug allowed developers to make requests to the server in background mode and once the results are ready they could use them to change the layout or run other tasks.

The most important part here is "in background mode" because the web page didn't wait and didn't freeze waiting to finish this task. The developers can now run a lot of tasks asynchronously and leverage the power of the browser to build the most important parts of the application like the user interface or show initial information quickly to the user, improving the user experience.

Once the asynchronous tasks are finished, the developers use this information to make other tasks, show more information to the user, or change the layout showing new blocks.

Imagine a web application like Twitter, Facebook, or Google+. You sign in and quickly you see the basic layout, the application menu with all the options, and few seconds later you begin to see your latest posts. While the browser is rendering the basic layout it made an asynchronous request to the server to get the latest news or posts. When this request has finished the application gets the retrieved information and uses it to build new HTML blocks with this information.

This asynchronous programming is now available in all modern web browsers; with JavaScript you can use the XMLHttpRequest object and build your asynchronous applications. Dart simplifies it a lot and gives this asynchronous programming the structured touch necessary for building complex and big web applications. The Future API is responsible for this. We think this is one of the most important parts of the language; in fact, all the SDK uses this same philosophy.

Thanks to this API you will build the most powerful asynchronous web applications in the easiest way ever. No matter how big your application is, with this API you can maintain your applications in the easiest possible way so far.

Until now developing web applications was like driving a car without wheels, you have brakes, an accelerator, and gears but you don't have the ability to handle the car easily. If you have developed web applications you know what we're talking about. You have the languages and the browsers but you couldn't be agile with your developments. For the few past years the browsers evolved rapidly making important changes for web developers.

Now we have Google Chrome with its Chrome Developer Tools, a very useful and important tool to make your web developments easier and allow for more control over your applications. Safari and Firefox, among other browsers, have similar applications and a lot of plugins and addons to improve your productivity.

The only thing we needed was for the programming languages to evolve too and Dart did. You now have everything you need all in one place, making your development experience amazing and extremely easy for anyone who wants to come up to Dart.

We consider this one of the most important features for a modern web programming language. Don't worry if your applications would run properly in all of the web browsers. Dart is a cross-browser language.

Your applications would be mobile *friendly*, with a *responsive design*, from the moment you start coding. In the present days is incomprehensible develop a web page, a web application with no support for all the mobile devices you can find outside. When a user visits your website from his or her phone and the web page he's visiting does not adapt the content to that device, the user could not view your web page as he expects. That bothered the user and you probably lost this user forever.

We need to write better code, we can do better and we need to improve the UX (User Experience). The only way to accomplish this task is using a better programming language; one with great tools and good manners to develop your applications, thinking in all those aspects but not making harder your development process.

Your development experience as the user experience we've mentioned must be great and simple; you only have to focus on your application and how it must works. And then your application would adapt and fit perfectly the target device, no matter if it is a phone, a tablet, an old small screen or a new one really big screen. Every device would render your web application according to the users' device, as shown in Figure 1-4.

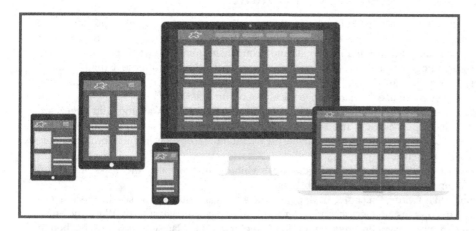

Figure 1-4. *The application adapts to different devices to provide an optimal viewing experience*

As you will see in the remaining chapters Dart has a lot of great tools to improve your development and your productivity. With those tools, and with a very simple and structured programming language you could control your applications as long as you start coding.

You can debug your applications step by step as you could do with other languages and platforms in a very simple way that lets you have the control of your applications.

No more black boxes in which you don't know how the things were working, no more using fools alerts or console logs like you have to do with JavaScript to test and debug your applications.

With the browser's developer tools everything was a very easy but you have to write your code, save it, load your web page or your application in the browser, open its developer tools, and add your breakpoints to the methods you want to test. Every time you need to test something you need to repeat that process; every time you bugfix something you need to repeat the process. It's very annoying.

This kind of work would be a memory of the past thanks to Dart. You only need to write your code in Dart Editor, set your breakpoints, and run it; that's all, and you could go step by step through your entire application, method by method, class by class or even entering from one library to another. During your debug process you always have all the local variables and objects and you can see everything that is happening.

We will see all of this mentioned in action in the coming chapters and we bet you will love these features too.

Summary

In this chapter we have learned:

Dart is a programming language:

- Developed by Google

- It would be an alternative to JavaScript

- Open-source

- With high performance

- It has its own virtual machine called DartVM

- It produces simple code and simplify maintenance tasks

- It follows structured programming model

- Cross-browser

- It could be compiled to JavaScript and run it in all the mainstream browsers.

- It emerged to support new trends that keep the server-side simple and add complexity in the client side.

PART I

Getting Started

CHAPTER 2

■ ■ ■

Setting up Dart Correctly

Now that you know and understand more about using Dart and all the utilities it brings to you, it's time to roll up your sleeves and start working with it.

We understand you may not know anything about the language yet, such as its syntax or quirks, but we think it's very important to show you the main tool you will use working with Dart, in order to take a comprehensive view of the language and the tools so you can make your tests.

Dart is extremely easy to start and has a lot of tools and very powerful SDK, but the most important advantage is that you only need to download one simple compressed ZIP file to start working with it. The first thing you need to do is get the software development kit (SDK) and the code editor (Dart Editor). In this chapter we will download and install them to become better familiar with our new software development environment. Then we're going to open our first sample application, just to have a look at the code.

Downloading and Installing the Software

The first thing you must do is visit `www.dartlang.org`, the official Dart programming language site, and get the latest version of the SDK and Dart Editor. The home page shown in Figure 2-1 will automatically detect your operating system and version in order to offer you the direct link to download everything you need to start with Dart.

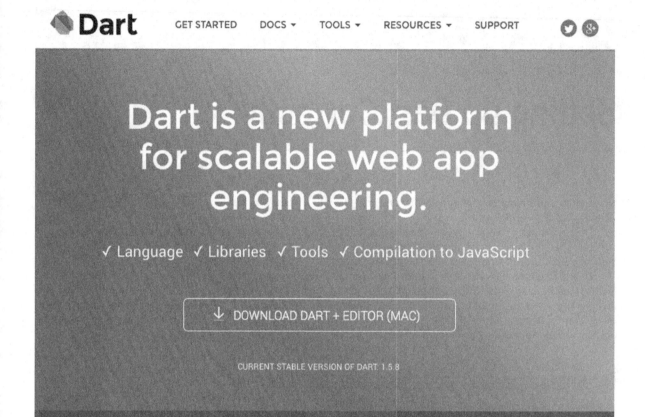

Figure 2-1. *Dartlang.org home page to download the tools*

Clicking on the download link we will start the download of a compressed ZIP file with Dart SDK and Dart Editor.

After downloading the file, you only need to unzip it. No installation is required. You do not need to follow any installation wizard steps and wait for a long time while the installation wizard does its job to enjoy your new development environment. Just download it, unzip into the directory you selected, and run it by clicking DartEditor application icon. You now have all you need to start with Dart.

Once you've unzipped the downloaded file you will see a directory structure similar to Figure 2-2.

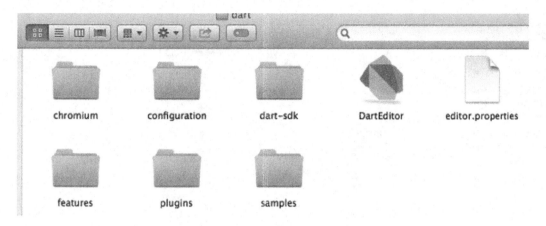

Figure 2-2. *Directory structure after unzipping the downloaded file*

At this moment we won't go into details of these directories, we just want you to start seeing and try Dart, so double click on the Dart Editor icon and it starts running.

This is the code editor you will use when you work with Dart. It is based on Eclipse, so if you know or have previously worked with Eclipse this will be very familiar.

■ **Note** Dart Editor is a Java based application. You must have Java 6 or higher for Dart to work properly. Go to www.java.com to download and install Java on your system.

When you try to run Dart Editor for the first time and don't have Java SE 6 runtime, Dart Editor will offer to install Java for you.

Setting Up a Previous Version of Dart Editor

If you have previously downloaded Dart Editor, you must check your version in order to work with the latest version of Dart SDK and Dart Editor. You can check your Dart version on Dart Editor menu and select *About Dart Editor* menu item, as shown in Figure 2-3. The *About Dart Editor* dialog will be displayed and you could check your version and if there is another most recent version available.

Figure 2-3. *Getting the new Dart version*

Click on the *Download update ...* button to get the latest and most recent version. Once the download has finished, you can apply it.

You also can check your version by clicking on the top right icon, as shown in Figure 2-3. This icon is the shortcut for Dart Editor Preferences. When a new version is available you can see a green arrow near that icon.

Clicking on that icon shows you the *Preferences* dialog (Figure 2-4) with the new update available.

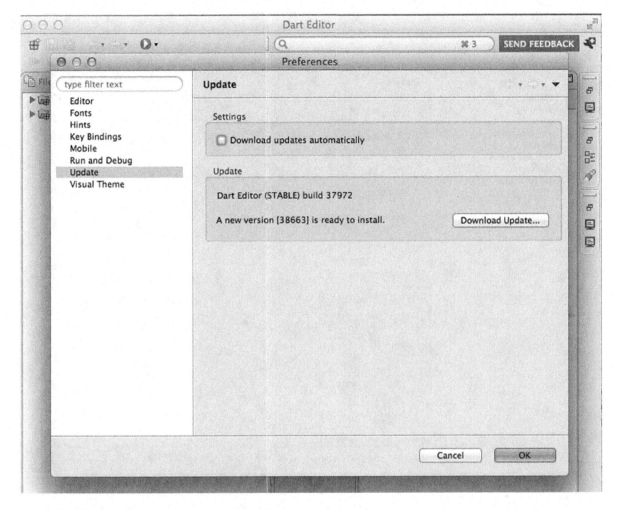

Figure 2-4. *Update preferences dialog to get the new Dart version*

In this dialog you can get the latest stable version of Dart by clicking on *Download update ...* button and you can check the option *Download updates automatically* to stay updated.

When the latest version has been downloaded and is ready to install simply click on the *Apply update* button, as shown in Figure 2-5.

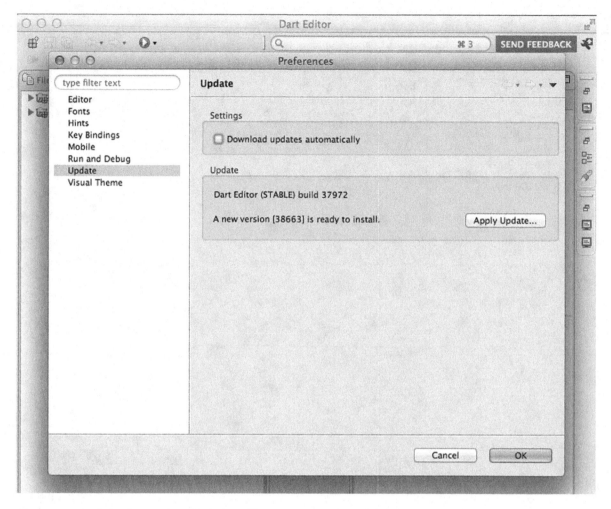

Figure 2-5. *Applying the new downloaded version*

This action will replace all the content of your installation directory with the new version just downloaded. Don't worry about your Dart Editor preferences because all of them are saved in a different place in your user home directory to avoid overriding them.

In order for this update to take effect Dart Editor will be closed and reopened again when you apply the update so be careful and remember to save all your work before applying a new update.

Dart Editor and the Software Development Environment

Dart Editor gives you everything you need; you can view the SDK directly on the editor. It helps you to develop your code and allows you to run and test your applications.

In the Dart installation directory, double click on the executable file Dart Editor ⬤. The application will be opened displaying the Welcome window, as shown in Figure 2-6.

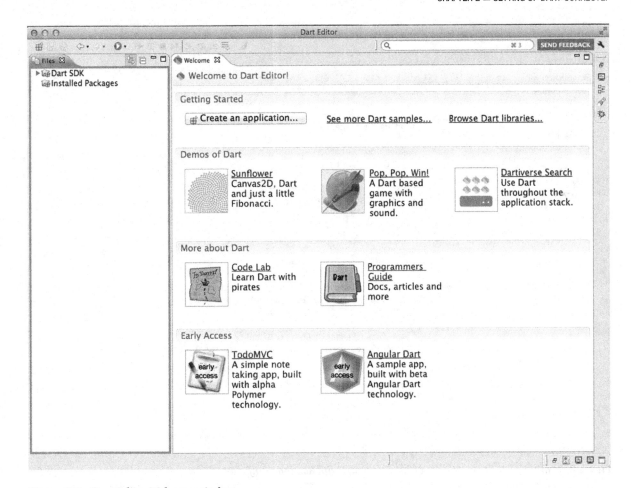

Figure 2-6. *Dart Editor Welcome window*

Opening and Running an Example

Dart Editor includes examples in the welcome page. In the section Demos of Dart simply select the first one and Dart Editor will do the rest.

The editor displays the contents of Sunflower.dart (Figure 2-7) and file view (left panel) shows the directory structure with the files of the Sunflower application.

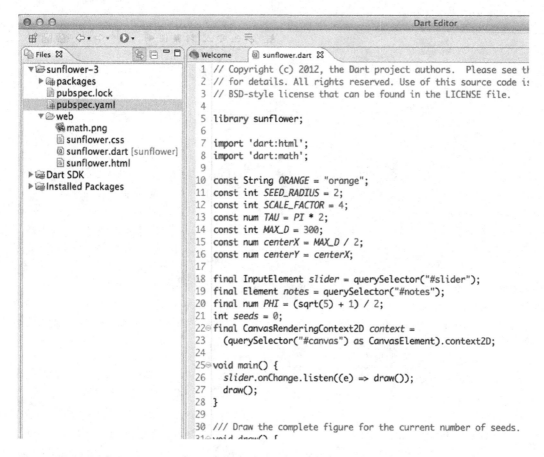

Figure 2-7. *Initial view in Dart Editor of our first sample application: Sunflower*

We do know you're eager to get started, so let's see this example running. Look at the Dart Editor toolbar and see a round green button ⊙ . This is the *Run* button, for running applications from Dart Editor.

The *Sunflower* application is a web application, so when you click on the button to run, the application will run in the web browser as if it were an HTML web page, as shown in Figure 2-8.

Figure 2-8. Dartium running Sunflower Dart application

Note that does not open your default web browser, it opens the sample application in Dartium, the web browser needed to run and test Dart applications. We'll talk about this later on Chapter *7: Optimizing for Dart VM and Dartium.*

The first time you click on the *Run* button you will need an active Internet connection to download the required dependencies.

■ **Note**   Dartium is a very specific Dart tool. Although similar to Google Chrome, please do not use Dartium as your primary web browser as you may have security and stability problems.

In Figure 2-8 you can see a slider bar. Use your mouse to drag left or right the sunflower bar and you will see how the drawn sunflower changes.

Congratulations! You've already installed the editor and all the tools you need to develop, run, and test your applications.

Creating Your First Application

Now that you've executed Dart Editor and tried to open and run a basic example, let's create our first test application. As you will see, it is really easy to create a new web application or a command line application with Dart Editor.

Creating a Web Application

First, we're going to create a simple web application. Click the button ⊞ to create new applications (it's located on the ToolBar similar to Run button) or select **File ➤ New Project**. A new window will appear (Figure 2-9) and you could select the application type you want to develop and the name you want for your first project. You must select **Web Application** as project type and named it *HelloWord*. A little different version from the famous Hello World !.

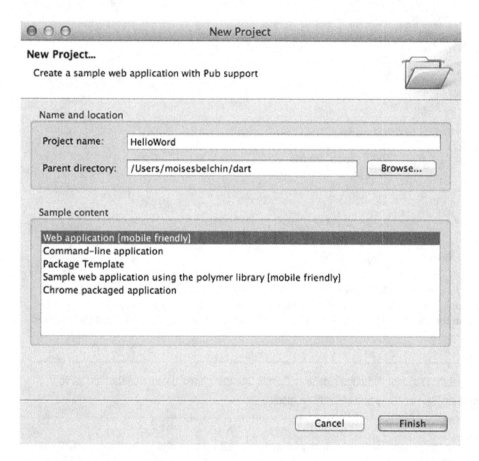

Figure 2-9. New Project dialog to create new applications

Once you've selected the type of application you want to create, Dart Editor will generate a basic structure and a small sample code. That makes it even easier to start coding. Finally click *Finish* and you will see the new project with content and sample code, as shown in Figure 2-10.

Figure 2-10. *Your first Dart web application: HelloWord*

Dart Editor has automatically created a basic directory structure for this new web application and a small sample code. Although you don't understand perfectly all the sample code, we're going to mention the most important parts to become familiar with the basics.

In this sample code you could see an import statement that imports the dart:html library to work with HMTL (because it is a web application) and creates two different methods.

The main method will be the unique and required method that all your applications will need in order to run properly and the reverseText method. Specifically this method retrieves the text of a DOM DIV element located on helloword.html file, reverses that text, and then sets it again on #sample_text_id DIV element.

Click the Run button on the toolbar and watch how Dartium runs this new application. In Figure 2-11, click the *"Click me!"* item and see how the text changes every time you click it.

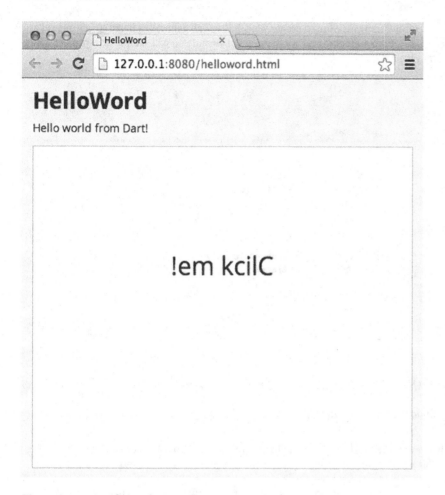

Figure 2-11. *Your first web Dart Editor project running on Dartium*

Creating Command-Line Applications

Now that you've seen the first simple web project example and have analyzed the sample code, we will create a different type of project.

Click the **New project** button to create a new application and this time in the New Project window (Figure 2-12), then select **Command-line application**.

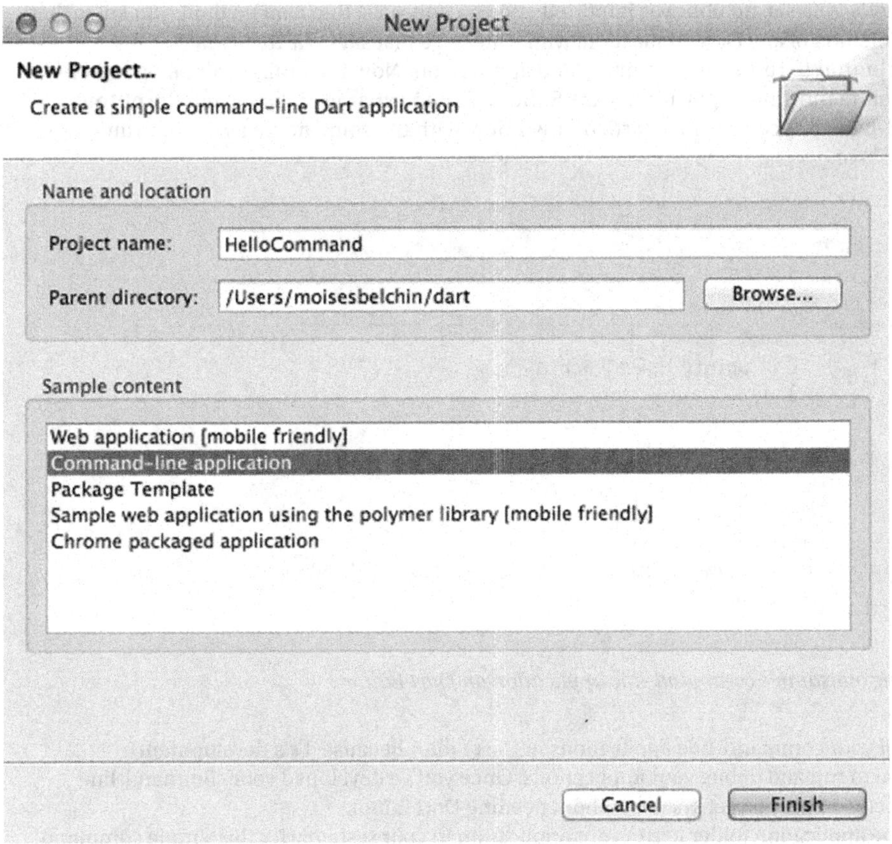

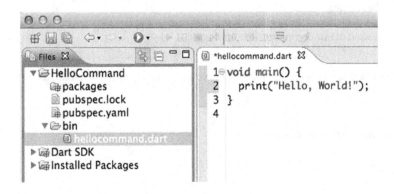

Figure 2-12. *Your new command-line application*

Similarly, Dart Editor will generate the sample content and directory structure to make our developing experience more comfortable and funny. Click the Finish button to see our new command-line project, as shown in Figure 2-13.

Figure 2-13. *Dart Editor showing our command-line application project*

In this case the sample code is easier, no library is imported and you only have the main method; you know that is the required and essential method of any Dart application, with a message that says *"Hello, World!"*.

Click again on the **Run** button to run your command-line application. Now Dartium won't be opened to show you the result of the command-line application, Dart Editor will be in charge of displaying the output messages of your command-line applications in a particular window with the same name as the file you're running, as shown in Figure 2-14.

Figure 2-14. *Result of running our sample command-line application on Dart Editor*

You can see the output of your command-line applications in Dart Editor because it's a development environment and it allows you to run and debug your applications. Once you've developed your command-line applications you can run directly on your target system without needing Dart Editor.

Go to your command-line application folder to run your application in your system with this simple command.

```
$ cd /path/to/your/command-line/application
$ /path/to/your/dart/installation/folder/dart-sdk/bin/dart hellocommand.dart
```

Change those paths with your system paths. In our particular case those commands would be:

```
$ cd /Users/moisesbelchin/dart/HelloCommand/bin/
$ /Applications/dart/dart-sdk/bin/dart hellocommand.dart
```

As you see in Figure 2-15, this will be the output of our command-line application.

```
MacBook-Pro-de-Moises:bin moisesbelchin$ /Applications/dart/dart-sdk/bin/dart hellocommand.dart
Hello, World!
MacBook-Pro-de-Moises:bin moisesbelchin$ ▊
```

Figure 2-15. *Output of your sample Dart command-line application*

Summary

In this chapter we have learned:

- how to download, unzip, and run our new development environment
- how to upgrade from an older version of Dart Editor
- how to run Dart Editor and open application samples from the Welcome view
- how to run web applications
- how to run command-line applications from Dart Editor
- how to run command-line Dart applications using your system terminal

PART II

Dart Tools

CHAPTER 3

■ ■ ■

Making the Most of the Dart Editor

A good programming language not only requires a simple, convenient, and quick syntax, or great libraries to do anything you can imagine but it also must have good documentation, a large community behind it, and a great set of tools that make you feel comfortable developing that language.

The first time you get closer to a new programming language, you want to see some code examples, read about their features and benefits, and, most importantly, you want to start working with this new programming language immediately.

In Chapter 2 described how to achieve this with Dart. You also learned how to download and install Dart Editor with all the tools and the SDK. Additionally, you could play with some examples and create your own small applications thanks to Dart.

Now we will dive into the use of the tools. This chapter is a little bit bigger than others chapters in the book because we'll show you the code editor in depth, which is the main tool you'll use all the time.

In this chapter we will see in detail the code editor and the other applications, such as compiling, package management, and documentation generation.

The Dart Editor in Detail

Dart Editor is the Dart code files editor that you'll work with most of the time. If you have previously worked or know the Eclipse development environment or any of its "friends" (Aptana Studio, Zend Studio, etc.) you're in luck! Dart Editor is a lightweight version of the Eclipse environment, as shown in Figure 3-1.

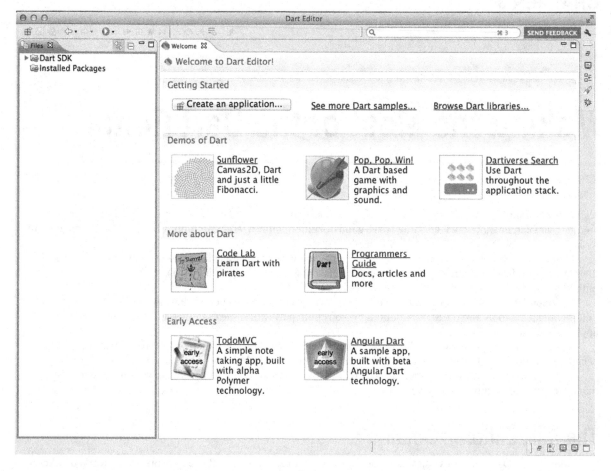

Figure 3-1. *First glimpse of Dart Editor*

Dart's development team picked up a version of Eclipse, they removed everything they considered superfluous, and created Dart Editor with the tools that are absolutely necessary for developing, debugging, and running Dart applications. If you do not know anything about Eclipse do not worry, you will learn all about it in a few minutes and see how powerful and useful it is.

Let's take a walk through our new development environment so you become familiar. You'll see it's very easy and powerful. The first time you open Dart Editor you see three main areas: left, top, and right. At the top you see the menu bar with some shortcuts to the main editor options (Figure 3-2).

Figure 3-2. *Top menu bar*

On the left is the **Files View** (Figure 3-3). In that area you see your open projects with their directories and files. You also see Pub installed packages and the SDK.

Figure 3-3. *Right left panel Files View*

On the right, the first time you open Dart Editor, you could see the **Welcome Page**, as shown in Figure 3-4. As you'll remember, we used it to open and play with some examples in the previous chapter.

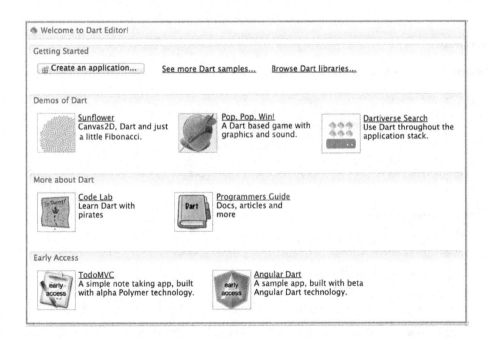

Figure 3-4. *Welcome view to open and see Dart in action*

Later in this chapter we will see all Dart Editor's views, and how to configure them in Dart Editor. For now, this overview is enough.

Opening Some Examples

We already have our development tool and we've taken a first look, so let's start playing with some of the examples on the welcome page. The Welcome Page displays some Dart examples. If you click on any of them you can open them and start see the potential of Dart. You see some Dart code samples and how Dart applications are structured, including their directories and their most important files. As you can see in Figure 3-5, we are going to open the Sunflower example to see how Dart works with the DOM and how Dart uses Canvas2D.

Figure 3-5. *Open Sunflower demo*

Click on the title of the example and see how the application appears in the Files view (Figure 3-6).

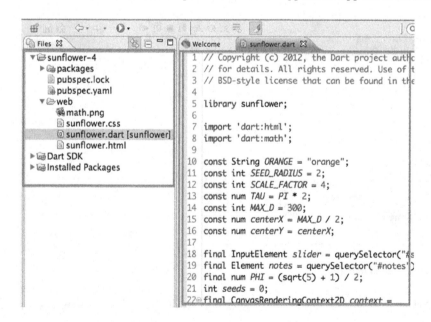

Figure 3-6. *Dart Editor loads Sunflower, the first Dart demo*

On the left panel you will see the application's files and directories. On the right, you'll see the main Dart file for this application. Every time you double click on one file it shows up in the right area.

■ **Note**   In the Files view you can also view the installed packages on your system and the full Dart SDK. This is one of the strengths of Dart, because you can browse and study the Dart SDK without leaving the workspace.

As you can see in this example, Dart applications have a web directory where we have .dart files (Dart code files), .html files (HTML files for the application), and .css files (files with the style definitions for the application template).

In addition, on this directory you can store the static files that your applications need, such as images, videos, and music.

Obviously you can organize your files and directories as you consider better options. For example, if you have a lot of css files you can make a CSS directory and put them into it. Or if you have a lot of images you can create all the directories you need to organize them properly.

The Dart applications, as you can see in Figure 3-7, have a special file called **pubspec.yaml**, where all the packages needed in our application will be defined. Automatically, Dart Editor takes care of those packages. It will find them, download them, and make them available for use. The downloaded packages will be available on the packages directory of each application. Later we will see in detail how to create and configure this special file.

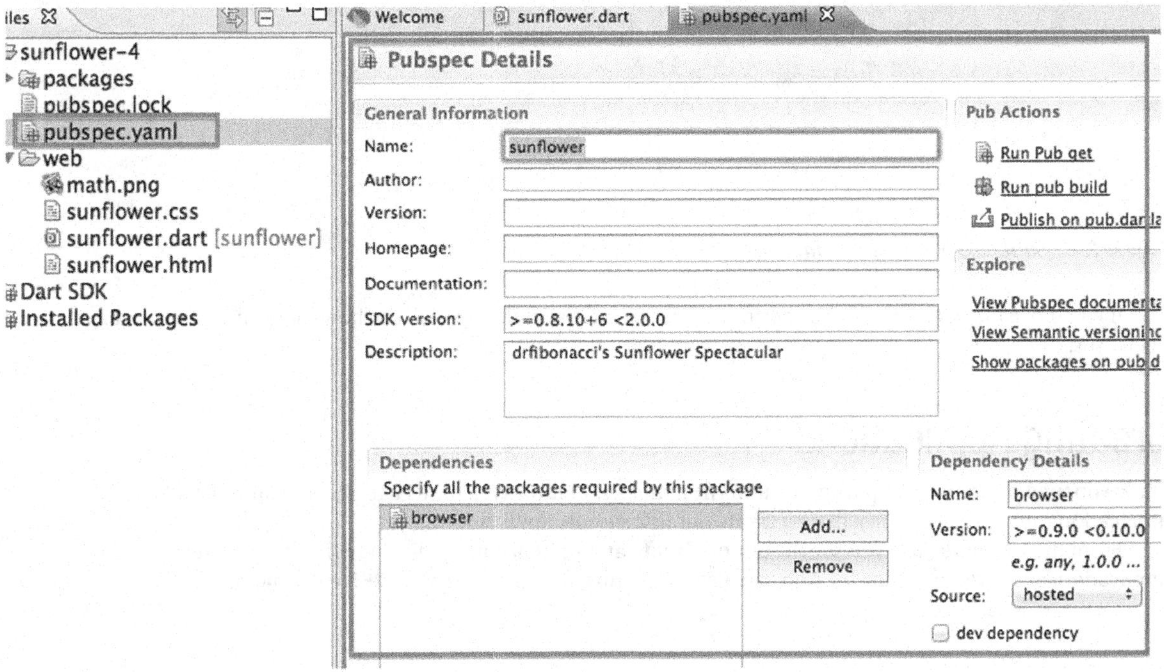

Figure 3-7. *pubspec.yaml and packages used in Sunflower*

Click the icon  located on the top menu bar. You'll see how Dart Editor opens a new browser window, called **Dartium**, where the Sunflower example will run (Figure 3-8).

Figure 3-8. *Sunflower running on Dartium*

If you move the bar located at the bottom of the example slightly, you will see how the graph increases or decreases.

Creating Applications

You've opened one of the sample applications from the Dart Editor Welcome Page and you know how Dart applications are organized. We will now create our first sample application.

From the welcome page you see the option **Create an application**. By clicking on it you will create a new application, as shown in Figure 3-9. You can also access this from the menu **File ➤ New project**.

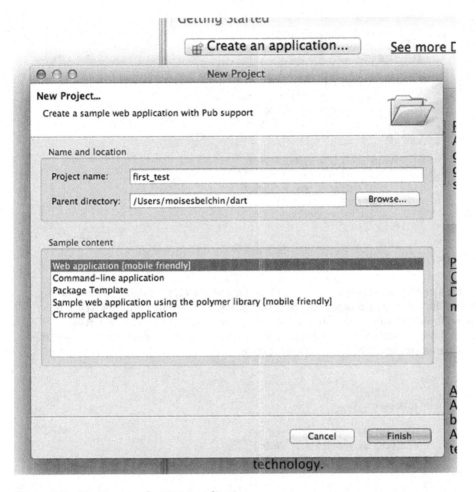

Figure 3-9. *Creating your first Dart application*

When you select the option **Create a new project**, a dialog will show up. In this dialog window you must enter the name of your new project. In our case we've selected `first_test`, select the destination folder for the project, by default Dart Editor will suggest one, and you must select the application type from the sample content frame. In this particular case, we'll select **Web application**.

■ **Note** As you see, Dart lets you create different types of applications, including web applications, command-line applications, your own libraries (Package Template), Chrome packaged applications, and web applications using the Polymer library. We will see all these of application types in the following section.

Once you've selected all the required information, Dart Editor will create your first example application with the basic directory structure, the pubspec.yaml file, and the directory that contains the required **packages**. Furthermore, Dart Editor will create the main HTML and Dart code files, as shown in Figure 3-10. If you take a quick look at the code you'll see that it imports the **dart:html** library needed to manage the DOM of the web document. It also creates two methods, main (this method is the entry point for Dart applications) and reverseText. This method will turn a string of text over.

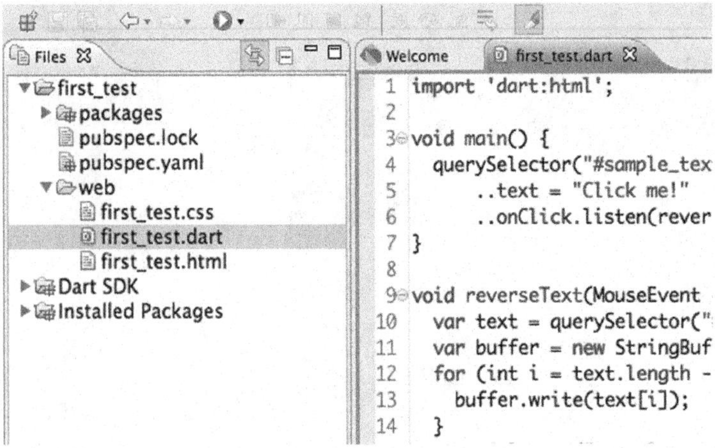

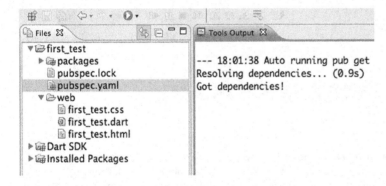

Figure 3-10. The code of your first test application

The first time you load the first_test sample application, Dart Editor automatically runs Pub (the Dart package manager) in order to download the necessary packages defined in **pubspec.yaml**. The Pub output, as well as other dart tools, will be shown in the **Tools Output** view (Figure 3-11). This view will only show up when a dart tool is running and has something to show you, but you can easily hold it if you want to see all the information from dart tools. We will see how to manage and organize the views in coming sections.

Figure 3-11. Dart Editor runs automatically Pub to download the necessary packages

Dart Editor Options and Main Views

You are familiar with your new development environment, you know how to open demos and create your own applications, before we continue testing or debugging our new applications it's time to know all the functions of Dart Editor, including its views and configuration options.

As you can see in Figure 3-12, Dart editor has a lot of views, windows, and options, but don't worry about that. For the moment we want to show you all the options you can use. Later you can configure them and add the views you need to a simple view or more complex view depending on your needs.

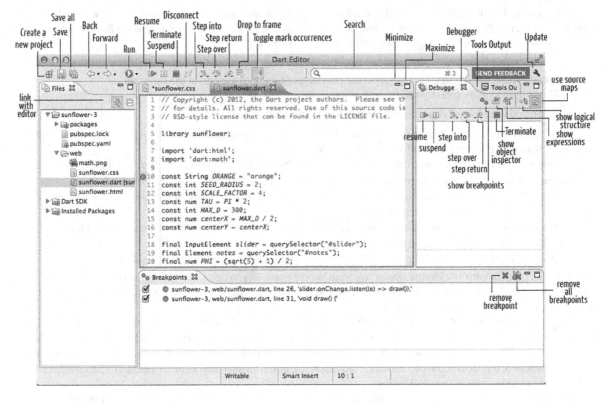

Figure 3-12. *Dart Editor options and views*

First, we will review all the options of Dart Editor and its three main areas. Later you'll learn you can have more areas. In Figure 3-13 you see Dart Editor's general options located at the top in the menu bar.

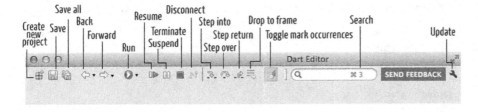

Figure 3-13. *Dart Editor top menu bar options and functions*

■ With this option you could create **new projects**.

■ **Save** the current active and open file.

■ **Save all** opened files.

⇦▾ Move to **previous file**.

⇨▾ Move to **next file**.

Those arrows let you move between all opened files. When you open several files, beside the arrow there is a drop-down menu that allows you to view all next or previous opened files and move directly to the file you select.

This is our well-known friend round green button to **Run** Dart applications.

This button will be active when you are running and debugging an application and lets you **continue running** your app from the actual breakpoint to the next breakpoint or to the end of the program.

This button lets you **pause** your running application.

And if you want to **end running** an application use this one.

The next buttons are activated when you have set breakpoints and you want to debug your application step by step. Don't worry we'll see this in detail in coming sections.

Step into button lets you to go into the function or method located in the current line. You'll go to this function or method. Once you are there you could step over or step into the lines of this function or method.

Step over button lets you continue to the next line. No matter what function or method is in this line, it will execute and Dart Editor will continue to the next line.

Step return will let you execute the body of the function or method you are in and go to the next line immediately after the end of the return statement.

Drop To Frame is a special button. With that feature you have the possibility to go back in time. You can simply go to a point in your stackframe where you have been before. So you can start debugging right at the entry point of the method. If you click on the preceding method call and click on the "Drop To Frame" button again. You can even go back to that preceding method call.

Toggle Mark Occurrences is a very useful function. It highlights all occurrences of a word you're looking for in the current file. When you have a very large code file Dart Editor helps you to quickly find what you're looking for.

The **Omnibox search** is a special search engine to find all you need in one place. It allows you to find Occurrences of the term you type, who declared this term, and who uses this term. In addition, this omnibox search function will search in Dart SDK types.

If you're looking for a "String" term the omnibox search will show you the three different types of search we've already mentioned (Figure 3-14), and all the Types in the SDK that match the word. If it finds something, it will show you the library in which it was found.

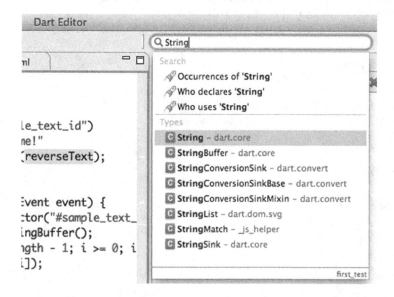

Figure 3-14. Omnibox search in action showing you "String" types and their libraries

SEND FEEDBACK By clicking this button you'll be able to send your **feedback** about Dart Editor to the development team. You also can report errors using this function. The errors you report with this option will be available in a public issue tracker located in www.dartbug.com. You can add your e-mail to your feedback or error reports in order to get a CC on the bug.

If you select this option to report an error you can attach a screenshot and additional information to help the development team with the bugs.

The wrench button is a shortcut to the Dart Editor **preferences** and to the updater function. When a new Dart Editor update is available you see a green and white arrow near to this button indicating there's a new update ready to download and install.

■ **Note**   If you placed your mouse over any of those buttons you see a tooltip showing you the name of the option and the keyboard shortcut. For example, to start searching a term on the Omnibox search you only need to type CMD+3 on MacOS or Ctrl+3 on Windows.

It's very common to get helper tools in the right panel, so Dart Editor would be divided into three main areas: at the left the Files view, at the center the Dart code files, and at the right additional views to help you with your development and debugging.

In our full Dart Editor sample screenshot (Figure *3-13*) we've shown you the **Debugger View** and the **Tools Output View**. You can use this particular configuration or add additional views that fit your needs. We're going to use this particular configuration to show you the Debugger View options and how you can stack up all the views you need (Figure 3-15).

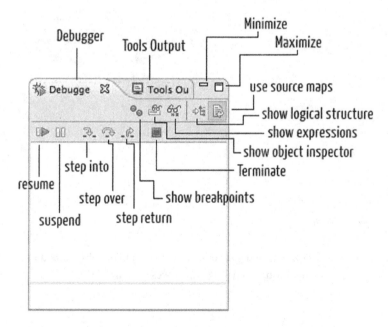

Figure 3-15. *Debugger and Tools output views*

As we previously saw, in the Debugger view you have shortcuts to the main debug functions. The resume, suspend, and stop buttons. The step-by-step debugging buttons with the step into, step over, and step return buttons. Furthermore, in this view you can find these new function buttons.

This button will show you a special view called **Breakpoints view** with all the breakpoints you have set in your code files. We'll see this view later.

The **object inspector** button will show you a new view with all the information regarding any object, as shown in Figure 3-16.

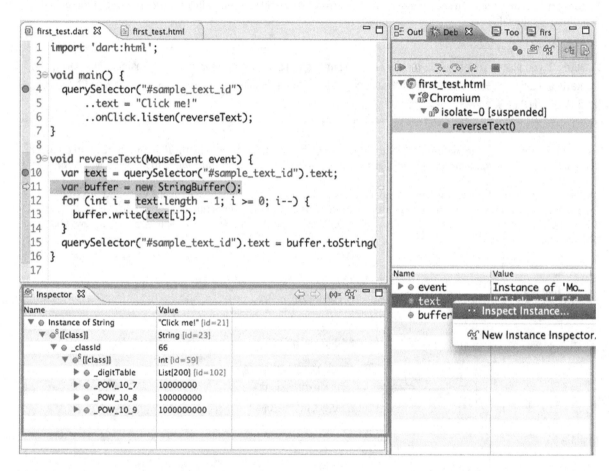

Figure 3-16. *Inspecting a String object in the object inspector*

Show expressions button will show a new special view in which you could add any variable, object, function, method, or statement you need in order to evaluate or execute during the debugging process (Figure 3-17).

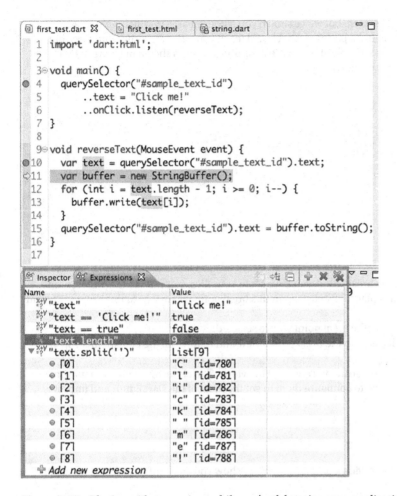

```dart
  first_test.dart ☒    first_test.html    string.dart
 1  import 'dart:html';
 2
 3⊖ void main() {
 4    querySelector("#sample_text_id")
 5        ..text = "Click me!"
 6        ..onClick.listen(reverseText);
 7  }
 8
 9⊖ void reverseText(MouseEvent event) {
10    var text = querySelector("#sample_text_id").text;
11    var buffer = new StringBuffer();
12    for (int i = text.length - 1; i >= 0; i--) {
13      buffer.write(text[i]);
14    }
15    querySelector("#sample_text_id").text = buffer.toString();
16  }
17
```

Inspector	Expressions ☒			
Name		Value		
"text"		"Click me!"		
"text == 'Click me!'"		true		
"text == true"		false		
"text.length"		9		
"text.split('')"		List[9]		
[0]		"C" [id=780]		
[1]		"l" [id=781]		
[2]		"i" [id=782]		
[3]		"c" [id=783]		
[4]		"k" [id=784]		
[5]		" " [id=785]		
[6]		"m" [id=786]		
[7]		"e" [id=787]		
[8]		"!" [id=788]		
➕ Add new expression				

Figure 3-17. *Playing with expressions while you're debugging your application*

Simply click the **Add new expression** button to add a new expression and you immediately will see the result of the expression. In *Figure* 3-17 we've added one variable to see its content, we've made some comparisons, and we've used a few methods of the string objects, namely, length and split. The string length method will return the length of the string. The string split method will split the string by a separator you specify and return a list of elements. We will explore all those methods in depth later in this book.

Show logical structure will show you the information you need to know about any object when you're debugging your applications. You don't need to know the internal representation of a List object; you need to know how many elements there are in the list and what each element contains. By activating this option you will see this kind of information instead of the internal representation of the objects.

When using **Source Maps** button you can see the original lines of code when a problem arises. As we mentioned and we'll see in the next section you could compile your application from Dart to JavaScript in order to distribute your applications. When you compile your application a .map file is generated and this .map files help Dart Editor to translate from one compiled line of code to the original line of code. For example, line 42 in your original code will be line 1456 in compiled code.

In previous figures and in our full sample screenshot we've shown you a bottom area in which we've placed Object inspector, the Expression views and the Breakpoints view. As we'll teach you, you can easily configure your views and place them wherever you want. Let's talk now about the **Breakpoints view**, as shown in Figure 3-18, in which contains our full Dart Editor sample screenshot.

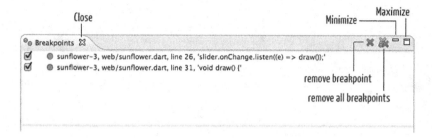

Figure 3-18. *Breakpoints view*

The breakpoints view will show you all the breakpoints you have set in your files, you can see the project name, the file name, and line where the breakpoint is placed. By clicking in this breakpoint you will go to this project, file and line.

    Remove breakpoint button will remove the breakpoint you've selected.

    Remove all breakpoints button will clean up the Breakpoints view and remove all the breakpoints you've set in your code.

We want you to show three special buttons that are present in all the views. The close, minimize, and maximize buttons. We'll talk later about each view and how to configure them to get the most of the Dart Editor and improve your developments.

Preferences and Views

You have learned the main Dart Editor functions, views, and tools. Let's see how you can configure the editor and predefined views.

If you want to see all the available views in Dart Editor, you can display them using the **Tools** menu, as shown in Figure 3-19.

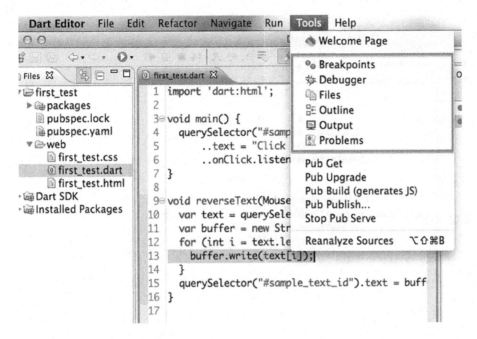

Figure 3-19. *Dart Editor views*

    Breakpoints: view that lets you to have quick access to the breakpoints set in your projects.

    Debugger: is the view that we used in the previous sections and it lets you work with the Dart Editor Debugger.

    Files: you've seen this view the first time you ran Dart Editor. In this view you can inspect the SDK, the installed packages and all files and directories of your projects.

    Outline: One of the most commonly used views. It provides a quick glance (Figure 3-20) at all the classes and methods and lets you go to any method or class by clicking on it.

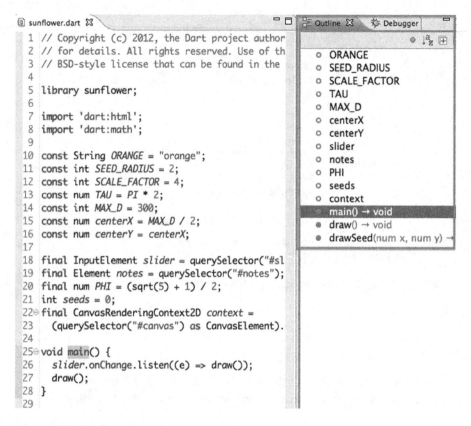

```
1  // Copyright (c) 2012, the Dart project author
2  // for details. All rights reserved. Use of th
3  // BSD-style license that can be found in the
4
5  library sunflower;
6
7  import 'dart:html';
8  import 'dart:math';
9
10 const String ORANGE = "orange";
11 const int SEED_RADIUS = 2;
12 const int SCALE_FACTOR = 4;
13 const num TAU = PI * 2;
14 const int MAX_D = 300;
15 const num centerX = MAX_D / 2;
16 const num centerY = centerX;
17
18 final InputElement slider = querySelector("#sl
19 final Element notes = querySelector("#notes");
20 final num PHI = (sqrt(5) + 1) / 2;
21 int seeds = 0;
22 final CanvasRenderingContext2D context =
23    (querySelector("#canvas") as CanvasElement).
24
25 void main() {
26    slider.onChange.listen((e) => draw());
27    draw();
28 }
29
```

Outline view options:
- ORANGE
- SEED_RADIUS
- SCALE_FACTOR
- TAU
- MAX_D
- centerX
- centerY
- slider
- notes
- PHI
- seeds
- context
- main() → void
- draw() → void
- drawSeed(num x, num y) →

Figure 3-20. Outline view

■ **Output**: you'll see the output of your projects in this view (Figure 3-21). It's useful mostly for command-line applications. When you run your command-line applications all the information will be shown in this window and the name of the tab will change from Output to the application's name.

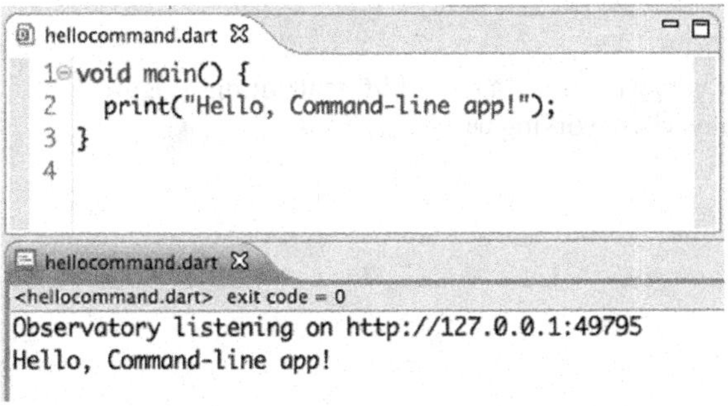

```
hellocommand.dart ⊠
1⊖ void main() {
2     print("Hello, Command-line app!");
3  }
4
```

```
hellocommand.dart ⊠
<hellocommand.dart> exit code = 0
Observatory listening on http://127.0.0.1:49795
Hello, Command-line app!
```

Figure 3-21. *Output view*

■ **Problems**: This view (Figure 3-22) lets you see any errors or problems existing in your applications and access it quickly by double clicking.

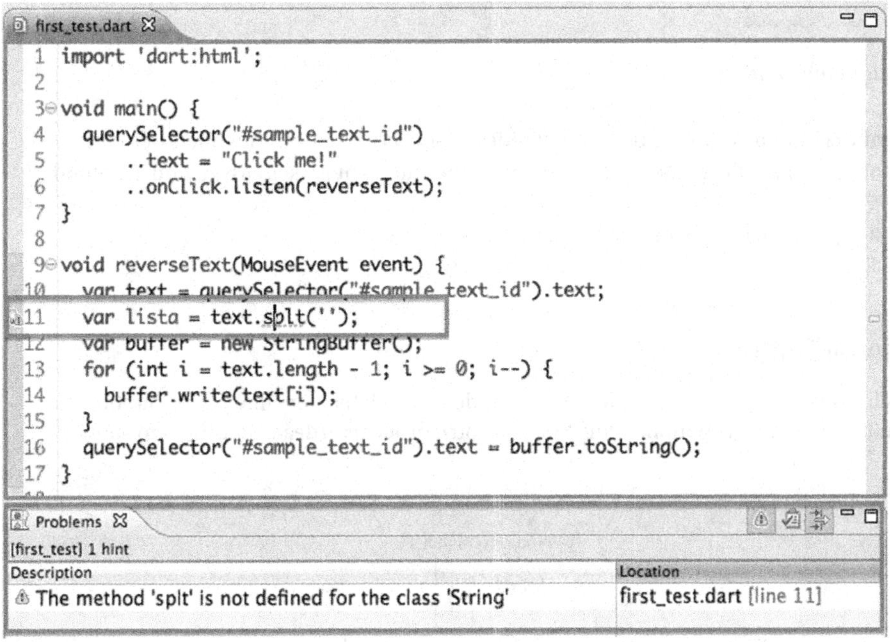

```
first_test.dart ⊠
1   import 'dart:html';
2
3⊖ void main() {
4     querySelector("#sample_text_id")
5         ..text = "Click me!"
6         ..onClick.listen(reverseText);
7  }
8
9⊖ void reverseText(MouseEvent event) {
10    var text = querySelector("#sample_text_id").text;
11    var lista = text.splt('');
12    var buffer = new StringBuffer();
13    for (int i = text.length - 1; i >= 0; i--) {
14      buffer.write(text[i]);
15    }
16    querySelector("#sample_text_id").text = buffer.toString();
17  }
```

Problems ⊠	
[first_test] 1 hint	
Description	Location
⚠ The method 'splt' is not defined for the class 'String'	first_test.dart [line 11]

Figure 3-22. *Problems view*

Outline View Additional Buttons

The outline view is a view you'll use a lot and it's worth to know very well. It has a few additional buttons (Figure 3-23) that let you manage this view and make your life easier especially when working with large files.

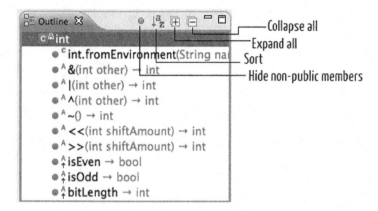

Figure 3-23. *Outline view's additional buttons*

⊙ **Hide non-public members** button is a toggle button that hides or shows non-public members of a class.

↓ᵃ𝓏 **Sort** button lets you sort in alphabetical order all the content of the Outline it makes easy to find a method, constant, or instance variables.

⊞ **Expand All** button will expand all the classes in the Outline view.

⊟ **Collapse All** button will collapse all the classes in the Outline view.

Problems View Additional Buttons

As you know all the problems in your projects will be shown in this window, which has very interesting buttons, as shown in Figure 3-24. These buttons are toggle buttons, which means you can activate/deactivate them to show or hide tips and tasks.

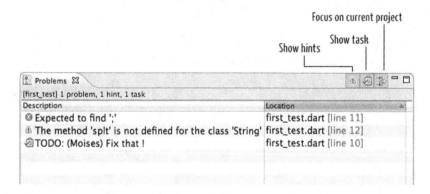

Figure 3-24. *Problem view's additional buttons*

Show hints will show you the advice from Dart Editor not only the errors.

Show tasks will show you the tasks you add to your code. If you want to add a task to tour code you only need to write a comment line with TODO word.

```
  8
  9⊖ void reverseText(MouseEvent event) {
◎10    // TODO: (Moises) Fix that !
```

Figure 3-25. *Adding tasks to Dart Editor problems view*

By clicking **Focus on current project** button you can see only the errors, tips, and tasks for the active project. If you deactivate this button you'll see all the errors, tips, and tasks for all the projects you have opened in Dart Editor.

Setting Up the Views

Now you know the main available views in Dart Editor. We will teach you how to configure views to create a comfortable workspace.

When you select a view in Dart Editor through **Tools** menu it could be appear in the left side, in the right side, or in the bottom of Dart Editor. This layout may be a problem because you'll end up with a chaotic workspace. The good news is you can configure and place your views as you want and wherever you want. You just have to click on the view's name tab and drag it to any other part of editor. You'll see how you can anchor each view at the right, left, or bottom area (Figure 3-26).

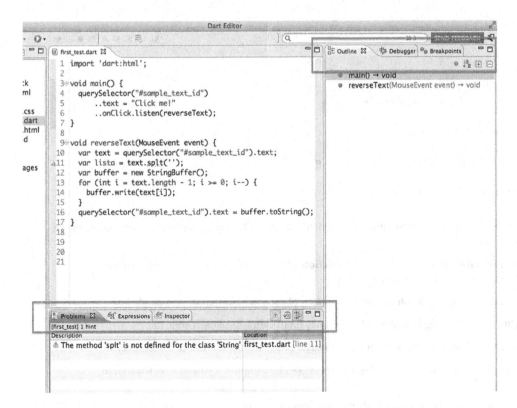

Figure 3-26. *Anchoring views to the bottom and to the right side panel*

When you have clicked the view's name tab and you're dragging it, Dart Editor will show you an arrow indicating where to place the selected view.

Dart Editor Preferences

The main functions of Dart Editor can be configured through the **Tools ➤ Preferences** menu, as shown in Figure 3-27.

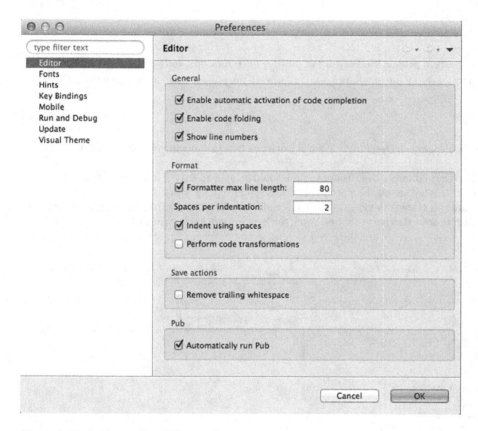

Figure 3-27. *Setting up Dart Editor preferences*

As you can see this window has several options in the left side panel. **Editor** preference will let you configure some options related to the code editor.

- **Enable automatic activation of code completion** will perform code completion proposals while you're writing your code and type a dot.

- **Enable code folding**. Code folding allows sections of code to be collapsed to a single line.

- **Show line numbers**. Toggle line numbers display on the left side of each code file.

- **Formatter max line length** will show you a vertical line at the max line length you specify.

- **Spaces per indentation**. Number of spaces to use per indentation if you've selected Indent using spaces.

- **Indent using spaces**. Indent your code using spaces instead of tabs.

- **Perform code transformations**. It performs behavior-preserving code transformations.

- **Remove trailing whitespace**. Cleans up your code of trailing whitespaces on save.

- **Automatically run Pub**. This option will automatically run Pub when you save, when you open a new folder, or when you create a new project.

Fonts preferences will allow you to change the font and size for the code editor and for the views, as you can see in the Figure 3-28.

Figure 3-28. *Fonts preferences*

Hints preferences allow you to configure what type of tips you want to see while you're working with Dart Editor, as shown in Figure 3-29.

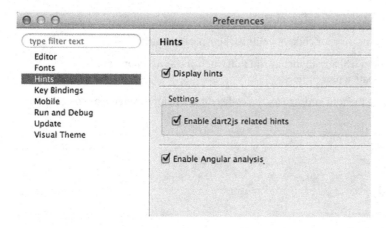

Figure 3-29. *Hints preferences*

Display hints will show you hints in the editor window and optionally in the problems view.

The **Enable dart2js related hints** will show you hints when your code will be compiled into JavaScript.

Finally the **Enable Angular analysis** option will allow you to enable/disable the Angular analysis and is also useful if you're working with Angular Dart.

The **Key Bindings** option is necessary to change the default keyboard shortcuts for any of the options available in Dart Editor (Figure 3-30).

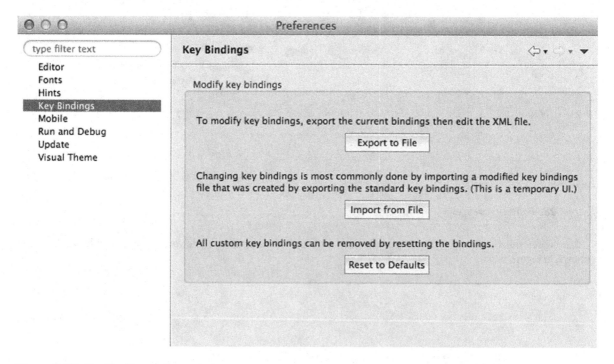

Figure 3-30. *Key Bindings preferences*

As you can see in the previous figure you can export the current bindings, modify the XML file, and then import it again into Dart Editor.

Mobile is a new preference incorporated with Dart Editor in the newest versions (Figure 3-31). With the responsive design coming up, Dart Editor provides the option to develop applications for mobile devices.

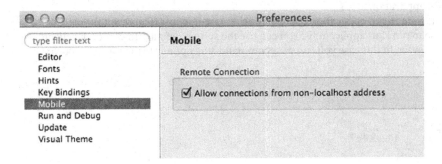

Figure 3-31. *Mobile preferences*

When working and running applications with Dart Editor, Dartium is the default browser used to run and debug your projects. Dart Editor has its own web server and with the **Allow connections from non-localhost address** option you can connect to this internal web server from any mobile device to test your applications.

Run and Debug allow you to configure certain options related to debugging or launching processes, as shown in Figure 3-32.

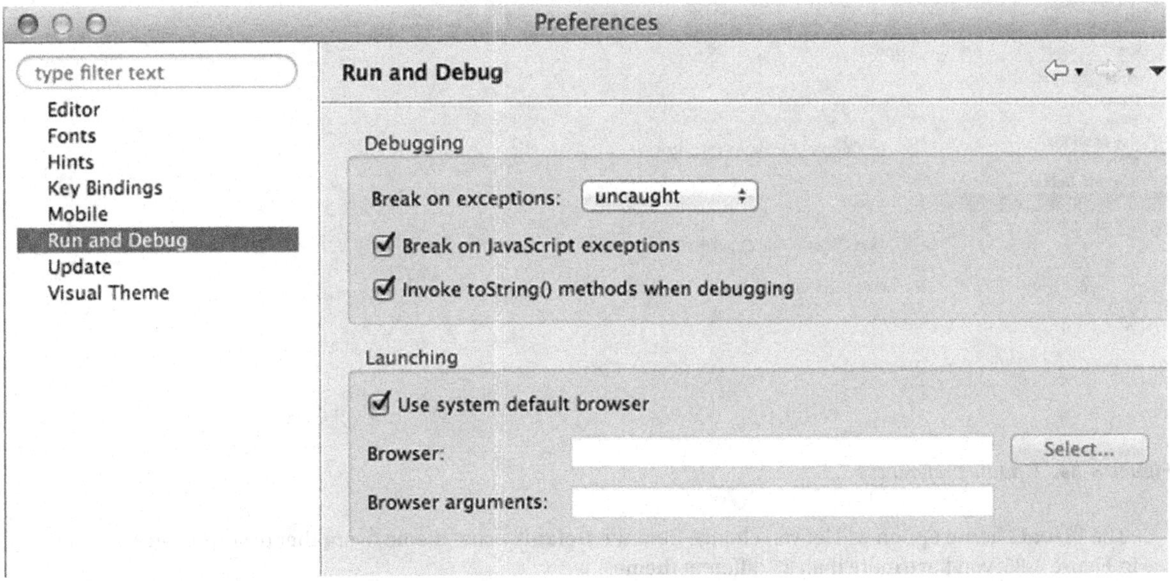

Figure 3-32. *Run and Debug configuration options*

Break on exceptions could take one of three different values: uncaught, none, and all. With this option you could define the behavior of the Dart Editor debugger.

For debugging you can configure whether to stop when a JavaScript exception occurs while running an application by clicking the option **Break on JavaScript exceptions**. This is useful when you use compiled code.

Invoke `toString()` methods when debugging option will auto execute `toString()` methods over the different objects when you're debugging your applications.

As we mentioned, Dart uses Dartium to run applications but in launching preferences (Figure 3-33), you can decide what browser you want to use to run Dart applications. You can use the system default browser or deactivate this option and use your own web browser. In this case you can pass command-line options to the browser you've selected.

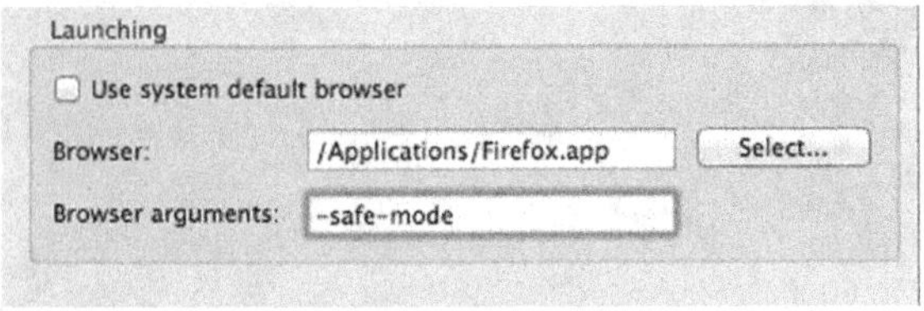

Figure 3-33. *Run a different web browser*

The **Update** option (Figure 3-34) allows you to decide if you want to download available updates automatically. In this preference window you can see your current version and access the new ones when they're ready to download and install.

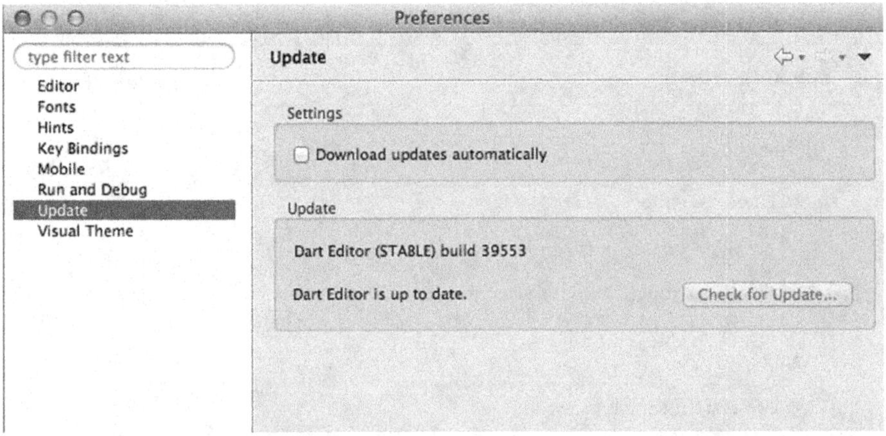

Figure 3-34. *Update preferences*

The **Visual Theme** option will let you change from the **Default** visual theme to another of your choice. As you can see in Figure 3-35, you have more than 25 different themes.

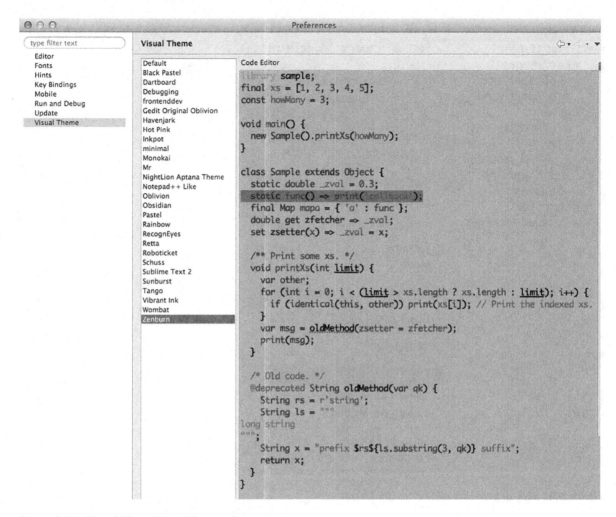

Figure 3-35. *Visual Theme Dart Editor preference*

Running Applications

As demonstrated previously, to run an application in Dart Editor you can press the green button **Run Application**, press **CMD + R** for MacOS, **Ctrl + R** on Windows, or click the menu **Run ➤ Run**. You also can place your mouse over the main dart file of your application, as you can see in Figure 3-36, **right click**, and select **Run in Dartium**.

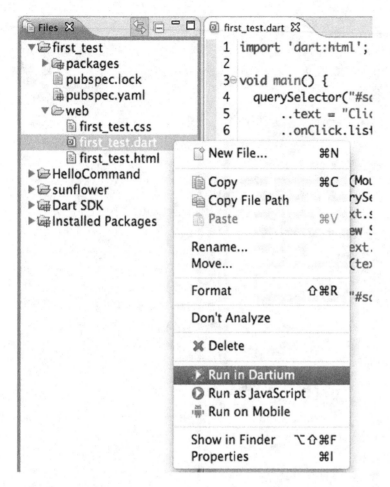

Figure 3-36. *Run an application use contextual menu*

With any of those methods, the dart application that you have opened in Dart Editor will run on Dartium.

■ **Note** Dartium is the default web browser used to run Dart applications because it has integrated the Dart virtual machine. This allows faster development iterations without the need to compile after each change.

How Does this Sample Application Run?

When you launch the application, Dart looks for the HTML file associated with this web application. It will load this file and all the files referenced within this HTML file (Figure 3-37), so it will load .dart, styles (.css), images, and videos.

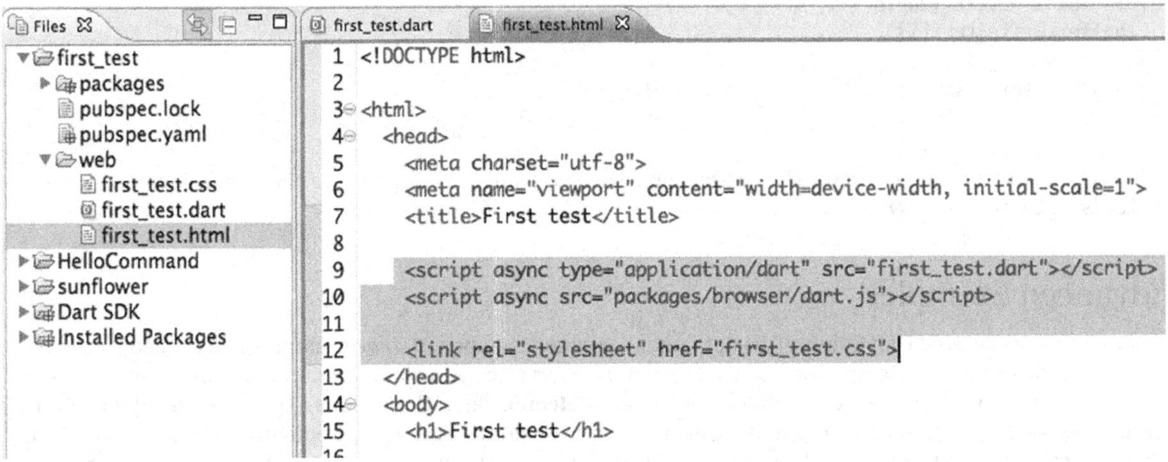

Figure 3-37. Main HTML file

In our first test application Dart also loads the **browser** package because it's necessary to properly run our application and we have it invoked in our HTML file. After loading the HTML file, Dart Editor loads the references to Dart files.

■ **Note**   We use async in the script tags to speed up the initial load.

In this example, Dart loads the file first_test.dart and starts executing the main method located in this file.

```
import 'dart:html';

void main() {
  querySelector("#sample_text_id")
    ..text = "Click me!"
    ..onClick.listen(reverseText);
}
```

The main method retrieves the paragraph element (<p></p>) sample_text_id from the first_test.html file. Set "Click me!" as this item text and binds the execution of reverseText method to the **click** event.

When you click on the `<p id="sample_text_id">Click me !</p>` element, the **reverseText** method is executed.

```
void reverseText(MouseEvent event) {
  var text = querySelector("#sample_text_id").text;
  var buffer = new StringBuffer();
  for (int i = text.length - 1; i >= 0; i--) {
    buffer.write(text[i]);
  }
  querySelector("#sample_text_id").text = buffer.toString();
}
```

This method turns the text of the `<p></p>` element over and then it sets again in the paragraph element `<p id="sample_text_id"></p>`.

Advanced Examples

Now that you've mastered Dart Editor, all its options and preferences, opened some examples, and created your own test applications, we would like to show you the full power of Dart through advanced examples. If we come back to the Welcome page, you can use the **Tools** menu and select **Welcome Page**. There is one application called **Pop, Pop, Win!** in the demo of Dart section and another called **Dartiverse Search**. As a brief introduction, we want to show you what Dart can do, including both the language and the tools with which you will work. Are you ready? Let's start with **Pop, Pop, Win!**. Open the Welcome Page in Dart Editor, select **Tools ➤ Welcome Page** and select the **Pop, Pop, Win!** Demo (Figure 3-38) to load all the files in Dart Editor.

 Pop, Pop, Win!
A Dart based game with graphics and sound.

Figure 3-38. *Select and open Pop, Pop, Win! demo*

Once it's open, you will see the magnitude of this application (Figure 3-39) and how they have organized and structured code and additional elements, such as audio and images.

```
 Files ☒              ⚙ ⊟ ⌐ □        index.html ☒
▼📂 pop_pop_win                    1  <!DOCTYPE html>
  ▶📦 packages                     2  <html lang="en-us">
    📄 pubspec.lock                3    <head>
    📄 pubspec.yaml                4      <meta charset="utf-8">
  ▶📁 chrome_app                   5      <title>Pop, Pop, Win!</title>
  ▼📁 lib                          6      <link rel="shortcut icon" href="favico
    ▼📂 assets                     7      <link rel='stylesheet' type='text/css'
      ▶📁 audio                    8      <link href='http://fonts.googleapis.co
      ▶📁 images                   9      <meta name="viewport" content="width=d
        📄 style.css              10      <script type="application/dart" src="g
    ▼📂 src                       11      <script src="packages/browser/dart.js"
      ▶📁 game                    12    </head>
      ▶📁 stage                   13    <body>
        📄 audio.dart [pop_pop_wi 14      <canvas id='gameCanvas' width='2048' h
        📄 game.dart [pop_pop_wi  15      <div id='popup'>
        📄 game_manager.dart [po  16        <div id='about'>
        📄 game_storage.dart [pop 17          <h1>About</h1>
        📄 platform.dart [pop_pop 18          <p class="difficulty">Set Difficul
        📄 stage.dart [pop_pop_wi 19          <p>Developed with <a href="http://
      📄 platform_target.dart [pop 20        </div>
      📄 pop_pop_win.dart [pop_p  21        <div id='help'>
    ▼📂 web                       22          <h1>Help</h1>
      🌐 favicon.ico              23          <img src='packages/pop_pop_win/ass
      📄 game_web.dart            24          <p>Click on balloons to pop them.<
      📄 index.html               25          <p>A revealed number tells you how
      📄 platform_web.dart [pop_p 26          <p>The count includes squares abov
    📄 LICENSE                    27          <p><em>One of these balloons is a
    📄 readme.md                  28          <img src='packages/pop_pop_win/ass
  ▶📦 Dart SDK                    29          <p>If you're certain a balloon is
  ▶📦 Installed Packages          30          <p>Freeze a balloon by shift- or r
                                  31          <p>Every time you freeze a balloon
```

Figure 3-39. *Directory and file structure of Pop, Pop, Win! demo*

As you can see, there are libraries and many classes to enjoy this great application. Don't be scared; for now, let's enjoy this game.

Click the **Run application** button and watch as the game loads. Then you just have to click on the balloons (Figure 3-40) that you want to explode. The operation is similar to the popular game *"Minesweeper"*.

Figure 3-40. *Playing Pop, Pop, Win! dart demo*

The game effects are really awesome: the dart flying, the exploding balloons, the audio, and other details are very elaborate. It shows that it is possible to start developing games in a native web platform thanks to Dart and the new features of HTML5 and CSS3.

Let's see now the **Dartiverse Search** example, which uses Dart to run a http server, and displays a home page with a search box to find terms related to Dart on StackOverflow and GitHub. At first it seems very simple, but the power of this example is how Dart is also useful to develop on the server side. To run this sample, open the **bin/server.dart** file and select **Tools ➤ Pub build (generates JS)** (Figure 3-41).

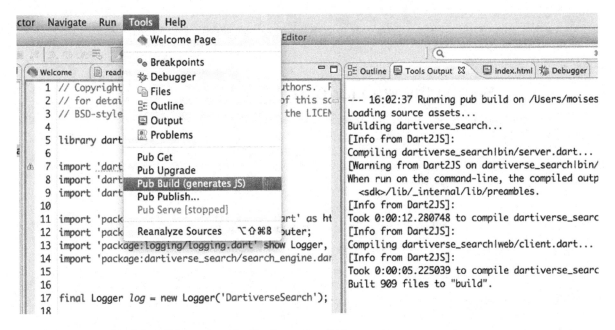

Figure 3-41. Running Pub Build command for Dartiverse Search demo

When **Pub Build** command has finished, click the **Run Application** button. After a few seconds you will see this initial message in the Output view (Figure 3-42).

```
INFO: 2014-09-01 16:05:40.791: Search server is running on 'http://127.0.0.1:9223/'
```

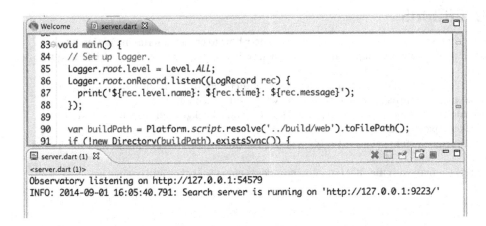

Figure 3-42. Running Dartiverse Search demo

That tells you that the server is running on the http://127.0.0.1:9223/ address. Open your browser and load this URL. You'll see a screen with a search box to locate resources related to Dart.

We searched the term "server dart" to locate more information about Dart on the server side and these are the resources we found (Figure 3-43).

Search the Web for Dart

Search StackOverflow and GitHub for Dart-related topics and repositories.

(server dart   ⊗)

server dart: 3 results found

Github

Dart fullstack (client + server) blog
sample using Polymer + MongoDB
+ websocket

Github

A sample Docker image of a Dart
server

Github

A client + server routing library for
Dart

This app sends your search request to a server-side Dart application, which forwards the
request to StackOverflow and GitHub.

Figure 3-43. *Searching for "server dart" in the Dartiverse Search demo*

Debugging Applications

We've shown you advanced samples written in Dart and you already know how to create and run in Dartium your own web projects. But you still don't know anything related to Dart syntax. It's time to show you how to debug your applications.

Let's go to the next level. We're going to modify our first test application by adding some new simple features to reverseText method. As you've seen, it turns a text paragraph over when you click on it.

What do you think if we add some color to this sample? The idea is to add a background color to the text paragraph every time you click the paragraph.

Inside the HTML file there is an element called <div id="sample_container_id"></div> that is the container of the paragraph.

We're going to retrieve this element with the DOM method document.querySelector and change its backgroundColor property.

This is our new application.

```
import 'dart:html';
import 'dart:math'; // Math library necessary for Random functions.

void main() {
  querySelector("#sample_text_id")
    ..text = "Click me!"
    ..onClick.listen(reverseText);
}
```

```
void reverseText(MouseEvent event) {
  // Change container background color
  var list = ['#5a82d7', '#d35a5a', '#d75a5a' , '#5ad7d5', '#5ad773', '#d7cf5a'];
  var index = new Random().nextInt(list.length - 1);
  var color = list[index];
  var container = querySelector("#sample_container_id");
  container.style.backgroundColor = color;

  var text = querySelector("#sample_text_id").text;
  var buffer = new StringBuffer();
  for (int i = text.length - 1; i >= 0; i--) {
    buffer.write(text[i]);
  }
  querySelector("#sample_text_id").text = buffer.toString();
}
```

We've marked in bold the new code we've created. First, we've added a new import to get math random functions available for our application.

```
import 'dart:math'; // Math library necessary for Random functions.
```

In the reverseText method we've defined a list of hexadecimal HTML colors.

```
var list = ['#5a82d7', '#d35a5a', '#d75a5a' , '#5ad7d5', '#5ad773', '#d7cf5a'];
```

We'll generate a new index value between 0 and 5 (the six elements of the list) every time reverseText is executed using Random class of the dart:math library. We store the random selected color in a variable called color.

```
var index = new Random().nextInt(list.length - 1);
var color = list[index];
```

Then we retrieve the container DIV by its ID with document.querySelector and set the backgroundColor style property of this element.

```
var container = querySelector("#sample_container_id");
container.style.backgroundColor = color;
```

Every time we click the paragraph our color will change randomly (Figure 3-44).

Figure 3-44. *Randomly change the background color*

It seems that everything works properly but let's think for a moment. After you modify your application something goes wrong. How could you debug your Dart applications? The answer is easy: use Dart Editor Debugger. On the left side of each line of code you can see the line number (Figure 3-45) if you double-click on the left side of this number you can set a breakpoint. Dart Editor will put a blue point where you have double-clicked. We added a new breakpoint in line 11.

```
10  void reverseText(MouseEvent event) {
11      var list = ['#5a82d7', '#d35a5a', '#d75a5a' , '#5ad7d5',
12              '#5ad773', '#d7cf5a'];
13      var index = new Random().nextInt(list.length - 1);
14      var color = list[index];
15      var container = querySelector("#sample_container_id");
16      container.style.backgroundColor = color;
17
18      var text = querySelector("#sample_text_id").text;
19      var buffer = new StringBuffer();
20      for (int i = text.length - 1; i >= 0; i--) {
21          buffer.write(text[i]);
22      }
23      querySelector("#sample_text_id").text = buffer.toString();
```

Figure 3-45. Setting breakpoints in Dart Editor

Now run your application again and click on the paragraph that says: *"Click me!"* you can see that Dart Editor stops in the breakpoint you've placed at line 11 in the code (Figure 3-46).

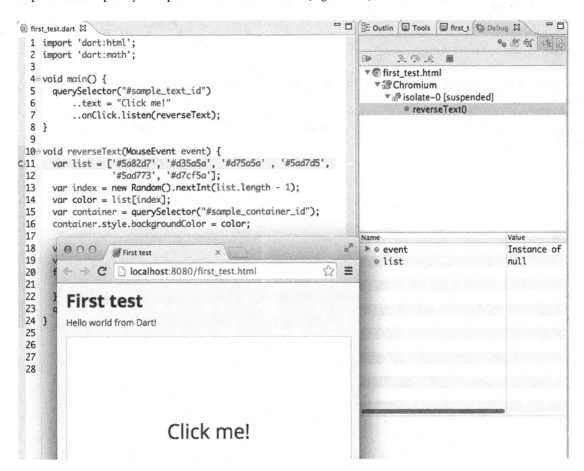

Figure 3-46. Dart Editor stops at line 11 where the breakpoint was placed

Note that we've shown the **Debugger** view (Figure 3-46) so you can see how Dart Editor stops at that point and shows all the debugger information.

- By pressing keys **F5, F6, F7, F8** you can control the debugger.

- **F5** (step into) go into the function is running.

- **F6** (step over) jumps to the next line.

- **F7** (step return) jump to the next return statement.

- **F8** (resume) runs to the next breakpoint and if there is no more, then runs to the end.

Obviously you can also use the Debugger view buttons (Figure 3-47).

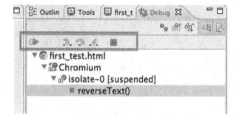

Figure 3-47. *Action buttons in debugger view*

As we mentioned in the previous section you can see the Debugger View through the **Tools** menu by selecting **Debugger**.

Press **F6** (step over) key several times to see how Dart Editor is moving line by line and the debugger view is showing you all the information related to this debugging session (Figure 3-48). You can see information about functions, objects, and variables.

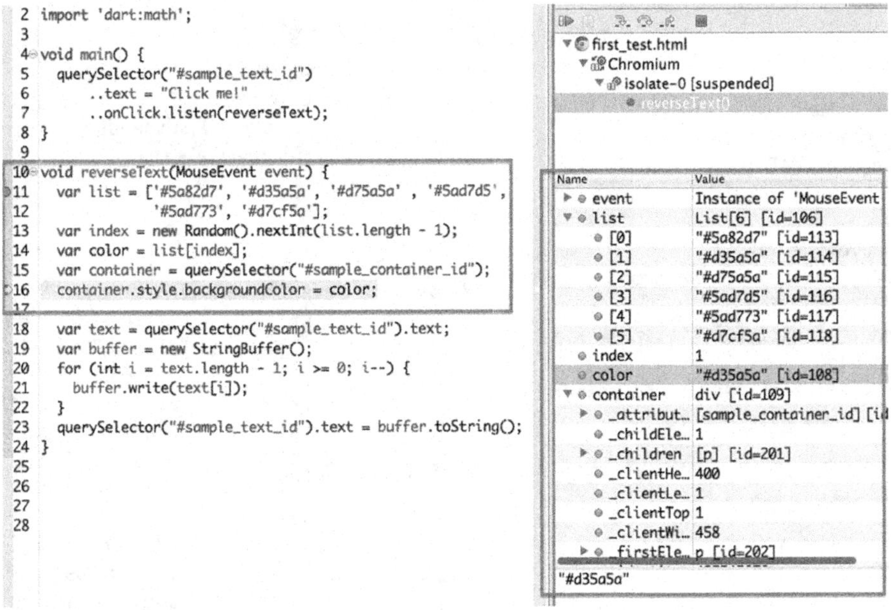

```
2  import 'dart:math';
3
4  void main() {
5    querySelector("#sample_text_id")
6      ..text = "Click me!"
7      ..onClick.listen(reverseText);
8  }
9
10 void reverseText(MouseEvent event) {
11   var list = ['#5a82d7', '#d35a5a', '#d75a5a' , '#5ad7d5',
12              '#5ad773', '#d7cf5a'];
13   var index = new Random().nextInt(list.length - 1);
14   var color = list[index];
15   var container = querySelector("#sample_container_id");
16   container.style.backgroundColor = color;
17
18   var text = querySelector("#sample_text_id").text;
19   var buffer = new StringBuffer();
20   for (int i = text.length - 1; i >= 0; i--) {
21     buffer.write(text[i]);
22   }
23   querySelector("#sample_text_id").text = buffer.toString();
24 }
25
26
27
28
```

Name	Value
▶ ● event	Instance of 'MouseEvent
▼ ● list	List[6] [id=106]
● [0]	"#5a82d7" [id=113]
● [1]	"#d35a5a" [id=114]
● [2]	"#d75a5a" [id=115]
● [3]	"#5ad7d5" [id=116]
● [4]	"#5ad773" [id=117]
● [5]	"#d7cf5a" [id=118]
● index	1
● color	"#d35a5a" [id=108]
▼ ● container	div [id=109]
▶ ● _attribut...	[sample_container_id] [i
● _childEle...	1
▶ ● _children	[p] [id=201]
● _clientHe...	400
● _clientLe...	1
● _clientTop	1
● _clientWi...	458
▶ ● _firstEle...	p [id=202]

"#d35a5a"

Figure 3-48. Debugger view showing information about executed lines

For a better debugging experience you can also use the **Expressions** View to evaluate comparisons, see objects, and execute object methods (Figure 3-49).

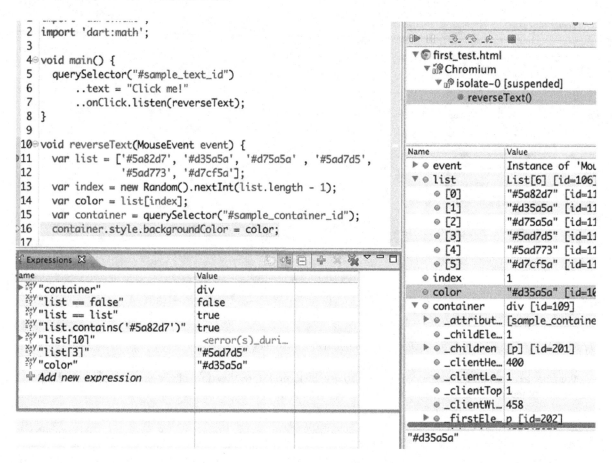

```
 2  import 'dart:math';
 3
 4⊖ void main() {
 5    querySelector("#sample_text_id")
 6        ..text = "Click me!"
 7        ..onClick.listen(reverseText);
 8  }
 9
10⊖ void reverseText(MouseEvent event) {
11    var list = ['#5a82d7', '#d35a5a', '#d75a5a' , '#5ad7d5',
12              '#5ad773', '#d7cf5a'];
13    var index = new Random().nextInt(list.length - 1);
14    var color = list[index];
15    var container = querySelector("#sample_container_id");
16    container.style.backgroundColor = color;
17
```

Figure 3-49. *Expressions View working together with Dart Editor Debugger*

Inspecting the SDK

As we discussed, one of the great advantages of Dart Editor is that it lets you explore the SDK while you're working in your applications. That's really awesome because you can resolve any doubt about a class or method immediately. For example, in your first test application, you've imported dart:math to use the Random class and generate random numbers to get a random color from the color list you defined. We've also used some dart:html methods, as querySelector, to handle the DOM and its elements. If you have any questions about a class or a method, put your cursor on that class or method and press **F3** or right click and select **Open Declaration**, as shown in Figure 3-50.

```
10⊖ void reverseText(MouseEvent event) {
11     var list = ['#5a82d7', '#d35a5a', '#d75a5a' , '#5ad7d5',
12                 '#5ad773', '#d7cf5a'];
13     var index = new Random().nextInt(list.length - 1);
14     var color = list[index];
15     var container = querySele                    "");
16     container.style.backgrou
17
18     var text = querySelector
19     var buffer = new StringBu
20     for (int i = text.length
21       buffer.write(text[i]);
22     }
23     querySelector("#sample_te                    ring();
24 }
25
26
27
28
```

For "querySelector" do:	
Find Uses	⇧⌘U
Open Declaration	**F3**
Browse Dart Doc	
⟲ Undo	⌘Z
Cut	⌘X
Copy	⌘C
Paste	⌘V
Inline...	⌥⌘I
Quick Fix	⌘1
Format	⇧⌘R
Outline File	⌥O
Revert File	

Figure 3-50. *Opening querySelector of dart:html library in Dart SDK*

You'll see how Dart Editor opens automatically the dart:html library and takes you to the document.
querySelector method (Figure 3-51).

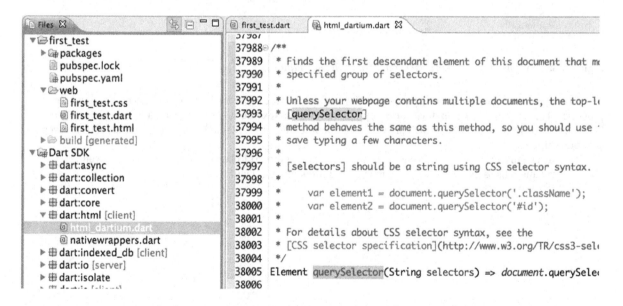

Figure 3-51. *Showing the document querySelector method in dart:html*

In fact, it doesn't show the definition of querySelector itself, which is a more involved, low-level function. But you can see information about the method on the code and even samples of use. If you press F3 on the Random class, you can see how Dart Editor takes you to Random class on the dart:math library (Figure 3-52).

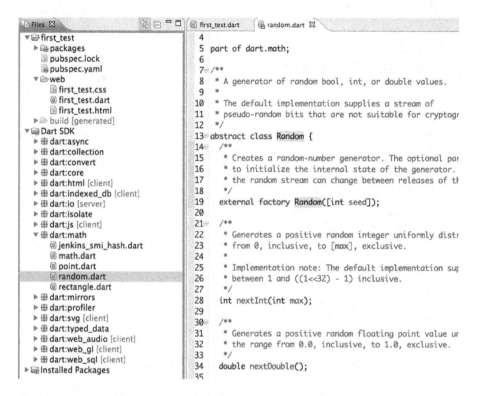

Figure 3-52. *Exploring the Random class of dart:math in Dart Editor*

Of course, when you're exploring the Dart SDK you can continue browsing between classes and methods by pressing **F3** or selecting the **Open declaration** option from the context menu. As you have seen, in Figures 3-51 and 3-52, all the classes and methods in SDK are very well documented and explained and, in most cases, you can even see code snippets.

To take a simple example, you can see the sort() method of the List class in dart:core. It's very well documented and it has a few code samples for a better understanding (Figure 3-53).

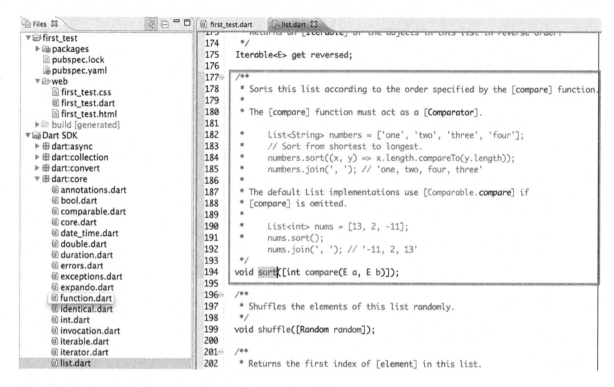

Figure 3-53. *Documentation and code samples in the Dart SDK*

Summary

In this chapter we have learned:

- the Dart Editor in depth, all the options, and its three main areas

- how to open examples with Dart Editor

- how to create your own Dart projects

- the default structure for your projects and what pubspec.yaml file is

- all the editor views with their options and buttons

- how to configure the editor views

- how to run complex applications

- how to debug applications using the Debug view and breakpoints

- how to inspect the SDK to learn more about classes, methods, or objects.

■ ■ ■

CHAPTER 4

Using Pub and dart2js to Compile Applications to JavaScript

You've already created your first Dart application, you used the sample content that Dart Editor loads by default, and you have added new features. You added color every time you clicked on the paragraph element.

Your application runs perfectly in Dartium, but you want everyone to enjoy it. It's time to talk about the Dart to JavaScript code compilation.

Currently. only Dartium can run Dart applications because it's the only web browser that has the Dart Virtual Machine (Dart VM) included. In the future Dart will run natively on other browsers. Soon Dart applications can run natively on Google Chrome because it will have the Dart VM included right out of the box.

For the moment, if you want your applications to run in other browsers you must compile your Dart code into JavaScript. Currently, all modern web browsers have a JavaScript engine to execute JavaScript applications.

Hey, wait a moment, didn't you say Dart was super easy? "compile" sounds horrible to me ! Do not worry, the compilation process is not complicated, it is an absolutely transparent process as easy as running your application in Dartium.

Reviewing the Compliation Process

To compile your Dart application into JavaScript, just open the main Dart code file for your application and click on **Tools** menu and select **Pub Build (generates JS)**, as shown in Figure 4-1.

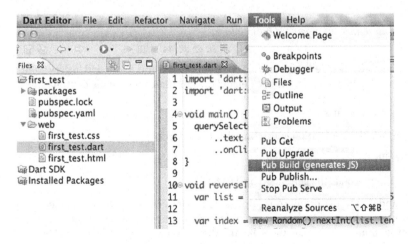

Figure 4-1. *Compiling Dart code into JavaScript*

The compilation process is done by **dart2js** through **Pub Build** command, another great tool that come with Dart. These tools convert Dart code into JavaScript code. The process to compile from one programming language to another can last from a few seconds to several minutes. It depends on the amount of code in your application. Don't worry about the time it's usually very fast.

When you run the JavaScript compilation you will see that it opens the **Tools Output** view where you will be informed about the evolution of the compilation process and the time it takes, as shown in Figure 4-2. Once the compilation process has been completed, you will see a new folder in the **Files** view, as shown in Figure 4-2. This new folder called **build** contains all the application folders, files, and the new JavaScript files generated during the compilation process.

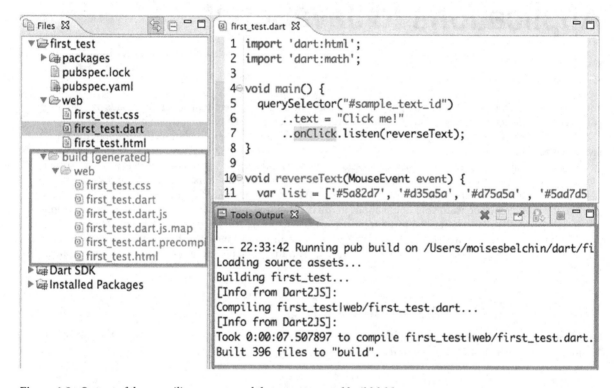

Figure 4-2. *Output of the compiling process and the new generated build folder*

The build folder has an indicator ([generated]) beside its name and Dart Editor marks this folder with a grey color indicating this is a generated folder. Any change you make here will be deleted the next time you run the compilation process.

Now, we will briefly comment on the generated files:

- first_test.dart.js. JavaScript file with the application code compiled to JavaScript.

- first_test.dart.js.map. Mapping file between files and names.

- first_test.dart.precompiled.js. Intermediate file generated by dart2js.

As the chapter's title says, Using Pub and dart2js to Compile our Applications to JavaScript, we're going to see these new command-line tools and how they work. When Dart was born, it used dart2js to compile code and Pub was used only as the package manager. The programming language, the SDK, and the tools have evolved and now they work together to make our lives easier.

Pub build

This is what the command-line tool uses to compile Dart code into JavaScript through **Tools ➤ Pub build (generates JS)** menu. You can also execute this function by right clicking on pubspec.yaml file and selecting **Pub Build (generates JS)**, as shown in Figure 4-3.

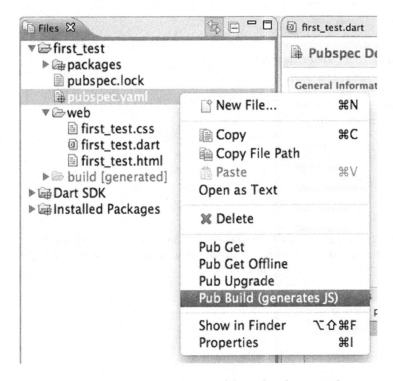

Figure 4-3. *Running Pub Build command through pubspec.yaml*

Now, we're going to see how these tools work internally. We'll see how to execute the same function from the command line console.

We're going to add our Dart SDK bin directory to the system paths in order to make things easier. As you'll remember we have Dart in this path /Applications/dart/dart-sdk/bin/ If you use Mac, open up Terminal and run the command shown in Figure 4-4.

```
MacBook-Pro-de-Moises:~ moisesbelchin$ sudo nano /etc/paths
Password:
```

Figure 4-4. *Editing /etc/paths*

Enter your root password. Go to the bottom of the file, and enter the path you wish to add, as shown in Figure 4-5. For us, it is */Applications/dart/dart-sdk/bin/*

```
GNU nano 2.0.6                          File: /etc/paths

/usr/bin
/bin
/usr/sbin
/sbin
/usr/local/bin
/Applications/dart/dart-sdk/bin/█
```

Figure 4-5. *Adding /Applications/dart/dart-sdk/bin/ to our system Path*

Hit *control-x* to quit and press *"Y"* to save the modified file.
Close the terminal and open it up again.
Run this command echo $PATH, as show in Figure 4-6.

```
MacBook-Pro-de-Moises:~ moisesbelchin$ echo $PATH
/usr/local/bin:/usr/local/sbin:~/bin:/usr/bin:/bin:/usr/sbin:/sbin:/usr/local/bin:
/Applications/dart/dart-sdk/bin/:/usr/local/git/bin
```

Figure 4-6. *Viewing new system paths*

Now you can run any dart-sdk bin command-line application from wherever you are located in your system without having to write the full path to the command you need to run, as you can see in Figure 4-7. If you use Linux you can add the SDK's bin directory to your system path with this command.

```
export PATH=$PATH:<path to sdk>/bin
```

```
MacBook-Pro-de-Moises:~ moisesbelchin$ pub --help
Pub is a package manager for Dart.

Usage: pub <command> [arguments]
```

Figure 4-7. *Running Dart tools without full path*

On Windows you can set the environment variable through the Control Panel. A quick search on your favorite search engine should find the instructions for your version of Windows.

If you execute the command pub --help you'll see all the information about this tool, the commands, the arguments, and the options you can use with it. You'll see all the commands for Pub. For now we're only interested in Pub build.

```
MacBook-Pro-de-Moises:~ moisesbelchin$ pub --help
Pub is a package manager for Dart.

Usage: pub <command> [arguments]

Global options:
-h, --help              Print this usage information.
    --version           Print pub version.
    --[no-]trace        Print debugging information when an error occurs.
    --verbosity         Control output verbosity.
```

```
    [all]       Show all output including internal tracing messages.
    [io]        Also show IO operations.
    [normal]    Show errors, warnings, and user messages.
    [solver]    Show steps during version resolution.

-v, --verbose       Shortcut for "--verbosity=all".

Available commands:
  build         Apply transformers to build a package.
  cache         Work with the system cache.
  deps          Print package dependencies.
  downgrade     Downgrade the current package's dependencies to oldest versions.
  get           Get the current package's dependencies.
  global        Work with global packages.
  help          Display help information for Pub.
  publish       Publish the current package to pub.dartlang.org.
  run           Run an executable from a package.
  serve         Run a local web development server.
  upgrade       Upgrade the current package's dependencies to latest versions.
  uploader      Manage uploaders for a package on pub.dartlang.org.
  version       Print pub version.

Run "pub help [command]" for more information about a command.
See http://dartlang.org/tools/pub for detailed documentation.
```

Run pub help build to get all the information about pub and more specifically about pub build command.

```
MacBook-Pro-de-Moises:~ moisesbelchin$ pub help build
Apply transformers to build a package.

Usage: pub build [options] [directories...]
-h, --help      Print usage information for this command.
    --mode      Mode to run transformers in.
                (defaults to "release")

    --all       Use all default source directories.
    --format    How output should be displayed.
                [text (default), json]

-o, --output    Directory to write build outputs to.
                (defaults to "build")
```

Those are the available options for Dart pub build command. When you select **Tools ➤ Pub build** on your opened application Dart Editor is running this command, as shown in Figure 4-8.

```
MacBook-Pro-de-Moises:first_test moisesbelchin$ pub build --mode "release" -o build web
Loading source assets...
Building first_test...
[Info from Dart2JS]:
Compiling first_test|web/first_test.dart...
[Info from Dart2JS]:
Took 0:00:07.344326 to compile first_test|web/first_test.dart.
Built 6 files to "build".
```

Figure 4-8. *Running Pub build through Terminal*

As you can see it shows you the same information that you can see in the Output tools view. The only difference between the command Dart Editor runs and the command we've executed in this example is the option --mode "release". By default Dart Editor uses --mode "debug" and it generates the files we've previously seen:

- first_test.dart.js
- first_test.dart.js.map
- first_test.dart.precompiled.js

Using --mode "release" option you'll get these new files:

- first_test.dart.js
- first_test.dart.precompiled.js

The most important difference between first_test.dart.js in "debug" mode and first_test.dart.js in "release" mode is the size of those files. The first one has 6394 lines of code and 218KB, the second one has 3238 lines of code and 93KB. The "release" mode removes all unnecessary information and minify the content of the file. It's now perfect to release your new Dart application to all web browsers. As you see the difference is very important, the size of the file was decreased by more than 50%.

dart2js

Dart Editor is the perfect tool to start working with Dart easily and quickly. When we talked about Dart Editor and gave some examples, we used **dart2js** to compile our Dart applications into JavaScript code. In fact, we didn't use this tool directly. We did it through **Pub build**.

Now it's time to see the power of **dart2js** and how it uses "magic" to decrease the size of our Dart applications when they're compiled to JavaScript. As you know, this tool will allow you to compile your applications written in Dart to JavaScript code and thus the applications will run in all modern web browsers.

Let's dig into this tool and see dart2js as a separate tool that you can use. As you can see, Dart is powerful not only for the programming language but also for all the tools that make up this fantastic development ecosystem.

Here's an example file with Dart code named *hello_world.dart*

```
void main() => print("Hello, World!");
```

Running this command you can convert this Dart file to JavaScript code.

```
MacBook-Pro-de-Moises:bin moisesbelchin$ dart2js hello_world.dart
Dart file (hello_world.dart) compiled to JavaScript: out.js
```

After executing this command, *dart2js* tells you that it has generated a file *out.js* very similar to what is shown in Figure 4-9.

```
 1// Generated by dart2js, the Dart to JavaScript
 2// The code supports the following hooks:
 3// dartPrint(message):
 4//    if this function is defined it is called
 5//    method.
 6//
 7// dartMainRunner(main, args):
 8//    if this function is defined, the Dart [ma
 9//    directly. Instead, a closure that will in
10//    [args] is passed to [dartMainRunner].
11(function($) {
12 function dart(){ this.x = 0 }var A = new dart;
13 delete A.x;
14 var B = new dart;
15 delete B.x;
16 var C = new dart;
17 delete C.x;
18 var D = new dart;
19 delete D.x;
20 var E = new dart;
21 delete E.x;
22 var F = new dart;
23 delete F.x;
```

Figure 4-9. out.js file, hello_world.dart file compiled to JavaScript

---

■ **Note**   The compile performance is improved with every new version of Dart so the generated output will change even for the same input file.

As you have seen, you can manually do the same actions that Dart Editor uses to compile. These tools are very useful when you need to create a script that automatically compiles all source files.

Let's look at some parameters that make our work better with dart2js. It's a command line tool, so we have some parameters and modifiers that you need to know so that you can take full advantage of this tool.

Running this command can get information from the available options.

```
MacBook-Pro-de-Moises:bin moisesbelchin$ dart2js --help
Usage: dart2js [options] dartfile

Compiles Dart to JavaScript.

Common options:
 -o <file> Generate the output into <file>.
  -c       Insert runtime type checks and enable assertions (checked mode).
  -m       Generate minified output.
  -h       Display this message (add -v for information about all options).
```

81

The -o (output) option, followed by the name of the destination file, lets you specify the JavaScript output file that will store the JavaScript generated code.

The -c (checked) option can enable checked mode.

The -m (minify) option will generate JavaScript code obfuscated and compressed version. This option is really interesting because your JavaScript code will reduce its size and this increases the loading speed of your applications.

Finally, the -h (help) option displays help and documentation about the dart2js application. Adding the -v parameter will provide more detail than is necessary.

```
MacBook-Pro-de-Moises:bin moisesbelchin$ dart2js -h -v
Usage: dart2js [options] dartfile

Compiles Dart to JavaScript.

Supported options:
 -o <file>, --out=<file>
   Generate the output into <file>.

 -c, --enable-checked-mode, --checked
   Insert runtime type checks and enable assertions (checked mode).

 -m, --minify
   Generate minified output.

 -h, /h, /?, --help
   Display this message (add -v for information about all options).

 -v, --verbose
   Display verbose information.

 -D<name>=<value>
   Define an environment variable.

 --version
   Display version information.

 -p<path>, --package-root=<path>
   Where to find packages, that is, "package:..." imports.

 --analyze-all
   Analyze all code.  Without this option, the compiler only analyzes
   code that is reachable from [main].  This option implies --analyze-only.

 --analyze-only
   Analyze but do not generate code.

 --analyze-signatures-only
   Skip analysis of method bodies and field initializers. This option implies
   --analyze-only.

 --suppress-warnings
   Do not display any warnings.
```

--suppress-hints
  Do not display any hints.

--enable-diagnostic-colors
  Add colors to diagnostic messages.

--terse
  Emit diagnostics without suggestions for how to get rid of the diagnosed
  problems.

--show-package-warnings
  Show warnings and hints generated from packages.

--csp
  Disables dynamic generation of code in the generated output. This is
  necessary to satisfy CSP restrictions (see http://www.w3.org/TR/CSP/).

The following options are only used for compiler development and may
be removed in a future version:

--output-type=dart
  Output Dart code instead of JavaScript.

--throw-on-error
  Throw an exception if a compile-time error is detected.

--library-root=<directory>
  Where to find the Dart platform libraries.

--allow-mock-compilation
  Do not generate a call to main if either of the following
  libraries are used: dart:dom, dart:html dart:io.

--enable-concrete-type-inference
  Enable experimental concrete type inference.

--disable-native-live-type-analysis
  Disable the optimization that removes unused native types from dart:html
  and related libraries.

--categories=<categories>
  A comma separated list of allowed library categories. The default
  is "Client". Possible categories can be seen by providing an
  unsupported category, for example, --categories=help. To enable
  all categories, use --categories=all.

--dump-info
  Generates an out.info.json file with information about the generated code.
  You can inspect the generated file with the viewer at:
  http://dart-lang.github.io/dump-info-visualizer/build/web/viewer.html

We're going to do some tests and see how the *out.js* file, created at the beginning of this section, changes. Let's change the target file and indicate to dart2js that we want the minified file.

```
MacBook-Pro-de-Moises:bin moisesbelchin$ dart2js -o hello_world.js -m -c hellow_world.dart
```

When dart2js finishes the work, after a few seconds, we have our application compiled to JavaScript and compressed into the file hello_world.js. If you look at the size of the files, you will be surprised as hello_world.js size (26K) compressed is larger than out.js (14K) generated uncompressed. Why? If you remember, we have enabled checking mode and this makes typing checks at runtime. If you re-run the command without the -c parameter.

```
MacBook-Pro-de-Moises:bin moisesbelchin$ dart2js -o hellow_world.js -m hellow_world.dart
```

Now look at the file sizes.

- out.js: 14KB

- hello_world.js: 6.8KB

In this small application, we have saved 7.2KB, this doesn't sound a lot, but we're talking about decreasing our application size by more than 50%. Imagine the size of the savings when we have an application with 15,000 lines of code.

This is amazing because the smaller the file we have the faster our application will load. Not only will this speed up our applications, but it'll also improve the user experience of our project when we release it.

Pub Serve

Now that you know how to compile, deploy, and make your applications available for all modern browsers we want to show you an additional Pub command called Pub serve.

Pub serve command will allow Dart web files to be accessed by Dartium or other browsers, due to compiling on the fly. This command starts up a development server for your Dart web applications.

The server is an HTTP server that will serve up your web application's assets. It will compile the assets on the fly by running transformers so your Dart web applications can be accessed by other non-Dartium browsers. That is an awesome functionality because you can test your Dart applications in other browsers to check compatibility without compiling your application each time.

Pub serve will do this for you, simply run pub serve command on your application's path. Now you can access your application from Safari, Firefox, Chrome, or Internet Explorer.

You can do any modification you need on your application and Pub serve will compile it into JavaScript by refreshing your browser. Let's see how to use this amazing functionality. Open your command line tool and go to any Dart web application or create a new one using Dart Editor. We're going to use the first_test sample we made in Chapter 3.

Once you're located on your application's path run the pub serve command as shown in Figure 4-10.

```
MacBook-Pro-de-Moises-3:first_test moisesbelchin$ pub serve
Loading source assets...
Serving first_test web on http://localhost:8080
Build completed successfully
```

Figure 4-10. *Running pub serve to access Dart web apps from other browsers*

Now you're ready to test your Dart web application in other browsers. We're going to use Safari to test the first_test Dart application, as shown in Figure 4-11. Open your preferred browser and navigate to http://localhost:8080/first_test.html.

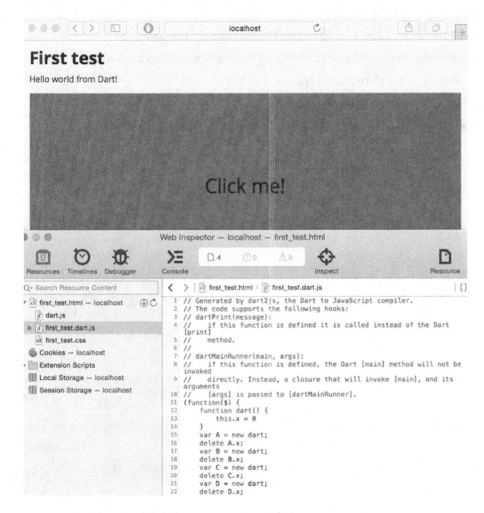

Figure 4-11. *First_test dart web app running on Safari*

In Figure 4-11 we've opened the Safari's developer tools to show you the first_test.dart.js compiled file auto generated by Pub serve command. When you finish your tests you can stop the development server by hitting CTRL+X on your command line tool.

Summary

In this chapter we have learned:

- how to compile Dart applications to JavaScript
- how to use Pub Build from Dart Editor to compile your Dart applications into JavaScript
- how to use dart2js from the command line to compile your Dart applications into JavaScript
- all the supported options for dart2js command line tool
- how to add Dart SDK's bin directory to your system path
- how to use Pub serve to test your Dart web applications in other non-Dartium browsers due to compiling on the fly.

CHAPTER 5

■ ■ ■

Application Launches

In this chapter we'll see all the available configurations for our applications, no matter if they are command-line applications or web applications. In fact, with the most recent versions of Dart Editor you could create several different configurations.

We'll dive into the Manage Launches configuration tool and see how to configure your applications. We'll also look at how to connect your Android mobile device with Dart Editor to run and test your Dart web applications.

Manage Launches

Every time you've typed **CMD+R** or clicked on the Run button throughout the examples in this book, you've seen how your Dart applications run, and you could see the output of the application on the Output view (if it's a command-line application) or you could see Chromium running your app (if it's a web application).

By this point, Dart Editor has created a particular configuration for your application. All of your applications are stored in the Manage Launches configuration window. Let's see what the application launches are and how you can work with them.

Application launches are configurations we make for our applications so that they run properly on Dartium, on the Dart virtual machine, or on an Android mobile device. Which platform is used depends on what application type we are developing.

To open the Manage Launches configuration window, go to **Run ➤ Manage Launches** (see Figure 5-1).

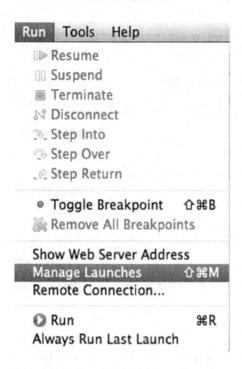

Figure 5-1. *Opening the Manage Launches configuration tool*

You can also use the drop-down menu near the round green Run button to see all the application launches already created as well as the Manage Launches... option (see Figure 5-2).

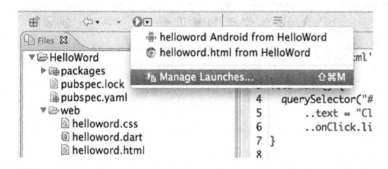

Figure 5-2. *Manage Launches tool from the Run button*

Once you've selected the Manage Launches… option, you should see the configuration tool shown in Figure 5-3:

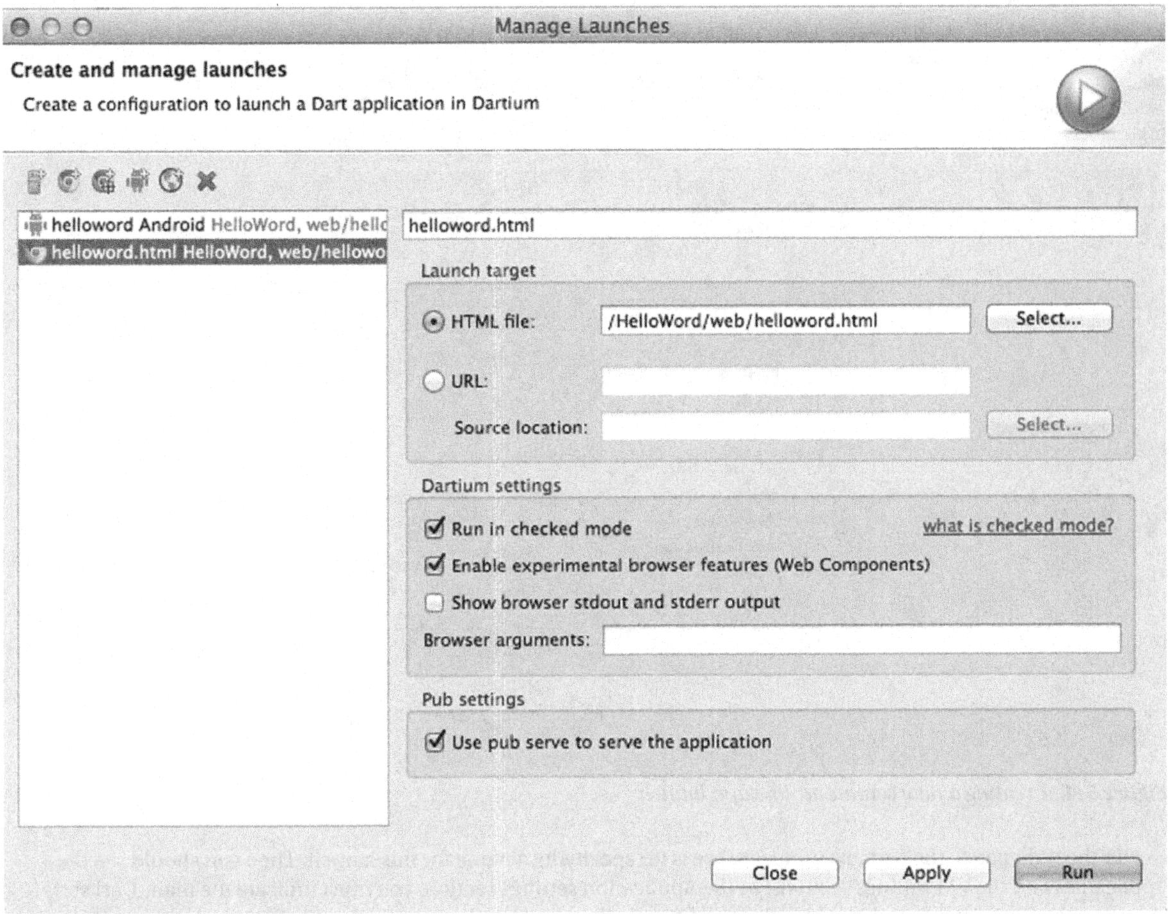

Figure 5-3. *Manage Launches tool*

From this new window we can create different launches for our Dart applications, and in addition we can specify additional parameters for these launches. As you know, Dart Editor does all the dirty work for us, but if you need more control over your applications, you can do this through the configuration tool.

In the Manage Launches window you should see two main sections: on the left, a sidebar with existing launches; on the right, the options for the selected launch. This window will change depending on the launch type you select.

Dart Command-Line Launch

We're going to use **HelloCommand**, the first Dart command-line application we made in Chapter 2. Open this application in Dart Editor. This application is very simple, but it is perfect for seeing how to manually create a launch.

Once you've opened your application in Dart Editor, go to the Manage Launches configuration tool and click on the first icon to create a new Dart command-line app launch, as shown in Figure 5-4.

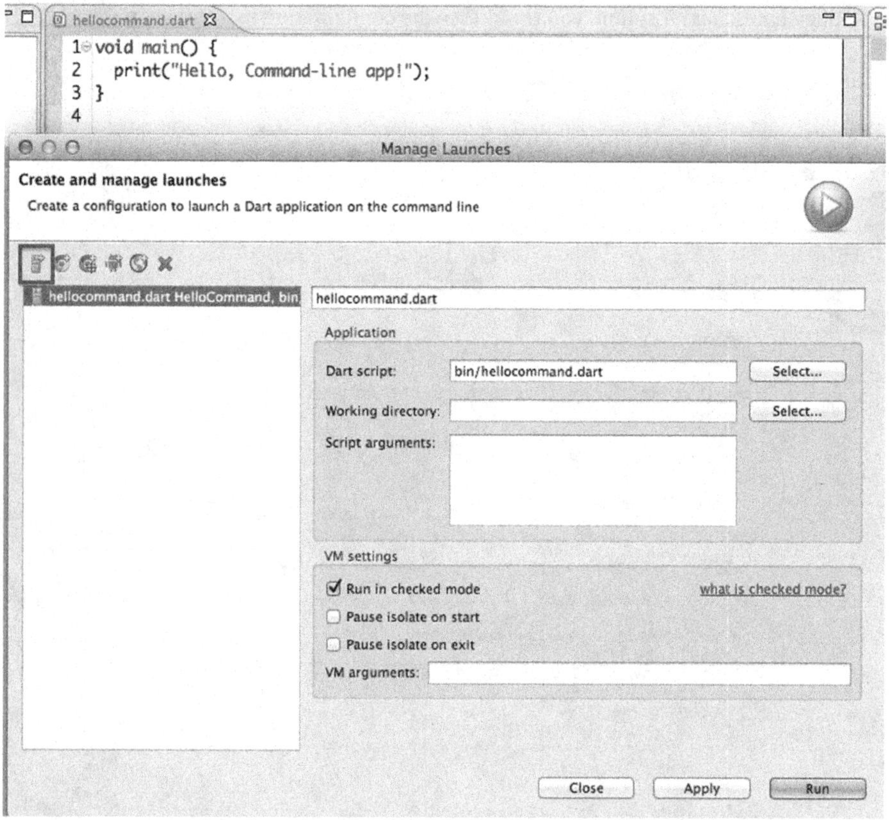

Figure 5-4. *Creating a new command-line app launch*

In the right panel, the first text input you see is for specifying a name for this launch. Then you should see the Application and the VM settings sections. In the Application settings section, you must indicate the main Dart script to run on the Dart virtual machine. You also need to specify a working directory, using the Select… button to navigate on your computer. Finally, if you need to, you could specify parameters for the application.

The VM section lets you configure specific options for the Dart virtual machine. You could run your app in checked mode or in production mode. You could pause the main isolate where your application is running on start or on exit using the appropriate checkbox. If you need to pass a special parameter to the virtual machine, you could use the VM arguments input text field.

WHAT IS CHECKED MODE?

This mode lets Dart make special checks on your applications during the development process, such as during data-type validations, when passing parameters to functions, when you make assignments, or when returning results from methods or functions.

When this mode is enabled and you're running and testing your application, Dart will stop and show you the error description if an error occurs. You have the opportunity to catch errors during development.

Obviously this extra functionality and checking comes at the cost of performance.

Now that we have our first launch ready we're going to use it to run our Dart application. Use the drop-down menu near to the green Run button and select the new command-line application launch you've just created (see Figure 5-5).

Figure 5-5. *Using our new command-line app launch*

You will see how your application is running with the given configuration and the output of your application will appear in the Output window.

Dartium Launch

Next we're going to use our first Dart web application, **HelloWord**, so open that back up. Also open the Manage Launches tool and select the new Dartium launch icon. You should see how the right panel has changed from our previous command-line app launch. Some fields are very similar, but other fields are totally different (see Figure 5-6).

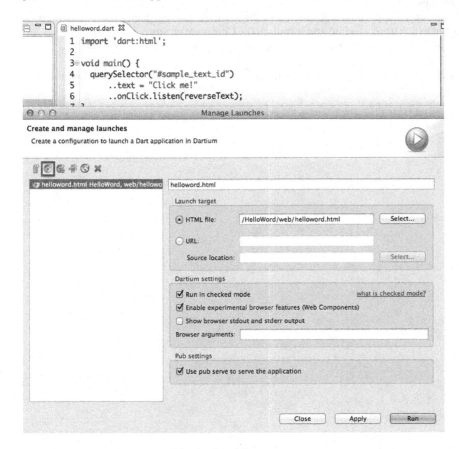

Figure 5-6. *New Dartium application launch*

In this case, we have to indicate a name for this new launch. Then we have three different sections to deal with.

- Launch target lets you select the main HTML file for your application; you should use the Select… button for this. This section lets you select a URL to which to load your Dartium application, which is used if your application is served by a web server.

- On the Dartium settings section you will find the available options you can change for Dartium when running your application. You could run your application in checked mode or in production mode. You could indicate whether you want to enable experimental features on Dartium or show the browser output on the Output view. As in the command-line application launches, you could specify additional arguments for the browser.

- Finally, you could change the default Pub setting if you want to use Pub to serve the application or not.

When you have your new Dartium launch ready, click the Apply and then Run buttons and you will see Dartium running your application with these new configuration options.

Chrome App Launch

Newer versions of Dart have incorporated a lot of new and very interesting functionality. Chrome Apps and Connect with Android Devices are our favorites.

Dart lets you create Chrome packaged applications; if you don't know, Chrome packaged apps are applications that run inside Google Chrome and which users can find and install via the Chrome Web Store. Thank to Chrome packaged applications, you can go beyond the browser and run your Dart applications as standalone desktop applications.

With Dart Editor, beginning development of a new Dart Chrome app is very simple. Just click on the "Create a new application" icon and select "Chrome packaged application" (see Figure 5-7). Dart Editor will create the project structure and the files for the sample application.

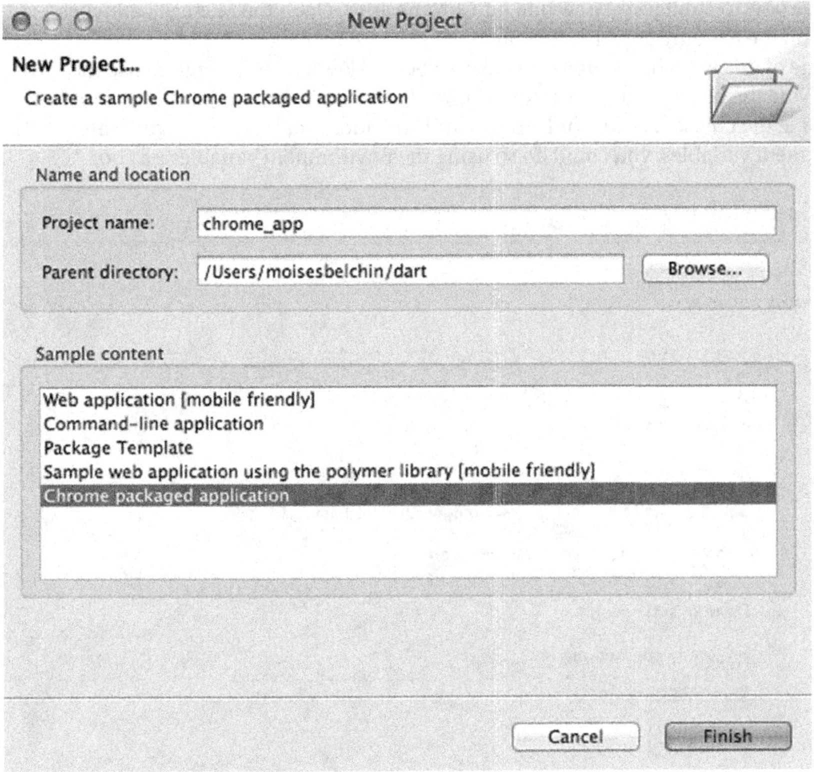

Figure 5-7. *Creating a Chrome packaged application*

This type of Dart application is like any other; the only difference is that Chrome packaged applications need some special pub packages in order to run, and they have a special file called **manifest.json**, which will describe your application (see Figure 5-8).

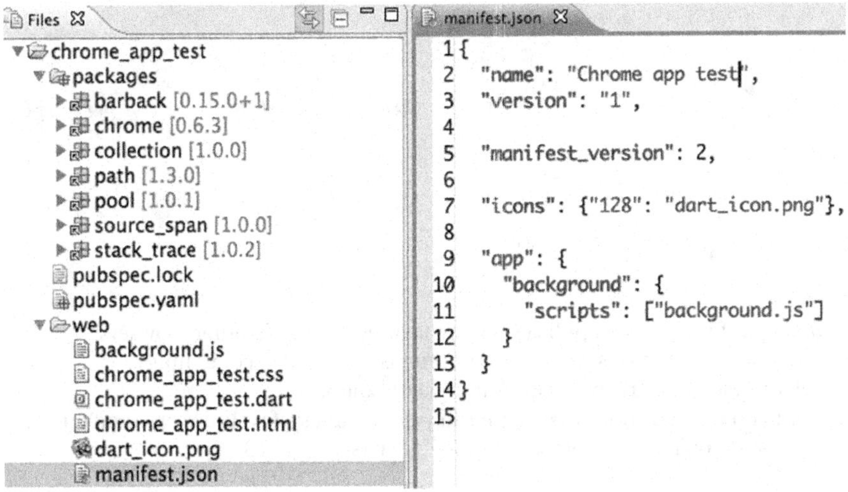

Figure 5-8. *manifest.json file for Chrome packaged applications in Dart*

Let's get back to launches and see how to configure a new one for Chrome apps. Open the Manage Launches configuration tool, this time clicking on the Chrome app launch icon.

As always, you could set the name of this launch, and you must also select the launch target, in this case the **manifest.json** file (see Figure 5-9). Note the next section, Dartium settings. The Chrome Dart applications run on Dartium, so you could enable or disable the checked mode for Dartium and add additional browser arguments. If you need to set any special environment variables, you could do so using the Environment variables text box.

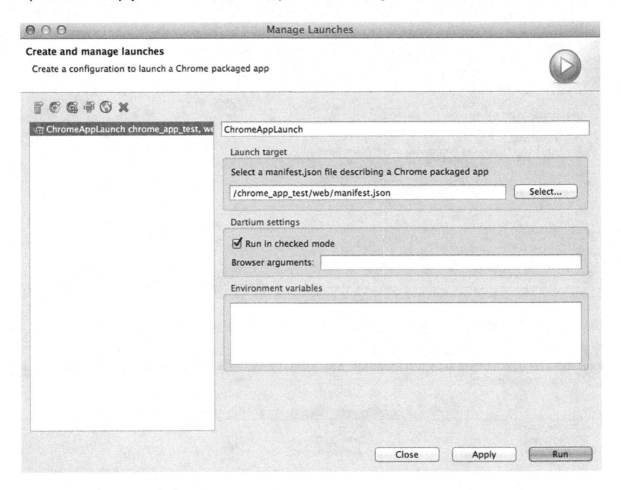

Figure 5-9. *Chrome app launch*

Browser Launch

Browser launches let you configure launches for your web applications so that they can run in other browsers you have installed on your computer, not only Dartium. As you know, Dartium is the result of combining **Dart + Chromium**, and it is the default browser for Dart applications from Dart Editor.

With this new launch you could run and test your Dart applications in your default system browser. Open the Manage Launches configuration tool and click on the "New browser launch" icon (see Figure 5-10).

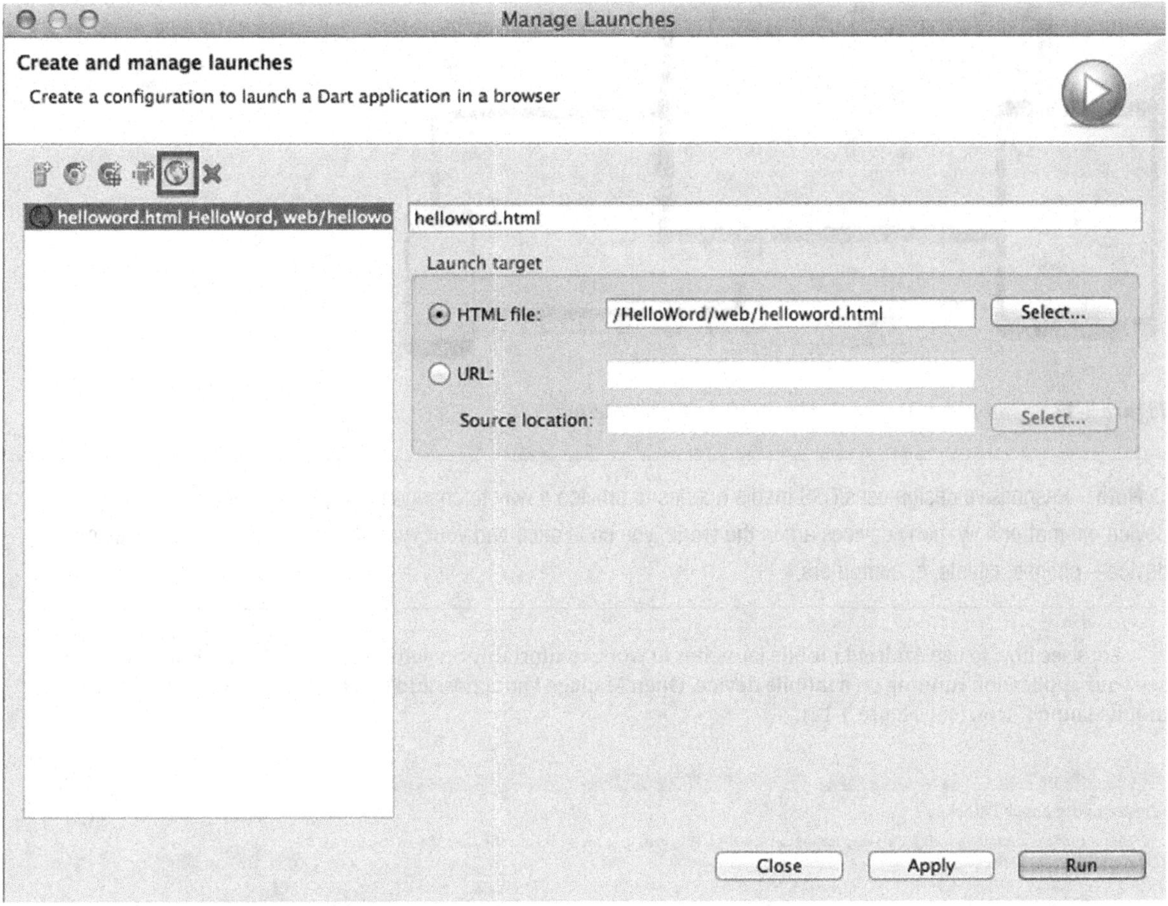

Figure 5-10. *Configuring browser launches*

Similar to how Dartium launches work, you can set the name of the launch and select the target to be either a file or a URL. Once you get your new browser launch ready, execute your Dart application; you'll see your app running on Chrome, Safari, Firefox, or IE—it depends on your default system browser and operating system.

Android Mobile Launch

With the Android mobile launch configuration you could run your Dart applications directly from Dart Editor to your Android mobile device, which is a really great feature.

It's very important to consider how your web application will look on a mobile device. Thanks to new HTML and CSS features, it is possible to build only one web application that will adapt to different devices, which is called **responsive and adaptive design** (see Figure 5-11 for examples).

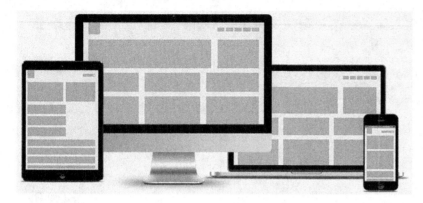

Figure 5-11. *Examples of responsive layout for adaptive design*

■ **Note**   Responsive design uses CSS media queries to provide a way to change the layout and adapt it to the user device; no matter how many devices are in the world, you code once and your web application will run perfectly on any device—phones, tablets, or computers.

Let's see how to use Android mobile launches to work comfortably on your desktop with Dart Editor so as to see your application running on a mobile device. Open Manage Launches, and this time click on the "Create a new mobile launch" icon (see Figure 5-12).

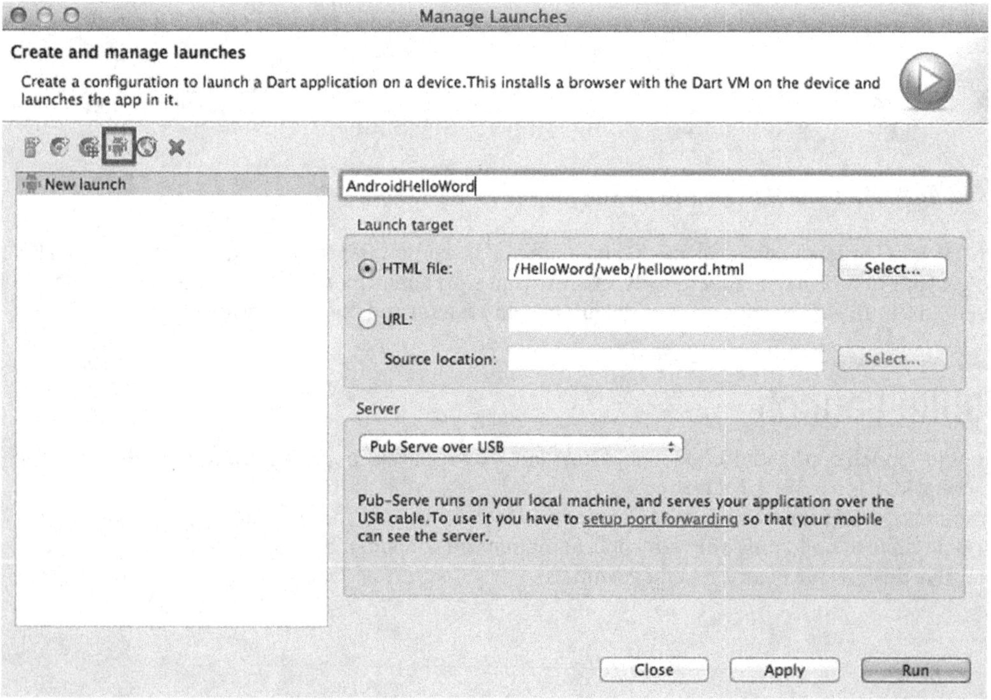

Figure 5-12. *Creating a new mobile launch*

Remember that you are creating a mobile launch, so you must select a Dart web application. As usual, you can set the name for the new launch you're creating. The Launch target section lets you select a file or URL; in this case we're going to select our **HelloWord** main HTML file.

Finally, you should see the Server section, where you can set how Dart Editor will communicate with your Android device.

■ **Note**   You must have an Android device connected to your computer and enable the USB debugging option on your Android device.

You can see Pub Serve over USB; this option is very interesting because every time you run your application by clicking the Run button, Dart Editor will communicate with your Android device and send the changes.

You also could configure the Server section to use Embedded server over WIFI network. With this option you will use the server embedded in the Dart Editor to connect over your network. This requires that your phone establish a direct connection by Wi-Fi to the computer where Dart Editor is running.

Once you get your launch ready, click the Apply button and then Run; you should see your application running on your phone (see Figure 5-13). Please be patient with this option, as it could take up to 30 seconds to properly run your app on your phone.

Figure 5-13. *Running our HelloWord app on an Android mobile phone*

Summary

In this chapter we have learned:

- what launches are in Dart and how to manage them
- what types of configurations are available for Dart applications
- how to configure a command-line launch
- how to configure a Dartium launch
- how to configure a Chrome app launch
- how to configure a browser launch
- how to configure an Android mobile launch

CHAPTER 6

■ ■ ■

Using the Dart Pub Package Manager

In this Chapter we'll see what the Dart Pub Package Manager is, how to use it, and how it can help you in your Dart projects. We'll create a new application and we will add an external dart package to see how Pub works. We'll also learn how to use pubspec.yaml files and the basic pub commands. Later we'll show you all the available Pub commands and what those commands can do.

What is Pub?

Pub is the package manager for Dart. It is the tool will let us add any library written by other developer to our applications in a very simple way. Pub automatically resolves dependencies and will keep us updated with the latest versions, if we want it.

A package for Dart is just a Dart application with a specific layout, a file of dependencies, a web directory with some files of code, and maybe other libraries. It may also contain other resources such as documentation, examples, tests, benchmarks, pictures, a configuration file that indicates the package version, extra interest information, and the dependency libraries to work properly. Thanks to this layout, we can use *Pub* to download a specific package, start using this package, and Pub will automatically download everything you need to make it work with your application. It is wonderful to work in this simple way!

Digging Deeper

Let's see a practical example of using Pub and see the different Pub commands to get the most of this tool. Like *dart2js*, Pub is a standalone application (you also could use it from the *command line*) and is perfectly integrated into Dart Editor to make your job easier.

Imagine that you are writing an *HTML5* application for an ecommerce online shop where the user gets a list of products to purchase, but he does not want to buy them right now. It would be great to store these items, so the next time the user accesses our shop we can remind him what he wanted buy. The first option that is to store the items in the client browser and *IndexedDB* would be perfect option. This great API lets you create small databases in the client browser and work with them.

■ **Note** IndexedDB is a new HTML5 feature lets you use the browser client to store items. It is useful to store pairs of keys and their corresponding values. `http://www.w3.org/TR/IndexedDB/`

Go to http://pub.dartlang.org and find something related to IndexedDB. The first result, as shown in Figure 6-1, is a package that looks great and this package allows us to manage IndexedDB, as well as, *local storage* and *websql*.

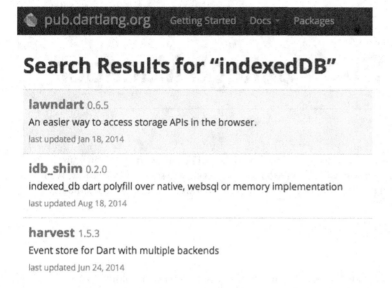

Figure 6-1. *Looking for a package to manage IndexedDB in pub.dartlang.org*

This looks good. We have located the **lawndart** package, but how do we include this package in our application? Go to Dart Editor, create a new project, tell Dart Editor to create the new web application called **testPub**, and create the sample content, as shown in Figure 6-2.

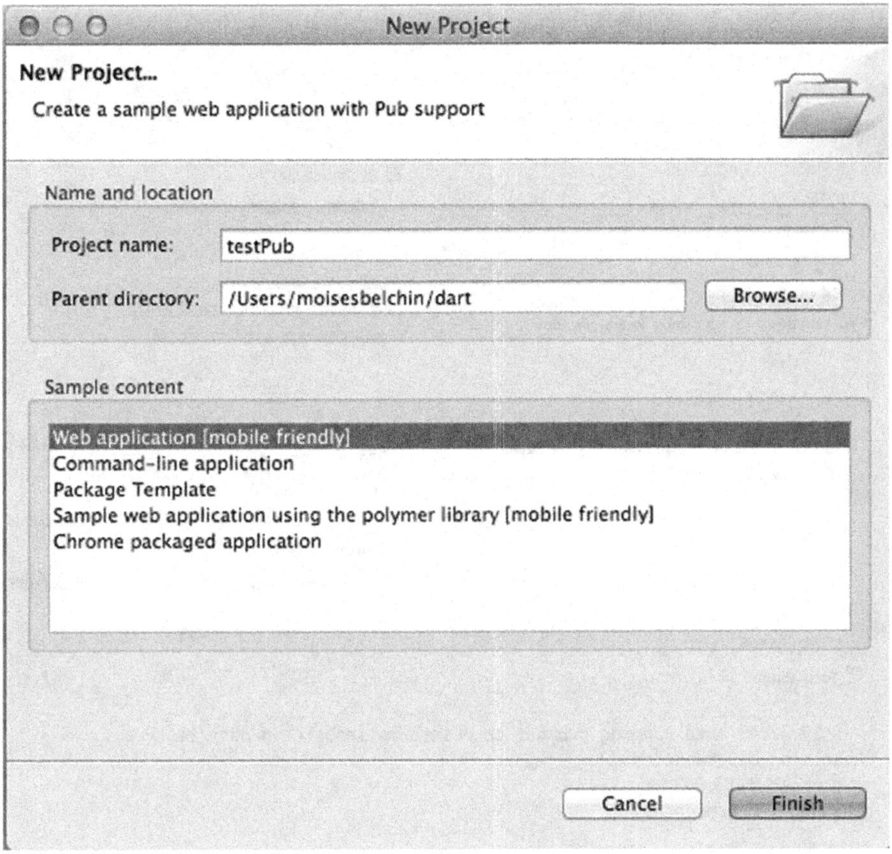

Figure 6-2. *Creating a new test web application to use Pub*

When the new application is created, we're going to create a file called pubspec.yaml. This file is necessary to indicate to Pub that we want to use a library in our new project.

In fact, this file was just created, as shown in Figure 6-3, and Dart Editor has executed pub get command as you can see in the *Tools Output view*. We will see all the Pub commands immediately.

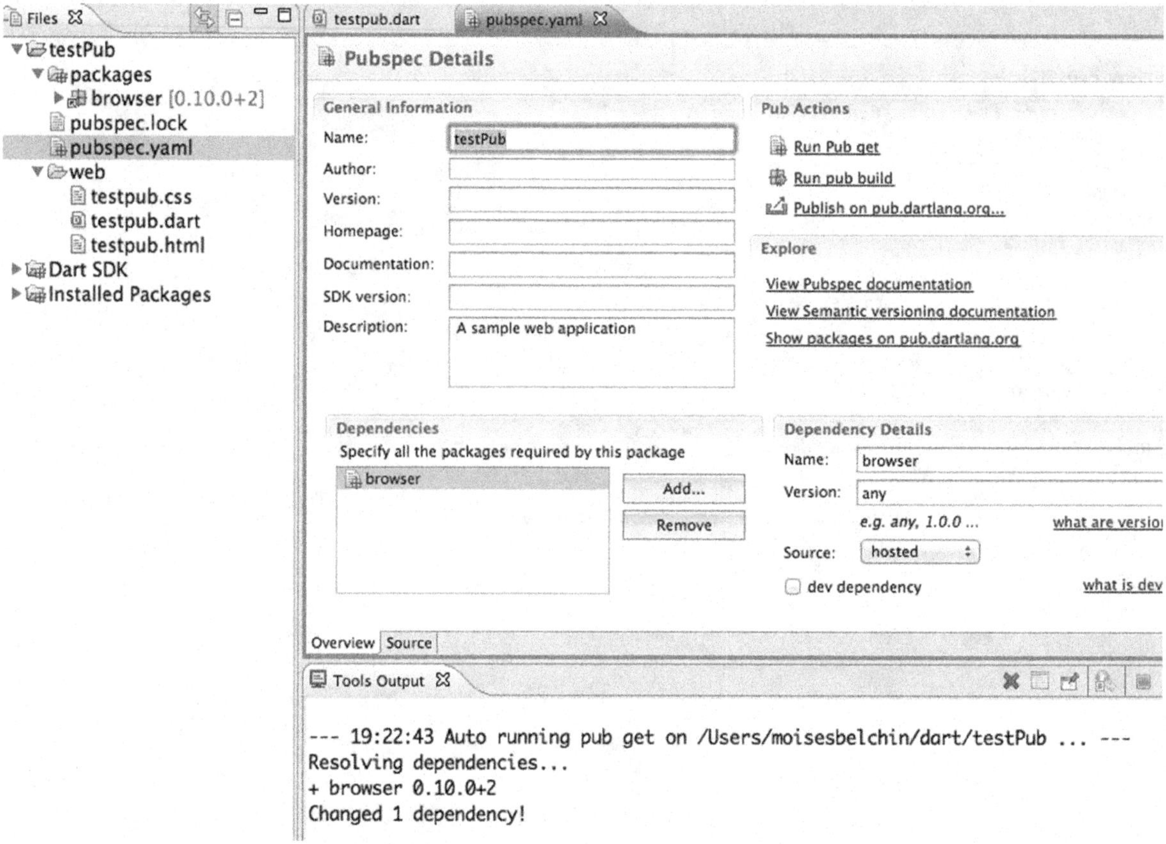

Figure 6-3. *The packages directory and the pubspec.yaml file*

Working With Commands and Packages

When you create the new file or run pub get or pub upgrade for the first time, Pub will automatically create a pubspec.lock file and the packages directory, as shown in Figure 6-3. The pubspec.lock file ensures that future gets will use the same versions of those dependencies. The packages directory will store all the needed libraries for your new project as specified on pubspec.yaml.

The pubspec.yaml file is a plain text file, but it is formatted by Dart Editor and easily indicates all the dependencies for our new project.

■ **Note**   You can change from the formatted view to the raw view by clicking the **Source** tab. This is needed when working with transformers for certain packages.

In the Dependencies section of pubspec.yaml we press the *Add...* button to add a new dependency. A search box will be opened to search, select, and add the lawndart package to manage IndexedDB in our application, as shown in Figure 6-4.

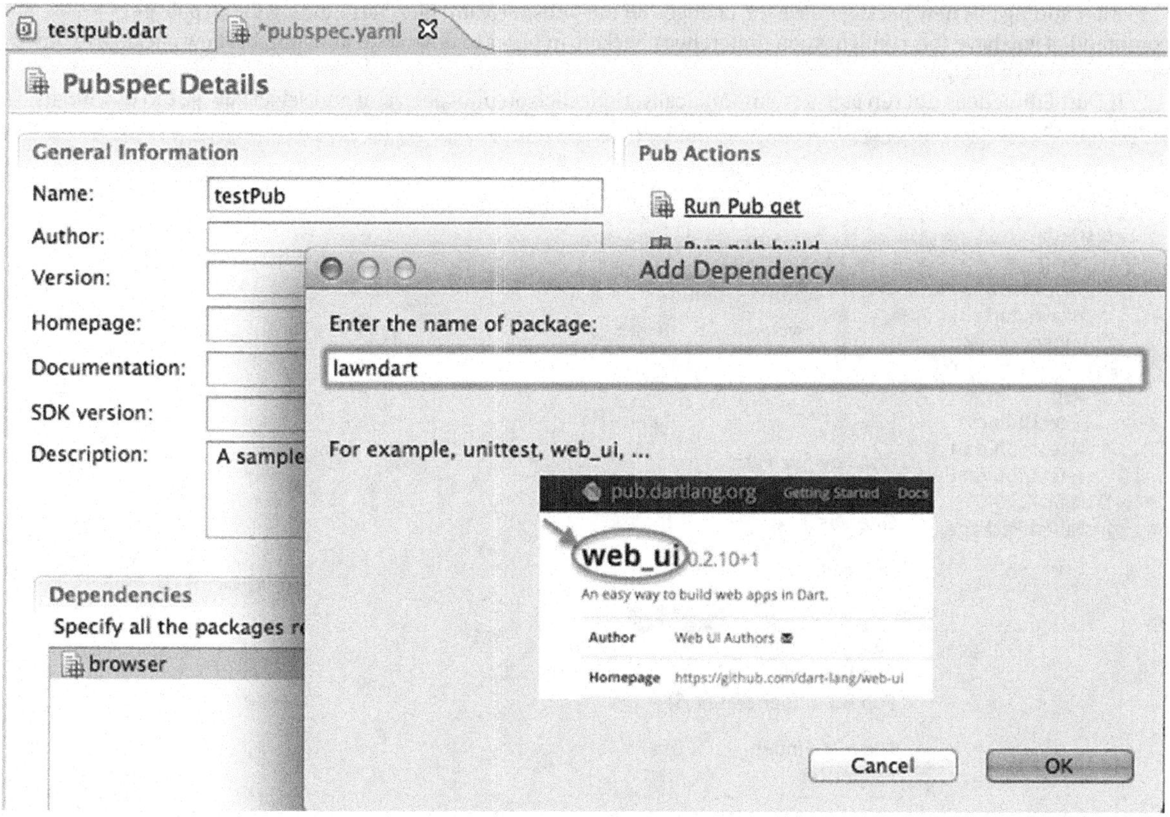

Figure 6-4. We added the lawndart package to our application

In the new opened window, type the exact package name we searched for in Figure 6-1. Once you've typed lawndart press OK. You can see that it now appears in the section dependencies of pubspec.yaml file, as shown in Figure 6-5.

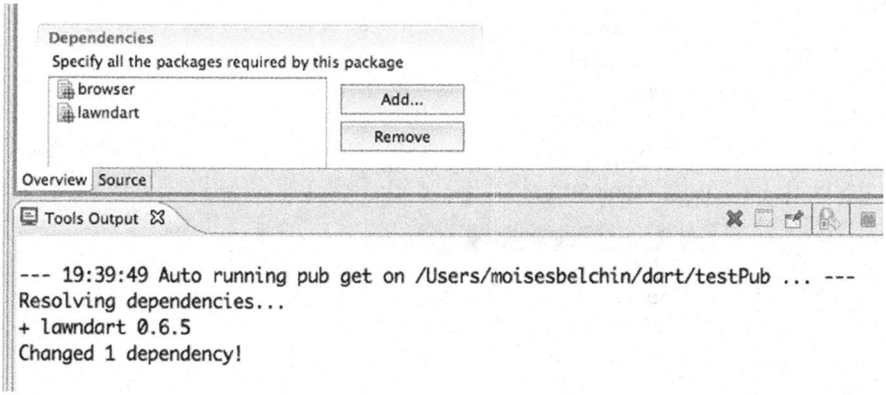

Figure 6-5. Dart Editor automatically downloading our new package lawndart

After adding this new package, save the changes on the pubspec.yaml file. Dart Editor will run pub get command, if you have this configuration preference checked, in order to download and add this new package to our project, as shown in Figure 6-5.

If Dart Editor does not run pub get automatically, right click on pubspec.yaml and select **Pub get** to download and install this new package, as you can see in Figure 6-6.

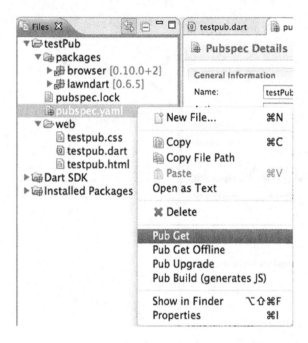

Figure 6-6. *Right clicking on pubspec.yaml lets you run some Pub commands*

You could run Pub commands from the ***Tools*** menu, as shown in Figure 6-7.

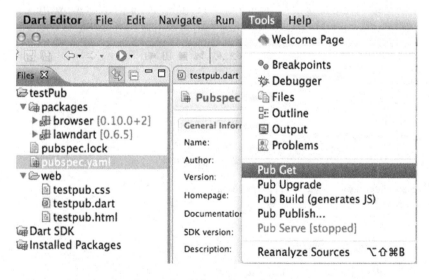

Figure 6-7. *Running Pub commands from the Tools menu*

We will see all the Pub commands in detail later in this chapter, but for the moment know that the **Pub Get** command is used to resolve and download dependencies and the **Pub Upgrade command** is used to download the latest versions of your current packages.

Now, as you can see in Figure 6-8, you have the new lawndart package in your new application. You can import it and start using it.

Figure 6-8. *Lawndart package ready for use in our project*

The import of these packages is similar to the import of any other Dart libraries except you just have to indicate the packages directory.

```
import 'package:lawndart/lawndart.dart';
```

Below you can find the code for our new application.

```
import 'package:lawndart/lawndart.dart';

void main() {
 // Load products on browser database.
 Store store = new IndexedDbStore('db_products', 'products');
 store.open()
   .then((_) => store.save('iPhone 6', 'VF32Gn95voEALOE'))
   .then((_) => store.save('iPhone 6 Plus', 'c6w3hE471WZe5VGsa'))
   .catchError((e) {
     print('Error saving products.');
   });
```

```
// Loading products from browser database
store.open()
  .then((_) {
    store.keys()
      .listen((key) {
        store.getByKey(key).then((String name) {
          print('ID: ${key} PRODUCT: ${name}');
        });
      })
      .onDone(() {
        print('Product loading finished ${new DateTime.now()}');
      });
  })
  .catchError((e) {
    print('Error loading products');
  });
}
```

In the first part of our program we created a new browser database called db_products, a table called products, and stored a few products. We used the store.open method to open the IndexedDB database and work with it, then we used store.save to store key and value pairs.

In the second part we used the local IndexedDB browser database to read all the keys stored and show them on the Dartium console. We used store.open to open the database and then we used store.keys to read all the keys of the database. Then we used store.getByKey to get the associated value for a given key.

Don't worry if you don't fully understand this example, we've created this to show you how to import and use an external Dart package in your projects. In this example, we're using the Future API. In coming chapters you will learn all about Future API and then you can come back to this example and practice with it.

If you run this example in Dartium you won't see anything spectacular, but open the chrome developer tools. *Chrome button ➤ Tools ➤ Developer Tools* or just hit *CMD+ALT+I*. Then go to the **Resources** tab and select **IndexedDB.** Expand this resource and you will see our new database db_products. Inside it you will see your new table products with our two new products, as shown in Figure 6-9.

Figure 6-9. *Storing and showing products in the local browser database*

Additional Pub Commands

Now that you know the Pub upgrade and get commands and you have learned about pubspec.yaml and import packages, it's time to learn the other commands that Pub supports and what you can do with them.

- pub build
- pub cache
- pub deps
- pub get
- pub global
- pub publish
- pub run
- pub serve

- pub upgrade

- pub uploader

- pub downgrade

- pub help

- pub version

Pub Build

You already know pub build. You used it in *Chapter 4*. This command generates assets for the current application, compiles your application to JavaScript, and puts them into a new directory called *build*.

Pub Cache

Pub uses an internal cache directory where the downloaded packages are physically stored. Then Pub uses symbolic links to this cache instead of copying those packages into packages directory for each project you create. This cache directory is located in ~/.pub-cache for Mac and Linux systems. On windows it goes in AppData\Romaing\Pub\Cache.

For some reasons in old Dart versions, when you upgrade Dart from one version to another in some cases this cache is broken and you will need to repair it manually. You do this by deleting all the cache directory contents and running pub get again.

In the most recent versions of Dart, Dart developers introduced pub cache to manage the pub system cache.
pub cache add lets you install a library in your cache.
pub cache repair will perform a clean reinstall of all the packages in the system cache.

Pub Deps

Pub deps will print a dependency graph of a package. It will draw a tree graph with all the package's dependencies. Open a Terminal and go to our **testPub** new project, then type pub deps and press enter. You will see all the package's dependencies for our application, as shown in Figure 6-10.

```
MacBook-Pro-de-Moises:testPub moisesbelchin$ pub deps
testPub 0.0.0
|-- browser 0.10.0+2
'-- lawndart 0.6.5
```

Figure 6-10. *Showing dependencies for our testPub package*

Pub Get

This command lets you get all the dependencies specified in your **pubspec.yaml**, download them, and have them ready to use in your applications. Pub get will download the dependencies of a pubspec.lock file if it exists. If this file doesn't exist, this command will create the pubspec.lock file after downloading the dependencies based on the version constraints present on pubspec.yaml.

Pub Global

This new command introduced in the latest Dart release lets you run Dart scripts and use packages from the command line when you are not inside a package.

Pub global command will allow you to activate packages, list all activated packages, run scripts from the command line, and finally deactivate activated packages. In order to accomplish these tasks pub global uses these commands.

- pub global activate <package>

- pub global list

- pub global deactivate <package>

- pub global run <package>:<script>

We're going to test these commands with a new Dart package called **simple_http_server**. This package lets you get ready to use a simple http server like python -m SimpleHTTPServer. Run this command in your terminal and you will see how it activates the simple_http_server, as shown in Figure 6-11, after downloading the required dependencies.

```
MacBook-Pro-de-Moises:testPub moisesbelchin$ pub global activate simple_http_server
```

```
MacBook-Pro-de-Moises:testPub moisesbelchin$ pub global activate simple_http_server
Downloading simple_http_server 0.1.0+3...
Resolving dependencies... (3.5s)
+ args 0.12.0+2
+ collection 1.0.0
+ crypto 0.9.0
+ http_parser 0.0.2+5
+ mime 0.9.0+3
+ path 1.3.0
+ shelf 0.5.4+3
+ shelf_static 0.2.0
+ source_span 1.0.0
+ stack_trace 1.0.2
+ string_scanner 0.1.0
Downloading shelf_static 0.2.0...
Downloading http_parser 0.0.2+5...
Downloading shelf 0.5.4+3...
Downloading string_scanner 0.1.0...
Activated simple_http_server 0.1.0+3.
```

Figure 6-11. *Running pub global activates the simple_http_server package*

Once you've activated the **simple_http_server** Dart package, run pub global run simple_http_server from any directory , as shown in Figure 6-12.

```
MacBook-Pro-de-Moises:testPub moisesbelchin$ pub global run simple_http_server
Server started on port 8080
```

Figure 6-12. *Running a simple http server Dart package from the command line*

Now get a simple http server running, as shown in Figure 6-13.

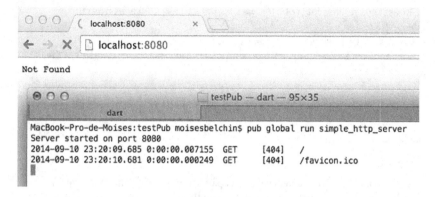

Figure 6-13. *Our new simple http server running*

To deactivate this activated package just run the command below and you'll see how the package is deactivated, as shown in Figure 6-14.

```
MacBook-Pro-de-Moises:testPub moisesbelchin$ pub global deactivate simple_http_server
```

```
MacBook-Pro-de-Moises:testPub moisesbelchin$ pub global deactivate simple_http_server
Deactivated package simple_http_server 0.1.0+3.
```

Figure 6-14. *Deactivating a simple_http_server Dart package*

Pub Publish

As you know you cannot only create Dart applications, you can also create your own packages and **pub publish** will publish your packages on http://pub.dartlang.org for anyone to download and use.

■ **Note**   If you want to publish your own packages it's important to follow the pubspec format and the package layout conventions.

```
https://www.dartlang.org/tools/pub/pubspec.html
https://www.dartlang.org/tools/pub/package-layout.html
```

Pub Run

With the pub run command you can run Dart scripts from the command line. It executes the files in bin directory for a given application or package, so you can only use this command to execute Dart command-line applications. Let's see an example.

If we execute pub run in our new testPub project folder, we see the error message shown in Figure 6-15.

```
MacBook-Pro-de-Moises:testPub moisesbelchin$ pub run testpub
```

```
MacBook-Pro-de-Moises:testPub moisesbelchin$ pub run testpub
Could not find bin/testpub.dart.
```

Figure 6-15. Error using pub run command

Go to the *HelloCommand* application directory, this is a Dart command-line application that we built in *Chapter 2*. Now you're ready to execute the pub run command and you'll see the output of the application shown in Figure 6-16.

```
MacBook-Pro-de-Moises:HelloCommand moisesbelchin$ pub run hellocommand
```

```
MacBook-Pro-de-Moises:HelloCommand moisesbelchin$ pub run hellocommand
1 : Hello, Command-line app!
2 : Hello, Command-line app!
3 : Hello, Command-line app!
4 : Hello, Command-line app!
5 : Hello, Command-line app!
```

Figure 6-16. Running pub run command for a Dart command-line application

Pub Serve

When you run your Dart web application from Dart Editor you've already used this command. By clicking the **Run ➤ Run** menu option you're invoking the pub serve command over the Dart web application, Figure 6-17.

Figure 6-17. Running web application in Dartium from Dart Editor

This command starts up a development server to execute your Dart web applications. Go to the *testPub* project folder and run pub serve to start running your Dart web application, as shown in Figure 6-18.

```
MacBook-Pro-de-Moises:testPub moisesbelchin$ cd ../testPub/
MacBook-Pro-de-Moises:testPub moisesbelchin$ pub serve
Loading source assets...
Serving testPub web on http://localhost:8080
Build completed successfully
```

Figure 6-18. *Running our new testPub Dart web application using pub serve*

Pub Upgrade

We've already discussed this command in this chapter and you can use it directly from Dart Editor. As you know this command downloads and installs the latest version of all the dependencies listed in your pubspec.yaml project file, as shown in Figure 6-19.

```
MacBook-Pro-de-Moises:testPub moisesbelchin$ pub upgrade
Resolving dependencies... (1.1s)
  browser 0.10.0+2
  lawndart 0.6.5
No dependencies changed.
```

Figure 6-19. *Running pub upgrade*

Pub Uploader

This command is a tool for managing uploaders of a package. The uploaders are people who can upload a package to http://pub.dartlang.org. With this command you can **add** or **remove** a person who will or won't be an uploader for that package.

- pub uploader add me@email.com will add this person as an uploader.
- pub uploader remove me@email.com will remove this person as an uploader for the package.

Pub Downgrade

This command is the opposite of Pub Upgrade. It lets you downgrade the current package's dependencies to the oldest versions.

Pub help

Pub help will display all the information, commands, and options for pub as shown in Figure 6-20.

```
Pub is a package manager for Dart.

Usage: pub <command> [arguments]

Global options:
-h, --help              Print this usage information.
    --version           Print pub version.
    --[no-]trace        Print debugging information when an error occurs.
    --verbosity         Control output verbosity.

        [all]           Show all output including internal tracing messages.
        [io]            Also show IO operations.
        [normal]        Show errors, warnings, and user messages.
        [solver]        Show steps during version resolution.

-v, --verbose           Shortcut for "--verbosity=all".

Available commands:
    build       Apply transformers to build a package.
    cache       Work with the system cache.
    deps        Print package dependencies.
    downgrade   Downgrade the current package's dependencies to oldest versions.
    get         Get the current package's dependencies.
    global      Work with global packages.
    help        Display help information for Pub.
    publish     Publish the current package to pub.dartlang.org.
    run         Run an executable from a package.
    serve       Run a local web development server.
    upgrade     Upgrade the current package's dependencies to latest versions.
    uploader    Manage uploaders for a package on pub.dartlang.org.
    version     Print pub version.

Run "pub help [command]" for more information about a command.
See http://dartlang.org/tools/pub for detailed documentation.
```

Figure 6-20. *Running the pub help command*

Pub version

Pub version will show you the current version of Pub that is installed.

Summary

In this chapter we have learned:

- what the Pub package manager is
- how to create the pubspec.yaml file for your dart projects
- how to add new pub packages in your projects
- how to run Pub from Dart Editor to get the new pub packages added to pubspec.yaml
- all the Pub commands to properly manage your pub packages

CHAPTER 7

Optimizing for Dart VM and Dartium

Throughout this book we mentioned Dartium and Dart Virtual Machine when we've talked about how to run our applications.

In this chapter we're going to look at what they are and how to use them. In addition we'll show you what the checked mode is and how to optimize your Dart applications deactivating this mode when you're ready to deploy them.

Dart Virtual Machine

Dart Virtual Machine or Dart VM is the virtual machine of Dart. As happens with Java, Dart needs an interpreter who can recognize and run Dart code.

WHAT IS A VIRTUAL MACHINE?

A virtual machine (VM) is an emulation of a particular computer system. A VM is a software implementation of a machine (for example, a computer) that executes programs like a physical machine.

For example, if you write a Dart command-line application and try to run it on a system, which has not installed Dart VM, that application will not run. It will be a simple text file with instructions inside that the operating system cannot recognize. To prevent this from happening, you have to install Dart VM. The Dart VM recognizes and executes command-line applications and server side scripts, applications, and servers. Just as pub or dart2js, the Dart VM has commands and options to use.

Note   Remember, the Dart Virtual Machine is executed from the directory where Dart is installed, in our case it's /Applications/dart/dart-sdk/bin.

Running this command you could see all the options available in the Dart Virtual Machine.

```
MacBook-Pro-de-Moises:bin moisesbelchin$ dart -h
Usage: dart [<vm-flags>] <dart-script-file> [<dart-options>]

Executes the Dart script passed as <dart-script-file>.

Common options:
--checked or -c
 Insert runtime type checks and enable assertions (checked mode).
```

```
--help or -h
 Display this message (add -v or --verbose for information about
 all VM options).
--package-root=<path> or -p<path>
 Where to find packages, that is, "package:..." imports.
--version
 Print the VM version.
```

The -c or --checked parameter enables the Dart VM assertions (checked mode). As we've mentioned, this mode is recommended during the development and testing phase.

By default, Dart VM runs in production mode, because the checked mode slows down execution of larger programs significantly.

The -h or --help parameter displays the dart VM help information.

The --version parameter displays your Dart VM installed version.

```
MacBook-Pro-de-Moises:bin moisesbelchin$ dart --version
Dart VM version: 1.6.0 (Tue Aug 26 22:30:33 2014) on "macos_x64"
```

Finally, --package-root or -p followed by the path will indicate to Dart where the packages are to import and use in our applications.

We'll take the *hello_world.dart* file we created in previous chapters and we'll see how to execute it through the Dart VM. We can make sure that our hola_mundo.dart application runs in our system by running this command.

```
MacBook-Pro-de-Moises:bin moisesbelchin$ dart /path/to/your/file/hellow_world.dart
Hello, World!
```

It doesn't look so impressive, but let's next see something amazing. We're going to create a simple web server and run it with Dart VM on your system.

This is the code for our simple web server:

```dart
import 'dart:io';

main() {
  HttpServer.bind('127.0.0.1', 8080).then((server) {
    server.listen((HttpRequest request) {
      request.response.write('Hello, Welcome to Dart');
      request.response.close();
    });
  });
}
```

The code is really simple. With HttpServer class and bind method we started listening HTTP requests in the address and port indicated. Every time our server gets a new request, it'll show a welcome message to the fantastic world of Dart and close the response to the client. Run this web server through Dart VM with this command.

```
MacBook-Pro-de-Moises:bin moisesbelchin$ dart server.dart
```

After running the command, you will see that Dart VM keeps waiting to receive HTTP requests. Now open a browser and browse to the address **http://127.0.0.1:8080**

Our little server written in Dart says hello to us, as shown in Figure 7-1.

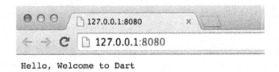

Hello, Welcome to Dart

Figure 7-1. *Greeting from our little Dart web server*

■ **Note** You can hit CTRL+C on the command line to kill the server after it's running.

Dartium

Now that we know Dart VM and know that this is essential to run our code, we're going to talk about Dartium, but what is Dartium? We've talked before about Dartium, but why is it included when I download and install Dart on my system? As we told you, in the future our Dart applications can run natively in the main browsers and then we won't need Dartium anymore, but for now we have two options to run and release our applications. First, you've already known and you used it in previous chapters: compile your Dart applications to JavaScript code and then, any modern browser with a JavaScript engine can understand and execute it. The second option is run your Dart web applications in a web browser that includes Dart VM.

This is Dartium. Dartium is the open source web browser Chromium (Google Chrome is based on this project) that includes the Dart VM. This explains the name: *Dart + Chromium = Dartiumn* Thanks to this combination of browser and virtual machine, we can execute our Dart web applications directly in the web browser without first compiling to JavaScript. As we mentioned Dartium is intended for development purposes only and is not safe to use on your day-to-day browsing. Dart VM and Dartium are included in our default Dart installation with the Dart Editor, SDK, pub, and dart2js. When you want to run a web application, this will be the default browser to run your Dart web applications. Like the other applications mentioned, you can run Chromium from the command-line using this command if your system is MacOS.

```
$ /Applications/dart/chromium/Chromium.app/Contents/MacOS/Chromium
```

Or this one if you're using Windows and your Dart environment is installed on the C:\dart.

```
C:\dart> chromium\chrome.exe
```

Checked Mode

We've previously talked about checked mode. This mode is intended only for development purposes because it adds warnings and errors to help you with your development and debugging process. In fact, an application with warnings running in checked mode could be stopped but will work fine in production mode. Let's see how to use and disable this checked mode to optimize your Dart applications before you deploy them. We're going to change Dartium flags to enable checked mode to verify type annotations and check assertions. Because Dartium is based on Chromium all Chromium flags should work. You can see the command-line flags and more information on Chromium by going to chrome://version, as you can see in Figure 7-2.

Figure 7-2. *Running chrome://version on Chromium*

To run Dartium in checked mode if you're running on MacOs or Linux you can use DART_FLAGS='--checked.' By running this command, if your system is MacOs, you're executing Dartium in checked mode.

```
DART_FLAGS='--checked' path/Chromium.app/Contents/MacOS/Chromium
```

If you use Linux you can use this command.

```
DART_FLAGS='--checked' path /chrome
```

In both cases replace path with your Chromium's path. Let's see now an example of using checked mode to activate on Dart VM. We're going to create a command-line application called Chapter_7 and this command-line application will contain this sample code.

```
void main() {
  int i = 'Hello, World!';
  print(i);
}
```

Now we're going to show you the difference between running this application with checked mode activated or not. And how an application with errors will work fine in production mode but will fail in checked mode.

Open up your command line tool and run this command.

```
$ dart chapter_7.dart
```

You will see this message, Hello World!. What does mean? Dart VM runs with checked mode off by default, so we're assigning a string message to a int i variable, but dart vm doesn't care about that.

Let's see what happens if we run the same command with the checked mode activated. Run this command on your terminal.

```
$dart -c chapter_7.dart
```

And you'll see something similar to Figure 7-3.

```
MacBook-Pro-de-Moises-3:bin moisesbelchin$ dart -c chapter_7.dart
Unhandled exception:
type 'String' is not a subtype of type 'int' of 'i'.
#0      main (file:///Users/moisesbelchin/dart/chapter_7/bin/chapter_7.dart:3:11)
#1      _startIsolate.isolateStartHandler (dart:isolate-patch/isolate_patch.dart:214)
#2      _RawReceivePortImpl._handleMessage (dart:isolate-patch/isolate_patch.dart:122)
```

Figure 7-3. Running dart code in checked mode

That's the main reason checked mode is helpful during the development and debugging phases. Our sample code had an error. We shouldn't assign a string to an int variable, and Dart VM is throwing a TypeError exception to warn us about that. The checked mode does a lot of type checkings and assertions and these operations slow down dramatically in larger applications.

As shown in Chapter 4, Pub has the --mode option and dart2js has the -c option to enable or disable the checked mode when you go to compile your application to deploy it. These options will change the size of the compiled files significantly. If you enable the checked mode a lot of runtime typechecks and assertions are included in the compiled files. Remember, use the checked mode only during development and debugging processes and disable it when you're going to compile your applications. That will optimize the size of the compiled files and speed up your first load applications.

Summary

In this chapter we have learned:

- what Dart Virtual Machine is

- what Dartium is

- what checked mode is and how you can deactivate when your applications go live to improve them

CHAPTER 8

Cleaning up with Dart Formatter

In this chapter we will show you a new Dart tool available from Dart 1.3 that will let you clean up your Dart code.

We'll see what this new tool is and how you can use it from the command-line with all its options and from Dart Editor.

Dart Formatter

From Dart 1.3 we have available a new tool with Dart that will let you format properly and automatically your Dart code. This tool is **Dart Formatter** and you can run it from the Dart sdk bin directory with these two modes.

```
dart-sdk/bin/dartfmt [flags] FILE.DART
```

```
dart-sdk/bin/dartfmt [flags] DIRECTORY
```

It is simple to use. If you specify a Dart file code, the tool will make corresponding changes in the file; if you indicate a directory, Dart Formatter will make changes in all the files it finds recursively in that directory. By default, all the changes made by dartfmt will be displayed on standard output. These are all the options or flags you can use with Dart Formatter:

```
-h, --help. Displays usage information
-w, --write. Write the result of reformatting directly over the files (overwritting contents) and
does not show the result on the standard output.
-t, --transform. Makes changes in the code. For example, if the control structures do not have
brackets, the added to.
-l, --max_line_length. Sets the length of the lines to the specified value, by default to 80
characters. If you do not want the lines to fit a specific length, you can indicate "Infinity" or
"Inf" value.
-m, --machine. The reformatting is saved in a particular format for a better parsing, it saves the
files as JSON format.
```

Let's see some examples.

Running dartfmt with -h option we can see all user information about this application.

```
MacBook-Pro-de-Moises:bin moisesbelchin$ dartfmt -h
dartfmt formats Dart programs.

Without an explicit path, dartfmt processes the standard input. Given a file, it operates on
that file; given a directory, it operates on all .dart files in that directory, recursively.
(Files starting with a period are ignored.) By default, dartfmt prints the reformatted sources to
standard output.

Usage: dartfmt [flags] [path...]

Supported flags are:
-w, --write              Write reformatted sources to files (overwriting contents). Do not print
                         reformatted sources to standard output.
-t, --transform          Perform code transformations.
-l, --max_line_length    Wrap lines longer than this length. To never wrap, specify "Infinity" or
                         "Inf" for short.
                         (defaults to "80")

-m, --machine            Produce output in a format suitable for parsing.
-h, --help               Print this usage information.
```

Running dartfmt with -w option writes the changes to the file.
Working with a file with this sample code:

```
/**
 * DocString for this file.
 */
import 'dart:html';

/// Application entrypoint.
void main() {
  int zero;
  if (0==0)
    zero=0;
  else if (0==1)
    zero=1;
  else if (0==2)
    zero=2;
}
```

When you run this command.

```
MacBook-Pro-de-Moises:bin moisesbelchin$ dartfmt -w test.dart
```

You'll get this result.

```
/**
 * DocString for this file.
 */
import 'dart:html';
```

```
/// Application entrypoint.
void main() {
 int zero;
 if (0 == 0) zero = 0; else if (0 == 1) zero = 1; else if (0 == 2) zero = 2;
}
```

Running dartfmt with the -t option, will make code transformations, such as adding brackets in control structures.

When you run this command.

```
MacBook-Pro-de-Moises:bin moisesbelchin$ dartfmt -w -t test.dart
```

You'll get this result.

```
/**
 * DocString for this file.
 */
import 'dart:html';

/// Application entrypoint.
void main() {
  int zero;
  if (0 == 0) {
    zero = 0;
  } else if (0 == 1) {
    zero = 1;
  } else if (0 == 2) {
    zero = 2;
  }
}
```

At last, if you run this command.

```
MacBook-Pro-de-Moises:bin moisesbelchin$ dartfmt -w -t -m test.dart
```

You'll get the result in JSON format:

```
{
"source":"/**\n * DocString for this file.\n */\nimport 'dart:html';\n\n/// Aplicattion
Entrypoint.\nvoid main() {\n int zero;\n if (0 == 0) {\n zero = 0;\n } else if (0 == 1)
{\n zero = 1;\n } else if (0 == 2) {\n zero = 2;\n }\n}\n",
"selection": {
"offset":-1,
"length":-1 }
}
```

You can also run Dart Formatter while you're working with Dart Editor. In the code editor you can right-click over the file you're editing and select **Format**. As you can see in Figure 8-1, this option is similar to run dartfmt with the -w option.

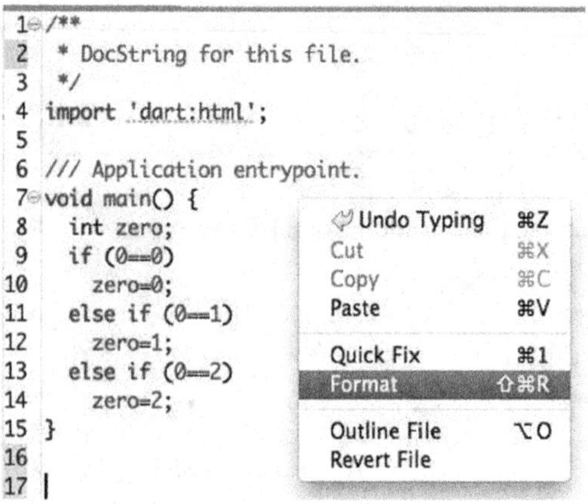

```
 1  /**
 2   * DocString for this file.
 3   */
 4  import 'dart:html';
 5
 6  /// Application entrypoint.
 7  void main() {
 8    int zero;
 9    if (0==0)
10      zero=0;
11    else if (0==1)
12      zero=1;
13    else if (0==2)
14      zero=2;
15  }
16
17  |
```

Undo Typing	⌘Z
Cut	⌘X
Copy	⌘C
Paste	⌘V
Quick Fix	⌘1
Format	⇧⌘R
Outline File	⌥O
Revert File	

Figure 8-1. *Running Dart Formatter during development*

Summary

In this chapter we have learned:

- what Dart Formatter is
- how you can use this tool from the command-line and what options it supports
- how to clean up your Dart code from Dart Editor

124

CHAPTER 9

Generating Dart Code Documentation

At the time of writing this book we are in the newest 1.7 Dart stable version. In this chapter we want to show the tools available to generate code documentation in Dart. We're going to talk about **docgen** (Documentation Generator). We'll cover docgen tool and its options, and we'll use it to generate the documentation of a simple library.

docgen

This tool came to replace the previous Dart documentation generator tool, called **dartdoc**, and this new tool changes completely the process of documentation generation. Dartdoc generated **HTML** static documentation files from the Dart files you selected, however docgen generates **YAML** or **JSON** files which are better for external tools and are easy to process. Furthermore, docgen has a new system that works as local server in order to process the JSON or YAML files and show the documentation through a web browser, similar to https://api.dartlang.org/. Obviously, docgen and its predecessor dartdoc use the code documentation comments (we'll see in our next chapters) to generate the documentation of your applications, libraries, or packages.

Documentation comments are generated using /// or /**/.

Here are some examples of documentation comments:

```
/**
 * Shift the bits of this integer to the right by [shiftAmount].
 *
 * Shifting to the right makes the number smaller and drops the least
 * significant bits, effectively doing an integer division by
 *`pow(2, shiftIndex)`.
 *
 * It is an error of [shiftAmount] is negative.
 */
int operator >>(int shiftAmount);

/// Returns true if and only if this integer is even.
bool get isEven;
```

Let's see how docgen works and its options. This is how you must use this tool.

```
MacBook-Pro-de-Moises:dart moisesbelchin$ docgen [OPTIONS] directory/file
```

If you select a directory, docgen will work in a recursive way in all the files in that directory; if you select a file, docgen will generate documentation for this file. These are all the options you could use with docgen. Run this command to see all the options.

```
MacBook-Pro-de-Moises:dart moisesbelchin$ docgen -h
```

You'll get all the information about how to use this tool.

```
-h, --help               Prints help and usage information.

-v, --verbose            Output more logging information.

   --include-private     Flag to include private declarations.

   --[no-]include-sdk    Flag to parse SDK Library files.(defaults to on)

   --parse-sdk           Parses the SDK libraries only.

   --package-root        Sets the package root of the library being analyzed.

   --compile             Clone the documentation viewer repo locally (if not already present)
                         and compile with dart2js

   --serve               Clone the documentation viewer repo locally (if not already present),
                         compile with dart2js, and start a simple server

   --no-docs             Do not generate any new documentation

   --introduction        Adds the provided markdown text file as the introduction for the
                         generated documentation. (defaults to "")

   --out                 The name of the output directory.(defaults to "docs")

   --exclude-lib         Exclude the library by this name from the documentation

   --[no-]include-
dependent-packages       Assumes we are documenting a single package and are running in the
                         directory with its pubspec. Includes documentation for all of its
                         dependent packages. (defaults to on)

   --sdk                 SDK directory

   --start-page          By default the viewer will start at the SDK introduction page. To start
                         at some other page, e.g. for a package, provide the name of the package
                         in this argument, e.g. --start-page=intl will make the start page of
                         the viewer be the intl package.

   --[no-]indent-json    Indents each level of JSON output by two spaces

Usage: dart docgen.dart [OPTIONS] fooDir/barFile
```

We'll show you in detail all the options.

DocGen Options

- -h, --help. Shows help and usage information.

- -v, --verbose. Shows more useful information during the generation process.

- --include-private. Includes private declarations in the documentation. The private declarations are private methods, variables, or classes at the library level you've written. We'll cover this topic in depth in Chapter 18.

- --[no-]include-sdk. It will include or not SDK files in your documentation. Defaults include SDK files.

- --parse-sdk. Parses only the SDK libraries.

- --package-root. Sets root directory for the library being analyzed.

- --compile. Clone the documentation viewer application and compile it with dart2js.

- --serve. Similar to --compile, download the application viewer, compile it, and run the simple web server to view the documentation through your web browser.

- --no-docs. Use this option to avoid generating any new documentation. This option is useful for faster start-up when used with --serve option if the docs have already been compiled previously.

- --introduction. Adds text as introduction for the generated documentation. Defaults to "". Later we'll see an example of this option.

- --out. Sets the name of the output directory. Defaults to "docs".

- --exclude-lib. It will exclude the library we set of the documentation.

- --[no-]include-dependent-packages. It will include or not the dependent packages in the documentation. It defaults to on.

- --sdk. Sets the SDK directory.

- --start-page. By default the viewer will start in the introduction page. With this parameter you could start the viewer in another page.

■ **Note** The --compile and the --serve options require you to have GIT installed on your system.

We're going to see some docgen usage examples. We'll start with a simple **test.dart** file with this content.

```
/**
 * An arbitrarily large integer.
 *
 * **Note:** When compiling to JavaScript, integers are
 * implemented as JavaScript numbers. When compiling to JavaScript,
 * integers are therefore restricted to 53 significant bits because
 * all JavaScript numbers are double-precision floating point
 * values. The behavior of the operators and methods in the [int]
 * class therefore sometimes differs between the Dart VM and Dart code
 * compiled to JavaScript.
 *
```

```
* It is a compile-time error for a class to attempt to extend or implement int.
*/
abstract class int {

 /**
  * Bit-wise and operator.
  *
  * Treating both `this` and [other] as sufficiently large two's component
  * integers, the result is a number with only the bits set that are set in
  * both `this` and [other]
  *
  * Of both operands are negative, the result is negative, otherwise
  * the result is non-negative.
  */
 int operator &(int other);

 /** Returns `this.toDouble()`. */
 double roundToDouble();

 /** Returns `this.toDouble()`. */
 double floorToDouble();

 /** Returns `this.toDouble()`. */
 double ceilToDouble();

 /** Returns `this.toDouble()`. */
 double truncateToDouble();

 /**
  * Returns a String-representation of this integer.
  *
  * The returned string is parsable by [parse].
  * For any `int` [:i:], it is guaranteed that
  * [:i == int.parse(i.toString()):].
  */
 String toString();
}
```

If you run this command.

```
MacBook-Pro-de-Moises:documentation moisesbelchin$ docgen test.dart
```

You'll see docgen is generated the **docs** directory (the default docgen output directory) with all the JSON format files that contain the documentation.

```
MacBook-Pro-de-Moises:documentation moisesbelchin$ docgen test.dart
WARNING: No package root defined. If Docgen fails, try again by setting the --package-root option.
Package Root: null
Added to libraries: file:///Users/moisesbelchin/dart/documentation/test.dart
SDK Root: /Applications/dart/dart-sdk
```

This is the new behavior of docgen. In previous versions of dart, docgen automatically generated the documentation adding the core libraries by default, as you can see below.

```
MacBook-Pro-de-Moises:documentation moisesbelchin$ docgen test.dart
WARNING: No package root defined. If Docgen fails, try again by setting the --package-root option.
Package Root: null
Added to libraries: file:///Users/moisesbelchin/dart/documentation/test.dart
Add to SDK: dart:async
Add to SDK: dart:collection
Add to SDK: dart:convert
Add to SDK: dart:core
Add to SDK: dart:html
Add to SDK: dart:indexed_db
Add to SDK: dart:io
Add to SDK: dart:isolate
Add to SDK: dart:js
Add to SDK: dart:math
Add to SDK: dart:mirrors
Add to SDK: dart:profiler
Add to SDK: dart:typed_data
Add to SDK: dart:svg
Add to SDK: dart:web_audio
Add to SDK: dart:web_gl
Add to SDK: dart:web_sql
SDK Root: /Applications/dart/dart-sdk
Cannot find MDN docs expected at /Applications/dart/utils/apidoc/mdn/database.json
```

With recent versions of docgen you can add the core libraries to your library documentation using the --include-sdk option.

dart-async.Completer.json	dart-async.DeferredLibrary.json	dart-async.DeferredLoadException.js...
dart-async.EventSink.json	dart-async.Future.json	dart-async.json
dart-async.Stream.json	dart-async.StreamConsumer.json	dart-async.StreamController.json
dart-async.StreamIterator.json	dart-async.StreamSink.json	dart-async.StreamSubscription.json
dart-async.StreamTransformer.json	dart-async.StreamView.json	dart-async.TimeoutException.json
dart-async.Timer.json	dart-async.Zone.json	dart-async.ZoneDelegate.json
dart-async.ZoneSpecification.json	dart-collection.DoubleLinkedQueue....	dart-collection.DoubleLinkedQueue...
dart-collection.HashMap.json	dart-collection.HashSet.json	dart-collection.HasNextIterator.json
dart-collection.IterableMixin.json	dart-collection.json	dart-collection.LinkedHashMap.json
dart-collection.LinkedHashSet.json	dart-collection.LinkedList.json	dart-collection.LinkedListEntry.json
dart-collection.ListBase.json	dart-collection.ListMixin.json	dart-collection.ListQueue.json
dart-collection.Maps.json	dart-collection.Queue.json	dart-collection.SplayTreeMap.json
dart-collection.SplayTreeSet.json	dart-collection.UnmodifiableListVie...	dart-convert.AsciiCodec.json
dart-convert.AsciiDecoder.json	dart-convert.AsciiEncoder.json	dart-convert.ByteConversionSink.json
dart-convert.ByteConversionSinkBas...	dart-convert.ChunkedConversionSin...	dart-convert.ClosableStringSink.json
dart-convert.Codec.json	dart-convert.Converter.json	dart-convert.Encoding.json
dart-convert.EventSink.json	dart-convert.HtmlEscape.json	dart-convert.HtmlEscapeMode.json
dart-convert.json	dart-convert.JsonCodec.json	dart-convert.JsonCyclicError.json

Figure 9-1. *JSON files generated with docgen*

Okay, but what about the JSON files? How can I view the documentation on a somewhat more human format?
Let's try something more interesting. We will use the --serve docgen option, but remember that you must have GIT installed on your system.

■ **Note**   GIT is a version control system designed by the creator of Linux, Linus Torvalds. If you want more information or instructions to use it, go to `http://git-scm.com/`

Why do I need GIT? The --serve option downloads the viewer documentation repository, compiles it with dart2js and starts a local web server to access and view the documentation with your web browser. The repository for the doc viewer application is a GIT repository so you need to have GIT installed on your system. Once you have installed GIT on your system, run this command.

```
MacBook-Pro-de-Moises:documentation moisesbelchin$ docgen --serve test.dart
```

At this time, in addition to generating the JSON files, it will download dartdoc-viewer, which is the application written in Dart to display, in a more legible format, the generated documentation JSON files. It will download the viewer launcher, run dart2js to compile dartdoc-viewer, and start the web server to view the generated documentation.

The result of the command is shown in Figure 9-2.

```
Downloading template_binding 0.11.0...
Downloading polymer_expressions 0.11.2...
Downloading web_components 0.4.0...
Downloading analyzer 0.15.7...
Downloading observe 0.10.1+2...
Downloading html5lib 0.11.0+2...
Downloading args 0.11.0+1...
Downloading utf 0.9.0+1...
Downloading csslib 0.11.0+2...
Changed 10 dependencies!

process stderr:
Compiling the app to JavaScript.
process output: Done! All files written to "out"
Running dart2js

Done

process stderr:
Docs are available at /Users/moisesbelchin/dart/documentation/dartdoc-viewer/client/out/web
Server launched. Navigate your browser to: http://localhost:8080
```

Figure 9-2. *docgen -serve output information*

As you can see in the output information you now can navigate with your browser to http://localhost:8080 to view the new documentation, as you can see in Figure 9-3.

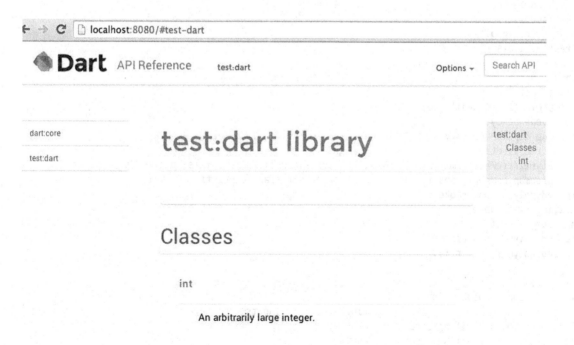

Figure 9-3. *New documentation for our test.dart library*

As we mentioned we can use --no-docs option combined with --serve for a faster start-up of our previously generated documentation.

If you run this command you can see how docgen launched the dartdoc viewer application without compiling the docs again.

```
MacBook-Pro-de-Moises:documentation moisesbelchin$ docgen --no-docs --serve test.dart
```

And you can see an output similar to this.

```
process output: Resolving dependencies...
  analyzer 0.22.4 (0.23.0-dev.13 available)
> args 0.12.1 (was 0.12.0+2)
  barback 0.15.2+2
  browser 0.10.0+2
  code_transformers 0.2.3+1
  collection 0.9.4 (1.1.0 available)
  csslib 0.11.0+2
  html5lib 0.12.0
  logging 0.9.2
  matcher 0.11.1
  observe 0.12.1+1
  path 1.3.0
  polymer 0.15.1+3
  polymer_expressions 0.13.0
  pool 1.0.1
  smoke 0.2.1+1
  source_maps 0.10.0
  source_span 1.0.0
  stack_trace 1.1.1
  template_binding 0.13.1
  unittest 0.11.0+5
  utf 0.9.0+1
  watcher 0.9.3
  web_components 0.9.0
  yaml 0.9.0+2 (2.1.0 available)
Changed 1 dependency!
Precompiling dependencies...
Loading source assets...
Loading polymer/src/build/mirrors_remover, polymer/src/build/delete_file, polymer/src/build/
remove_sourcemap_comment, observe and smoke/src/default_transformer transformers...
Precompiled polymer and smoke.
Precompiling executables...
Loading source assets...
Precompiled polymer:new_element.
Precompiled polymer:new_entry.

process stderr:
Compiling the app to JavaScript.
process output: info Took 0.3s (0.0s awaiting secondary inputs).
info Took 1.0s (0.8s awaiting secondary inputs).
info Took 1.0s (0.8s awaiting secondary inputs).
```

```
warning line 10, column 3 of web/index.html: No need to include "dart_support.js" by hand anymore.
See http://goo.gl/5HPeuP#polymer_43 for details.
  <script src="packages/web_components/dart_support.js"></script>
  ^^^^^^^^^^^^^^^^^^^^^^^^^^^^^^^^^^^^^^^^^^^^^^^^^^^^^^^
info Took 1.9s (0.0s awaiting secondary inputs).
Done! All files written to "out"
Running dart2js

Done

process stderr:
Docs are available at /Users/moisesbelchin/dart/documentation/dartdoc-viewer/client/out/web
Server launched. Navigate your browser to: http://localhost:8080
```

Let's see now how to use the --introduction option to add text to the generated documentation. We'll create a new file called intro.txt and add this text to the created file.

```
This is our test library with great documentation generated.
```

Now run this command to see how to use this new option and see the content of the new intro.txt file on the generated documentation.

```
MacBook-Pro-de-Moises:documentation moisesbelchin$ docgen --introduction=intro.txt --serve test.dart
```

As you can see in Figure 9-4 the new documentation contains the custom introduction text.

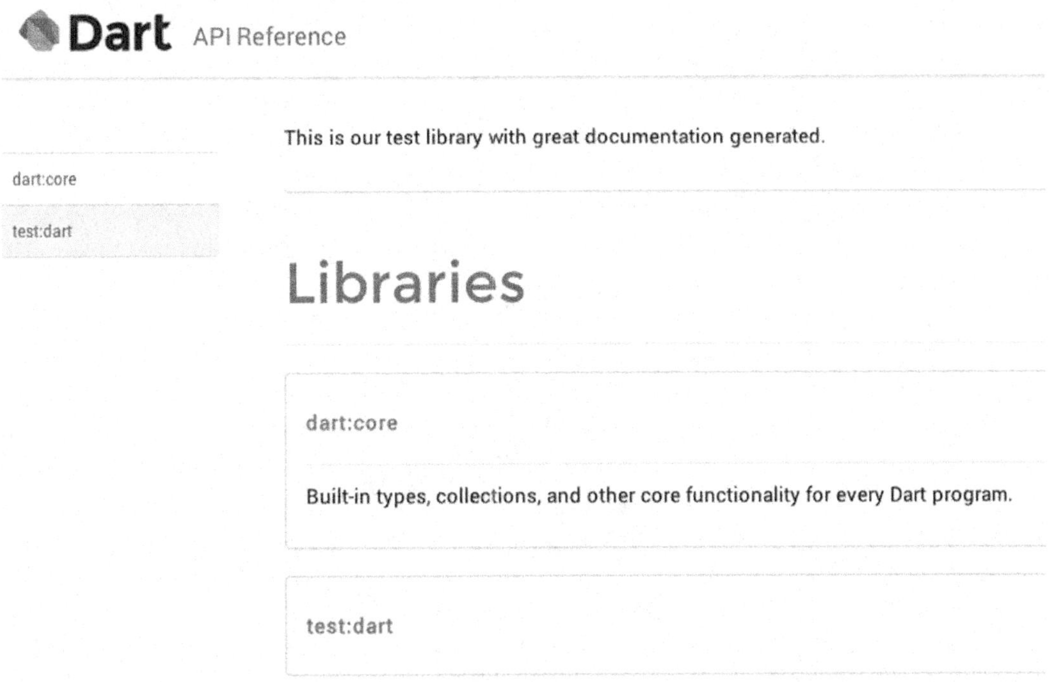

Figure 9-4. *The new documentation with custom introduction*

Summary

In this chapter we learned:

- what docgen is and all its options
- how to generate documentation for our libraries
- how to serve the generated documentation using --serve option
- how to speed up the docgen start-up viewer
- how to add custom text to the generated documentation using --introduction option

CHAPTER 10

■ ■ ■

Monitoring Your Applications with Observatory

In this chapter we will see a relatively new tool introduced in Dart called Observatory. We will see how take advantage of using it to debug and profile our web and command-line applications.

Observatory

Observatory, a tool for profiling and debugging Dart applications, was introduced in Dart 1.4. As you know, Dart is an interpreted programming language that needs the Dart VM to run. Diving into the virtual machine is very important as it is useful to know how everything works in order to try to improve it. Sadly, not everyone has the knowledge or the time to investigate how things work inside the virtual machine.

Every engineer knows that without mastering how things work, it would be very difficult to fix problems that arise, and nearly impossible to attempt to improve them. In order to know how the virtual machine works and how you could improve your applications, Dart's development team has brought you Observatory.

This tool allows you to see in real time how your applications run inside the virtual machine and to investigate where the application is spending more time, consuming more memory, and so forth.

Observatory will allow you to:

- Determine where an app is spending its time

- Examine allocated memory

- See which lines of code have executed

- Debug memory leaks

- Debug memory fragmentation

This amazing new tool will allow you to debug Dart web applications as well as Dart command-line applications. We're going to see how Observatory works using two different sample applications.

Observatory and Command-Line Applications

First of all, we're going to open a command-line application that has sample content, as shown in Figure 10-1.

```
Files ⌗                                    hellocommand.dart ⌗
▼ HelloCommand                        1  void main() {
    packages                          2    String msg = "Hello, Command-line app!";
    pubspec.lock                      3    List greetings = [1, 2, 3, 4, 5];
    pubspec.yaml                      4
▼ bin                                 5    greetings.forEach((c) {
    hellocommand.dart                 6      print("${c} : ${msg}");
▶ Dart SDK                            7    });
▶ Installed Packages                  8  }
                                      9
```

Figure 10-1. *Opening a new sample command-line applicationby*

We changed the default sample application a little bit by adding some variables, running a forEach loop, and showing a message. Here you can find the code:

```dart
void main() {
  String msg = "Hello, Command-line app!";
  List greetings = [1, 2, 3, 4, 5];

  greetings.forEach((c) {
    print("${c} : ${msg}");
  });
}
```

Let's now run this sample application and see all the information about it that shows up in our new friend Observatory. Note that we've set a breakpoint at line 2 of our example, as you can see in Figure 10-2. Run this application from Dart Editor, and in the Output view click on the Open Observatory button, shown in Figure 10-2, in order to open this new tool.

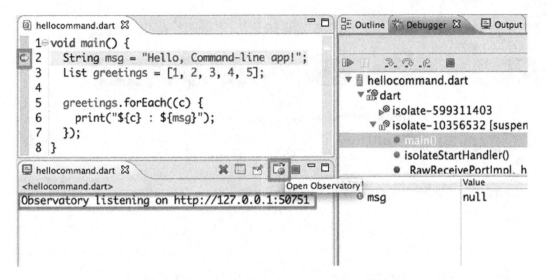

Figure 10-2. Opening Observatory to view our command-line application

Every time you run an application you can see this message in the Output view, informing you where Observatory is running:

```
Observatory listening on http://127.0.0.1:50751
```

Once you've clicked the Open Observatory button, you can see the new tool running, showing you all the important information, as shown in Figure 10-3.

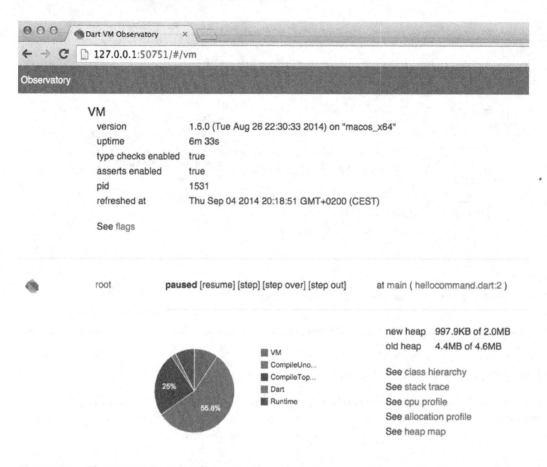

Figure 10-3. Observatory showing information about the hellocommand.dart application

---

■ **Note**   Observatory requires an Internet connection for the Google charts API you can see in Figure 10-3; without that the page will just display as a blank page.

Go back to your application, click on the debugger Step Over button (or press F6 few times) to run two statements, and then go to your browser to see how Observatory changes and shows you more information about memory. You'll also see how its graph changes. In addition, Observatory has different options for viewing all information regarding classes, stack trace, CPU profiling, and memory management, as shown in Figure 10-4.

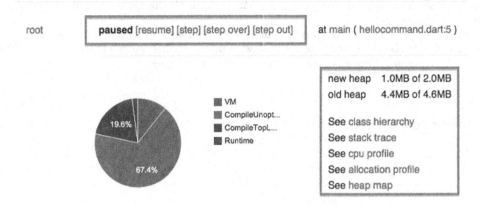

Figure 10-4. *Observatory in action*

You could manage your application through Observatory directly using the resume, step, step over, and step out buttons, shown in Figure 10-4, much as you were doing in Dart Editor debugger.

Observatory and Web Applications

It's time to run a web application and explore the information we can get via Observatory. We're going to open the Sunflower Dart Editor demo application to test it through Observatory. Go to Tools ➤ Welcome Page and open the Sunflower demo web application.

Once the application is open click on Run ➤ Run. Note that in the Output view the Open Observatory button is now disabled, as shown in Figure 10-5. So, how can you get information from Observatory when running web applications?

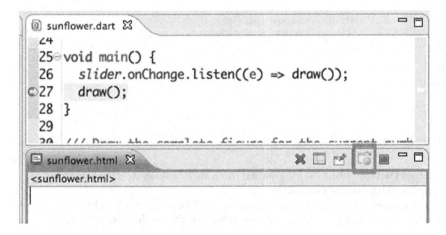

Figure 10-5. *Open Observatory button disabled when running web applications*

When you're running web applications and you want to inspect what's going on via Observatory, you'll need to open the Chrome Developer Tools in Dartium.

Hit Alt+CMD+I for Mac OS, CTRL+Shift+I for Linux/Windows, or select on the Dartium menu Tools ➤ Developer Tools. You should see a new panel on the bottom of the Dartium window. In this new panel you should see the Observatory option, as shown in Figure 10-6. Click this button in order to access Observatory.

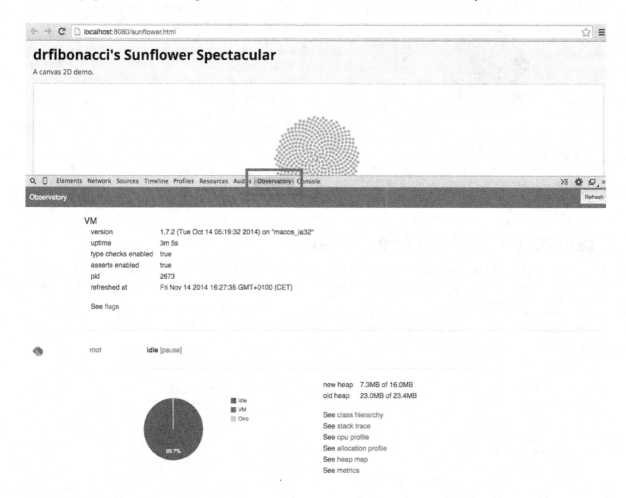

Figure 10-6. *Opening Observatory on Dartium*

Once you have Observatory open on Dartium, select the information you want to investigate–class hierarchy, stack trace, CPU profile, allocation profile, heap map, or metrics.

Once you have selected one of those items, you should see all its information. Observatory will add a navigation menu, as shown in Figure 10-7, in order to make it easier to change between the items to see different information.

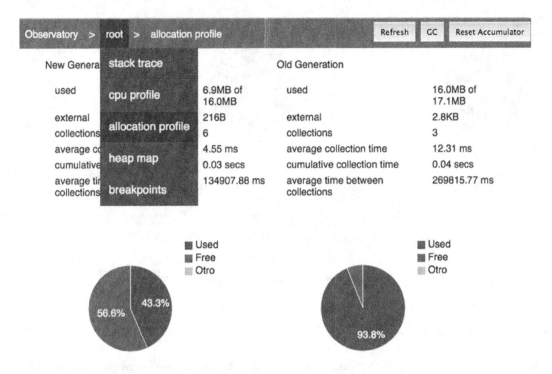

Figure 10-7. *Observatory navigation menu and memory management*

■ **Note** The Class Hierarchy and Metrics screens won't show the navigation breadcrumbs we talked about, but you can go back by clicking on the main Observatory link.

In the allocation profile screen, shown in Figure 10-8, you will see how an isolate is using memory in a given moment. This option also provides accumulator values that you can use to study the allocated memory. This helps you to detect leaking memory bugs.

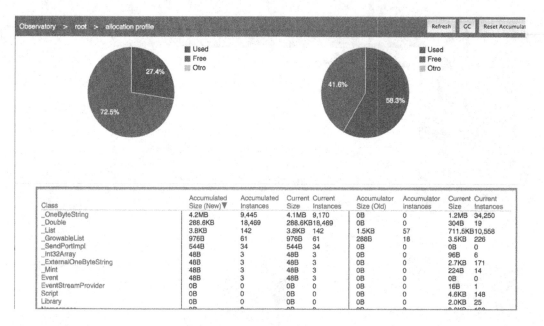

Figure 10-8. *Observatory ➤ allocation profile*

The Stack Trace screen, shown in Figure 10-9, displays the active stack frames as a tree for any given isolate. This window lets you expand any of the frames by clicking on the + icon.

Observatory > root > stack trace

```
#0          main ( hellocommand.dart:5 ) { ⊟
              msg        "Hello, Command-line app!"
              greetings  _GrowableList (5) { ⊞ }
            }

#1          isolateStartHandler ( isolate_patch.dart:214 ) { ⊞ }

#2          _RawReceivePortImpl._handleMessage ( isolate_patch.dart:122 ) { ⊞ }
```

Figure 10-9. *Observatory ➤ stack trace*

The CPU profile screen, shown in Figure 10-10, allows you to investigate the time spent by the virtual machine when executing an isolate.

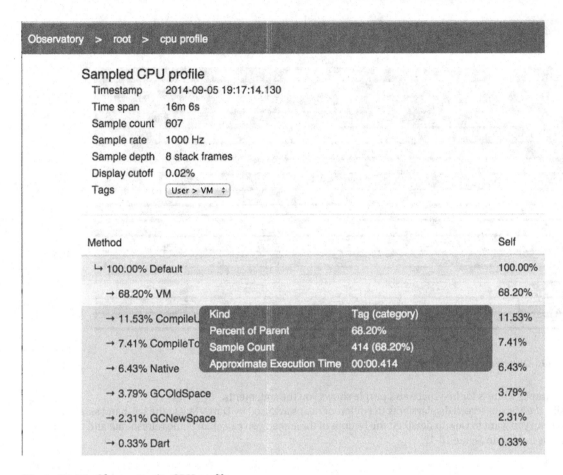

Figure 10-10. Observatory ➤ CPU profile

The Heap Map screen, shown in Figure 10-11, lets you see the memory fragmentation at any time for a particular isolate. This screen will show you blocks of memory represented by colors. A page of memory is 256 KB, and a horizontal black line separates each page. Each color on this screen represents different objects, free space, or instructions.

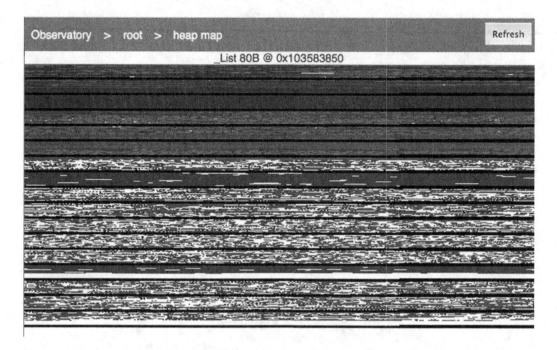

Figure 10-11. *Observatory* ➤ *heap map*

For example, white is for free space and purple shows you the statements.

Finally, the Metrics screen displays how the different heaps are used by Dart VM. On the left-hand side you can select the heap you want to view in detail. At the bottom of the screen you can change the refresh rate and the sample buffer size, as marked in Figure 10-12.

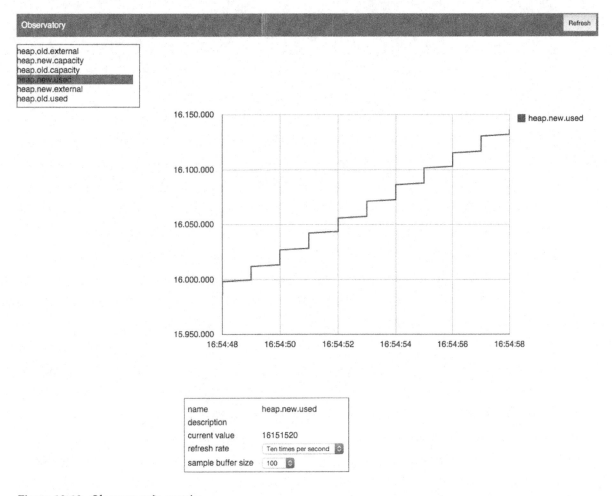

Figure 10-12. *Observatory* ➤ *metrics*

Summary

In this chapter we have learned the following:

- What Observatory is

- How you can use Observatory to profile your web or command-line applications

- How to run Observatory from command-line applications and from web applications

- How to use the different screens on Observatory to monitor your application's class hierarchy, stack trace, CPU profile, allocation profile, heap map, and metrics.

PART III

The Dart Language: Basics

CHAPTER 11

The Dart Comment System

In this chapter we will cover the Dart comment system–the different types of comments available when you write your Dart code. We'll see inline, block, and documentation comments and how to use them to properly document your applications. In addition, at the end of the chapter we'll see the markdown syntax you would use to add extra functionality to your programs' documentation.

Comments Overview

As you know, comments are an essential part of the source code of any application. They help to clarify some tricky parts of the code, especially if you have to return to them later to change anything.

They also help to other team members. In development groups where there are many people involved in the same projects, it is essential that each person develops his work, but also facilitates the work of others, leaving clear comments on the construction of the code to avoid any confusion.

Comments are used in all languages, even for something as simple as to auto generate the system documentation. For example, PHP, Java, and JavaScript use PHPDoc, JavaDoc, and JSDoc, respectively. As you know, in Dart we would use docgen for this same purpose.

In any case, we always need to document, so we will learn how to create these types of comments.

Inline Comments

In Dart, we can create comments that extend to a single line by beginning them with the characters //.

```
String htmlEscape(String text) {
  //More efficient implementation.
  return text.replaceAll("&", "&amp;")
          .replaceAll("<", "&lt;")
          .replaceAll(">", "&gt;")
          .replaceAll('"', "&quot;")
          .replaceAll("'", "&apos;");
}
```

In this example we have created an inline comment in a function indicating the reason why we used this type of implementation.

Block Comments

In Dart, as in other programming languages, there are also block comments. We can use them when we need to detail more information about our code. These comments begin with /* and are closed with */.

```dart
/*
 * We modify the method htmlEscape in version 1.2
 * Modified the replacement methods
 * for a more efficient and secure implementation.
 */
String htmlEscape(String text) {
  //More efficient implementation.
  return text.replaceAll("&", "&amp;")
             .replaceAll("<", "&lt;")
             .replaceAll(">", "&gt;")
             .replaceAll('"', "&quot;")
             .replaceAll("'", "&apos;");
}
```

In this example you can see a multiple-line comment is created to add more information. The leading * is stylized and is not specifically required, as you can see below. This is a format type, but another format is possible. Below you can see another way to format block comments:

```dart
/* We modify the method htmlEscape in version 1.2. Modified the replacement
 methods for a more efficient and secure implementation. */
String htmlEscape(String text) {
  //More efficient implementation.
  return text.replaceAll("&", "&amp;")
             .replaceAll("<", "&lt;")
             .replaceAll(">", "&gt;")
             .replaceAll('"', "&quot;")
             .replaceAll("'", "&apos;");
}
```

Documentation Comments

Previously, we learned there are applications for generating system documentation automatically by using the comments in our code. You could improve your application by adding a lot of comments about your system, and in addition you would benefit by getting great system documentation.

You know that in Dart this is possible thanks to the docgen tool, which uses in documentation the comments you insert when you write your code. These documentation comments are similar to block comments, with a small difference– they begin with /** and are closed with */, and each line is preceded by *.

Unlike above, when we saw the block comments, now the * followed by a single space is required at the beginning of each line. This type of comments is shown in Figure 11-1.

```
/**
 * The [Collection] interface is the public interface of all
 * collections.
 */
interface Collection<E> extends Iterable<E> {
  /**
   * Applies the function [f] to each element of this collection.
   */
  void forEach(void f(E element));

  /**
   * Returns a new collection with the elements [: f(e) :]
   * for each element [e] of this collection.
   *
   * Note on typing: the return type of f() could be an arbitrary
   * type and consequently the returned collection's
   * typeis Collection.
   */
  Collection map(f(E element));
```

Figure 11-1. *Documentation block comments*

Use the triple slash /// to create inline documentation comments. The Dart style guide currently recommends the triple slash for documentation comments, even for multi-line comments. This style, shown in Figure 11-2, is the preferred method for documentation.

```
_checkOpen() {
  if (!isOpen) throw new StateError('$runtimeType is not open');
}

/// Returns a Future that completes when the store is opened.
/// You must call this method before using
/// the store.
Future open();

/// Returns all the keys as a stream. No order is guaranteed.
Stream<String> keys() {
  _checkOpen();
  return _keys();
}
Stream<String> _keys();

/// Stores an [obj] accessible by [key].
/// The returned Future completes with the key when the objects
/// is saved in the store.
Future<String> save(V obj, String key) {
  _checkOpen();
  if (key == null) {
    throw new ArgumentError("key must not be null");
  }
  return _save(obj, key);
}
```

Figure 11-2. *Documentation inline comments*

The documentation comments can appear in any part of your code. Generally, the programmers use them at the beginning of the classes, methods, or functions; however, you could also add documentation comments inside classes, functions, or methods. For example, if you wanted to add documentation comments to any property of a class, you would add them in the appropriate part of your program, as shown in Figure 11-3.

```
/**
 * A parsed URI, such as a URL.
 *
 * **See also:**
 *
 * * [URIs][uris] in the [library tour][libtour]
 * * [RFC-3986](http://tools.ietf.org/html/rfc3986)
 *
 * [uris]: http://www.dartlang.org/docs/dart-up-and-running/contents/ch0:
 * [libtour]: http://www.dartlang.org/docs/dart-up-and-running/contents/(
 */
class Uri {
    // The host name of the URI.
    // Set to `null` if there is no authority in a URI.
    final String _host;
    // The port. Set to null if there is no port. Normalized to null if
    // the port is the default port for the scheme.
    // Set to the value of the default port if an empty port was supplied.
    int _port;
    // The path. Always non-null.
    String _path;
```

Figure 11-3. *Adding documentation comments on instance variables*

Comments are also very important at the library level. You can see a lot of inline, block, or even documentation comments placed before the library declaration, as shown in Figure 11-4.

```
//Copyright 2012 Seth Ladd
//
//Licensed under the Apache License, Version 2.0 (the "License");
//you may not use this file except in compliance with the License.
//You may obtain a copy of the License at
//
//    http://www.apache.org/licenses/LICENSE-2.0
//
//Unless required by applicable law or agreed to in writing, software
//distributed under the License is distributed on an "AS IS" BASIS,
//WITHOUT WARRANTIES OR CONDITIONS OF ANY KIND, either express or implied.
//See the License for the specific language governing permissions and
//limitations under the License.

/**
A unified, asynchronous, easy-to-use library for offline-enabled
browser-based web apps. Kinda sorta a port of Lawnchair to Dart,
but with Futures and Streams.

Lawndart uses Futures to provide an asynchronous, yet consistent,
interface to local storage, indexed db, and websql. This library is designed
for simple key-value usage, and is not designed for complex transactional
queries. This library prefers simplicity and uniformity over expressiveness.

You can use this library to help deal with the wide array of client-side
storage options. You should be able to write your code against the Lawndart
interface and have it work across browsers that support at least one of the
following: local storage, indexed db, and websql.

# Example

    var db = new IndexedDbStore('simple-run-through', 'test');
    db.open()
      .then((_) => db.nuke())
      .then((_) => db.save("world", "hello"))
      .then((_) => db.save("is fun", "dart"))
      .then((_) => db.getByKey("hello"))
      .then((value) => query('#text').text = value);

See the `example/` directory for more sample code.

*/
library lawndart;
```

Figure 11-4. *Comments at the library level*

Markdown

Docgen tool also recognizes other Dart Doc comment syntax inspired by the markdown package
(https://pub.dartlang.org/packages/markdown). This syntax is used by docgen to format documentation
comments and add extra capabilities to the documentation, such as links, code snippets, code font, italics, boldface,
ordered and unordered list item, and so on.

We'll show you how to use this new functionality to improve the documentation of your own APIs.

Links

You can add links to your Dart Doc comments, which could point to an identifier, constructor, or external hyperlink. [id] or [id](uri) will generate a hyperlink to a Dart identifier, a class, a method, or a property.

In the coming example we've created two classes, and the Dart Doc for FirstClass has links to both FirstClass and SecondClass identifiers.

```
/// First class is used to create [FirstClass] objects.
/// This class also uses [SecondClass] to accomplish other tasks.
class FirstClass {}

class SecondClass {}
```

After running docgen you can view the links in the generated documentation, as shown in Figure 11-5.

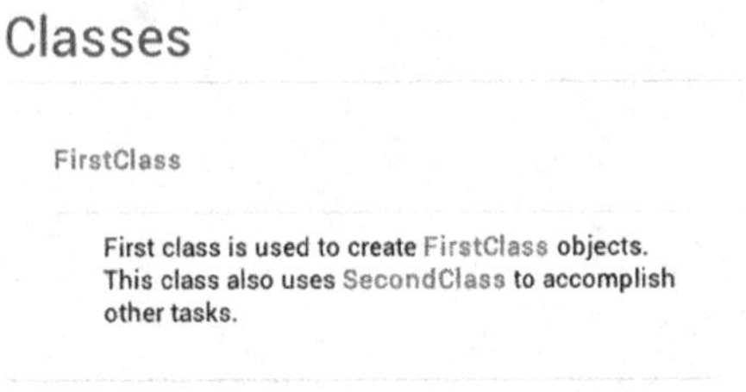

Classes

FirstClass

First class is used to create FirstClass objects.
This class also uses SecondClass to accomplish
other tasks.

Figure 11-5. *Links to Dart identifiers*

The links you add into your Dart Doc comments can point to constructor methods or external hyperlinks, as you can see in the code example below. [new c] or [new c](uri) will create a new link to the constructor for c. [text] (uri) or <uri> will create an external hyperlink using text as the link text in the first case, and the uri as link text in the second case.

Using these kinds of links in your code will generate the documentation you can see in the code below and in Figure 11-6.

```
/// First class is used to create [FirstClass] objects.
/// This class also uses [SecondClass] to accomplish other tasks.
class FirstClass {

  /// The [new FirstClass] constructor is inspired on
  /// [Uri class](https://api.dartlang.org/apidocs/channels/stable/dartdoc-viewer/dart:core.Uri)
  /// You can find this class on <https://api.dartlang.org/apidocs/channels/stable/dartdoc-viewer/
dart:core>
  FirstClass();

}

class SecondClass {}
```

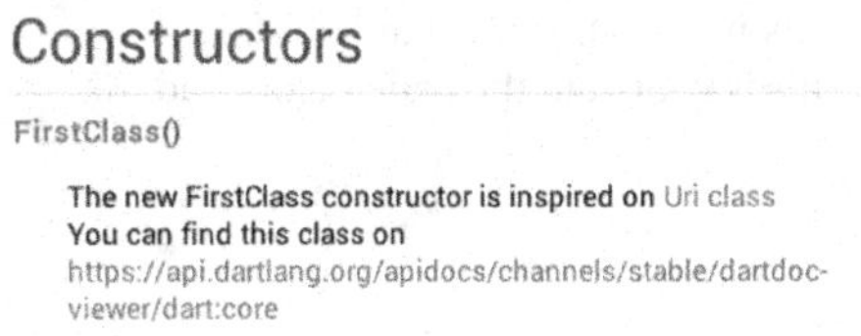

Constructors

FirstClass()

The new FirstClass constructor is inspired on Uri class
You can find this class on
https://api.dartlang.org/apidocs/channels/stable/dartdoc-
viewer/dart:core

Figure 11-6. *External links*

Block Styles

You can use a blank line to denote the end of a paragraph:

```
/// This is a paragraph.
///
/// This is another paragraph.
```

You can add code snippets into your Dart Doc comments using four blank spaces after the line's comment. It means five spaces after the * or /, as seen below:

```
/**
 *
 * Example:
 *
 *     Uri uri1 = Uri.parse("a://b@c:4/d/e?f#g");
 *     Uri uri2 = uri1.replace(scheme: "A", path: "D/E/E", fragment: "G");
 *     print(uri2);  // prints "A://b@c:4/D/E/E/?f#G"
 *
 */
```

You can specify header text using ## as you can see below and in Figure 11-7:

```
/**
 * ## Other resources
 *
 * See [StringBuffer] to efficiently build a string incrementally. See
 * [RegExp] to work with regular expressions.
 *
 */
```

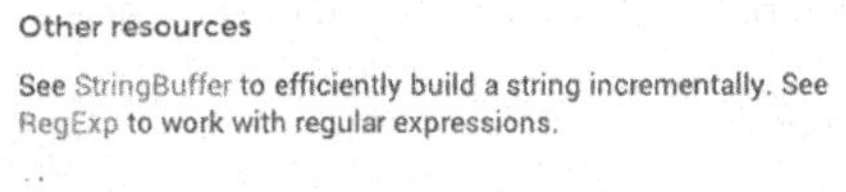

Other resources

See StringBuffer to efficiently build a string incrementally. See
RegExp to work with regular expressions.

Figure 11-7. *Adding header text to Dart Doc comments*

You can also add ordered or unordered lists to your Dart Doc comments using * as the first character for unordered lists, or using numbers such as 1., 2., and so on for ordered lists. This is shown in the code below and in Figure 11-8.

```
/// This class is used to create:
///
///     * FirstClass objects
///     * User objects
///     * SecondClass objects
///
/// This class is also used to create:
///
///     1. Objects with one property
///     2. Objects with two properties
///     3. Objects with three properties
///
class FirstClass {}
```

FirstClass class

Extends: Object

This class is used to create:

- FirstClass objects
- User objects
- SecondClass objects

This class is also used to create:

1. Objects with one property
2. Objects with two properties
3. Objects with three properties

Figure 11-8. *Using ordered and unordered lists*

Inline Styles

In our Dart Doc comments we can use inline styles to emphasize notes or warnings as well as use code-style font. Let's see some examples.

`code` or [:code:] will use code-style font for the code you write. Using a single underscore or single asterisk will mark the word or sentence as italics, and double underscore or double asterisks will mark the word or sentence as boldface.

Let's see these inline styles in action in the code below and in Figure 11-9.

```
/// This class is used to create [FirstClass] objects.
///
/// `new FirstClass();` will create a new [FirstClass] object.
///
```

```
/// **Warning** This class uses cache.
///
/// Remember _clear the cache_ after using these objects.
///
class FirstClass {}
```

FirstClass class

Extends: Object

This class is used to create FirstClass objects.

`new FirstClass();` will create a new FirstClass object.

Warning This class uses cache.

Remember *clear the cache* after using these objects.

Figure 11-9. *Inline styles*

Summary

In this chapter we have learned the following:

- What Dart Doc is
- The different types of comments you can use in your applications
- How to create inline comments
- How to create block comments
- How to use the documentation comments
- What Markdown is and how to use it to improve your program's documentation
- How to use links, block styles, and inline styles

■ ■ ■

CHAPTER 12

Understanding Operators and Expressions

In this chapter we will see what operators and expressions are and the different types we can use in our Dart applications. At the end of the chapter we'll review how to create your own operators.

An Introduction to Dart Operators

Operators are an essential part of any programming language. With them, you can do arithmetic operations with numbers, assign values between variables, and make decisions in a particular moment so that your program will execute one or another block of instructions.

Dart is an object-oriented language; everything in Dart is an object, so the operators are aliases (shortcuts) to methods of instance. These methods are special in that they cannot be assigned to a variable as other objects can, and they have special names, for example, +, -, *,%, and so on.

Essentially, an instance method is a classification that is applied to specific methods defined by a class. Instance methods work on object instance variables, but also have access to the class variables.

Do not worry if you have not understood anything so far, as we will see it in more detail when we study classes, methods, instance variables, and object-oriented programming with Dart. The operators, defined by default in Dart, can be overridden or redeclared. If you want to override an operator in one of your classes, you must use the reserved keyword operator, as shown in Figure 12-1.

```
abstract class double extends num {
  static const double NAN = 0.0 / 0.0;
  static const double INFINITY = 1.0 / 0.0;
  static const double NEGATIVE_INFINITY = -INFINITY;
  static const double MIN_POSITIVE = 5e-324;
  static const double MAX_FINITE = 1.7976931348623157e+308;

  double remainder(num other);

  /** Addition operator. */
  double operator +(num other);

  /** Subtraction operator. */
  double operator -(num other);

  /** Multiplication operator. */
  double operator *(num other);

  double operator %(num other);

  /** Division operator. */
  double operator /(num other);
```

Figure 12-1. *Defining a class with its operators*

In Figure 12-1 we can see how to define the double class, which has different operators, or methods with special names: addition operator [+], subtraction operator [-], multiplication [*], division [/], and module operator [%].

■ **Note**   Not all operators can be overridden, only a certain subset such as, <, +, |, [ ], >, /, ^, [ ]=, <=, , ~/, , &, ~, >=, , *, <<, , ==, −, %, >>

Operator Types

Types of operators in Dart are classified as:

- Arithmetic
- Equality and relational
- Type test
- Assignment
- Conditional
- Bit
- Other

Let us explore these in more detail.

Arithmetic

Below you can see Table 12-1 with the Arithmetic operators.

Table 12-1. *Arithmetic operators*

+	Addition
-	Subtraction
-expr	Unary negation
*	Multiplication
/	Division
~/	Integer division
%	Remainder
++var	Increment before executing other operation
var++	Increment after running the statement
--var	Decrement before executing other operation
var--	Decrement after running the statement

Let's see some examples of arithmetic operators.

```
void main() {
  num a = 3;
  num b = 15;

  print(a + b);  // 18
  print(a - b);  // -12
  print(-a);     // -3
  print(a * b);  // 45
  print(a / b);  // 0.2
  print(a ~/ b); // 0
  print(a % b);  // 3

  print(a);      // 3
  print(++a);    // 4
  print(a);      // 4
  print(a++);    // 4
  print(a);      // 5

  print(b);      // 15
  print(--b);    // 14
  print(b);      // 14
  print(b--);    // 14
  print(b);      // 13
}
```

Equality and Relational

In Table 12-2 you can see the equality and relational operators.

Table 12-2. *Equality and relational operators*

==	Equal to
!=	Not equal to
>	Greater than
<	Less than
>=	Greater than or equal to
=<	Less than or equal to

Below you can see examples of equality and relational operators in action.

```
void main() {
  num a = 3;
  num b = 15;

  print(a == b); // false
  print(a != b); // true

  print(a > b); // false
  print(a < b); // true

  print(a >= b); // false
  print(a <= b); // true
}
```

Type Test

Type test operators are described in Table 12-3.

Table 12-3. *Type test operators*

as	Type casting, converts an object of one type into an object of another type
is	True if the object is of the indicated type
is!	False if the object is of the indicated type

Here are some examples of type test:

```
void main() {
  int a = 3;

  print((a as num).toDouble()); // 3.0

  print(a is double); // false
  print(a is! double); // true

}
```

Assignment

We'll show you the assignment operators in Table 12-4.

Table 12-4. *Assignment operators*

=	Assigns a value to a variable
*=	Multiplication assignment
~/=	Integer-division assignment
%=	Module assignment
+=	Addition assignment
-=	Subtraction assignment
/=	Division assignment
<<=	Bitwise left-shift assignment
>>=	Bitwise right-shift assignment
&=	Bitwise AND assignment
^=	Bitwise XOR assignment
!=	Bitwise OR assignment

Let's see some examples of assignment operators:

```
void main() {
  var a;

  a = 15;
  print(a); // 15

  a *= 3;
  print(a); // 45

  a ~/= 2;
  print(a); // 22
```

```
  a %= 3;
  print(a); // 1

  a += 14;
  print(a); // 15

  a -= 7;
  print(a); // 8

  a /= 2;
  print(a); // 4.0

  a = a.toInt();
  a <<= 2;
  print(a); // 16

  a >>= 1;
  print(a); // 8

  a &= 0;
  print(a); // 0

  a ^= 1;
  print(a); // 1

  a != 1;
  print(a); // 1

}
```

Conditional

In Table 12-5 you'll see the conditional operators.

Table 12-5. *Conditional operators*

!expr	Reverses the value of the conditional expression
||	Logical OR
&&	Logical AND

Here you can see an example of the use of conditional operators:

```
void main() {
  num a = 3;

  print(a == 3); // true
  print(!(a == 3)); // false

  print(a > 2 || a < 4); // true

  print(a > 2 && a < 4); // true
}
```

Bit

Bit operators are described in Table 12-6.

Table 12-6. *Bit operators*

&	AND
|	OR
^	XOR
~expr	Reverses the value of Bit
<<	Left shift
>>	Right shift

Below you can find examples of bit operator usage.

```
void main() {
  print(1 & 0); // 0

  print(0 | 1); // 1

  print(1 ^ 0); // 1

  print(4 << 1); // 8

  print(4 >> 1); // 2
}
```

Others

Dart has other operators commonly used, shown in Table 12-7.

Table 12-7. *Other operators*

()	Call a function
[]	Reference a value from a list
cond?exp1:exp2	If the condition is true, expression 1 is executed; otherwise expression 2 is executed.
.	Accessing the members of an object
..	Making multiple operations on an object, known as cascade operator

An Introduction to Expressions

The expressions in Dart are code snippets. They are evaluated at runtime to get a value, which is always an object. Each expression has a static type associated, and each value has a dynamic type associated.

An expression is a set of data or functions connected by arithmetic, logic, or any other operator.

We will go deep into the data types later, so do not worry too much for now, and let's continue with expressions. Below we'll describe the different type of expressions you can use in your Dart programs.

Conditional

Evaluates one of two expressions based on a Boolean condition.

```
expr1 ? expr2 : expr3
```

If expr1 is true, then it executes expr2; in any other case, it will execute expr3.

Logical

Logical expressions combine Boolean objects with conjunction and disjunction operators.

```
expr1 || expr2
```

```
expr1 or expr2
```

```
expr1 && expr2
```

```
expr1 and expr2
```

Bit

You can manipulate the individual bits of numbers using bit expressions.

```
expr1 & expr2
```

Multiply bits logically, for example, 12 & 10 makes 8.

```
expr1 | expr2
```

Add bits logically, for example, 12 | 10 makes 14.

```
expr1 ^ expr2
```

Exclusive addition of the bits, for example, 12 ^ 10 makes 6.

Equality

This checks equality or identity on objects.

```
expr1 == expr2
```

This expression returns a Boolean object `true` if `expr1` is equal to `expr2` and return `false` in any other case.

```
expr1 != expr2
```

This expression returns a Boolean object `true` if `expr1` is different than `expr2`, and returns `false` otherwise.

Relational

This invokes relational operators on the expression objects.

```
expr1 > expr2
```

Returns `true` if `expr1` is greater than `expr2`, `false` otherwise.

```
expr1 >= expr2
```

Returns `true` if `expr1` is greater than or equal to `expr2`, `false` otherwise.

```
expr1 < expr2
```

Returns `true` if `expr1` is less than `expr2`, `false` otherwise.

```
expr1 <= expr2
```

Returns `true` if `expr1` is less than or equal to `expr2`, `false` otherwise.

Bitwise

Invokes shift operators on the expression objects.

```
expr1 >> expr2
```

Moves a bit pattern to the right, discarding the bits to the left.

```
expr1 << expr2
```

Moves a bit pattern to the left and fills with zeros to the right.

Addition

Invokes addition operators on expression objects.

```
expr1 + expr2
expr1 - expr2
```

Multiplication

Invokes multiplication operators on expression objects.

```
expr1 * expr2
expr1 / expr2
expr1 ~/ expr2
expr1 % expr2
```

Pre-Expressions and Post-Expressions

Also known as unary expressions, these work on the expression objects. You could get different results depending if you uses pre- or post-expressions.

++expr. Increments expr by one and returns expr

expr++. Returns expr and then increments its value by one

--expr. Decrements expr by one and returns expr

expr--. Returns expr and decrements its value by one

Assignment

Assigns value to expression objects. With this, you can change the value of a variable or property whenever it is mutable, which means it can be changed.

The main operator is [=], but there are more, for example, [*=], [/=], [~/=], [%=], [+=], [-=], [<<=], [>>=], [&=], [^=], [|=].

expr1 += 5. Gets expr1 value, adds 5, and assigns the new value to expr1.

```
void main() {
  var a;

  a = 15;
  print(a); // 15

  a *= 3;
  print(a); // 45

  a ~/= 2;
  print(a); // 22

  a %= 3;
  print(a); // 1

  a += 14;
  print(a); // 15

  a -= 7;
  print(a); // 8
```

```
  a /= 2;
  print(a); // 4.0

  a = a.toInt();
  a <<= 2;
  print(a); // 16

  a >>= 1;
  print(a); // 8

  a &= 0;
  print(a); // 0

  a ^= 1;
  print(a); // 1

  a != 1;
  print(a); // 1

}
```

How to Create Your Own Operators

At the beginning, we mentioned that Dart lets you overwrite or redefine operators for any use you need. Let's see an example of how easy it is.

We will create a class Address that will store the street where a person lives, and we will use the operator [+] to get the full address, including street, number, floor, and city, as shown below.

```
/// Address class
class Address {
  /// Instance variable with the address.
  String _dir;

  /// Simple class constructor.
  Address(this._dir);

  /// Add operator, concatenates our address with more information.
  Address operator + (Address more_info) {
    return new Address("$_dir, $more_info");
  }

  /// Overrides Object.toString() method.
  String toString() => _dir;
}

void main() {
  var adrs = new Address("Main street");
  print(adrs); // Main street

  adrs += new Address("number 3, 4th floor, Madrid");
  print(adrs); // Main street, number 3, 4th floor, Madrid
}
```

169

In this example we've created our `Address` class in order to create a custom addition operator. This method needs two special things. One of them is that it must return an `Address` object. Second, it must require an `Address` object as a parameter. This is an operator method that operates on `Address` objects, adding two new `Address` objects.

Do not worry about class definition, constructor, overriding, etc. in the example, just look the `Address` operator + method.

```
///Add operator, concatenates our address with more information.
Address operator + (Address more_info) {
  return new Address("$_dir, $more_info");
}
```

And, just look at how in the main function we could add two different `Address` objects.

```
adrs += new Address("number 3, 4th floor, Madrid");
```

Summary

In this chapter we have learned the following:

- What the Dart operators are

- What the Dart expressions are

- Some examples combining operators and expressions

- How you can create your own operators

■ ■ ■

CHAPTER 13

Mastering Dart's Variables and Data Types

In this chapter we will see all of Dart's basic data types such as string, numbers, and Boolean. We will also look at how to define variables in Dart and how to use `final` and `const` reserved keywords.

Later, we will see more complex types such as lists, sets, and maps as well as how to work with regular expressions and `DateTime` objects.

An Introduction to Variables and Data Types

We will start with a very basic and simple definition about what variables are.

> *The variables are just storage places, memory places that we'll use to store information.*

You already know operators are necessary and basic in all programming languages, but without the variables the operators would not make sense. We store strings, numbers, results of other functions, instances, etc. in memory. To access them you must use references, which are the variables. Variables are names that we give to those parts of our computer's memory where data is stored.

If we have access to the data, we can operate with them. If we store number 5 in a variable and number 2 in another variable, we could use the addition operator to work with those variables and add the numbers contained in them, getting a result. This new result could be stored in another variable to use it later if you need it.

Dart also supports different types of data to define the many variables we use in our programs. The data type is like an annotation that you can use so as to know whether the value contained in the variable is a number, a string, or other data type, and thus you can work properly with this data type. For example, you could do mathematics operations such as subtraction or division with numbers but not with strings of text.

Dart uses data types to improve your development experience, warning you about errors while you're writing your applications. Data types also help Dart translate Dart code to JavaScript code.

Let's look at some simple examples using variables:

```
void main() {
  var variable1 = 5;
  var variable2 = 2;
  print(variable1+variable2); // The result is 7
}
```

We have defined two variables without specifying their data type and have added these variables, displaying the results on screen.

In the next example we work with two different variables, one of which is a `String` variable and the other of which is a variable of type num. We'll show a message by interpolating the contents of both variables:

```
void main() {
  String variable1 = 'Welcome to Dart';
  num variable2 = 1.6;
  print('$variable1 $variable2'); // The result is "Welcome to Dart 1.6"
}
```

Variables Definition

As we have seen in the previous examples, there are two ways to define the variables in Dart; the first is with the word var followed by the variable name.

```
void main() {
  var my_variable;
  var other_variable = 'This is the content of the variable';
}
```

You can also specify the data type of the variable at definition time, as follows:

```
void main() {
  double my_variable;

  String other_variable = 'This is the content of the variable';
}
```

Therefore, Dart is an optional typed language. If you want, you can specify the type annotations or not and write your applications as you would do in JavaScript.

■ **Note**   Using data type annotations is useful for maintaining your applications. The editor and the compiler use data types to help you in checked mode while you are writing code by autocompleting the code and giving you warnings or errors. If checked mode is disabled then the type annotations will be ignored and will not generate errors or warnings.

Notice that when you define a variable, you can indicate its value, or not. In the first case, the variable has no value assigned, so to Dart the value will be null, whatever the data type. In the second case, the variable is initialized with the string of text *"This is the contents of the variable."*

Types of Variables: Final and Const

There are two modifiers by which to change the normal behavior of a variable: final and const. When writing code, you should determine whether a variable will change during execution. If the variable will never change, you can use final or const to indicate to Dart that these variables will never change, instead of using var. See here:

```
void main() {
  final app_title = 'My first Dar application';
  final String app_subtitle = 'So cool!';
}
```

Notice that you can choose to use the data type annotation when you define the variable with `final`.

What is the difference between `const` and `final`? A variable declared as `final` is initialized only once. However, a variable declared as `const` is considered as a constant in run-time. The global-scope variables, local-scope variables, or class members declared as `final` are initialized the first time they are used. This is called *lazy initialization* and helps applications to start up faster.

For any value that you want to be constant at runtime, use `const` followed by the variable name and the value of the variable. Let's see an example.

We're going to create a small application to calculate the area of a circle. As you may know, the area of a circle can be calculated using this formula, $A = \Pi * r^2$. The number *pi* is a mathematical constant, so we'll define it as `const` in our Dart program.

```
void main() {
  const pi = 3.14159265358979;
  var r = 2.59;
  var a = pi * r * r;
  print(a); // 21.07411767954567
}
```

Data Types

Dart has several data types that you can use, and they each have special uses:

- Numbers
- Strings
- Booleans
- Lists (also known as *arrays*)
- Maps (in Python you know them as *dictionaries*)

In Dart, every variable is a reference to an object. As you know, Dart is an object-oriented language, and everything in Dart is an object, even the most basic data type. An object is an instance of a class, which we will discuss later.

When you create this object (instances of classes), you use a constructor method to initialize the object and its class members. Some of the Dart data types have their own builders; for example, to create a list you will use the constructor `new List ()`.

But you can also initialize these special data types with what is called a literal.

```
void main() {
  var string = 'This is a string'; // String Object.

  var number = 15;    // Number Object.

  var correct = true; // Bool Object.

  var list = [1,2,3]; // List Object.

  var map = {         // Map Object. Key-value pairs.
    'name': 'Juan',   // String object for name.
    'age': 29,        // Number object for age.
    'sick': false     // Bool object for sick.
  };
}
```

Numbers

In Dart numbers can be int or double, which are a subtype of num. An integer or decimal numeric value that is assigned to a variable defines that variable as being of type num. The num type includes most of the operations you will use when working with numbers. Mathematical operations you cannot find in num you will find in Dart's library:math (discussed in detail later), such as *sin, cos, pow, min, max,* and so on.

int are numbers without a decimal point.

```
void main() {
  var number = 15;
  var other_number = 159763213;
  var hexadecimal_number = 0x3F;
}
```

double are numbers with a decimal point.

```
void main() {
  var double_1 = 15.83;
  var double_2 = 159763213.764398216;
  var double_3 = 1.3e-5;
  var double_4 = -98.72;
}
```

Working with Numbers in Dart

Let's look at some of the methods that we can use when working with numbers in Dart. All of these methods are located in dart:core, the main Dart library that offers a great set of predefined functions. This library is automatically imported into all programs.

This library defines three basic classes with which to work with num, int, and double data types. The num class is the super class of int and double, which means that int and double inherit all the methods that we can find in the num class.

Convert a string to a number:

```
int.parse('189'); // returns 189 as int object.
```

double.parse('15.48'); // returns 15.48 as a double object. These parse methods have their own error handling in case you cannot parse and convert the string to a number. Here's an example:

```
var int_number = int.parse('15');
print(int_number);        // shows 15 as int object.
print(int_number is int); // shows true;

var error_int_number = int.parse('15€', onError: (_) {return null;});
print(error_int_number);        // shows null because it can not parse the string.
print(error_int_number is int); // shows false.

var double_number = double.parse('15.42');
print(double_number);            // shows 15.42 as double object.
print(double_number is double); // shows true;
print(double_number is num);     // shows true;
```

```
var error_ double_number = double.parse('15.42$', (_) {return null;});
print(error_ double_number); // shows null because it can not parse the string.
print(error_ double_number is double); // shows false.
```

num.parse also works, which will first try to convert a string to an integer, and if it fails it'll try to convert to a double, and if that fails then it'll run the onError handler, if defined. These methods, with their own error handling, are very useful when trying to collect information from the user and when you need to work with it properly.

If you want to convert a number to string, you can use the .toString() method:

```
int num = 5;
String mystring = num.toString();
print(mystring); // shows object String 5.
```

Let's now consider the common methods available on class num to work with numbers in Dart. Start with a number like this:

```
num number = -15.84;
```

With these methods you can find out if a number is *finite, infinite, negative,* or *NaN* (is not a number). The method will always return a bool value of True or False:

```
print(number.isFinite);    // True
```

```
print(number.isInfinite); // False
```

```
print(number.isNegative); // True
```

```
print(number.isNaN);       // False
```

If you want to know the sign of a number you can use this method:

```
print(number.sign); // -1.0
```

It returns -1.0 if the number is less than zero, returns +1.0 if it's greater than zero, or returns the number itself if it is -0.0, 0.0, or NaN.

If you want to get the absolute value of a number, use the following code:

```
print(number.abs()); // 15.84
```

See how to round to the next integer greater than the number:

```
print(number.ceil()); // -15
```

See how to round to the previous integer number lowest than the number:

```
print(number.floor()); // -16
```

Now round to the nearest integer number:

```
print(number.round()); // -16
```

Now return the integer part and discard the decimal part of the number:

```
print(number.truncate()); // -15
```

All of these methods will return an integer number, but the toDouble variant will return a double number for these same operations, as follows:

```
print(number.ceilToDouble());      // -15.0

print(number.floorToDouble());     // -16.0

print(number.roundToDouble());     // -16.0

print(number.truncateToDouble()); // -15.0
```

You can also convert a double number to integer, using toInt:

```
print(number.toInt()); // -15
```

And you can get a string from a number indicating the decimal part digits:

```
number = 3.14159265358979;

print(number.toStringAsExponential(6)); // 3.141593e+0

print(number.toStringAsFixed(4));        // 3.1416

print(number.toStringAsPrecision(2));    // 3.1
```

Two new methods were introduced on the latest Dart releases: remainder and clamp. The first one returns the remainder of the truncating division of one number by another. The second one clamps a number so as to be in the range between lowerlimit, upperlimit that you indicate.

```
int number = 18;
var result = 18.remainder(2.5);
print(result); // shows 0.5

int number = 18;
print(number.clamp(1, 9));   // 9
print(number.clamp(10, 30)); // 18
print(number.clamp(18, 50)); // 18
```

The int class contains the methods we have learned and some others:

```
int number = 15;
```

To find out if a number is even or odd, use the following:

```
print (number.isEven); // False

print (number.isOdd);  // True
```

You can get the bit length of the integer number in binary mode by using the following code:

```
print (number.bitLength); // 4 - binary number 1111
```

You can also convert the number to a string object in the given representation, as follows:

```
print(number.toRadixString(5));  // 30
print(number.toRadixString(2));  // 1111
print(number.toRadixString(16)); // f
```

The double class contains the same methods that we have already learned, and the only difference is the use of a constant to work with this type of numbers:

```
static const double NAN = 0.0 / 0.0;
static const double INFINITY = 1.0 / 0.0;
static const double NEGATIVE_INFINITY = -INFINITY;
static const double MIN_POSITIVE = 5e-324;
static const double MAX_FINITE = 1.7976931348623157e+308;
```

The double data type is contagious, which means that when you perform operations with double numbers you'll get results of type double, as follows:

```
int num1 = 15;
double num2 = 2.0;
print(num1 * num2); // 30.0
```

dart:math Library

Now that we have seen the basic Dart class for working with numbers, let's take a look at the dart:math library that allows you to make advanced mathematical calculations with numbers. This library provides functionality to generate random numbers, trigonometric functions, and oft-used math constants such as *pi* and *e*. To be able to use this library in your applications, you need to import it this way:

```
import 'dart:math';
```

Besides the functions of dart:math we have learned, there are other classes that allow you to work with bidimensional representations of positions and rectangles for 2D graphic designs. Let's see some dart:math methods. For mathematical constants to use in your applications, see here:

```
print(E);  // 2.718281828459045
print(PI); // 3.141592653589793
```

For trigonometric functions to calculate cosine, sine, tangent, arc cosine, arc sine, and arc tangent use the following:

```
var degrees = 30;
var radians = degrees * (PI / 180); // 0.5235987755982988

print(cos(radians)); // 0.8660254037844387

print(sin(radians)); // 0.49999999999999994
```

```
print(tan(radians)); // 0.5773502691896257
```

```
print(acos(radians)); // 1.0197267436954502
```

```
print(asin(radians)); // 0.5510695830994463
```

```
print(atan(radians)); // 0.48234790710102493
```

To calculate square root, exponential function, logarithmic, and power use the following:

```
print(sqrt(25)); // 5.0
```

```
print(exp(3)); // 20.085536923187668
```

```
print(log(10)); // 2.302585092994046
```

```
print(pow(2, 3)); // 8
```

It also includes functions to calculate the minimum and the maximum of two numbers:

```
print(min(2, 8));    // 2
print(max(15, 10)); // 15
```

Random Numbers

We have learned some of the things we can do using dart:math, but there is more; one of them is to work with random numbers using the Random class.

Instantiate an object of Random type by calling its constructor:

```
var rand = new Random();
```

Then you can generate ten random int numbers between 1 and 100 with a code like this:

```
for(var i=0; i<10; i++) {
  print(rand.nextInt(100));
}
```

This code could return a sequence of numbers like this:

```
40, 84, 35, 26, 58, 86, 77, 28, 68, 28
```

With this code you will get a list of ten random double numbers between 0 and 1:

```
for(var i=0; i<10; i++) {
  print(rand.nextDouble());
}
```

And this example would return a list of numbers like this:

```
0.35400081214332246, 0.2540705633345569, 0.15263890994501117, 0.265262387358984, 0.9386646648924302,
0.8545231577991513, 0.5948728139929099, 0.04713641533447943, 0.6284813334686553, 0.5992417288687604
```

Random also lets you to generate random bool values:

```
for(var i=0; i<10; i++) {
  print(rand.nextBool());
}
```

And this little snippet of code will return a list of values like this:

```
true, false, false, false, false, true, false, true, true, false
```

Strings

Dart strings are sequences of UTF-16 characters. To initialize a string you can use a literal enclosed in double quotes or single quotes, as follows:

```
var str_1 = "Example of string enclosed in double quotes";

var str_2 = 'Example of string enclosed in single quotes';

// You can include a quote type inside another.
var str_3 = 'This is a "string"';

// You can escape quotes with backslash.
var str_4 = 'Escaping \'single quotes\' inside single quotes';
```

Dart supports *string interpolation*, which means that in a string you can include the value of another variable or expression using the format $variableName or ${expression}:

```
var my_number = 4000;

var str_1 = 'Dart is used for more than $my_number people!';

print(str_1); // Dart is used for more than 4000 people!
```

You can also define multi-line strings using triple single quotes or triple double quotes, like you do in Python. Within these strings you can also use interpolation. Note that the new line at the beginning is trimmed off; however, the new line at the end of the triple quote is significant (will display an empty line). See here:

```
var name = 'John';

var template = '''
<html>
 <head>
   <tittle> Dart </tittle>
 </head>
 <body>
   <h1> Welcome to Dart $name !! </h1>
 </body>
</html>
''';
```

Later, we will see the `StringBuffer` class and how efficient it is when used to concatenate strings, but if you need to make a simple string concatenation you can use adjacent strings' literals. No '+' sign is needed—it's valid but not required.

```
var address = 'Picasso Street, 12'
'Postal Code: 28001'
'Madrid'
'Spain';

print(address); // Picasso Street, 12 Postal Code: 28001 Madrid Spain
```

Working with Strings

In `dart:core` you can find the classes you previously learned for working with numbers, but in addition you can find other classes useful for working with other basic data types. In this case, you will see how you can work with strings and all the methods available to the `String` class located in `dart:core`.

Something to keep in mind is that strings are *immutable*—you cannot change a string, but you can create operations on strings and assign the result to another string. See here:

```
var my_string = 'Welcome to Dart';
var new_string = my_string.substring(11, 15);
print(new_string); // Dart
```

Internally, the strings work as lists of characters so you can access a particular position in the string and get the character with the operator [ ]

```
var my_string = 'Welcome to Dart';

print(my_string[0]); // W
```

Strings are sequences of characters (using UTF16) so you can get the code of the character at that position:

```
print(my_string.codeUnitAt(0)); // 87
```

You can also get all the character codes on the string:

```
print(my_string.codeUnits); // [87, 101, 108, 99, 111, 109, 101, 32, 116, 111, 32, 68, 97, 114, 116]
```

You can get the length of the string with this method:

```
print(my_string.length); // 15
```

You can find out if a string ends with a specific character, if it ends with another string, or if it ends with a regular expression. The `endsWith`, `startsWith`, `split`, `replace`, `contains`, `lastIndexOf`, and `indexOf` methods let you specify a simple string or regular expression as an argument:

```
print(my_string.endsWith('t'));    // True
```

```
print(my_string.endsWith('bye')); // False
```

```
print(my_string.startsWith('Wel'));                    // True

print(my_string.contains(new RegExp(r'\bto\b'))); // True

print(my_string.contains(new RegExp(r'[0-9]')));  // False
```

You can discover the position of a string or a particular character in this way:

```
print(my_string.indexOf('Dart')); // 11

print(my_string.indexOf('hello')); // -1

print(my_string.lastIndexOf('a')); // 12
```

You can also find out if a string is empty or not:

```
print(my_string.isEmpty);      // False

print(my_string.isNotEmpty); // True
```

You can use the following method to retrieve only one string fragment. You can specify the optional end index parameter as well:

```
print(my_string.substring(11));      // Dart
print(my_string.substring(11, 13)); // Da
```

And you can remove blank characters at the beginning and end using trim():

```
var my_string2 = 'Dart';

print(my_string2.trim()); // Dart
```

With the arrival of Dart 1.4 two more trim methods were added to the String class: trimLeft() and trimRight(). The first one returns the string without any leading whitespace. The second one returns the string without any trailing whitespace. See here:

```
print(my_string2.trimLeft());    // Dart
print(my_string2.trimRight());   // Dart
```

When you work with strings you probably need to fill them with a certain number of characters, like zeros or whitespaces, to get them in the perfect format. Dart brings to you padLeft() and padRight() methods to accomplish these tasks. The padLeft() method will prepend the character you indicate, or whitespace by default, onto the string one time for each position the length is less than a given width. See the following:

```
var str_num = '12';
print(str_num.padLeft(5, '0')); // 00012
str_num = '37546';
print(str_num.padLeft(5, '0')); // 37546
```

On the other hand, with padRight() you can append a character, or whitespaces by default, after the string:

```
var name = 'Moises';
  var age = '30';
  var row = '| ${name.padRight(20, '_')}${age.padRight(5,'_')} |';
  print(row); // | Moises_____30___ |
```

With the following methods you can find out whether a string contains a particular character or other string. You can also replace only the first occurrence or all existing in a given string. You can also split the string from a character or string. See the following:

```
print(my_string.contains('hello')); // False

print(my_string.contains('Dart')); // True

print(my_string.replaceFirst('to', 'to the amazing')); // Welcome to the amazing Dart

print(my_string.replaceAll('e', '3')); // W3lcom3 to Dart

print(my_string.split('e')); // [W, lcom,  to Dart]
```

Converting the string to lowercase or uppercase works as follows:

```
print(my_string.toLowerCase()); // welcome to dart

print(my_string.toUpperCase()); // WELCOME TO DART
```

Now that we've taken a look at the methods of the String class on dart:core, we want to show you the great potential of the StringBuffer class, which, as we mentioned before, is a very efficient implementation for string concatenation.

To create a new StringBuffer you must make a call to the constructor:

```
StringBuffer result = new StringBuffer();
```

Once you have created the object, you can start writing content inside the StringBuffer with the write method. When you want to show the content of the StringBuffer object, you can use .toString() method. In the example below it's not necessary because the print statement automatically calls the toString method:

```
result.write('Welcome');
result.write('to');
result.write('Dart');

print(result); // Welcome to Dart
```

You can even write new lines using the writeln() method:

```
result.writeln(); // This method add new line at the end of the string buffer.

result.write('version 1.7');
print(result.toString()); // Welcome to Dart
                           // version 1.7
```

You can get the size of the string buffer and whether is empty or not.

```
print(result.length);      // 27

print(result.isEmpty);     // False

print(result.isNotEmpty);  // True
```

You can also write a list of strings (List<string>) in the string buffer object using the writeAll method:

```
result.writeAll(['. the ', 'new ', 'programming ', 'language']);
print(result.toString()); // Welcome to Dart
                          // version 1.7. the new programming language
```

To clean and empty the StringBuffer object you can use the clear() method:

```
print(result..clear());    // '' [Empty string]
```

Regular Expressions

We have seen how to work with strings and StringBuffer. In previous examples, we learned that some methods can accept strings, characters, or regular expressions. To work with regular expressions in Dart, dart:core includes the **RegExp** class. Dart regular expressions have the same syntax and semantics as JavaScript.

▪ **Tip**   See the specification of JavaScript regular expressions at
http://www.ecma-international.org/ecma-262/5.1/#sec-15.10

Brackets

Brackets are used to search a range of characters. See Table 13-1.

Table 13-1. *Brackets*

[abc]	Search any character specified between the brackets. You can use a hyphen to specify alphabetical ranges, such as [A-Z].
[^abc]	Search for any character that is not indicated between the brackets.
[0-9]	Search for any digit specified between the brackets.
[^0-9]	Search for any digit that is not indicated between the brackets.
(x|y)	Search any of the indicated alternatives.

Metacharacters

Regular expressions use some special characters for searches. See Table 13-2.

Table 13-2. *Metacharacters*

.	Search for a character, except the line termination character or newline character
\w	Search for a letter.
\W	Find a non-word character.
\d	Search for digits.
\D	Find a non-digit character.
\s	Search for whitespace characters.
\S	Search for non-whitespace characters.
\b	Search for matches at the beginning or end of a word.
\B	Search for matches not at the beginning or end of a word.
\0	Search for the NUL character.
\n	Search for the newline character.
\f	Search for the line-feed character.
\r	Search for the carriage-return character.
\t	Search for the tab character.
\v	Search for the vertical tab character.
\xxx	Search for the character specified by the octal number xxx.
\xdd	Search for the character specified by the hexadecimal number dd.
\uxxxx	Search for the Unicode character specified by the hexadecimal number xxxx.

For example, to search for numbers in a string you can use a regular expression like this:

```
var text = 'Welcome to Dart';
var re = new RegExp(r'\d+');
print(re.hasMatch(text)); // False
text = 'Welcome to Dart 1.7';
print(re.hasMatch(text)); // True
```

The constructor method of the RegExp class lets you create a new regular expression and determine whether you want it to be case-sensitive or support searching across multiple lines.

```
var re = new RegExp('e');
```

In this sample text you can see how the RegExp object is handled:

```
var mytext = 'Welcome Dart';
```

You can find out if the regular expression has matches in the text using the hasMatch method:

```
print(re.hasMatch(mytext)); // True
```

The stringMatch method will return the first occurrence:

```
print(re.stringMatch(mytext)); // e
```

And allMatches lets you work with all the occurrences found. In this particular case, we will iterate over all the matches; we've shown the start and end indexes on the string:

```
re.allMatches(mytext).forEach((m) {
  print(m.start);
  print(m.end);
}); // 1, 2
    // 6, 7
```

These following methods tell you the regular expression pattern, whether it has multi-line support, and whether it's case sensitive:

```
print(re.pattern);         // 'e'
print(re.isMultiLine);     // False
print(re.isCaseSensitive); // True
```

Booleans

Variables defined as *Boolean* with a bool data type usually represent a variable that differs between two statements: *true* or *false*. Boolean variables are defined in Dart with the literal true or false.

```
var my_bool = true;
bool other_bool = false;
```

■ **Note**   Dart only considers as a true value the true value for the bool variables; everything else is interpreted as false (opposite that which happens in JavaScript).

This should be kept in mind when you work with Dart because you will be forced to check the values you expect. See below for an example of the use of conditional expressions on non-Boolean values.

```
var name = 'Juan';
if(name) {
  print(name);
}
```

If you use a code like that, you will get a Dart error displaying that the variable of type String is not a Bool subtype for use in a conditional expression. This error occurs because the name variable is a string; if this variable were a bool variable, this type of conditional expression would be evaluated without errors. However, these types of conditional expressions are very common in JavaScript and work perfectly.

You could change the example and run it like this:

```
var name = 'Juan';
if(name != null && name.isNotEmpty) {
  print(name);
}
```

Working with Bool Values

In dart:core you can find the **bool** class that you will use when you want to work with Boolean values. This class has no methods, such as int, num, or string classes. Actually these data types are often used in conditional expressions to determine whether a particular block of code is executed. The only method of the class bool is the toString() method, which returns a string object with the value of the Boolean variable. See the following:

```
bool done = false;
if(done) {
  print(' Well done you've finished!');
} else {
  print(' Sorry, but you have to keep trying !');
}
print(done.toString()); // "false"
```

Lists

One of the most commonly used data structures in all programming languages is the list. In other languages you know them as *arrays*. In Dart, the arrays are collections of objects and are called lists. As you have seen, you can initialize a variable of type list with a literal using brackets and commas to separate the values. See here:

```
main() {
  var people = ['Patricia', 'Moises'];

  List pets = ['Benchara', 'Erik', 'Lily'];

  List empty_list = new List();

  // Add elements to empty list.
  empty_list.add('First element');
  empty_list.add(28);

  print(people);     // [Patricia, Moises]
  print(pets);       // [Benchara, Erik, Lily]
  print(empty_list); // [First element, 28]
}
```

In this example, you can see how to create and initialize a list from the literal or by using the constructor new List(). We added the add() method so you can see how to add elements of any type to a list. Also, you can nest lists, which means that within a list another list or other data type can be included.

As you know, Dart has an *optional typing* system, but if you want even to just define the values that will go into your lists, you can do it using angle brackets and the data type, as in this example:

```
main() {
 List<int> numbers_list = [1, 2, 3, 4, 5];
 List<String> names_list = ['Peter', 'John', 'Mary'];
}
```

Working with the List Class

We will now see all the methods available in dart:core for the List class, which has four different constructors with which to create Dart lists.

The default constructor allows you to create a list with no elements, and you won't need to indicate the list size:

```
var empty_list = new List();
print(empty_list); // []
```

You can also define a list with a fixed-size element:

```
var empty_list _2_elements = new List(2);
print(empty_list_2_elements); // [null, null]
```

You can create a list of fixed size, and also have it be initialized with a value, a number, a string or a map; for example:

```
var my_filled_list_num = new List.filled(3, 0);
var my_filled_list_str = new List.filled(3, 'A');
var my_filled_list_map = new List.filled(3, {});
print(my_filled_list_num); // [0, 0, 0]
print(my_filled_list_str); // [A, A, A]
print(my_filled_list_map); // [{}, {}, {}]
```

You can use the List.from constructor and create a list from another list. This constructor has a parameter so as to create a list of fixed or variable length, allowing the list to grow, or not:

```
var my_list_from_another = new List.from(my_filled_list_str, growable:true);
print(my_list_from_another); // [A, A, A]
my_list_from_another.add('B');
print(my_list_from_another); // [A, A, A, B]
```

Finally, you can use the List.generate constructor method to create a list from another by using an iterator and ensuring certain conditions are met. The method passed to the generate constructor receives the index of the element in the list. See a sample list:

```
var other_list = ['/etc/', '/home/pi/'];
```

From this you can create a new list using elements of the first and separating them by a backslash:

```
var my_iterator_list_1 = new List.generate(other_list.length, (e) {
 return other_list[e].split('/');
}, growable: true);
print(my_iterator_list_1); // [[, etc, ], [, home, pi, ]]
```

Or you can create a new list, separating each element by a backslash and discarding empty elements:

```
var my_iterator_list_2 = new List.generate(other_list.length, (e) {
 return other_list[e].split('/').where((e) => e != '').toList();
}, growable: true);
print(my_iterator_list_2); // [[etc], [home, pi]]
```

Besides the constructors, there are other methods for working with lists in Dart. We will work on examples about list management with a simple list, like this:

```
var my_list = [1, 2, 3];
```

This method shows the length of the list, i.e., how many elements it contains:

```
print(my_list.length); // 3
```

You can also change the length of the list, as follows:

```
my_list.length = 5;
print(my_list.length); // 5
```

And if you want to access a specific position and get its value, you can use brackets that indicate the index:

```
print(my_list [1]); // 2
```

Using brackets, you can also assign values to these positions:

```
my_list [3] = 4;
my_list [4] = 5;

print(my_list); // [1, 2, 3, 4, 5]
```

Or you can use the add() method to add items to the list. If the list is non-growable, the add() method will throw an error.

```
my_list.add(6);
print(my_list); // [1, 2, 3, 4, 5, 6]
```

There is also a method to add one list to another:

```
my_list.addAll([7, 8, 9]);
print(my_list); // [1, 2, 3, 4, 5, 6, 7, 8, 9]
```

You can turn over the list with the reversed method:

```
print(my_list.reversed); // (9, 8, 7, 6, 5, 4, 3, 2, 1)
```

This next method allows you to sort a list:

```
my_list.sort();
print(my_list); // [1, 2, 3, 4, 5, 6, 7, 8, 9]
```

The .sort() method can take a function that can be used to manually compare values to determine sorting order. Let's see an example. We have this list of applications with their names and versions:

```
List apps = [
  {'name': 'WordPress', 'version': 4},
  {'name': 'SourceTree', 'version': 2},
  {'name': 'Google Chrome', 'version': 38},
  {'name': 'Safari', 'version': 8},
];

apps.forEach((a) => print(a['name'])); // WordPress
                                       // SourceTree
                                       // Google Chrome
                                       // Safari
```

We can sort them by their names in ascending mode using this compare function:

```
// Sort apps by name ascending
var compare = (a, b) => a['name'].compareTo(b['name']);
apps.sort(compare);

apps.forEach((a) => print(a['name'])); // Google Chrome
                                       // Safari
                                       // SourceTree
                                       // WordPress
```

Now we're going to sort them by their version number in descending mode with another compare function:

```
// Sort apps by version descending
compare = (b, a) => a['version'].compareTo(b['version']);
apps.sort(compare);
apps.forEach((a) => print(a['name'])); // Google Chrome
                                       // Safari
                                       // WordPress
                                       // SourceTree
```

You can also shuffle the list elements randomly with the shuffle() method:

```
my_list.shuffle();

print(my_list); // [3, 6, 8, 7, 5, 1, 2, 4, 9]
```

Now let's say you have listed these values:

```
my_list = [3, 6, 8, 7, 5, 1, 2, 4, 9];
```

With the following method you can find the position of item 7. It will return -1 if unable to find that item:

```
print(my_list.indexOf(7)); // 3
```

You can get the last position of an item using lastIndexOf(), or -1 if it is not present:

```
print(my_list.lastIndexOf('Z')); // -1
```

The insert() method lets you to insert a value in a specific position. In this example we insert at position 0 the value of 9:

```
my_list.insert(0, 9);
print(my_list); // [9, 3, 6, 8, 7, 5, 1, 2, 4, 9];
```

You can also insert a list of values into another list, and place those values in a certain position, with the insertAll method:

```
my_list.insertAll(5, [3, 3, 3]);
print(my_list); // [9, 3, 6, 8, 7, 3, 3, 3, 5, 1, 2, 4, 9]
```

The previous two methods also let you insert content into a list by expanding the size of the list.

The following method, setAll, allows you to replace values in a list with other values, and to do so at a specific position:

```
my_list.setAll(3, [5, 5, 5]);
print(my_list); // [9, 3, 6, 5, 5, 5, 3, 3, 5, 1, 2, 4, 9]
```

To delete a specific value from a list you can use the remove method, indicating the item to delete. Note that we're indicating the element to remove, not the index or position of this element:

```
my_list.remove(6);
print(my_list); // [9, 3, 5, 5, 5, 3, 3, 5, 1, 2, 4, 9]
```

You can also remove an element at a given position using removeAt:

```
my_list.removeAt(0);
print(my_list); // [3, 5, 5, 5, 3, 3, 5, 1, 2, 4, 9]
```

You can remove the last element of a list using removeLast:

```
my_list.removeLast();
print(my_list); // [3, 5, 5, 5, 3, 3, 5, 1, 2, 4]
```

When you're working with lists, you can remove specific elements of a list using the removeWhere method and define the condition that must be met to remove those elements:

```
my_list.removeWhere((e) => e==5);
print(my_list); // [3, 3, 3, 1, 2, 4]
```

On the other hand, by using the method `retainWhere` you can get elements that satisfy the defined condition:

```
my_list.retainWhere((e) => e!=3);
print(my_list); // [1, 2, 4]
```

You can keep a specific part of a list indicating the index range. The end index of a sublist is optional; if it's not specified it will provide a sublist, including everything from the start index to the end of the list:

```
print(my_list.sublist(1, 2)); // [2]
```

The getRange method will return an iterable that lets you work with the elements indicated in the index from-to range. Note that in this method, as in the previous one, the final index is excluded from the range returned:

```
print(my_list.getRange(0, 2)); // (1, 2)
```

setRange lets you copy iterable values in the from-to range. If you also specify the last parameter (`skipCount`), these values are discarded:

```
print(my_list); // [1, 2, 4]
var my_list2= [7, 8, 9, 6];
my_list.setRange(1, 2, my_list2, 2);
print(my_list); // [1, 9, 4]
```

Delete the elements in the from-to range with the `removeRange` method:

```
my_list.removeRange(1, 2);
print(my_list); // [1, 4]
```

Set the values in the from-to range with the specified value as follows:

```
my_list.fillRange(1, 2, 2);
print(my_list); // [1, 2]
```

Delete the values in the from-to range and insert the values given as follows:

```
my_list.replaceRange(1, 2, [7, 8, 9]);
print(my_list); // [1, 7, 8, 9]
```

In addition, you can convert a list into a dictionary where the keys are consecutive numbers and the values of Map are the elements of the list, as follows:

```
var my_map = my_list.asMap();
print(my_map.keys); // (0, 1, 2, 3)
print(my_map.values); // (1, 7, 8, 9)
```

If you want to empty a list you can use clear:

```
my_list.clear();
print(my_list); // []
```

Iterable

The methods that we have seen are the built-in methods defined by Dart on dart:core for the List class, but when you work with lists or sets, there are more methods available because List and Set implement the Iterable interface. This interface is very important because it is also implemented by the classes contained in dart:collection.

An Iterable is an object that, using an iterator, allows for working with objects one at a time. In other words, it allows you to iterate using the for-in loop on objects and then do something with them. Here are some examples of iterables using the for-in loop:

```dart
var my_list = [1, 2, 3];
for(var my_element in my_list) {
  print(my_element); // 1
                               // 2
                               // 3

}

Set my_set = new Set.from([true, false]);
for(var value in my_set) {
  print(value); // true
                      // false
}

var my_map = {'1': 'one',
                        '2': 'two',
                        '3': 'three'};
for(var my_element in my_map.values) {
  print(my_element); // one
                               // two
                               // three

}
```

Let's see all the methods available to work with this type of object. With the map method you could obtain a new iterable where each iterable element is replaced by the result of the function executed in map:

```dart
var dicc = {'1': 'one',
                    '2': 'two',
                    '3': 'three'};
dicc.keys.toList().forEach((k) {
  print('${k} :: String? ${k is String} :: Int? ${k is int}');
});
```

For each key in the dictionary it will show this result:

```dart
// 1 :: String? true :: Int? false
// 2 :: String? true :: Int? false
// 3 :: String? true :: Int? false
```

Now let's transform this map where its keys are strings to a new map where the keys will be `int`:

```
var keys = dicc.keys.map((key) => int.parse(key));
dicc = new Map.fromIterables(keys, dicc.values);
dicc.keys.toList().forEach((k) {
 print('${k} :: String? ${k is String} :: Int? ${k is int}');
});
```

The `Map.fromIterables(keys, dicc.values)` method will work as expected because Dart's default map is a `LinkedHasMap`, which guarantees the order of values. For each key of the map you will see this result:

```
// 1 :: String? false :: Int? true
// 2 :: String? false :: Int? true
// 3 :: String? false :: Int? true
```

You can get a new `Iterable` for those items that meet a specific condition using the `where` method:

```
var dicc = {'1': 'one',
            '2': 'two',
            '3': 'three'};
var odd = dicc.keys.where((e) => int.parse(e).isOdd);
print(odd); // (1, 3)
```

The `expand` method lets you to create a new `Iterable` from the elements of the initial `Iterable`, expanding each element in zero or more elements from the result of a function. See here:

```
var queryString = 'arg1=value1&arg2=value2&arg3=value3';
var arguments = queryString.split('&');
print(arguments); // [arg1=value1, arg2=value2, arg3=value3]
arguments = arguments.expand((String arg) => arg.split('=')).toList();
print(arguments); // [arg1, value1, arg2, value2, arg3, value3]
```

If you need to check whether an iterable contains a certain element, you can use the `contains` method:

```
var dicc = {'1': 'one',
            '2': 'two',
            '3': 'three'};

print(dicc.values.contains(4));      // false
print(dicc.values.contains('two')); // true
```

You can also iterate over each element and apply a specific function using `forEach`:

```
dicc.keys.forEach((key) {
 key = int.parse(key);
 print(key); // 1
             // 2
             // 3
});
```

The reduce method allows you to reduce a data set to a single value by iterating over the elements and combining them using the given function:

```
var dicc = {1: 'one',
                 2: 'two',
                 3: 'three'};
var keys_sum = dicc.keys.reduce((total, element) => total + element);
print(keys_sum); // 6
```

There is a similar method that also allows you to initialize the variable so as to store the result to a specified value.

```
var dicc = {1: 'one',
                 2: 'two',
                 3: 'three'};

var keys_sum = dicc.keys.fold(45, (total, element) => total + element);
print(keys_sum); // 51
```

You can get a Boolean value if all items (every) of Iterable meet a certain condition:

```
var dicc = {1: 'one',
                 2: 'two',
                 3: 'three'};

var keys = dicc.keys.every((e) => e.isEven);
print(keys); // false

keys = dicc.keys.every((e) => e is int);
print(keys); // true
```

Yet another method allows you to get a Boolean value of true or false if any items (any) of Iterable meet a certain condition:

```
var dicc = {1: 'one',
                 2: 'two',
                 3: 'three'};

var keys = dicc.keys.any((key) => key.isOdd);
print(keys); // true

keys = dicc.keys.any((key) => key.isEven);
print(keys); // true
```

Using the join method you can convert each element to a string and join all the iterable elements with the specified separator, as follows:

```
var dicc = {1: 'one',
                 2: 'two',
                 3: 'three'};

var keys = dicc.keys.join("--");
print(keys); // 1--2--3
```

You can convert an iterable to a list or a set using the .ToList() and .toSet() methods, respectively:

```
var dicc = {1: 'one',
               2: 'two',
               3: 'three'};

print(dicc.keys.toList()); // [1, 2, 3]
print(dicc.keys.toSet());  // {1, 2, 3}
```

You can find the length of an iterable and whether it's empty or not:

```
var dicc = {1: 'one',
               2: 'two',
               3: 'three'};

print(dicc.keys.length);     // 3
print(dicc.keys.isEmpty);    // false
print(dicc.keys.isNotEmpty); // true
```

To get the first and last element you could use first and last methods, respectively. If you need to get only one element contained in the iterable, you can use the single method. If the iterable is empty or has more than a single element, the method will run an exception:

```
print(dicc.keys.first);  // 1
print(dicc.keys.last);   // 3
print(dicc.keys.single); // Bad state: More than one element
```

See here how to access the iterable and get a specific element at a given position using the elementAt method:

```
print(dicc.values.elementAt(1)); // two
```

Using the take method you can retrieve a specified number of elements:

```
var dicc = {1: 'one',
               2: 'two',
               3: 'three'};

print(dicc.values.take(2)); // (one, two)
```

You could retrieve a certain number of items using takeWhile, which requires the indication of one condition. This method will stop when the condition is not met anymore. See the following:

```
print(dicc.keys.takeWhile((k) => k.isEven)); // ()
print(dicc.keys.takeWhile((k) => k.isOdd));  // (1)
```

You can keep some elements of the object, but you can also discard some elements:

```
var dicc = {1: 'one',
               2: 'two',
               3: 'three',
               4: 'four'};
```

```
print(dicc.values.skip(2));                     // (three, four)
print(dicc.keys.skipWhile((k) => k.isEven));    // (1, 2, 3, 4)
print(dicc.keys.skipWhile((k) => k.isOdd));     // (2, 3, 4)
```

Finally, you can keep the first, the last, and the only element that meets a specific condition with these methods:

```
var dicc = {1: 'one',
            2: 'two',
            3: 'three'};

print(dicc.keys.firstWhere((k) => k.isOdd));    // 1
print(dicc.keys.lastWhere((k) => k.isOdd));     // 3
print(dicc.keys.singleWhere((k) => k.isEven));  // 2
```

Sets

Let's look at the Set data type, which lets you work with data sets and operate them as if they were lists. The main features of sets are that they:

- do not allow storage of duplicate elements, and

- are messy

Sets inherit from iterables and share all the methods just learned in the previous section. Let's look at some examples of sets and how to work with them.

To create a new set, we can use any of their constructors; for example, new Set() or Set.from().

```
var con = new Set();
con.addAll([1, 1, 2, 3]);
print(con); // {1, 2, 3}

con = new Set.from([1, 1, 2, 2, 3, 3, 4]);
print(con); // {1, 2, 3, 4}
```

■ **Note** When creating the set, duplicate items will disappear.

When working with sets you can check if they contain a specific item using the contains method, or if it contains a set of elements by using containsAll:

```
print(con.contains(1)); // true
print(con.contains(5)); // false

print(con.containsAll([2, 3])); // true
```

You can look for a specific value and, if the value is within the set, the Set class will return the found element or null if it's not found. See here:

```
print(con.lookup(9)); // null
print(con.lookup(4)); // 4
```

To add items to the set you can use add or addAll. They work the same way as we've previously seen working with lists. See here:

```
con.add(5);
print(con); // {1, 2, 3, 4, 5}

con.addAll([6, 7, 8, 9]);
print(con); // {1, 2, 3, 4, 5, 6, 7, 8, 9}
```

To remove items from a set you can use the following methods. You can delete a single item, delete multiple items, or delete items that meet a specific condition.

```
con.remove(9);
print(con); // {1, 2, 3, 4, 5, 6, 7, 8}

con.removeAll([8, 7, 6]);
print(con); // {1, 2, 3, 4, 5}

con.removeWhere((e) => e==5);
print(con); // {1, 2, 3, 4}
```

You can return only some elements of a set using retainAll followed by an Iterable, or you can use retainWhere followed by a condition to get a new set that has only those elements specified:

```
con.retainAll([1,2,3]);
print(con); // {1, 2, 3}

con.retainWhere((e) => e.isOdd);
print(con); // {1, 3}
```

Finally, this class offers you the methods of intersection, union, and difference necessary to work with data sets:

```
var con = new Set.from([1, 3]);
var con2 = new Set.from([3, 4]);

print(con.intersection(con2)); // {3}
print(con.union(con2));        // {1, 3, 4}
print(con.difference(con2));   // {1}
```

Maps

A Map is an object that associates keys and values; if you know Python, this will be familiar because it is similar to a Python dictionary and very similar to JavaScript Objects too.

In this case a map can be defined by a string literal or by using the constructor new Map(). If you use a string to initialize, the keys and values can be of any data type (including lists or other maps). Let's see an example:

```
var literal_map = {
  1: 'values',
  'key': 12,
  true: 'true',
```

```
  'false': false,
  12.45: 12,
  [1, 2]: [1, 2],
  {1: 'one'}: {2: 'two'}
};
```

Let's see how to add more key-value pairs to a map:

```
var p1 = {
 'name': 'John',
 'age': 29
};
// You can add Key-Value pair to a map this way.
p1['surname'] = 'Smith';

Map p2 = new Map();
p2['name'] = 'Peter';
p2['age'] = 32;

Map results = new Map();
results [1] = 'Ranked first 1500 points';
results [2] = 'Ranked second 990 points';
results [3] = 'Ranked third 786 points';

// Access to the keys of map.
print(p1['name']);     // John
print(p1['surname']); // Smith

print(p2['old']);     // 32
print(p2[surname]); // null
```

You can add more keys to a map at any time in your application, and if you try to access an undefined property of a map, Dart will return null.

Just as with lists, you can specify the data type of the key values and the map values using angular brackets:

```
Map<String, double> champions = {
   'Sebastian Vettel': 397.0,
   'Fernando Alonso': 242.0,
   'Mark Webber': 199.0
};

Map<int, List> positions = {
  1: [1, 3, 4, 1, 7, 8],
  2: [4, 13, 1, 2, 4, 5],
  3: [7, 8, 9, 10, 2, 4]
}
```

The Map class has several methods to work with, some of which you should know already. Let's look at them now.

In addition to the constructor methods we've just discussed, the Map class has constructors by which to create new maps from other maps or from iterables. See here:

```
var p1 = {
 'nombre': 'John',
 'age': 29
};

var p2 = new Map.from(p1);
p2['age'] = 32;

print(p1);
print(p2);

var my_list = ['one', 'two', 'three', 'four'];

var my_map = new Map.fromIterable(my_list,
    key: (item) => item.toString().length,
    value: (item) => item);

print(my_map); // {3: two, 5: three, 4: four}

var keys = [1, 2, 3];
var values = ['one', 'two', 'three'];
var my_map2 = new Map.fromIterables(keys, values);
print(my_map2); // {1: one, 2: two, 3: three}
```

You can see if it contains a specific key or value with these methods.

```
var my_map = {1: 'one', 2: 'two', 3: 'three'};
print(my_map.containsKey('7')); // false
print(my_map.containsKey(2));    // true

print(my_map.containsValue('7'));       // false
print(my_map.containsValue('three')); // true
```

The Map class has a method to add a key if it does not exist on the object; this method simultaneously associates a value:

```
my_map.putIfAbsent(4, () => 'four');
print(my_map); // {1: one, 2: two, 3: three, 4: four}
```

It also lets you add other key-value pairs with the addAll method:

```
my_map.addAll({5: 'five', 6: 'six'});
print(my_map); // {1: one, 2: two, 3: three, 4: four, 5: five, 6: six}
```

You can delete a key from the map object using remove. The key and the associated value are removed. Note that you must indicate the *key* to remove, not the index, position, or element.

```
my_map.remove(5);

print(my_map); // {1: one, 2: two, 3: three, 4: four, 6: six}
```

You can also apply a function to each key-value pair with forEach:

```
my_map.forEach((k, v) {
 print('Key ${k} = ${v}'); // Key 1 = one
                                      // Key 2 = two
                                      // Key 3 = three
                                      // Key 4 = four
                                      // Key 6 = six
});
```

On the Map class there are several methods by which to know the keys and values of the object, the length of key-value pairs, and whether the map is empty or not:

```
print(my_map.keys);       // (1, 2, 3, 4, 6)
print(my_map.values);     // (one, two, three, four, six)
print(my_map.length);     // 5
print(my_map.isEmpty);    // false
print(my_map.isNotEmpty); // true
```

Finally, you can completely empty a map with the clear method:

```
my_map.clear();
print(my_map); // {}
```

Date and Time

In addition to the basic Dart data types, we have learned some of the most interesting dart:core classes, such as Lists, Sets, Maps, RegExp, and so forth. These classes allow you to work with other very useful data structures.

Now let's see a class that you will use very often when you need to work with dates and times: the DateTime class. This class is located on dart:core and has a set of constructors to define DateTime objects.

You can define a DateTime object with the current time with the constructor DateTime.now():

```
var my_date = new DateTime.now();
print(my_date); // 2014-10-07 19:31:17.610
```

You can define it explicitly by indicating the year, month, day, hour, minute, second, and millisecond. If a value is not specified, the default is initialized to 0:

```
my_date = new DateTime(2014, 3, 14, 17, 30, 0);
print(my_date); // 2014-03-14 17:30:00.000
```

This class also lets you define DateTime objects from strings that fit the ISO 8601 format:

```
my_date = DateTime.parse('2014-12-09 09:00:00');
print(my_date); // 2014-12-09 09:00:00.000
```

You can define DateTime objects directly in universal time with DateTime.utc() constructor:

```
my_date = new DateTime.utc(2014, 10, 7, 17, 30, 0);

print(my_date); // 2014-10-07 17:30:00.000Z
print(my_date.isUtc); // true
```

Or you can define them from a timestamp indicating milliseconds:

```
my_date = new DateTime.fromMillisecondsSinceEpoch(1394280000000);
print(my_date); // 2014-03-08 13:00:00.000
```

Note that the time in the comment above may vary from computer to computer due to time zones, unless the isUtc optional parameter is passed to indicate the time zone, as below:

```
my_date = new DateTime.fromMillisecondsSinceEpoch(1394280000000, isUtc: true);
print(my_date); // 2014-03-08 12:00:00.000Z
```

Besides these DateTime constructor methods, this new class offers you getters and methods so as to work with dates. To obtain the values of the DateTime object you can use these getters. As you can see, the days of the week in Dart begin on 1 for Monday and end at 7 for Sunday:

```
var today = new DateTime.now(); // 2014-03-08 18:52:33.906
print(today.year);              // 2014
print(today.month);             // 3
print(today.day);               // 8
print(today.hour);              // 18
print(today.minute);            // 52
print(today.second);            // 33
print(today.millisecond);       // 906
print(today.weekday);           // 6 - Saturday
```

You can get local time or universal time from a DateTime object in this way:

```
print(today.toLocal()); // 2014-03-08 18:52:33.906
print(today.toUtc());   // 2014-03-08 17:52:33.906Z
```

And you can convert the DateTime object into an String object with the toString() method:

```
print(today.toString()); // 2014-03-08 18:52:33.906
```

We will now define another DateTime object and see the operations we can do with it:

```
var yesterday = new DateTime(2014, 3, 7, 18, 23, 0);
```

We can compare both objects easily in this way. You'll get a Boolean value indicating if a date-time is equal to, less than, or greater than another. See here:

```
print(today==yesterday);               // false
print(today.isAtSameMomentAs(today));  // true
print(today.isBefore(yesterday));      // false
print(today.isAfter(yesterday));       // true
```

DateTime implements other methods that enable comparisons between date-time objects and then returns int values as a result, as follows:

```
print(today.compareTo(yesterday)); // 1
print(yesterday.compareTo(today)); // -1
print(today.compareTo(today));     // 0
```

When working with DateTime objects, it is common to add or subtract dates-hours or calculate differences between DateTime objects to accomplish some tasks on your programs. All these operations can be easily done in Dart, but before we see them we have to talk about another new class also available in dart:core called Duration. This class is used as a parameter, or it can be returned as a result indicating differences between dates.

The Duration class has its own methods and operators to compare, convert to String objects, and make operations such as add, subtract, multiply or divide. This class is used by other parts of the Dart library, such as Timers and Futures.

The most interesting aspect of the Duration class is its constructor, which defines a Duration object from the specified parameter; if none is specified, the default will be 0. Let's see an example:

```
var dur = new Duration(days: 20, hours: 4, minutes: 2, seconds: 17, milliseconds: 300,
microseconds: 155897);

print(dur); // 484:02:17.455897
```

You can get the value in days, hours, minutes, seconds, milliseconds, or microseconds with these methods:

```
print(dur.inDays);         // 20
print(dur.inHours);        // 484
print(dur.inMinutes);      // 29042
print(dur.inSeconds);      //  1742537
print(dur.inMilliseconds); // 1742537455
print(dur.inMicroseconds); // 1742537455897
```

If you want to add a day to a date, you must use the .add() method and a Duration object as the parameter indicating the number of days to add. According to our previous today variable:

```
print(today.add(new Duration(days:1))); // 2014-03-09 18:52:33.906
```

You can also add hours by indicating as the parameter a Duration object expressed in hours:

```
print(today.add(new Duration(hours:10))); // 2014-03-09 04:52:33.906
```

You already know how to add days, hours, or whichever parameter you specify with your `Duration` objects. Now let's see how you can subtract. The process is very similar; you can subtract a specific value of a date with the `subtract()` method, using a `Duration` object as the parameter containing the desired value to subtract—for example, days or hours. See here:

```
print(today.subtract(new Duration(days:1)));    // 2014-03-07 18:52:33.906
print(today.subtract(new Duration(hours:10)));  // 2014-03-08 08:52:33.906
```

Note that the `add` and `subtract` methods return a new instance of the `DateTime` object and do not modify the existing instance.

If you want to know the difference between two dates, you can use the `difference()` method; you'll get a `Duration` object as the result. You can use the `Duration` object as needed, for example, in hours, seconds, or days, with the corresponding getter method. See the following:

```
var today = new DateTime(2014, 10, 9, 18, 23, 0);
var yesterday = new DateTime(2014, 10, 7, 18, 23, 0);
print(today.difference(yesterday).inDays);     // 2
print(today.difference(yesterday).inHours);    // 48
print(today.difference(yesterday).inSeconds);  // 172800
```

Now let's look at two other methods for the `DateTime` class: one of them to get the name of the client time zone and the other to get the offset, which will return a `Duration` object. See here:

```
print(today.timeZoneName); // CET
print(today.timeZoneOffset.toString()); // 1:00:00.000000
```

Summary

In this chapter we have learned:

- About all the basic Dart data types: string, numbers, and Boolean.

- About all the methods available on Dart SDK to work with string, numbers, and Boolean.

- How to define variables in Dart and how to use `final` for lazy initialization and `const` to define constants.

- About more complex Dart types, such as lists, sets, and maps.

- About all the methods you can use to work with lists, sets, and maps.

- About the regular expression objects and how they are similar to JavaScript specifications.

- About DateTime objects and how to add, subtract, or calculate difference between dates.

■ ■ ■

CHAPTER 14

Flow Control Statements

In this chapter we'll see the flow control statements used in our programs to change the execution flow or to repeat sentences. We'll see if-else and switch statements.

Later we'll see the loops statements in Dart for loop and while loop that allow you to repeat blocks of code in your applications. We'll also see for-in and forEach loops that work with collections.

As you know, a program is a sequence of statements executed sequentially. There are two types of statements:

- **Simple statements**: run one after another

- **Control statements**: allow you to change the flow of program execution by introducing cycles and conditions that must be met in order for some blocks of code to be executed.

We'll start by talking about conditional statements, a type of control statement.

If and Else

The if statement lets you choose whether a block of instructions is executed or not. If this statement includes an else block, then this statement will execute one block of instructions if the condition is true and a different one if the condition is false. Dart allows if statements with optional else statements.

The peculiarity is that with Dart, we must be more explicit when we work with conditions and if statements, because Dart believes that all values different from True are False. This is different in JavaScript and, as we discussed in the "Mastering Dart's Variables and Data Types" chapter, if you use these types of conditions you will get an error.

```
var name = 'John';
if(name) {
  print(name);
}
```

Let's see how to use if-else conditional statements in Dart, and per the standard style recommendation, we should always use explicit curly brackets.

```
var weather = 'risk';
if(weather == 'risk') {
  caution();
} else {
  withoutCaution();
}
```

Dart also supports nested if-else-if statements, so you can use them in this way:

```
var color = '#0000ff';
if(color == '#ff0000') {
 print('Red');
} else if(color == '#00ff00') {
 print('Green');
} else if(color == '#0000ff') {
 print('Blue');
} else {
 print('I dont know this color!');
}
```

This type of structure is not the perfect solution, because to do this we must use the switch statement, which is faster than an if-else-if chain and generates a more readable code, as we'll see below.

Switch Statement

As mentioned, the switch statement allows one to make decisions between multiple alternatives, thus avoiding nested if-else-if statements. This improves the readability of the code, and it is a structure that executes faster than using nested if-else-if. Let's see an example of a switch statement.

```
var action = 'Open';

switch (action) {
  case 'Paid':
    pay();
    break;

  case 'Unpaid':
    unpay();
    break;

  case 'Rejected':
    rejected();
    break;

  default:
    check();
}
```

As you can see, this statement defines some matching cases (case) and some actions to take in case one of them is fulfilled. Having met the case and executed the action, you should always include the break statement to exit switch.

■ **Note**　In other languages, not including the break statement after each case will result in strange or inappropriate behavior. In Dart, while you're writing your code you can see how Dart Editor warns you about missing break statements. Even if you try to run your code, it'll throw an error and will stop the execution.

Optionally you can specify the **default** case, which will be executed if none of the other options coincide. In this particular case it is not necessary to include the break statement because there are no more cases after it.

The switch statement can contain empty cases, as you can see below in the case of *Unpaid*.

```
switch (invoiceStatus) {
  case 'Paid':
    pay();
    break;

  case 'Unpaid':
  case 'Rejected':
    unpaid();
    break;

  default:
    throw(' Error invoice Status !');
}
```

That means that the function unpaid() will be executed if the invoice status is Unpaid or Rejected.

A case of coincidence can contain calls to other functions, as you saw in the previous examples, but also can contain any block of code you want to execute. You can even define local variables that you need. These local variables will only be visible within the scope of that case.

```
switch (invoiceStatus) {
  case 'Paid':
    pay();
    break;

  case 'Paid':
  case 'Rejected':
    unpaid();
    break;

  default:
    var error = 'Error Invoice Status !';
    sendEmail(subject:error, to:'error@company.com');
    throw(error);
}
```

For Loop

Now that we've reviewed conditional statements, it's time to see looping statements. A loop is used to repeat a given sentence or sentences a specified number of times. Dart has several different types of loops, but for now we focus on the for loop. This loop has a very familiar format to you because it inherits the syntax of JavaScript, C, and so on.

```
for (var i=0; i < 3; i++) {
  print(i); // 0
            // 1
            // 2
}
```

The for loops also allow you to iterate over List, Map, and Set objects.

```
var my_list = ['one', 'two', 'three', 'four'];

for (var i=0; i < my_list.length; i++) {
 print('$i :: ${my_list[i]}');   // 0 :: one
                                 // 1 :: two
                                 // 2 :: three
                                 // 3 :: four
}
```

Actually, if the object that you go through is a collection, you can use the forEach() method. This is a perfect choice if you don't need to know the current iteration count.

```
var my_list = [one', two', 'three', 'four'];
my_list.forEach((item) {
 print(item);   // one
                // two
                // three
                // four
});
```

To iterate over a collection, or any iterable, without knowing the iteration count, you can use a for-in loop.

```
var documents = ['orders', 'invoices'];
for (var doc in documentos) {
 print(doc); // orders
             // invoices
}
```

You could use this for-in loop over any Iterable.

While Loop

The while loop repeats a block of code while a condition remains true. This statement will evaluate the condition before entering the loop, and will repeat it while the condition is true.

```
while (missingCalls()) {
  blinkLight();
}
```

If you want to evaluate the condition after executing the loop cycle (i.e., execute the loop at least once), you can use do-while statement.

```
do {
  blinkLight();
} while (missingCalls());
```

When you are working with loops you can also use these two statements: break and continue. These statements will serve to control the execution of the loop.

Break is used to stop the execution of the loop:

```
var i = 100;
while(true) {
  i -= 5;
  print(i);
  if(i < 75) {
    break;
  }
}
```

This example will return this result:

```
95
90
85
80
75
70
```

However, continue allows you to jump to the next iteration of the loop:

```
for (var i = 100; i > 0; i--) {
  if (i.isEven) {
    continue;
  }

  print(i);
  if (i < 75) {
   break;
  }
}
```

This version will show a result like this:

```
99
97
95
93
91
89
87
85
83
81
79
77
75
73
```

Summary

In this chapter we have learned the following:

- About flow control statements
- About `if-else` and `switch` statements
- How to use loops to repeat sentences using `For` or `While` loops
- How to use `for-in` and `forEach` loops when we're working with collections

■ ■ ■

CHAPTER 15

Working with Functions

In this chapter we'll talk about functions in Dart: how you can create them, how to define them, and which types of parameters they can receive.

We'll see in detail the difference between positional arguments and named arguments. We'll also see default values for the function parameters. Later we'll see the returned values for functions, and at the end of the chapter we'll look at recursive functions in Dart. So far, you've seen single statements, control statements, and loop structures. With these tools you can start to build an application in Dart, but as the application grows up you will need to organize your code better and reuse code you've written elsewhere in the application. Thanks to the functions, you could do this type of thing and get a cleaner, more efficient, and easier maintained code.

A function is a set of instructions that performs a specific task. Functions are executed by calling them from another part of the code, a class method, or other function. Functions can be called as many times as you need and can even call themselves (recursive functions).

Functions can work with parameters and can return results. The function parameters in Dart may be required or optional. If function parameters are optional, they may be optional by their position, known as positional arguments, or optional by name, known as named arguments.

We usually use functions to split a large task into simpler operations or to implement operations that we will use repeatedly in our application.

Defining Functions

Let's see how to define functions in Dart.

```
function_name(function_arguments) {
  // Body of the function
}
```

Here you can see a very simple function example:

```
greet(name) {
  print('Welcome to Dart $name');
}
```

If you want to execute this function from your main program, you only need to call it, like this:

```
void main() {
  greet('Peter'); // Executing our sample function.
}
```

Although the above code is perfectly valid, it is recommended to use the Dart code style guide. Therefore, you should always specify the return data type of the function and the data types of the parameters passed to the function when you define your functions. Thus, our function declaration should look like this:

```
return_type function_name(argument_type argument) {
  // body of the function.
}
```

Continuing with our example, let's change the greeting:

```
void greet(String name) {
  print('Welcome to Dart $name');
}
```

To properly declare a function in Dart and following the code style guide you must specify:

- Function return type or void if the function did not return any value.

- Function name.

- Function parameters specifying data type and name of each parameter.

- Body of the function, between curly braces.

To show you the return data type and how a function will return any value, our sample function will be redeclared as follows:

```
String greet(String name) {
  var msg = 'Welcome to Dart $name';
  return msg;
}
```

In cases of simple functions that have only a single statement, you could use the abbreviated definition. Here is an example:

```
void welcome() => print('Welcome to Dart!');
```

And then you could use this function by calling it like this:

```
void main() {
  welcome(); // Welcome to Dart!
}
```

As we previously mentioned, any function could receive required or optional parameters. Required parameters are indicated between parentheses. You could specify as many as you need, and every argument would be separated by a comma.

```
void greet(String required_parameter_1, num required_parameter_2) {
  // Function body
}
```

Optional parameters are also indicated between parentheses, but in this case we have to indicate them according to a specific nomenclature. As we know, optional parameters can be of two different types: optional by position (positional arguments) or optional by name (named arguments).

Positional Optional Parameters

Positional optional parameters are enclosed between square brackets and follow the same description as the required parameters: data type and parameter name.

```
void greet(String name, [String lastname, num age]) {
  if(lastname != null && age != null) {
    print('Welcome to Dart $name $lastname you are $age years old.');
  } else {
    print('Welcome to Dart $name.');
  }
}
```

If you make some calls to this function with these different parameters you could get these results:

```
void main() {
  greet('Peter');                // Welcome to Dart Peter.
  greet('Peter', 'Smith');       // Welcome to Dart Peter.
  greet('Peter', 'Smith', 28); // Welcome to Dart Peter Smith you are 28 years old.
}
```

What would happen if we changed the position of the arguments when we call the function? We would have unexpected results:

```
void main() {
  greet('Smith', 'Peter');      // Welcome to Dart Smith.
  greet('28', 'Peter', 28);     // Welcome to Dart 28 Peter you are 28 years old.
  greet(28, 'Peter', 'Smith'); // This will throw an exception.
}
```

What would happen if our function had 150 parameters? It would be almost impossible to not make mistakes when you call your function, right? To handle those situations, and as a means of further API self-documentation, Dart introduced optional parameters which are called by their name.

Named Optional Parameters

In addition to positional optional parameters, we have named optional parameters. They really are very useful because you do not need to call the function in the same way as with positional parameters, and this kind of parameter improves the documentation of the function when the call is made, mainly if the function has a lot of parameters.

Another important benefit is that for positional parameters, if you want to pass the last parameter, all preceding parameters must also be passed. Named parameters allow only the used parameters to be passed.

In our next sample code you can see our function does not have any required arguments, so all the arguments would be optional; in this particular case, they would be called optional arguments.

```
void greeting({String name, String lastname, num age}) {
  var greet = new StringBuffer('Welcome to Dart');
  if (name != null) {
    greet.write(' $name');
  }
```

```
  if (lastname != null) {
    greet.write(' $lastname');
  }

  if (age != null) {
    greet.write(' you are $age years old.');
  }
  print(greet.toString());
}

void main() {
  greeting(name:'Peter');                          // Welcome to Dart Peter
  greeting(lastname:'Smith', name:'Peter');        // Welcome to Dart Peter Smith
  greeting(lastname:'Smith', age: 29, name:'Peter'); // Welcome to Dart Peter Smith you are 29 years old.
  greeting(); // Welcome to Dart
  // If we want to pass only the last parameter we can do easily without
  // passing preceding parameters.
  greeting(age:29); // Welcome to Dart you are 29 years old.
}
```

Note that the order of the parameters passed to the function is not important, because you are mapping the parameter name with the value. This is something really great, because in functions that can accept many optional parameters, remembering the exact order in which to pass the parameters to the function is a task that is heavy and ripe for errors.

If we call our functions through named optional arguments, we can forget the exact parameter order. Furthermore, we would have even better documentation if we used very descriptive names for the optional parameters. This would improve our code-maintenance process.

Default Values

The functions with optional parameters also can get default values. A default value is assigned to the optional parameter if the parameter is not specified when you execute the function. The default value must be specified when you declare your function.

To specify the default value of an optional parameter, we use the equal sign (=) or a colon (:) depending on if it is an optional parameter by position or optional by name.

This is an example of a default value for a positional optional parameter:

```
void greeting([String name= 'ANONYMOUS']) {
  var greet = new StringBuffer('Welcome to Dart');
  if (name != null) {
    greet.write(' $name');
  }
  print(greet.toString());
}

void main() {
  greeting();          // Welcome to Dart ANONYMOUS
  greeting('John'); // Welcome to Dart John
}
```

And here we see an example of a default value for named optional arguments:

```dart
void greeting({String name: 'ANONYMOUS'}) {
  var greet = new StringBuffer('Welcome to Dart');
  if (name != null) {
    greet.write(' $name');
  }
  print(greet.toString());
}

void main() {
  greeting();              // Welcome to Dart ANONYMOUS
  greeting(name: 'John'); // Welcome to Dart John
}
```

Functions can be used as arguments to other functions. Let's see an example:

```dart
void welcome(element) => print('Welcome to Dart element $element');

void main() {
  var list = [1, 2, 3];
  list.forEach(welcome);   // Welcome to Dart element 1
                           // Welcome to Dart element 2
                           // Welcome to Dart element 3
}
```

Note that the function signature must exactly match the expected signature of the method. For instance, you could not pass a function to the forEach method that expected two required arguments, or that returned a value. Let's see an example:

```dart
void welcome(element, position) => print('Welcome to Dart element $element');

void main() {
  var list = [1, 2, 3];
  list.forEach(welcome); // This will throw an exception and stop execution.
}
```

This following example also will throw an exception:

```dart
int welcome(element) => element * 2;
void main() {
  var list = [1, 2, 3];
  list.forEach(print(welcome));
}
```

To properly run the above code, it should be changed to this version:

```
int welcome(element) => element * 2;
void main() {
  var list = [1, 2, 3];
  list.forEach((i) => print(welcome(i))); // 2
                                          // 4
                                          // 6
}
```

You can also assign a function to a variable. In this particular case, our function does not have name, so it will be identified by the variable name. Thus, if we need to execute this function we will call the variable followed by parentheses and parameters if the function has them.

```
var hello = (element) => print('Welcome to Dart element $element');
void main() {
  hello(1); // Welcome to Dart element 1
}
```

Return Values

Earlier we learned that when a function does not return any value, as a rule of syntax and style we should indicate the reserved word void. Actually, this is not quite true, because all functions in Dart will return a value; when your function doesn't explicitly indicate a return value, the function will return null.

```
num sum(num a, num b) {
  return a+b;
}
void main() {
  var result = sum(1, 5);
  print(result); // 6
}
```

In the previous example, the sum function returns a number.

```
void greeting() {
  print('Hello!');
}

void main() {
  var result = greeting(); // Executes print Hello!
  print(result);           // null
}
```

In this case, the function executes the print statement, showing us the 'Hello!' message, but it doesn't return any value, and therefore Dart will return null.

In the same way that you could use a function as an argument to another function, you also could use a function as a return value for other function. See the following.

```
String formatNums(num digit) {
  return digit.toStringAsPrecision(3);
}

String sum(num a, num b) {
  return formatNums(a+b);
}

void main() {
  print(sum(5, 3));              // 8.00
  print(sum(1.34578, 0.7863123)); // 2.13
}
```

In the previous sample we've shown you a function call as a return value for another function, but you can even return a function itself, as you can see below.

```
dynamic sum (num a) {
  return (b) => a + b;
}

void main() {
  var sumThree = sum(3);
  print(sumThree);     // Closure: (dynamic) => dynamic
  print(sumThree(5)); // 8

  // We can do the same as above in this way
  print(sum(3));       // Closure: (dynamic) => dynamic
  print(sum(3)(5)); // 8
}
```

Recursive Functions

As was mentioned earlier, you could have a function that calls itself. This type of function is known as a recursive function, and they're useful for showing how you could resolve a problem using only one function that executes itself repeatedly. The most important part of a recursive function is the base case, which will stop the recursion and solve the problem. If you do not properly define your base case, the recursive function will execute over and over again, similar to an infinite loop.

```
num factorial(num f) {
  if(f < 1) {
    return 1;                 // base case
  } else {
    return f * factorial(f-1); // recursive call
  }
}

void main() {
  print(factorial(5));
}
```

If we haven't properly defined the base case, we could have problems with our isolates, and thus Dart will stop our execution and inform us of a StackOverFlow error.

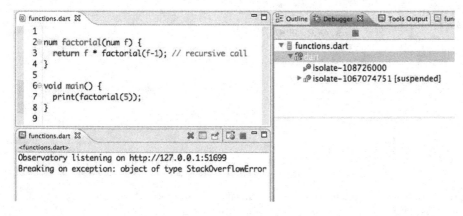

Figure 15-1. Stack overflow error in Dart

Summary

In this chapter we have learned the following:

- How to define functions in Dart

- What optional parameters are and which types we can use

- How to use positional parameters in functions and how to use them with default values

- How to use named parameters in functions and how to use them with default values

- What the return values are

- How to use functions as return values for other functions

- What recursive functions are and how to create recursive functions in Dart

CHAPTER 16

■ ■ ■

A Syntax Summary and Cheat Sheet

In this chapter we want to give you a handy cheat sheet with the syntax learned in this book thus far (see Table 16-1 and Table 16-2). When you learn a new programming language, it is very useful to have such a thing so you can quickly check the main instructions. Here's the summary of syntax we have learned until now.

Table 16-1. *Operators cheat sheet*

Negation	[!, -]
Multiplication	[*]
Division	[/]
Integer Division	[~/]
Modulo	[%]
Addition	[+]
Subtraction	[-]
Bitwise left shift	[<<]
Bitwise right shift	[>>]
Greater than	[>]
Greater than or equal to	[>=]
Less than	[<]
Less than or equal to	[<=]
Equal to	[==]
Not equal to Sheet	[!=]

Table 16-2. *Syntax Cheat Sheet*

Inline comments	`// This is an inline comment`
Block comments	`/* This is a block comment */`

Documentation comments	`/**`
	`* Doc comment`
	`* each line preceded by *`
	`* /`
	
	`/// inline doc comment`

Override an operator	`return_type` **`operator`** `name (parameters and types)`
Increments expr by one and returns expr	`++expr`
Returns expr and increments by one its value	`expr++`
Decrements expr by one and returns expr	`--expr`
Returns expr and decrements by one its value	`expr--`
Assignment	`[=]`
Other operators to assign value	`[*=], [/=], [~/=], [%=], [+=], [-=], [<<=], [>>=], [&=],` `[^=], [|=]`
Defines a variable	`var nameOfVariable`
Defines a constant	`const nameOfConstant valueOfConstant`
Defines a string variable	`string_1 = "Example"` `string_1 = "Example ${other variable value} of string"`

Defines string variables with multiple lines	`string_1="'`
	`  content`
	`  of the`
	`  string variable`
	`"';`

Types of numbers	`num, int, double`
Boolean values	`true, false`
Creates a new List object	`List l = new List()` `List l = [];`
Defines a Map object	`Map m = new Map()` `Map m = {};`
Defines a Set object	`new Set()`

(continued)

Table 16-2. (*continued*)

| If-else statement | ```
if (condition) {
  // instructions
} else {
  // instructions
}
``` |
| Switch statement | ```
switch(variable) {
  case value1:
    // instructions
    break;
  case value2:
    // instructions
    break;
  default:
    // instructions
}
``` |
| While loop | ```
while(condition) {
  // instructions
}

do {
  // instructions
} while(condition);
``` |
| For loop | ```
for(initialization; condition; inc./dec.) {
  // instructions
}
``` |
| For-in loop | ```
for(element in Iterable) {
  // instructions
}
``` |
| ForEach method | ```
Iterable.forEach((e) {
  // instructions
});
``` |
| Function definitions | ```
return_type function_name(parameters and types) {
  // function body
}
``` |
| Simple functions | ```
return_type function_name(parameters and types) =>
body_of_the_function;

void greet(name) => print("Hello $name!");
``` |

(*continued*)

Table 16-2. (*continued*)

Positional optional parameters	```return_type function_name([type param1, type param2, ...]) { // function body } ```
Named optional parameters	```return_type function_name({type named_param1, type nane_param2, ...}) { // function body } ```
Default function values	```return_type function_name([type param1=value, type param2=value, ...]) { // function body } return_type function_name({type param1: value, type param2: value, ...}) { // function body } ```

PART IV

The Dart Language: Advanced

■ ■ ■

CHAPTER 17

Processing Exceptions and Error Control

Thus far we've looked at important aspects of Dart, at what we consider to be the first part of the language. Now we're going to dive in a little deeper. In this second part of the book we'll learn about error control and exceptions—everything related to the creation and use of classes, constructors, and inheritance.

We'll also talk about generics, isolates, typedefs, and how libraries work in Dart. Do not be scared by these weird names, as you will soon see what they are and how you can use them to improve your knowledge of Dart.

Exceptions and Error Control

All modern and object-oriented languages, as Dart is, should include exceptions and error control. When you are programming an application, in spite of the fact that you've tried to exert as much control as possible, there will always be a set of data that you have not tried or a user behavior on a certain screen that won't be something you defined for. In these cases, there will be errors, and your application will fail or will be blocked.

Dart incorporates an exceptions mechanism to capture exceptional error cases not previously considered, and it'll act accordingly. As a result, you can display a more appropriate error message for the user and keep the system running.

In other cases, you can throw exceptions within specific blocks of your application. Dart also incorporates mechanisms to do this. When something unusual happens in your application, Dart throws an exception, and if the exception is not caught, the isolate that generated the exception will be interrupted and the program will end.

Dart provides Exception and Error for managing errors and exceptions. It also lets you create your own exceptions. Dart's mechanisms to manage errors and exceptions are called throw, catch, and finally. You may know these methods because they're similar to those found in PHP.

Throw lets you hurl exceptions anywhere in your code. Lets see a very simple example:

```
if(user == null) {
  throw new Exception('User not recognized in the system !!');
}

if(password == null) {
  throw new Exception('The password is incorrect !!');
}

if(data == null) {
  throw new ArgumentError();
}
```

```
if(data is! Map) {
  throw new TypeError();
}
```

Catch is Dart's mechanism to capture and handle exceptions, thus the propagation of the exception stops and you can manage it. To be more exact, Dart catchs exceptions using the try {} on {} catch {} blocks. These blocks can be nested and thus can capture more than one type of exception. See here:

```
try {
  login();
} on PasswordEmptyException { // Catchs a specific exception.
  reLogin();
} on Exception catch(e) { // Catchs any type of exception.
  print('What happend here?');
} catch(e) { // Catchs anything else than will happen.
  print('Something has gone wrong. I have no idea what happened !');
}
```

As you can see from this example, you can chain together try-catch blocks, depending on the types of exceptions you want to capture and handle.

During the capture of an exception you can use on, catch, or both. Use on when you need to specify the exception type. Use catch when your exception handler needs the exception object.

Finally, Dart gives you an opportunity to execute a code snippet at the end of the try-catch block, whether the exception occurs or not. With finally, you will always execute the code snippet, as follows:

```
var myresult;
try {
  // I try to gain access to the system.
  myresult = login();
} on Exception catch(e) {
  // An error occurs in the system.
  myresult = 'You did not say the magic word !';
} finally {
  // Displays the answer to the user.
  print(myresult);
}
```

You can find the Exception class and the Error class on dart:core. Use them to manage exceptions or errors in the system; these classes also allow you to define your own exceptions and errors.

Exceptions Types

There are three types of exceptions in Dart within the exceptions package on dart:core, as follows:

- Exception is the abstract class that represents a system failure. You must inherit from Exception class in order to create your own exceptions.

- FormatException defines a format error when a string or other value does not represent the correct format.

- IntegerDivisionByZeroException represents a division by zero exception.

Error Types

In the errors package on dart:core there are some classes that define different types of common errors:

- AssertionError is used when an assert statement fails.

- TypeError is used when a type assert statement fails.

- CastError is used when trying to convert a value from one type to another and failure occurs.

- NullThrownError is used when you throw null on your code.

- ArgumentError will occur when an error occurs in function arguments.

- RangeError is used when you try to access an index that is outside the range of indexes of the object.

- FallThroughError is used when control reaches the end of a switch case.

- AbstractClassInstantiationError is used when trying to instantiate an abstract class.

- NoSuchMethodError is used when you try to access a nonexistent method on an object.

- UnsupportedError is used when an operation is not allowed by an object.

- UnimplementedError is used when the method is not implemented in the object.

- StateError will throw when the operation was not allowed by the current state of the object.

- ConcurrentModificationError occurs when a collection is modified during iteration.

- OutOfMemoryError is used when the system is out of memory.

- StackOverflowError is used when a stack overflow failure occurs.

- CyclicInitializationError will be thrown when a lazily initialized variable cannot be initialized.

Exceptions and Error Definitions

Creating exceptions and errors in Dart is really simple—you just need to create the class of exception or error that you want to define and then extend the basic Dart error or exception classes.

What's the difference between an error and an exception? In particular, errors are meant to be fatal and halt program execution (and will not be caught in most cases). Exceptions are designed to be used for cases in which an error is expected, such as parsing user input (formatException).

Let's look at some simple examples of defining exceptions and errors and how to use them. To define your own exception class you must implement the base class Exception:

```
class MyException implements Exception {
 final msg;
 const MyException([this.msg = ""]);
 toString() => 'Fatal Exception in the system.$msg';
}
```

227

And then you can use it on your system in this way:

```
throw new MyException(); // Exception: Fatal Exception in the system.
throw new MyException('Access Error.'); // Exception: Fatal Exception in the system.Access Error
```

To define your own error classes you must extend the base class Error as follows:

```
class MyError extends Error {
 final msg;
 MyError([this.msg = " UNKNOWN "]);
 toString() => 'Error: $msg';
}
```

Then use your new error class as follows:

```
throw new MyError(); // Exception: Error: UNKNOWN
throw new MyError('Access Denied.'); // Exception: Error: Denied Access.
```

We know we haven't previously discussed clases, yet in this chapter we have talked about Exception and Error classes and used **extends** and **implements** keywords—do not worry about that, as we'll see these items in the next chapter.

Now let's get started talking about classes and explaining the difference between extends and implements!

Summary

In this chapter we have learned:

- How to control errors and manage exceptions

- When you should use on or catch to handle errors and exceptions

- What types of exceptions there are in Dart

- What types of errors there are in Dart

- How to create custom error classes

- How to create custom exception classes

■ ■ ■

CHAPTER 18

Understanding Dart Classes

In this chapter we will cover Dart classes, what constructors are, and how to create constructors for your classes. We'll see named constructors, instance variables, and instance methods as well. Later we'll see how inheritance works in Dart, and we'll talk about static variables and methods.

As you know, Dart is an object-oriented language with classes and single inheritance. Everything in Dart is an object, including the built-in data types. An object is an instance of a class. To create an object, use the keyword new followed by the constructor of the class. See the following:

```dart
class Person {
  Person() {
    // Do stuff here
  }
}

void main() {
 Person john = new Person(); // John is an object, an instance of Person.
}
```

Note that we can even use the Person class as a type annotation of our new variables.

Objects have members, functions, and data. The methods of a class are the functions, and instance variables are the data.

```dart
class Person {
  // Instance variables.
  String name;
  num age;

  // Empty constructor.
  Person();

  // Method that displays a greeting.
  void sayHello() => print('Hi my name is $name');
}

void main() {
  Person john = new Person(); // John is an object, the instance of Person.
  john.name = 'John Doe';
  john.age = 29;
  john.sayHello(); // Hi my name is John Doe
}
```

■ **Note** The style guide recommends using a semicolon rather than empty braces for empty constructors.

In this example we created a simple class with some instance variables and one method in addition to the constructor. Once you define the object, you can access its instance variables or methods using the object name followed by a dot and the method or instance variable you want to get.

Just as with variables, you can define objects as being either const or final, and with classes you can do the same thing. You can define a class that has a constant constructor so that a constant object is created at runtime. It creates the object by using the word const instead of new when calling the constructor of that class.

```dart
class DaVinci {
  final name = 'Leonardo da Vinci';
  const DaVinci(); // Constant Constructor.
}

void main() {
  var leo = const DaVinci();
  print(leo.name); // Leonardo da Vinci
}
```

Instance Variables

We have previously commented that the instance variables are the "data" of the object. These instance variables are defined in the class and are declared like variables, as we have already learned.

We indicate (optionally) the type, the name, and an assigned value; if you don't indicate a value, the default value will be null.

All instance variables defined will generate an implicit getter method (to get the value of the instance variable), so you will not have to declare it. Dart simplifies things a lot.

All instance variables defined with a data type of var also will generate an implicit setter method (to set the value of the instance variable).

We have seen in the above example the Person class and how we could set the value of the name and the age, thus displaying them without creating these getter or setter methods.

```dart
class Person {
  // Instance variables.
  String name;    // Variable initialized to null.
  num age;        // Variable initialized to null
  num childs = 0; // Variable initialized to 0.

  // Constructor.
  Person();

  // Method that displays a greeting.
  void sayHello() => print('Hi my name is $name');
}
```

```
void main() {
  Person john = new Person(); // John is an object, an instance of Person.

  // we can set the name and the age without having to define setter methods.
  john.name = 'John Doe'; // we set the name
  john.age = 29;          // we set the age

  // we can display the name and the age without having to define getter methods.
  print('Name: ${john.name}'); // Name: John Doe
  print('Age: ${john.age}');   // Old: 29
}
```

Instance variables can be visible or not visible from other libraries, which means you have the option of accessing them from the instance created or not. The instance variables that are not visible are called *private*.

If you start the variable name with an underscore (_) you are indicating that this instance variable is private.

```
class Person {
  // Instance variables.
  String name;
  num age;
  num _id; // Private variable

  // Constructor.
  Person();

  void sayHello() => print('Hi my name is $name');
}
```

You can identify private variables in the Outline by the red icon assigned to private instance members, as shown in Figure 18-1.

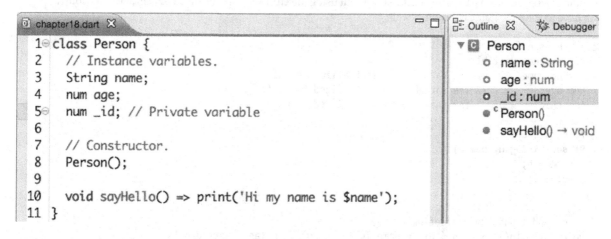

Figure 18-1. Dart editor outline displaying private/public instance variables

Constructors

In our previous examples we have also seen something about class constructors. The constructor of the class is a class method that is executed when the object is created and the class is instantiated. The constructor is a special method that has the same name as the class. Here's an example:

```dart
class Person {
  // Instance Variables
  String name;        // the variable is initialized to null.
  num age;            // the variable is initialized to null.
  num children = 0;   // the variable is initialized to 0.

  // Constructor.
  Person(String name, num age) {
    this.name = name;
    this.age = age;
  }

  // Method launching a greeting.
  void sayHello() => print('Hi my name is $name and i\'m $age years old.');
}

void main() {
  Person p = new Person('John Doe', 26);
  p.sayHello();  // Hi my name is John Doe and i'm 26 years old
}
```

Inside the constructor we can refer to instance variables using the keyword this. If you have worked with JavaScript, Java, or C# before, this will be familiar for you.

The Dart style guide discourages using this regularly and recommends it for use only when you have a name conflict. Here you can see the same example without using the this keyword inside our constructor; obviously we have to solve the name collision as well.

```dart
class Person {
  // Instance Variables
  String name;      // the variable is initialized to null.
  num age;          // the variable is initialized to null.
  num chidren = 0;  // the variable is initialized to 0.

  // Constructor.
  Person(String n, num a) {
    name = n;
    age = a;
  }

  // Method launching a greeting.
  void sayHello() => print('Hi my name is $name and i\'m $age years old ');
}
```

In the same way as you define instance variables with its type annotation or with the var keyword, if you do not specify a constructor for the class, Dart implicitly creates one without arguments, and this will be the first method to be executed when the object is created.

Within constructors you should pay attention to named constructors, constructors with names that define multiple constructors for a class.

Named constructors are not new to you, as you saw them earlier when we covered the DateTime class. As you may recall, there are different ways of defining a DateTime object: DateTime.now(), DateTime.utc(), or DateTime.fromMillisecondsSinceEpoch().

Named constructors can be used for different reasons—to initialize instance variables or to clarify the functions of the class.

```dart
class Person {
  // Instance Variables
  String name;      // the variable is initialized to null.
  num age;          // the variable is initialized to null.
  num children = 0; // the variable is initialized to 0.

  // Constructor.
  Person(String n, num a) {
    name = n;
    age = a;
  }

  // Named constructor.
  Person.json(Map data) {
    name = data['name'];
    age = data['age'];
    children = data['children'];
  }

  // Method launching a greeting.
  void sayHello() => print('Hi my name is $name and i\'m $age years old.');
}

void main() {
  Person p = new Person('John Doe', 26);
  p.sayHello(); // Hi my name is John Doe and I'm 26 years old

  var p2 = new Person.json({
    'name': 'Michael',
    'old': 45,
    'children': 2
  });
  p2.sayHello(); // Hi my name is Michael and I'm 45 years old.
}
```

Let's talk now about *constructor shortcuts*. These shortcuts allow us to save on typing when we're writing our Dart classes. Check this sample out:

```
class Person {
  String name;
  num age;

  Person(String name, num age) {
    this.name = name;
    this.age = age;
  }
}
```

We can use constructor shortcuts to avoid repetition when the constructor argument's name is the same as the name of the field. Let's see now how our sample looks using the constructor shortcuts:

```
class Person {
  String name;
  num age;

  Person(this.name, this.age);
}
```

We've used the this keyword on the constructor parameters. Note that the this keyword refers to the current instance. The Dart style guide usually omits the this keyword, and you must use it only when there is a name conflict.

Let's see now another great feature you can use on class constructors, the *initializer list*. In some cases you can also initialize instance variables before the constructor body runs. You can separate the initializers with commas, and you can use the contructors' parameters to initialize instance variables. See here:

```
class User {
  String name;
  String password;
  bool loggedin = false;

  User.fromJSON(Map json)
      : name = json['name'],
        loggedin = true,
        password = json['password'] {
    print('User initialized');
  }
}
```

When you define a constructor, you can redirect it, which is especially useful when there is an inheritance from the constructor of the child class. In this case we can redirect to the constructor of the parent class. You can also do it within the class itself if the utility of the class is clarified.

```
class Person {
  //Instance Variables.
  String name;       // the variable is initialized to null.
  num age;           // the variable is initialized to null.
  num children = 0;  // the variable is initialized to 0.
```

```
  // Constructor.
  Person(String n, num a) {
    name = n;
    age = a;
  }

  Person.withoutChildren(String n, num a):this(n, a);

  // Method launching a greeting.
  void sayHello() => print('Hi my name is $name and I\'m $age years old.');
}

void main() {
  var p = new Person.withoutChildren('Alice', 19);
  p.sayHello(); // Hi my name is Alice and I'm 19 years old.
}
```

As we discussed earlier, there are also constant constructors. You must use these if you know that an object does not change throughout the execution of the application. Create the class with its constant constructor, using const, and make sure all instance variables are constant with either final or const.

```
class Origin {
  final num x;
  final num y;
  const Origin(this.x, this.y);
}
```

Finally, let's talk about the factory constructors. When you use factory constructors to instantiate a class, a new instance won't be created; instead, the object is retrieved from a cache, so this can save a lot of memory in your applications.

The factory constructors are usually used when you are interested in separating the creation of an object from its implementation, and they are very useful when you need to choose between a number of interchangeable classes at runtime.

In other languages, the factory pattern is also used, but you must use a combination of static methods, class utilities, and so forth. Dart has already included this pattern, and you can use it natively. Here's an example:

```
class Boss {
  // Boss name
  String name;

  // cache to store the created instance.
  static final Map<String, Boss> _cache = <String, Boss>{};

  Boss._internal(this.name);

  // This is our factory constructor.
  factory Boss(String name) {
    if(_cache.containsKey(name)) {
      return _cache[name];
```

```
    } else {
      final boss = new Boss._internal(name);
      _cache[name] = boss;
      return boss;
    }
  }

  void sayHello() => print('Hi I\'m $name, the Boss!!');
}

void main() {
  var j1 = new Boss('Bruce Springsteen');
  var j2 = new Boss ('Bruce Springsteen');

  j1.sayHello(); // Hi I'm Bruce Springsteen, the Boss!!
  j2.sayHello(); // Hi I'm Bruce Springsteen, the Boss!!
  print(j1==j2); // true.
}
```

Note that j1 and j2 are in fact the same object.

Methods

Throughout the previous examples we have seen various class methods. Methods endow functionality to your objects. It is a function defined inside a class that ensures that the object has useful features.

```
class Person {
  // Instance Variables
  String name;       // the variable is initialized to null.
  num age;           // the variable is initialized to null.
  num children = 0; // the variable is initialized to 0.

  // Constructor.
  Person(this.name, this.age);

  void sayHello() => print('Hi my name is $name and I\'m $age years old.');
  void work() => print('Working ..');
  void eat() => print('Ummm delicious !');
  void sleep() => print('Good Night.. ZZZZZZZZ');
  void getSomeFun() => print('I love play HayDay');
}

void main() {
  var p1 = new Person('Mary', 19);
  p1.sayHello();    // Hi my name is Mary and I'm 19 years old.
  p1.eat();         // Ummm delicious !
  p1.work ();       // Working...
  p1.eat();         // Ummm delicious !
  p1.getSomeFun(); // I love play HayDay
  p1.sleep();       // Good Night.. ZZZZZZZZ
}
```

In addition to instance methods for your objects, there are also getters and setters, which we previously discussed and which Dart will create automatically. However, if you needed to create a getter or a setter for any of your classes, you can do so. See here:

```
class Person {
  // Instance Variables
  String name;      // the variable is initialized to null.
  num age;          // the variable is initialized to null.
  num children = 0; // the variable is initialized to 0.

  Person(this.name, this.age);

  bool get isParent => (children > 0);
      set parent(bool p) => (p==true)?children=1:children=0;
}

void main() {
  var p1 = new Person('Mary', 19);
  print(p1.isParent); // false

  p1.parent = true;
  print(p1.isParent); // true
  print(p1.children); // 1
}
```

When you define your getter and setter methods, you should use the abbreviated form as recommended in the Dart style guide; you must define type annotations for the return value in the getter methods and for the parameters in the setter methods.

When you define a class you can also those override operators that you learned in the first chapters, for example, +, -, and so forth.

Imagine you have a class that defines a GPS position. You may be interested in defining the operators + and - if you want to add or subtract two GPS positions and get a third GPS position as a result. Here's an example of how to do that:

```
class GPS {
  num latitude;
  num longitude;

  GPS(this.latitude, this.longitude);

  GPS operator +(GPS g) {
    return new GPS(latitude + g.latitude, longitude + g.longitude);
  }

  GPS operator -(GPS g) {
    return new GPS(latitude - g.latitude, longitude - g.longitude);
  }
}
```

```
void main() {
  var g1 = new GPS(40.311235, 32.87578786);
  var g2 = new GPS(38.642331, 41.79786401);
  var g3 = g1 + g2;
}
```

The Operators you can override in your classes are shown in Table 18-1.

Table 18-1. *Override Operators*

Operators				
<	+	|	[]	>
/	^	[]=	<=	~/
&	~	>=	*	<<
==	-	%	>>	

Inheritance

Inheritance allows you to create new classes from existing ones by adding a new behavior, more information, or more functionality to classes that inherit from parent classes, thus avoiding the redesign, modification, and verification of code already implemented.

In Dart you can create subclasses using the word extends, and you can refer to the parent class with the word super:

```
// Base class for animals
class Animal {
  String species;
  String variety;

  Animal(this.species, this.variety);

  void breathe() {
    print('Configuring respiratory system...');
    print('Respiratory system configured !');
  }

  void eat() {
    print('Configuring digestive system...');
    print('Digestive system configured !');
  }
}

// Concrete class for Dogs
class Dog extends Animal {
  String colour;
  num paws;
```

```
  Dog(String variety, String color, num paws) : super('mammal', variety) {
    this.colour = colour;
    this.paws = paws;
  }

  void breathe() {
    super.breathe();
    print('I\'m breathing by muzzle');
  }
}

void main() {
  var p = new Dog('Golden Retriever', 'yellow',  4);
  p. breathe(); // Configuring respiratory system...
                // Respiratory system configured !
                // I'm breathing by muzzle
  p.eat();      // Configuring digestive system...
                // Digestive system configured !
}
```

In the child class you can create new instance variables or new methods; you can also rewrite the parent methods. Whenever you need to refer to a method or instance variable of the parent class, use the word super.

In talking about inheritance we must say that constructors are not inherited, and neither are named constructors.

A subclass does not inherit the constructors of the parent class. If a constructor is not defined to the new subclass, then it will have the implicit constructor that Dart creates, without parameters:

```
class Animal {
  String name;
  String type;
  String breed;
  num age;
  num paws;

  Animal();

  Animal.json(Map data) {
    name = data ['name'];
    type = data ['type'];
    breed = data ['breed'];
    age = data ['age'];
    paws = data ['paws'];
  }
}

class Dog extends Animal {
  Dog.json(Map data) : super.json(data);
}
```

Variables and Static Methods

In Dart it is possible to create static methods and static variables when you define your classes. Static means you do not need to instantiate the class to use them, and they have a local scope to the class where they are defined, but their existence is permanent.

To create static methods or variables it is only necessary to use the word static.

```
class Car {
  static num maximum_speed = 120;
}

void main() {
  print(Car.maximum_speed); // 120
}
```

The static methods do not operate on the instances, so they cannot use the reserver keyword this.

```
class _CryptoUtils {

  static String bytesToHex(List<int> bytes) {
    var result = new StringBuffer();
    for (var part in bytes) {
      result.write('${part < 16 ? '0' : ''}${part.toRadixString(16)}');
    }
    return result.toString();
  }

}

void main() {
  print(_CryptoUtils.bytesToHex([6,4,7,8,1,0])); // 060407080100
}
```

■ **Tip** The Dart style guide recommends using global functions instead of classes with static methods for tasks or utilities commonly used in your applications.

Summary

In this chapter we have learned:

- How to create classes in Dart

- What the instance variables and the instance methods are

- The different types of constructors we can use in Dart

- About constructor shortcuts and initializer lists

- How to create subclasses from a parent class and how to call methods or constructors on the parent class

- What static variables and methods are and how to define them in your classes

CHAPTER 19

Implicit Interfaces and Abstract Classes

In this chapter we'll cover interfaces and abstract classes in Dart. We'll also see the difference between implementing interfaces and extending from a parent class. When you define a class, Dart implicitly defines an interface that contains all members of the instance and methods of the class and of the rest of the interfaces that implements. In short, if you want to write a class *A* that supports the API of a class *B* without inheriting the implementation of *B*, the *A* class must implement the *B* interface. To do this, when you define the class you can add the word implements followed by the classes you want implement and define the interfaces implementation.

Let's see an example to clarify this. We'll create a class and its implicit interface. Then we'll create another class which will implement the first one.

```
// In the implicit interface of Animal class is located the speak() method
class Animal {
  String _name;        // It is present in the interface
// but it's only visible in Animal class.
  Animal(this._name); // The constructor is not prensent in the interface.
  void speak() => print('Hi I\'m an Animal and my name is $_name');
}

// Implementation of the Animal interface.
class Dog implements Animal {
  String _name; // It should be defined because
                // it was only visible in the Animal class.
  void speak() => print('Hi I\'m a Dog and I have no name');
}

// Function that receives an object and executes its speak() method
sayHello(Animal animal) => animal.speak();

void main() {
  sayHello(new Animal('Boby')); // Hi I'm an Animal and my name is Boby
  sayHello(new Dog());          // Hi I'm a Dog and I have no name.
}
```

In this simple example, we've implemented the `Animal` interface in the class Dog. We must implement everything in the implicit interface from the Animal class methods and instance variables. We implemented the speak()methodand the instance variable _name, although later it is not used. If you look at the Dart SDK, you can see how this mechanism is very common. Figure 19-1 provides an example of implementing multiple interfaces, available in dart:html.

```
@DocsEditable()
/**
 * An abstract class, which all HTML elements extend.
 */
@DomName('Element')
abstract class Element extends Node implements GlobalEventHandlers, ParentNode, ChildNode {

  /**
   * Creates an HTML element from a valid fragment of HTML.
   *
   *     var element = new Element.html('<div class="foo">content</div>');
   *
   * The HTML fragment should contain only one single root element, any
   * leading or trailing text nodes will be removed.
   *
   * The HTML fragment is parsed as if it occurred within the context of a
   * `<body>` tag, this means that special elements such as `<caption>` which
   * must be parsed within the scope of a `<table>` element will be dropped. Use
   * [createFragment] to parse contextual HTML fragments.
   *
   * Unless a validator is provided this will perform the default validation
   * and remove all scriptable elements and attributes.
   *
   * See also:
   *
   * * [NodeValidator]
   *
   */
  factory Element.html(String html,
      {NodeValidator validator, NodeTreeSanitizer treeSanitizer}) {
    var fragment = document.body.createFragment(html, validator: validator,
        treeSanitizer: treeSanitizer);

    return fragment.nodes.where((e) => e is Element).single;
  }
}
```

Figure 19-1. *The Element class inherits from Node and implements the interfaces of GlobalEventHandlers, ParentNode and ChildNode*

In the previous example you can see how `Element` extends from `Node` and implements the interfaces of `GlobalEventHandlers`, `ParentNode`, and `ChildNode`. Implements allows your classes to inherit from multiple classes.

So, what's the difference between extends and implements? As we've seen in Chapter 18 the keyword extends is used when you want to create subclasses from a parent class inheriting instance members from the parent class.

The subclass will have all the methods and instance variables located on the parent class, but you don't need to define them again as you must do with `implements`. Let's see a simple example of extends and implements.

```
class Animal {
  String name;
  Animal(this.name);
  void greet() => print('Hi!');
}

class Dog extends Animal {
  Dog(String name):super(name);
  void eat() => print('eating...!');
}
```

The Dog class can use `name` and `greet()` and it doesn't need to define them again.

```
class Animal {
  String name;
  Animal(this.name);
  void greet() => print('Hi!');
  void eat() => print('eating...');
}

class Dog implements Animal {
  String name;
  Dog(this.name);
  void greet() => print('Woof!');
  void eat() => print('ummmm....');
}
```

In this case theDogclass must define the `name`, `greet()`, and `eat()` methods which are present in the interface. Extends is mainly used to reduce codebase by factoring common code into a super class. Interfaces are used to describe functionalities that are shared by a number of classes. With any discussion of interfaces, you must know what *abstract classes*are. An abstract class is defined as a regular class, but you must use the keyword `abstract` before the class definition

WHAT DOES ABSTRACT CLASS MEAN?

When we do a class hierarchy, sometimes there is a behavior that will be present in all the classes but it materializes differently for each one. For these purposes, we use abstract classes.

The abstract classes defining a common behavior to all classes will inherit or implement this class. Abstract classes are also very useful for defining interfaces. Not only can the classes be abstract, ***methods*** also can be ***abstract***. The process is the same, an abstract method will be a common function present in all classes, but it will work differently in each different class. When you're going to define your abstract classes or abstract methods, usually they will be defined without implementation and classes which implement this abstract class will define the code. Only the class is defined using the `abstract` keyword. Abstract methods can only be defined implicitly by omitting their bodies.

```
// Defines GeometricFigure interface. It won't be never instantiated.
abstract class GeometricFigure {
  // Define constructors, methods and instance variables.
  void draw(); // Abstract method.
}

class Circle extends GeometricFigure {
  void draw() {
    // Put your code here to draw a circle.
  }
}
```

We're going to see another example of abstract classes and how to use them. We're going to create two abstract classes to represent musical instruments and stringed instruments and how other classes, such as ElectricGuitar, SpanishGuitar, and BassGuitar can use these abstract classes.

```
// Abstract class for all the musical instruments.
abstract class Instrument {
  String name;
  void play();
}

// Abstract class for all the stringed instruments.
abstract class StringedInstrument extends Instrument {
  int number_of_strings;
}

// Concrete class for electric guitars.
class ElectricGuitar extends StringedInstrument {
  String name;
  int number_of_strings;

  ElectricGuitar(this.name, this.number_of_strings);

  void play() {
    print('$name Electric Guitar with $number_of_strings strings playing rock !');
  }
}

// Concrete class for Spanish guitars
class SpanishGuitar extends StringedInstrument {
  String name;
  int number_of_strings;

  SpanishGuitar(this.name, this.number_of_strings);

  void play() {
    print('$name Spanish Guitar with $number_of_strings strings playing flamenco !');
  }
}
```

```dart
// Concrete class for bass
class BassGuitar extends StringedInstrument {
  String name;
  int number_of_strings;

  BassGuitar(this.name, this.number_of_strings);

  void play() {
    print('$name Bass Guitar with $number_of_strings strings playing Jazz !');
  }
}

void main() {
  ElectricGuitar eg = new ElectricGuitar('Fender', 6);
  eg.play(); // Fender Electric Guitar with 6 strings playing rock !

  SpanishGuitar sg = new SpanishGuitar('Manuel Rodriguez', 6);
  sg.play(); // Manuel Rodriguez Spanish Guitar with 6 strings playing flamenco !

  BassGuitar bg = new BassGuitar('Ibanez', 4);
  bg.play(); // Ibanez Bass Guitar with 4 strings playing Jazz !
}
```

We've talked about implicit interfaces and abstract classes. Now it's time to talk about Mixins. *Mixins* is a way of reusing a class's codein multiple class hierarchies.

You can use mixins to inject functionalities into your classes without using inheritance.

To define a mixin in Dart you can use an abstract class with a few restrictions.

- Create a class that extends Object. In Dart all the classes extends from Object by default.

- The class has no declared constructors.

- The class contains no super calls.

According to our previous example where we define musical instruments we can change our StringedInstrument abstract class and use them as a mixin for the guitar instrument classes. Let's see how to define and use mixins.

```dart
// Instrument extends from Object
// Has no declared constructors
// Has no calls to super
// It's a Mixin!
abstract class Instrument {
  String name;
  void play() => print('Playing $name ... ');
}

// StringedInstrument extends from Object
// Has no declared constructors
// Has no calls to super
// It's a Mixin!
```

```
abstract class StringedInstrument {
  int number_of_strings;
  void tune() => print('Tunning $number_of_strings strings instrument ... ');
}

// Concrete class for electric guitars.
class ElectricGuitar extends Object with Instrument, StringedInstrument {
  String name;
  int number_of_strings;

  ElectricGuitar(this.name, this.number_of_strings);
}

void main() {
  ElectricGuitar eg = new ElectricGuitar('Fender', 6);
  eg.tune(); // Tunning 6 strings instrument ...
  eg.play(); // Playing Fender ...

  print(eg is ElectricGuitar);      // true
  print(eg is StringedInstrument);  // true
  print(eg is Instrument);          // true
}
```

As you can see in this example you can use play() and tune() methods in the ElectricGuitar object without inheritance because of the mixins. Notice that a class that uses a mixin is also a member of the mixin's type.

We changed our instruments example to use mixins in order to show you how you can modify your classes from inheritance to mixins. But this is not the best example to perfect understand mixins.

Generally you should use mixins when your classes don't fit well in a *is-a* relationship. For this reason we said the above code is not the perfect example for mixinis because ElectricGuitar is an Instrument so it fits in a *is-a* relationship.

Let's another example to use mixins for a class that not fit in a *is-a* relationship. Imagine you havean application to manage products. You have different types of products,for example, discs and books. Your classes looks like this.

```
class Product {
  String name;
  double price;
  Product(this.name, this.price);
}

class Disc extends Product {
  String artist;
  String title;
  Disc(name, price, this.artist, this.title):super(name, price);
}

class Book extends Product {
  String isbn;
  String author;
  String title;
  Book(name, price, this.isbn, this.author, this.title):super(name, price);
}
```

```
void main() {
  var d = new Disc('Planes, trains and Eric', 19.95, 'Eric Clapton',
      'Planes, trains and Eric');
  var b = new Book('Web Programming with Dart', 31.99, '978-1-484205-57-0',
      'Moises Belchin & Patricia Juberias', 'Web Programming with Dart');
}
```

You have a new backend and now you have to send informationabout your products in a JSON format to the backend. So you write a class called JSONSupport for converting Product objects into JSON and send to the backend and viceversa.

None of your products fit well in a is-a relationship with your newJSONSupport class. So you can use Mixins to add this new functionality into your classes without change your class hierarchy. This is our new code.

```
abstract class JSONSupport {
  convertToJSON() => print('Converting to JSON object ...');
  sendToBackend() => print('Sending to Backend ...');
}

class Product extends Object with JSONSupport {
  String name;
  double price;
  Product(this.name, this.price);
}

class Disc extends Product {
  String artist;
  String title;
  Disc(name, price, this.artist, this.title):super(name, price);
}

class Book extends Product {
  String isbn;
  String author;
  String title;
  Book(name, price, this.isbn, this.author, this.title):super(name, price);
}

void main() {
  var d = new Disc('Planes, trains and Eric', 19.95, 'Eric Clapton',
      'Planes, trains and Eric');
  var b = new Book('Web Programming with Dart', 31.99, '978-1-484205-57-0',
      'Moises Belchin & Patricia Juberias', 'Web Programming with Dart');
  d.convertToJSON();
  b.sendToBackend();
}
```

As you can see now you can use .convertToJSON() and .sendToBackend() methods on your Disc and Bookobjects without change these classes thanks to Mixins.

Summary

In this chapter we have learned:

- What implicit interfaces are and how to use them.

- How to implement an interface.

- The difference between extends and implements.

- What abstract classes are and how to create and use them in Dart.

- What mixins are and how you can use them in Dart by adding new functionalities into your classes without inheritance.

CHAPTER 20

■ ■ ■

Implementing Generics and Typedefs

As we've mentioned several times throughout this book, Dart is an optional-typed language, which means that you are not required to specify variables' data types in your applications. However, data typing can be very useful for self-documenting your source code and can make your life easier if you have to maintain the application.

If you indicate data types in your applications, something amazing will happen—all the Dart tools will begin to work for you and will provide various alerts while you work. These alerts might indicate typing errors between the parameters of a function or between a function result and assignment to a variable. Providing definitive data types in a language like Dart is like making a note to yourself, *"Hey, remember that this is a number!"*

They can also called type annotations, which are not to be confused with metadata annotations. Metadata consists of a series of annotations, each of which starts with @, followed a constant expression that starts with an identifier. This means you can use a class with a constant constructor as annotation. Metadata annotations are used to give additional information about your code.

In Dart there are three annotations available to all Dart code: @deprecated, @override, and @proxy. Let's see an example:

```
class Person{

  @deprecated // makes Dart Editor warn about using sayHello().
  void sayHello(String msg) => print(msg);

  void greet(String new_msg) => print(new_msg);
}
```

You can create your own metadata annotations, which can be as simple as creating a class with a constant constructor as you can see below. Let's create a class called FixMe to add annotations to within our code in order to fix bugs or create a better implementation. See here:

```
class FixMe {
  final String note;
  const FixMe(this.note);
}

class Person{
  @FixMe("Find better name")
  void eat() => print('eating...');
}
```

Generics

The **generics** are annotations for collections. When we covered maps and lists you saw how you can indicate the data type of the elements of that map or list. That is what the generics are.

Using angle brackets followed by the data type (`<..>`) we indicate to Dart that our list or our map will contain elements of that type. There are two different ways to make type annotations for collections:

```
List<int> l_num_1 = [1, 2, 3, 4, 5];

var l_num_2 = <int>[1, 2, 3, 4, 5];
```

What's the difference between them? The first indicates that the variable l_num_1 is a List<int>, whereas the second indicates that the variable is any type that at the moment contains a list of ints. When adding a string to the list, the first will create a warning while the second will create only a hint. If assigning a string to the variable (replacing the list), the first will create a warning while the second will not generate a warning or hint.

Generics will let Dart easily verify the operations you perform with the elements of the collections. Dart will verify whether you are adding elements that are nums or Strings and will warn you if you're running an invalid operation over those objects.

The generics also help you to reduce the amount of code. Imagine you create a class that manipulates a data structure. You decide to define the data type of this structure to take advantage of data-type checks and warnings during development. You decide to establish types, and you're going to use String. Later, you realize that you've written an awesome class. This class could also be used to manipulate other data structures with nums. You should duplicate the class and change only the data type, right?

If you use generics there's no need to duplicate the class you've created. You can use a **generic** as a parameter in your class. With that generic parameter, you're telling Dart that this class could manage any data type. Let's see a very simple example to better understand this. We're going to create a cache class to manage the cache on the client side. This cache class is amazing, and we would like to use it with any data type. To do this we'll use generic as a parameter for our cache class:

```
// We define the class and indicate that parameter would be any data type.
class Cache<T> {
  Map <String, T> _cache;

  // getByKey will return any data type value.
  T getByKey(String key) {
    if(_cache.containsKey(key)) {
      return _cache[key];
    }
    return null;
  }

  // setByKey will store any data type value.
  void setByKey(String key, T value) {
    _cache[key] = value;
  }

  Cache() {
    if(_cache == null) {
      _cache = {};
    }
  }
}
```

```dart
void main() {
  var strings = new Cache<String>();
  strings.setByKey('one', '1');
  print(strings.getByKey('one')); // '1'

  // This statement will throw an exception
  // type 'int' is not a subtype of type 'String' of 'value'.
  strings.setByKey('two', 2);

  var numbers = new Cache<num>();
  numbers.setByKey('two', 2);
  print(numbers.getByKey('two')); // 2
  print(numbers.getByKey('one')); // null
  // This statement will throw an exception
  // type 'String' is not a subtype of type 'num' of 'value'.
  numbers.setByKey('one', '1');
}
```

By indicating this generic as a parameter, we can avoid duplicating code and can continue getting the benefits of type annotations. You will see many examples of using generics in the Dart SDK. For example, the List, Map, and Iterable classes are good examples of using generics.

These data-type annotations are very useful and you can benefit from them by debugging your applications during design and programming phases, before they are executed. Data typing is truly something great and powerful! Now let's look at another useful tool, typedef.

Typedef

In order to provide a bit more information about functions in your application, you can use a typedef. A typedef essentially provides an alias for a function signature. Functions in Dart are first-class objects, which is why they may be passed as parameter to a function or be assigned to a variable. Let's see an example to better understand typedefs; we'll use a **callback** function that many JavaScript developers are accustomed to using.

A **callback** is a function passed as a parameter to another function. In the JavaScript world, due to memory leaks, the function is assigned to a variable, which is passed as a parameter. Here is a simple JavaScript example:

```javascript
var out = console.log;
function login(user, password, out) {
  if (user == ''  or password == '') {
    out('Access error. Enter username and password');
  }
}
```

Let's see a similar case in Dart and see what happens if we do not use typedef:

```dart
String formatLog(String msg, {int pos: 2}) {
  String cad = '';
  for(var i=0; i<pos; i++) {
    cad += '-';
  }
  return '${cad}${msg}';
}
```

```
void main() {
  var log = formatLog;
  var cad = 2 + log('My test message');
}
```

If you take a look at the example, you will notice that it has a clear error. In the line we've marked as bold, Dart Editor should alert you that you cannot concatenate a num with a String (the value returned by the formatLog function). In fact, if you run this example you'll get this exception on Dart Editor: type 'String' is not a subtype of type 'num' of 'other'.

Why didn't Dart Editor warn us about this while programming? Because we've assigned a function to a variable without data-type annotation, Dart Editor loses the data type of the original function. So, how can we avoid this?

The answer is simple: using **typedef**.

Typedef allows us to indicate that a function, although it's assigned to a variable or passed as a function parameter, should return a String type result.

Let's see now how to use typedef to take advantage of type annotations, even if we assign the function to a variable:

```
String formatLog(String msg, {int pos: 2}) {
  String cad = '';
  for(var i=0; i<pos; i++) {
    cad += '-';
  }
  return '${cad}${msg}';
}

typedef String LoggerOutputFunction(String msg, {int pos});

void main() {
  LoggerOutputFunction log = formatLog;
  var cad = 2 + log('My test message');
}
```

Thanks to typedef we can get alerts from Dart Editor while we are designing and programming our application. Dart Editor will alert us that we cannot concatenate a String with a num.

```
11  void main() {
12    LoggerOutputFunction log = formatLog;
⚠13    var cad = 2 + log('My test message');
```

Figure 20-1. Dart Editor displays the type warning thanks to the new typedef

Let's see how we can use typedefs to take advantage of data-type checking when we're passing a function as a parameter to another function. See this example:

```dart
void log(String msg) => print(msg);

num sum(num a, num b, logger) {
  logger(a);
  logger('+');
  logger(b);
  var res = a + b;
  logger('=');
  logger(res);
  return res;
}

void main() {
 sum(4, 9, log);
}
```

We now have two functions: log that prints out a message, and sum that adds two numbers. We're passing log as a parameter to sum. What's wrong with this code? If you run the example, you'll get an exception from Dart telling you that type int is not a subtype of type String of msg.

At the moment we passed the log function as a parameter to sum, Dart lost information about return types and parameter types for our log function. For this reason, we're not getting warnings while we're coding our application.

Let's see what happen if we add a typedef:

```dart
void log(String msg) => print(msg);

typedef void Logger(String msg);

num sum(num a, num b, Logger logger) {
  logger(a);
  logger('+');
  logger(b);
  var res = a + b;
  logger('=');
  logger(res);
  return res;
}

void main() {
 sum(4, 9, log);
}
```

In our new code, we've defined a typedef for the log function and used it in the sum function definition. With that simple code, Dart Editor can now warn us about the errors inside the sum function, as shown in Figure 20-2.

```
 1  void log(String msg) => print(msg);
 2
 3  typedef void Logger(String msg);
 4
 5  num sum(num a, num b, Logger logger) {
 6    logger(a);
 7    logger('+');
 8    logger(b);
 9    var res = a + b;
10    logger('=');
11    logger(res);
12    return res;
13  }
14
15  void main() {
16    sum(4, 9, log);
17  }
```

Figure 20-2. *Dart Editor warns us about issues inside the sum function thanks to typedef*

Summary

In this chapter we have learned:

- What generics and typedefs are

- How we can use generics to reuse code and to take advantage of data-type checking

- How our classes can manage different data types using generics

- How to define typedef to avoid losing data-type annotations on functions when they're assigned to variables or passed as parameters to another functions

CHAPTER 21

Using Dart's Libraries

In this chapter we'll cover Dart's libraries, what libraries are, and how to create your own libraries. We'll show you how to package functions, classes, or constants into a library for later use. Then we'll see how to create more complex libraries, conformed by multiple source files, and how to re-export a library so that it shows or hides some namespaces.

At the end of the chapter you'll see an example of how to use several concepts we've seen throughout this book, such as abstract classes, libraries, and pub packages. We have already seen how to define variables and functions, use the flow control and iteration statements, and create classes in Dart. This is much of what Dart offers.

Dart is a language that wants to become a standard for the development of next-generation web applications and therefore must present a mechanism to organize code, especially for large projects. In Dart, most of the time when you write an application, you will have multiple classes, some of which will inherit from others, and you will have different sections of your entire application in separate files, and so forth. Dart offers you the concept of a **library** to organize it all.

Now, in JavaScript we have a serious limitation, in that we have to work very hard to organize our entire project in code files. Libraries allow you to create modular code that can be easily shared and reused. A library is simply a package that you create from interfaces, classes, and global functions for reuse in another project using the keyword **library** followed by a name.

This is a simple example of creating a library, in which we have omitted the classes' implementation, or global functions bodies:

```
library animals;

num MAX_NUMBER = 12;

void createAnimal() {}

class Animal {}

class Dog extends Animal {}

class Cat extends Animal {}
```

Note The style guide recommends prefix library names with the package name and a dot-separated path.

So, according to this style guide, our previous library example would be called `chapter21.animals`, assuming the package's name is `chapter21`. See the example:

```
library chapter21.animals;

num MAX_NUMBER = 12;

void createAnimal() {}

class Animal {}

class Dog extends Animal {}

class Cat extends Animal {}
```

As you can see, you can pack everything you need into your library. You can add classes, global functions, or constants. A library can contain as many files as you need for solid organization of your code. In our example, our library will be formed only for one file, which is called `animals.dart`.

When a library has several files, they always have a file with the same name as the library. Let's see a more complex library example.

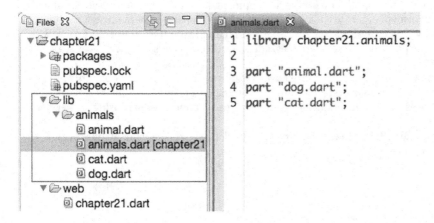

Figure 21-1. *Creating a more complex library with several files*

We'll create a new directory called `animals` in which to store our new library with all of its files. We'll place the new animals library inside `lib` directory according to Dart style guide. Then we'll create a main file with the same name as our library, `animals.dart`, which is the code of `animals.dart`.

```
library chapter21.animals;

part "animal.dart";
part "dog.dart";
part "cat.dart";
```

We'll indicate the name of the library prefixed with the package name, along with all the files that belong to this library. Then we'll create each file with its content. The `animal.dart` file will contain the Animal class.

```
part of chapter21.animals;

class Animal {

}
```

The `dog.dart` file will contain the Dog class. As you can see, on this file the first line will indicate that the file is part of the `animals` library by using the reserved keywords `part of`:

```
part of chapter21.animals;

class Dog extends Animal {

}
```

Finally the `cat.dart` file will contain the Cat class. As in our previous example, we avoid the implementations:

```
part of chapter21.animals;

class Cat extends Animal {

}
```

Using Libraries

Now that you are familiar with what libraries are and how to create them, let's see how you can work with them. Once you have defined a library that includes a series of interfaces, classes, functions, constants, and so forth, you can use it anywhere in your application simply by importing the library with the `import` keyword followed by the path of where it is stored.

We saw an example when talking about the library `dart:math` and learned to work with random numbers:

```
import 'dart:math';
```

The only thing remarkable is that Dart-native libraries are imported using the name **dart:** followed by the library name. The same thing happens when you want to work with a package downloaded using pub:

```
import 'package:lawndart/lawndart.dart';
```

You also can use this pattern when working with your own package or application. Any entry point (anything in `bin/`, `web/`, or another folder like `test`, `benchmark`, or `examples`) should also be able to import your own packages with the package uri. For example:

```
import 'package:chapter21/animals/animals.dart';
```

This should be used with the package-layout recommendation of putting libraries in the `lib/` directory. You will use the special name **package:** followed by the name or path of the library you want to use.

Regarding our previous `animals` library example, we could use this library using the `import` keyword followed by the path and the first file of the library, as follows:

```
import '../lib/animals/animals.dart';

void main() {
  // Using our library
  Dog d = new Dog();
  Cat c = new Cat();
  Animal a = new Animal();
}
```

As we've followed the package-layout recommendations, we also can import the library in this way:

```
import 'package:chapter21/animals/animals.dart';

void main() {
  // Using our library
  Dog d = new Dog();
  Cat c = new Cat();
  Animal a = new Animal();
}
```

When you work on your system, the most common problem you will run into is that you use many libraries, some of which may conflict with others because they have similar names. There are two different types of conflicts. The first involves internal library names (for example, you can't import two libraries each defined as 'library `animal`'). The second conflict involves the symbols libraries introduce to the namespace (for example, there are two conflicting variables named PI, or two different classes named Random).

To fix these conflicts, you can specify a prefix for the library when you import it. Imagine you are working in a scientific application where you will use `dart:math` and another library, also called `math`. You could resolve the name conflict in this way:

```
import 'dart:math' as math;
import 'math.dart' as math_lib;
```

Later you can refer to any of the functions, classes, or constants of each library using the prefix you have defined at the time of importation.

```
math.PI;
math_lib.ALPHA;
```

At other times you may want to import only a part of a library. To do this you must use the keyword **show**, which indicates to Dart the part of that library to show. See the following:

```
import 'dart:convert' show JSON;

void main() {
  print(JSON.encode({'msg': 'Hello'})); // String: {"msg":"Hello"}
  print(JSON.decode('{"msg":"Hello"}')); // Map: {msg: Hello}
}
```

Dart also supports hide in order to import everything except a particular namespace. Let's see an example:

```
import 'dart:convert' hide JSON;
void main() {
  print(ASCII.encode("Hello")); // [72, 101, 108, 108, 111]
  // This will throw an exception because JSON is not defined.
  print(JSON.encode({'msg': 'Hello'}));
}
```

Creating Libraries with Multiple Files

At the beginning of this section we saw how to easily create a library. We created a single file called animals.dart with the library directive followed by its library name. Within this file we defined all the classes that make up our library. We've also seen that in Dart you can define libraries with multiple files. In the main library file you must specify which files compose the library with the part directive followed by the file name. In each file of your library you must also indicate the part of directive and its name in order to indicate that the file is part of that library.

Let's look at a simple example that follows the definition from our library of animals. Create a basic file that will be the animals.dart library with the indicated content, as follows:

```
library chapter21.animals;

part 'dogs.dart';
part 'birds.dart';

class Animal {}
```

Now create the files dogs.dart and birds.dart, making sure they include classes that define our dogs and our birds and are part of our Animals library.

The dogs.dart file looks like this:

```
part of chapter21.animals;

class Yorkshire extends Animal {}
class Beagle extends Animal {}
```

The birds.dart file will contain this code:

```
part of chapter21.animals;

class Canary extends Animal {}
class Blackbird extends Animal {}
```

Note that this example differs a little bit from the example we showed you at the beginning of this chapter. In this new example, we've created the animals.dart file with the part directives and added a class inside. No matter that this file is the main library file, as you can use it to add classes, global functions, or constants.

In addition, in this new example we've added several classes to each file belonging to the library. You can use these files to add all the code you need to your application. Now, from any part of your system or another application, you can use this library via the import statement followed by the path and name of the main library file. See the following:

```dart
import 'package:chapter21/animals.dart';

void main() {
  var ani = new Animal();
  var dog = new Yorkshire();
  var bird = new Canary();
}
```

Re-exporting Libraries

It may happen that you want to make a new library with similar functions as another library and you want to use it in another application. Or you want to create a small library from a subset of another library's functions. To do these types of things, Dart incorporates the export mechanisms that we will see below in a simple example.

From our animals library we're going to create a new library using the most interesting entries; we will package it and create a new library. Let's create a new file called canine_mammals.dart with this content:

```dart
library chapter21.canine_mammals.dart;

import 'package:chapter21/animals.dart';
export 'package:chapter21/animals.dart' show Animal, Yorkshire, Beagle;

class CanineMammal extends Animal {}
```

We have created a new library based on our previous animals library and re-exported the Animal base class and the two classes of dogs that we need. Note that the **show** clause is optional and that an entire library can be re-exported if desired by omitting this keyword.

Now we can use this new library in any application in this simple way:

```dart
import 'package:chapter21/canine_mammals.dart';

void main() {
  var ani = new Animal();
  var dog_y = new Yorkshire();
  var dog_b = new Beagle();
}
```

In this particular application, we cannot define objects of type Canary or Blackbird because they are not visible in our canine_mammals library.

EXERCISE: CREATING OUR FIRST LIBRARY USING MYSQL DRIVER

Throughout the following chapters we're going to show you different Dart code samples to reinforce your knowledge. At the end of the book, we'll put all it together to create a complete functional application. This application will let us manage our contacts.

To build off its functionalities, we'll use IndexedDb for local storage on the browser and MySQL for storing our contacts on MySQL server database, and we'll also use Future Asynchronous API, libraries, HTML5, CSS3, web services, and so on.

Now we're going to create our first library for this final project application. This library lets us work with a MySQL database to store our contacts. In this example, we're going to show you how to use abstract classes as well as how you can use external packages from Pub in your applications to best utilize Dart.

We're going to create a new command-line project called chapter21_contacts. After that we'll create the contacts.dart file inside the lib/ directory. This new file will contain our library with chapter21_contacts. mysql_contacts.

In this library we'll have an abstract class and a concrete class for managing our contacts on MySQL. This is how our abstract class will look:

```dart
library chapter21_contacts.mysql_contacts;

import 'dart:async';
import 'package:sqljocky/sqljocky.dart';

/// Abstract class to manage contacts.
abstract class Contacts {
  /// Creates a new contact.
  Future add(Map data);

  /// Updates an existing contact.
  Future update(var id, Map data);

  /// Deletes an existing contact.
  Future delete(var id);

  /// Gets data for a given contact id.
  Future get(var id);

  /// Lists the existing contacts.
  Future list();

  /// Search for contacts,
  Future search(String query);
}
```

This abstract class defines the main methods by which to work with our contacts. We can add new contacts by passing a Map as a parameter with the new contact information to the add method.

```
{
  'fname': 'Moises',
  'lname': 'Belchin',
  'address': 'paseo del prado, 28',
  'zip': '28014',
  'city': 'Madrid',
  'country': 'Spain'
}
```

In our abstract class we also have an update method that is used to update the contact information; in this case, we'll pass as parameters the primary ID for the contact and a Map with the information to update.

The delete method lets us remove a contact from our database. In this case only the primary ID is necessary. We could retrieve a contact using a get method indicating the primary ID contact to retrieve.

Finally, we have developed two additional methods by which to get all the contacts from the database and search for contacts. Those methods are list and search.

As you can see, our abstract class Contacts will use Future API and the sqljocky package to work with MySQL.

■ **Note** You must install MySQL on your computer as well as sqljocky package from Pub. You can find the right version of MySQL for your system on http://dev.mysql.com Go to Chapter 6. Using Pub, the Dart Package Manager, learn how to install the sqljocky package. See here: https://pub.dartlang.org/packages/sqljocky

---

In the same contacts.dart file, we're going to develop our MySQLContacts class. This will be the concrete class we'll use to manage our contacts. It will look like this:

```
/// Concrete class to manage contacts stored on physical storage using MySQL.
/// This class requires sqljocky package.
/// https://pub.dartlang.org/packages/sqljocky
///
/// MySQL DB structure:
///
/// CREATE DATABASE  `dbContacts` ;
/// CREATE TABLE  `dbContacts`.`contacts` (
/// `id` INT( 11 ) NOT NULL AUTO_INCREMENT ,
/// `fname` VARCHAR( 150 ) NOT NULL ,
/// `lname` VARCHAR( 150 ) NULL ,
/// `address` TEXT NULL ,
/// `zip` VARCHAR( 10 ) NULL ,
/// `city` VARCHAR( 150 ) NULL ,
/// `country` VARCHAR( 150 ) NULL ,
/// PRIMARY KEY ( `id` )
/// ) ENGINE = MYISAM ;
class MySQLContacts extends Contacts {
```

```dart
/// MySQL sqljocky database object.
ConnectionPool _db;
/// MySQL host.
String _host;
/// MySQL port.
int _port;
/// Database name.
String _dbName;
/// MySQL default table name.
String _tableName;
/// MySQL User name.
String _user;
/// MySQL Password.
String _password;

/// Constructor.
MySQLContacts({String host:'localhost', int port:3306,
               String user:'root', String password:'',
               String db:'dbContacts', String table:'contacts'}) {
  _host = host;
  _port = port;
  _dbName = db;
  _tableName = table;
  _user = user;
  _password = password;

  if(_password != null && _password.isNotEmpty) {
    _db = new ConnectionPool(host:_host, port:_port, user:_user,
        password:_password, db:_dbName, max:5);
  } else {
    _db = new ConnectionPool(host:_host, port:_port, user:_user,
        db:_dbName, max:5);
  }
}

/// Deletes all the information on the `contacts` table.
Future dropDB() {
  return _db.query("TRUNCATE TABLE $_tableName").then((_) => true);
}

/// Closes DB connection.
void close() => _db.close();

/// Creates a new contact.
Future add(Map data) {
  var c = new Completer();
  var fields = data.keys.join(",");
  var q = data.keys.map((_) => '?').join(", ");
```

```
  var values = data.values.toList();
  _db.prepare("INSERT INTO $_tableName ($fields) VALUES ($q);").then((query) {
    c.complete(query.execute(values));
  });
  return c.future;
}

/// Updates an existing contact.
Future update(int id, Map data) {
  var c = new Completer();
  var fields = data.keys.map((v) => "$v = ?").join(", ");
  var values = data.values.toList();
  values.add(id);
  _db.prepare("UPDATE $_tableName SET $fields WHERE id = ?;").then((query) {
    c.complete(query.execute(values));
  });
  return c.future;
}

/// Deletes an existing contact.
Future delete(int id) {
  var c = new Completer();
  _db.prepare("DELETE FROM $_tableName WHERE id = ?;").then((query) {
    c.complete(query.execute([id]));
  });
  return c.future;
}

/// Gets data for a given data or null if not exist.
Future get(int id) {
  var element;
  return _db.prepare("SELECT * FROM $_tableName WHERE id = ?")
  .then((query) => query.execute([id]))
  .then((result) => result.forEach((row) {
    element = {
      'fname': row.fname,
      'lname': row.lname,
      'address': row.address,
      'zip': row.zip,
      'city': row.city,
      'country': row.country};
  }))
  .then((_) => element);
}

/// Lists the existing contacts.
Future list() {
  var results = [];
  return _db.query("SELECT * FROM $_tableName")
  .then((rows) => rows.forEach((row) {
    results.add({
```

```
            'id': row.id,
            'fname': row.fname,
            'lname': row.lname,
            'address': row.address,
            'zip': row.zip,
            'city': row.city,
            'country': row.country
        });
      }))
      .then((_) => results);
  }

  /// Search for contacts,
  Future search(String query) {
    query = query.toLowerCase().trim();
    var matches = [];
    var where = """LOWER(fname) like '%$query%' OR
    LOWER(lname) like '%$query%' OR LOWER(address) like '%$query%' OR
    LOWER(zip) like '%$query%' OR LOWER(city) like '%$query%' OR
    LOWER(country) like '%$query%'""";

    return _db.query("SELECT * FROM $_tableName WHERE $where")
    .then((rows) => rows.forEach((row) {
        matches.add({
          'id': row.id,
          'fname': row.fname,
          'lname': row.lname,
          'address': row.address,
          'zip': row.zip,
          'city': row.city,
          'country': row.country
        });
      }))
    .then((_) => matches);
  }
}
```

Our concrete `MySQLContacts` class extends from our abstract `Contacts` class and implements all its methods; in addition, this class adds the necessary instance variables and its constructor method.

All the methods of this class will return a `Future` object to make our code asynchronous, which means that we are not waiting for the MySQL operations to finish their jobs. We'll see the `Future` class and asynchronous programming more in depth in coming chapters.

We now have the abstract class and the concrete class, and to properly use them we're going to put them in a library called `sql_contacts`.

This class will import `dart:async` and `sqljocky` package:

```
contacts.dart
 1  library chapter21_contacts.mysql_contacts;
 2
 3  import 'dart:async';
 4  import 'package:sqljocky/sqljocky.dart';
 5
 6  /// Abstract class to manage contacts.
 7  abstract class Contacts {
 8    /// Creates a new contact.
 9    Future add(Map data);
10
11    /// Updates an existing contact.
12    Future update(var id, Map data);
13
14    /// Deletes an existing contact.
15    Future delete(var id);
16
17    /// Gets data for a given contact id.
18    Future get(var id);
19
20    /// Lists the existing contacts.
21    Future list();
22
23    /// Search for contacts,
24    Future search(String query);
25  }
26
27  /// Concrete class to manage contacts stored on
28  /// This class requires sqljocky package.
29  /// https://pub.dartlang.org/packages/sqljocky
30  ///
31  /// MySQL DB structure:
32  ///
33  /// CREATE DATABASE  `dbContacts` :
```

Figure 21-2. Creating our chapter21_contacts.mysql_contacts library with Contacts and MySQLContacts classes

We'll see now how to use this class and store our contacts on MySQL database server with Dart and `sqljocky`.

■ **Note**   Remember you must have MySQL server running on your system before running our Dart application, and you also need to create the database structure.

You could create the required database structure by running this sequence on MySQL server:

```
CREATE DATABASE `dbContacts` ;
CREATE TABLE `dbContacts`.`contacts` (
`id` INT( 11 ) NOT NULL AUTO_INCREMENT ,
`fname` VARCHAR( 150 ) NOT NULL ,
`lname` VARCHAR( 150 ) NULL ,
`address` TEXT NULL ,
`zip` VARCHAR( 10 ) NULL ,
`city` VARCHAR( 150 ) NULL ,
`country` VARCHAR( 150 ) NULL ,
PRIMARY KEY ( `id` )
) ENGINE = MYISAM ;
```

The following is an example to show you how to create a new contact, update its information, and delete it.

```
import 'package:chapter21_contacts/contacts.dart' show MySQLContacts;
void main() {

  // Managing contacts
  var id;
  var myc = new MySQLContacts();

  // Cleanup database and adding new contact.
  myc.dropDB().then((_) => myc.add({'fname': 'Moises'}))
  .then((contact) {
    id = contact.insertId;
    print(id);
    // getting info for the give ID contact
    return myc.get(id);
  })
  .then((contact) {
    print(contact);
    // updating contact info
    return myc.update(id, {'fname': 'Moisés', 'lname': 'Belchín'});
  })
  .then((_) {
    print('updated');
    // showing changes after updating.
    return myc.get(id);
  })
  .then((contact) {
    print(contact);
    // Deleting the contact.
    return myc.delete(id);
  })
  .then((_) {
    // getting a nonexistent key will return NULL
    return myc.get(id);
  })
```

```dart
    .then((contact) {
      print(contact); // NULL
      // Close DB connection.
      myc.close();
    });
}
```

After you run this code, you should see result on the Output view window similar to the following:

```
1
{fname: Moises, lname: null, address: null, zip: null, city: null, country: null}
updated
{fname: Moisés, lname: Belchín, address: null, zip: null, city: null, country: null}
null
```

Now we'll show you how to add multiple contacts to your databases and list all the information:

```dart
import 'dart:async';
import 'package:chapter21_contacts/contacts.dart' show MySQLContacts;

void main() {

  var myc = new MySQLContacts();

  // Adding multiple contacts
  Future.wait([
    myc.dropDB(),
    myc.add({
      'fname': 'Moises',
      'lname': 'Belchin',
      'address': 'paseo del prado, 28',
      'zip': '28014',
      'city': 'Madrid',
      'country': 'Spain'
    }),
    myc.add({
      'fname': 'Patricia',
      'lname': 'Juberias',
      'address': 'Castellana, 145',
      'zip': '28046',
      'city': 'Madrid',
      'country': 'Spain'
    }),
    myc.add({
      'fname': 'Peter',
      'lname': 'Smith',
      'address': 'Cyphress avenue',
      'zip': '11217',
      'city': 'Brooklyn',
      'country': 'EEUU'
    }),
  ]).then((_) {
```

```
    // Listing all the contacts from our database.
    myc.list().then((results) {
      results.forEach((r) => print(r));
      myc.close();
    });

  });
}
```

After running this code you should see something similar to the following:

```
{id: 1, fname: Moises, lname: Belchin, address: paseo del prado, 28, zip: 28014, city:
Madrid, country: Spain}
{id: 2, fname: Peter, lname: Smith, address: Cyphress avenue, zip: 11217, city: Brooklyn,
country: EEUU}
{id: 3, fname: Patricia, lname: Juberias, address: Castellana, 145, zip: 28046, city: Madrid,
country: Spain}
```

Finally, you could use this class to search for some contacts on your MySQL database server:

```
import 'dart:async';
import 'package:chapter21_contacts/contacts.dart' show MySQLContacts;
void main() {
  var myc = new MySQLContacts();
  Future.wait([
    myc.dropDB(),
    myc.add({
      'fname': 'Moises',
      'lname': 'Belchin',
      'address': 'paseo del prado, 28',
      'zip': '28014',
      'city': 'Madrid',
      'country': 'Spain'
    }),
    myc.add({
      'fname': 'Patricia',
      'lname': 'Juberias',
      'address': 'Castellana, 145',
      'zip': '28046',
      'city': 'Madrid',
      'country': 'Spain'
    }),
    myc.add({
      'fname': 'Peter',
      'lname': 'Smith',
      'address': 'Cyphress avenue',
      'zip': '11217',
      'city': 'Brooklyn',
      'country': 'EEUU'
    }),
  ]).then((_) {
```

```dart
    // Searching for contacts located in Madrid
    var query1 = 'madrid';
    myc.search(query1).then((results) {
      print('Looking for: $query1');
      if(results.length <= 0) {
        print('No results found');
      } else {
        results.forEach((r) => print(r));
      }
      myc.close();
    });

    // Searching for contacts which contains `cyp`
    var query2 = 'cyp';
    myc.search(query2).then((results) {
      print('Looking for: $query2');
      if(results.length <= 0) {
        print('No results found');
      } else {
        results.forEach((r) => print(r));
      }
      myc.close();
    });

  });
}
```

After executing this code, you could see something similar to these results:

```
Looking for: madrid
{id: 2, fname: Moises, lname: Belchin, address: paseo del prado, 28, zip: 28014, city:
Madrid, country: Spain}
{id: 3, fname: Patricia, lname: Juberias, address: Castellana, 145, zip: 28046, city: Madrid,
country: Spain}

Looking for: cyp

{id: 1, fname: Peter, lname: Smith, address: Cyphress avenue, zip: 11217, city: Brooklyn,
country: EEUU}
```

Summary

In this chapter we have learned:

- What Dart's libraries are

- How to create your own libraries in Dart

- How to create more complex libraries with multiple files

- How to use your own libraries on your projects

- How to re-export libraries showing or hiding some namespaces of the original library

CHAPTER 22

■ ■ ■

Leveraging Isolates for Concurrency and Multi-Processing

In this chapter we'll cover what isolates are and how you can use them—along with concurrency and multi-processing—to run your Dart programs. We'll learn everything about isolates through two simple examples so that you will know how to use multi-processing in your programs. Dart also lets you work concurrently and use all multi-processing capabilities, thanks to the multi-core in our modern computers.

In other programming languages this is known as *threads*. The difference between the threads in other languages and the Dart isolates is that the latter do not share memory; each isolate is independent of other isolates, and they communicate through messages.

When threads share memory, the application is prone to errors and the code becomes very complicated, making debugging difficult. Each Dart's isolate has its own memory and executes in an isolated way from the rest, hence their name. Isolates are possible in Dart and in the JavaScript translation because web workers are available in HTML5. Web workers are JavaScript tasks that run in the background to avoid the webpage being locked until a process finishes. When Dart code is compiled to JavaScript, dart2js use web workers to operate, although the ideal is to use *futures* and *streams* (more on those later).

Here you can see a simple example of Dart isolates:

```dart
import 'dart:async';
import 'dart:isolate';

void CostlyProcess(SendPort replyTo) {
  var port = new ReceivePort();
  replyTo.send(port.sendPort);
  port.listen((msg) {
    var data = msg[0];
    replyTo = msg[1];
    if (data == "START") {
      replyTo.send("Running costly process....");
      // Costly stuff here
      replyTo.send("END");
      port.close();
    }
  });
}
```

```
void main() {
  print('Start application');

  // Create reply port for the isolate.
  var reply = new ReceivePort();

  // We'll run the costly process in an Isolate.
  Future<Isolate> iso = Isolate.spawn(CostlyProcess, reply.sendPort);
  iso.then((_) => reply.first).then((port) {

    // Once we've created the Isolate, we send the start message process and
    // we're waiting to receive a reply from the costly process.
    reply = new ReceivePort();
    port.send(["START", reply.sendPort]);
    reply.listen((msg) {
      print('Message received from isolate: $msg');
      if (msg == "END") {
        print('Costly process completed successfully !!!');
        reply.close();
      }
    });

  });

  // We can continue executing more instructions while we're waiting for the
  // execution reply of our costly process in background.
  print ('Continue running instructions');
}
```

We've defined a function called CostlyProcess, which represents a costly process that will be executed by taking advantage of the concurrent programming. As you can see, this function uses ports—SendPort and ReceivePort—to communicate with the main process.

SendPorts are created from ReceivePorts. Any message sent through a SendPort is delivered to its corresponding ReceivePort. There could be many SendPorts for the same ReceivePort. SendPorts can be transmitted to other isolates, and they preserve equality when sent.

The send() method for the SendPort class sends an asynchronous message through this SendPort to its corresponding ReceivePort. The content of the message can be primitive values (null, num, bool, double, String), instances of SendPort, and lists or maps whose elements are any of these.

Later, we created the ReceivePort to communicate with our costly process resulting from the main function, executing the costly function in a separate isolate using the Isolate.spawn function.

ReceivePorts have a SendPort getter, which returns a SendPort. Any message that is sent through this SendPort is delivered to the ReceivePort it was created from. There, the message is dispatched to the ReceivePort's listener.

A ReceivePort is a non-broadcast stream. This means that it buffers incoming messages until a listener is registered. Only one listener can receive messages. If you run the above process you will get this result:

```
Start application
Continue running instructions
Message received from isolate: Running costly process....
Message received from isolate: END
Costly process completed successfully !!!
```

In this case, we've shown how to run a process in concurrent processing. The process we're executing is available in the same file where we have the **main()** function. Dart also allows you to run concurrent processes using isolates located in different source files.

Let's look at a simple example of a file structure like this. The chapter22.html file has this content. It is the basic example that Dart Editor loads when you select "Build a sample application code." See the following:

```html
<!DOCTYPE html>

<html>
  <head>
    <meta charset="utf-8">
    <meta name="viewport" content="width=device-width, initial-scale=1">
    <title>Chapter22 isolates</title>

    <script async type="application/dart" src="chapter22_isolates.dart"></script>
    <script async src="packages/browser/dart.js"></script>

    <link rel="stylesheet" href="chapter22.css">
  </head>
  <body>
    <h1>Chapter22 isolates</h1>

    <p>Hello world from Dart!</p>

    <div id="sample_container_id">
      <p id="sample_text_id"></p>
    </div>

  </body>
</html>
```

We also have the chapter22.css file with this CSS style:

```css
body {
  background-color: #F8F8F8;
  font-family: 'Open Sans', sans-serif;
  font-size: 14px;
  font-weight: normal;
  line-height: 1.2em;
  margin: 15px;
}

h1, p {
  color: #333;
}

#sample_container_id {
  width: 100%;
  height: 400px;
  position: relative;
  border: 1px solid #ccc;
  background-color: #fff;
}
```

```css
#sample_text_id {
  font-size: 15pt;
  text-align: center;
  margin-top: 140px;
  -webkit-user-select: none;
  user-select: none;
}
```

Then we have a chapter22_isolates.dart file with this code:

```dart
import 'dart:isolate';
import 'dart:html';
import 'dart:async';

main() {
 Element myresult = querySelector('#sample_text_id');

 // Define send/reply ports.
 SendPort sendPort;
 ReceivePort receivePort = new ReceivePort();
 receivePort.listen((msg) {
   if (sendPort == null) {
     sendPort = msg;
   } else {

     switch(msg) {
       case "FROM PROCESS: START":
         myresult.appendHtml(' Running costly process....<br/><br/>');
         break;

       case "FROM PROCESS: END":
         myresult.appendHtml(' Costly process completed successfully<br/><br/>');
         receivePort.close();
         break;

       default:
         myresult.appendHtml(' Received from the isolate: $msg<br/><br/>');
     }
   }
 });

 // This is a costly process that we want to execute.
 String Costlyprocess = 'costly_process.dart';
 int counter = 0;
 var timer;
 Isolate.spawnUri(Uri.parse(Costlyprocess), [], receivePort.sendPort).then((isolate) {
   print('Isolate running !!');
   timer = new Timer.periodic(const Duration(seconds: 1), (t) {
```

```
    switch (counter) {
      case 0:
        sendPort.send("START");
        break;

      case 5:
        sendPort.send("END");
        timer.cancel();
        break;

      default:
        // Every second we send a message to the costly process.
        sendPort.send('From application: ${counter}');
    }
    counter += 1;

  });
});

// We can continue executing more code while waiting for the
// reply execution of our process in background.
print('Continue executing more instructions');
print('.....');
print('Application completed');
}
```

Finally, we have another file called **costly_process.dart** that contains our costly process code, and this is what we'll call from the new isolate created on **chapter22_isolate.dart**:

```
import 'dart:isolate';

main(List<String> args, SendPort sendPort) {
  ReceivePort receivePort = new ReceivePort();
  sendPort.send(receivePort.sendPort);
  receivePort.listen((msg) {
    sendPort.send('FROM PROCESS: $msg');
  });
}
```

In this case we have the main() function in one file and the costly process in another one. In the main file we've used a timer to send information each second from main() to costly process. If you run this code in the Dart Editor Output view you will see the text of the print statements we have made in the code:

```
Continue executing more instructions
.....
Application completed
Isolate running !!
```

Figure 22-1 is the window in which you will see this result executed second by second.

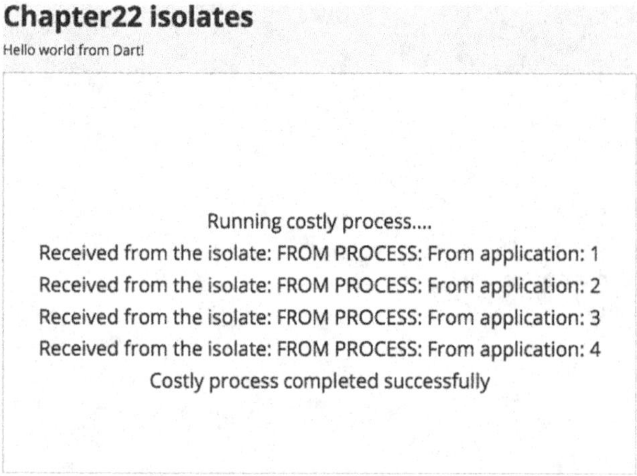

Chapter22 isolates

Hello world from Dart!

Running costly process....
Received from the isolate: FROM PROCESS: From application: 1
Received from the isolate: FROM PROCESS: From application: 2
Received from the isolate: FROM PROCESS: From application: 3
Received from the isolate: FROM PROCESS: From application: 4
Costly process completed successfully

Figure 22-1. *The result of the communication between chapter22_isolates.dart file and the costly_process.dart file*

The examples you've seen above don't do anything amazing, but they're perfect for teaching you how to configure your environment and play with concurrent programming in Dart.

Summary

In this chapter we have learned:

- What isolates are and how they allow you to use concurrent programming in Dart
- How to make an isolate run in concurrent-mode costly processes
- What `ReceivePort` and `SendPort` are
- How to use multi-threading in Dart to run costly processes located in either the same code file or different files

CHAPTER 23

■ ■ ■

Asynchronous Programming with Dart

In this chapter we'll cover the asynchronous programming in Dart, what Future and Stream are and how you can work with them. We'll see how you can create your own asynchronous functions in Dart using the Future API and Completers.

At the end of the chapter we'll show you an example of creating your own library based on Future API to manage contact information stored in IndexedDb.

When we began working with Dart we noticed this language would have great potential, not only for the great tools it offers but also how this new language unify all the mixture of tools, languages , and browsers we use to make web development.

Also it currently includes APIs that we can use and they're not available in JavaScript until the new language version is published.

If we consider this upcoming version 6 of JavaScript, which we hope will be available by the end of 2014, there are many functions and APIs already available in Dart, including:

- Block scope variables.

- Default values in functions.

- Optional Parameters by name.

- String Interpolation.

- Arrow functions.

- Promises API.

And these are just a few examples.

What is Asynchronous Programming?

Asynchronous programming, as presented by Dart and JavaScript 6 with its API Promises, is a way to work, creating and executing asynchronous processes in a natural, simple, and structured way. Dart offers the dart:async API with Future and Stream classes that you can use to do asynchronous programming. Actually, is essential that you understand what Future and Stream are and how they work because this is a common way to work in Dart's SDK. When you begin running and using them you will realize that these classes have a huge potential. They offer a very structured way to work asynchronously and avoid the callbacks hell very common in JavaScript.

Future

A Future object represents a process, function, or return value to be recovered in a future period of time. We will execute a function, for example, and we don't get immediately the return value of the function, we will get it in another moment during the application execution. Consider how a website works with links to other documents. The browser renders the document and displays it to the user. The user can start reading a text within two minutes and then click on a link. If you want to know when the user clicks on that link, you must capture the click event of the user. The event is the result of listening on that link (Future) until the user clicks it. When the user clicks on the link, you get a result at a future time that could be 5 seconds or 45 minutes from the web page loading, depending on what the user is doing in the website.

Except for the few minor differences, that is how a Future object works in Dart. You execute a process that does some action and you await the results. Best of all, while waiting for the result, your application is not stuck, it's continuously running more actions and your users don't notice anything. Using the Future class you can handle these objects and add asynchronous functions to your applications.

Working with Future

Let's look at some examples of Future and how we can work with them. We have commented that in the Dart SDK you can find many classes returning Future objects as an execution result. In dart:html you can find an example of this. We're going to use the HttpRequest class located on dart:html to make asynchronous requests and work with the results of these requests.

```
import 'dart:html';

void main() {
  print('1. Run a request asynchronously ');
  var result = HttpRequest.getString('response.json');
  result.then((future_result) {
    print('2. The Future has been completed and I get the result.');
    print(future_result);
  }).catchError((_) {
    print('3 Error running the request.');
  });
  print('4. I continue running more actions.');
}
```

To run this example properly you have to create a file called response.json with this content.

```
{'message': 'Welcome to the asynchronous programming with Dart'}
```

If you run this little application you'll get these messages.

```
1. Run a request asynchronously
4. I continue running more actions.
2. The Future has been completed and I get the result.
{'message': 'Welcome to the asynchronous programming with Dart'}
```

As you can see, regardless of the message we display, our little application is not waiting for the response of the HttpRequest.getString, it continues running more actions and when the server responds with a valid value or with an error, then the .then or .catchError methods of the returned Future object are executed. In the Future class you'll find interesting methods to work with these objects and it is imperative that you learn them to master the asynchronous programming.

First, we have several constructors to create Future objects. Using the default **Future** constructor we can create a future object containing the result of calling a computation asynchronously with Timer.run. Let's see an example of this constructor.

```
import 'dart:async';

int myfunc() {
  print('Making a lot of stuff here');
  print('...');
  print('...');
  var result = 159;
  return result;
}

void main() {
  print('1');
  var fut = new Future(myfunc);
  fut.then((r) => print('Result of myfunc: $r'));
  for(var i = 0; i<5; i++) {
    print('making other tasks');
  }
}
```

We've created myfunc, a function that will be the computation of the new Future. On the main method we've created a future object with new Future myfunc function as parameter. This creates a Future object and schedules a Timer to execute the function we give as an argument. If you run the above code you'll get this result.

```
1
making other tasks
making other tasks
making other tasks
making other tasks
making other tasks
Making a lot of stuff here
...
...
Result of myfunc: 159
```

We can see the first statement, later we've created the Future object and we continue executing other statements or tasks. As soon as the results of new Future(myfunc) are available we'll get it.

Into the Future class we have Future.microtask which is very similar to the Future constructor. It creates a future containing the result of calling a computation asynchronously with scheduleMicrotask. Let's see an example.

```
import 'dart:async';
void main() {
  print('1');
  var fut = new Future.microtask(() => 12);
  fut.then((v) => print('Result: $v'));
  print('2');
}
```

After running this example you can see this output.

```
1
2
Result: 12
```

As you can see the print statements are executed first, then when the future object is ready we'll see the Result: 12 statement. Future API has another constructor Future.value this constructor creates a future object whose value is available in the next event-loop iteration. Let's see an example.

```
import 'dart:async';
void main() {
  print('1');
  var fut = new Future.value(12);
  fut.then((v) => print('Result: $v'));
  print('2');
}
```

If you run this code you can see these results:

```
1
2
Result: 12
```

You'll see at first the print statements and in the next event-loop iteration you'll see the result of Future.value.

We have another interesting constructor that allows us to create future objects that run its computation after a delay. Let's see an example.

```
import 'dart:async';

int costly_function() => 12;

void main() {
  print('start');
  var fut = new Future.delayed(new Duration(seconds:5), costly_function);
  fut.then((v) => print(v));
  for(var i=0; i<8; i++) {
    print('Other tasks');
  }
  print('end');
}
```

If you run that program you can see all the print statements and after 5 seconds you can see how Dart shows you in the Output Tools view the result of the `costly_function`.

```
start
Other tasks
Other tasks
Other tasks
Other tasks
Other tasks
Other tasks
Other tasks
Other tasks
end
12
```

You have the static method `wait` to launch multiple asynchronous functions and await the result of all of them.

```
var futures = [HttpRequest.getString('response.json'),
               HttpRequest.getString('response.json'),
               HttpRequest.getString('response.json')];
Future.wait(futures).then((response) {
  response.forEach((e) => print(e));
});
```

___

Note Remember if you want to execute these examples you must import dart:html and dart:async in your dart applications.

___

We've seen `.then` method in our first example. This method lets you get the result returned when the `Future` object is completed and returns a value.

```
var fut = HttpRequest.getString('http://www.google.es');
fut.then((response) => handleResponse(response));
```

Before we also saw the `.catchError` method, which is very useful to detect if an error occurs during the execution of the asynchronous function.

```
var fut = HttpRequest.getString('http://www.google.es');
fut.catchError((error) => handleError(error));
```

We've seen the .catchError method to handle errors produced with Futures but if you need to complete your own futures with an error you can use the new Future.error constructor. This method creates a future object that completes with an error in the next event-loop iteration. Let's see an example.

We're going to create a future function and that function will make some parameter validations. If we have a problem with parameters we'll throw an Exception. As we are developing a future function but we have to throw the exceptions with Future.error constructor, so the .catchError will properly handle the errors.

```
import 'dart:async';

Future costly_calculation(Map parameters) {
  if(parameters.isEmpty) {
    return new Future.error(new Exception('Missing parameters'));
  }
  print('Doing costly calculation...');
  print('At some point we have an error');
  return new Future.value(12);
}

void main() {
  costly_calculation({})
    .then((v) => print('Result: $v'))
    .catchError((error) => print('Error: $error'));
}
```

The .whenComplete method allows you to register a function that will execute when the object Future has completed its task, whether it is completed successfully or not.

```
var fut = HttpRequest.getString('http://www.google.es');
fut.whenComplete(() => handleTask ());
```

The .asStream method allows you to generate a Stream from the Future object.

```
var fut = HttpRequest.getString('response.json');
fut.asStream().listen((v) => print(v));
```

Finally, you have the .timeout method to register a function to be executed after a specified period of time. For example, if you want to get a resource from the Internet and your connection is disrupted, the future won't wait forever; after 10 seconds it will print out the TimeOUT! message.

```
var fut = HttpRequest.getString('response.json');
fut
  .then((v) => print(v))
  .timeout(new Duration(seconds:10), onTimeout: () => print('TimeOUT!'));
```

Before finishing this section we want to talk about chaining futures. In some circumstances you need to execute some future functions and with the result of the first future function work in the second one and so on. You have two ways of doing that, as described in the following section.

```dart
import 'dart:async';

Future<int> one()   => new Future.value(1);
Future<int> two()   => new Future.value(2);
Future<int> three() => new Future.value(3);

void main() {
  one().then((v) {
    print('Result from one: $v');
    two().then((v) {
      print('Result from two: $v');
      three().then((v) {
        print('Result from three: $v');
        print('End');
      });
    });
  });
}
```

In this example we start executing one( ) when this future is completed then we execute two( ) when it's completed execute three( ). Nested calls work but they're harder to read. We can chain calls instead.

```dart
import 'dart:async';

Future<int> one()   => new Future.value(1);
Future<int> two()   => new Future.value(2);
Future<int> three() => new Future.value(3);

void main() {
  one().then((oneValue) {
    print('Result from one: $oneValue');
    return two();
  }).then((twoValue) {
    print('Result from two: $twoValue');
    return three();
  }).then((threeValue) {
    print('Result from three: $threeValue');
    print('End');
  });
}
```

When Future-returning functions need to run in order, use chained then( ) calls because they're more readable.

Stream

A Stream object is similar to a Future object. The only difference is that it is designed for repetitive data sets, but conceptually it is like a Future object in that it will return the result of an asynchronous execution at a particular time. For this reason you can convert a Stream into a Future and a Future into a Stream. Actually Stream is the class that you use when you add an event handler on a button in an HTML document in dart:html. In fact all the HTML event management applications use this class. It is also used for managing files and directories on dart:io, open, create, copy files, or create directories and list their contents.

Working with Stream

Let's look at some examples of event management in dart:html and how to work with Stream when we register a new event handler.

We'll start from an HTML document where we'll add a button and create a handler for the button click event. We'll stay listening to this event type in our button using the Stream class.

Each time the user clicks on this button, we will get a StreamSubscription object that will allow us to obtain the event that occurs in the HTML element, cancel the listening to this event, or pause it temporarily.

Here are some examples of using Stream and StreamSubscription in dart:html over ButtonElement.

```
var button = document.querySelector('#button');

button.onClick.listen((event) {
  print('Button clicked !!!');
});
```

With the .listen method of the Stream class we can create a new subscription and every time the user clicks the button, the function onData of StreamSubscription will be executed displaying the message Button clicked !!!.

In addition to the onData function, this method provides the onError, onDone, and cancelOnError functions, which as you can imagine register functions to be executed when an error occurs in the Stream, when the Stream is closed the onDone method will be executed and finally cancelOnError allows you to finish the subscription when an error occurs.

If you take a look at the Stream class you will see a lot of methods that we saw in dart:core when we worked with Iterable. These methods on Stream class are similar to the Iterable methods designed for repetitive data sets. In other words, a Stream allows you to work with each element placed in the Stream, so there are methods such as where, map, fold, join, forEach, every, any, last, first, and single.

```
void main() {

  print('1. Actions');
  var serie = [1, 2, 3, 4, 5];
  var stream = new Stream.fromIterable(serie);

  // We subscribe to the events of Stream
  stream.listen((value) {
    print("2. Stream: $value");
  });
  print('3. More actions');
}
```

After executing this code you'll get this result.

```
1. Actions
3. More actions
2. Stream: 1
2. Stream: 2
2. Stream: 3
2. Stream: 4
2. Stream: 5
```

As you can see, the result is similar to the execution of the Future examples. Our main program is not waiting for the Stream; it is completely asynchronous and when the data is received from the Stream the onData registered function is executed.

Creating Asynchronous Functions

We've learned the Future and Stream classes and it's time to create and use your own asynchronous functions and take advantage of all their functionality. A class that we have not discussed so far and is available in dart:async is Completer, which lets you to create Future objects and complete them later with a particular value or failed, as appropriate. We're going to create a very simple function but we're going to make it fully asynchronous. With this simple example you will understand how to make asynchronous applications.

```dart
import 'dart:async';

Future getUser() {
  final c = new Completer();
  c.complete({'user': 'Moises'});
  return c.future;
}

void main() {
  print('1. Doing some stuff');
  var u = getUser();
  u.then((v) {
    print('2. Result future.');
    print(v['user']);
  });
  print('3. Doing more stuff');
}
```

First we create a function that returns a Future object. In this function we use the Completer class to create a Completer object which will return value and we return the future of the Completer object. Then, from our application we call that function and we use the Future objects methods to work with it.

If you run this code you can see how the function is executed asynchronously the main program continues executing more actions and then, when the future value is ready we receive it and print it out.

```
1. Doing some stuff
3. Doing more stuff
2. Result future.
Moises
```

While completer's are extremely powerful for creating a Future-based API, they are often more complex than required for the majority of Future-based APIs. It is recommended to use Future constructors and chains. Let's see how we can make the getUser() function asynchronous without using Completer class.

```dart
Future getUser() => new Future.value({'user': 'Moises'});

void main() {
  print('1. Doing some stuff');
  var u = getUser();
  u.then((v) {
    print('2. Result future.');
    print(v['user']);
  });
  print('3. Doing more stuff');
}
```

In this case we can use one of the constructors we've seen in the previous section such as new `Future.value` to make our function asynchronous without using Completer. Completers are beneficial primarily when converting a callback based API to a Future based one (such as when creating a wrapper).

EXERCISE: CREATING AN ASYNCHRONOUS CLASS USING INDEXEDDB AND GOOGLE MAPS LIBRARIES

As we mentioned in *Chapter 21* you can find a big project to manage your contacts information. In that chapter we developed a class to store our contacts on the MySQL database server. We saw abstract classes and how to extend from them to create a more concrete class and how to use libraries to give more potential to our Dart applications.

We already know what asynchronous programming is and how to create our own asynchronous functions so now is a good time to come back to this chapter and study again how the futures objects work. In this exercise we're going to dive into these concepts again, including abstract classes, libraries, and asynchronous programming. We'll use Streams not just Futures, create our own asynchronous functions, and use two different libraries. We're going to create a new Web application project called chapter_23_sample and we'll create a `contacts.dart` file inside the `lib/` directory. This will be our main abstract class called `Contacts`. This is the same class we used in the Chapter 21 example.

```
library chapter_23_sample.idb_contacts;

import 'dart:async';
import 'dart:html';
import 'package:lawndart/lawndart.dart';
import 'package:google_maps/google_maps.dart';

/// Abstract class to manage contacts.
abstract class Contacts {
  /// Creates a new contact.
  /// It'll return the new conctact ID.
  Future add(Map data);

  /// Updates an existing contact.
  Future update(var id, Map data);

  /// Deletes an existing contact.
  Future delete(var id);

  /// Gets data for a given contact id.
  Future get(var id);

  /// Lists the existing contacts.
  Future list();
```

```
/// Search for contacts,
Future search(String query);

/// Gets map from contact location.
Future map(String address, String container);
}
```

Note that in this class we've added a new method called map to get the map from the contact address location. We'll use Google Maps to draw the map on our application. We've created a new class to manage our contacts that extends from Contacts abstract class but in this case we're going to use IndexedDb on our browser to store the contacts and all of their information. This is our IdbContacts class using IndexedDb through the lawndart pub package and Google maps through the google_maps pub package. To use these packages you must add them to your pubspec.yaml and import them on your class.

```
import 'dart:async';
import 'dart:html';
import 'dart:math';
import 'package:lawndart/lawndart.dart';
import 'package:google_maps/google_maps.dart';
```

As you can see our IdbContacts class will use dart:async and dart:html packages. Below you can see the IdbContacts class with its methods, instance variables, and constructors.

```
/// Concrete class to manage contacts stored on browser using IndexedDb.
/// This class requires lawndart package.
/// https://pub.dartlang.org/packages/lawndart
class IdbContacts extends Contacts {

  /// IndexedDb database object.
  IndexedDbStore _db;
  /// Database name.
  String _dbName;
  /// Database table name.
  String _tableName;

  /// Constructor.
  IdbContacts([String dbName='idbContacts',
               String tableName='contacts']) {
    _dbName = dbName;
    _tableName = tableName;
    _db = new IndexedDbStore(_dbName, _tableName);
  }

  /// Delete all the information on the DB
  Future dropDB() => _db.open().then((_) => _db.nuke());
```

```dart
/// Creates a new contact.
Future add(Map data) {
  var now = new DateTime.now().millisecondsSinceEpoch;
  var rand = new Random().nextDouble().toString().split('.')[1].substring(0, 10);
  var id = 'c_$now$rand';
  return _db.open().then((_) => _db.save(data, id));
}
/// Updates an existing contact.
Future update(String id, Map data) {
  return _db.open().then((_) => _db.save(data, id));
}

/// Deletes an existing contact.
Future delete(String id) {
  return _db.open().then((_) => _db.removeByKey(id));
}

/// Gets data for a given contact.
Future get(String id) {
  return _db.open().then((_) => _db.getByKey(id));
}

/// Lists the existing contacts.
Future<Map> list() {
  var results = {};
  var c = new Completer();
  _db.open().then((_) {
    _db.keys().listen((key) {
      results[key] = _db.getByKey(key);
    }, onDone: () => Future.wait(results.values).then((vals) {
      var i = 0;
      results.forEach((k, v) {
        results[k] = vals[i];
        i++;
      });
      c.complete(results);
    }));
  });
  return c.future;
}

/// Search for contacts.
Future<Map> search(String query) {
  var matches = {};
  var c = new Completer();
  list().then((results) {
    results.forEach((k, v) {
```

```dart
      v.values.forEach((f) {
        if(f.toString().toLowerCase().contains(query.toLowerCase())) {
          matches[k] = v;
        }
      });
    });
    c.complete(matches);
  });
  return c.future;
}

Future map(String address, String container) {
  var c = new Completer();
  var req = new GeocoderRequest();
  req.address = address;
  new Geocoder().geocode(req, (results, status) {
    // Get lat,long for the address geocoder
    var latlng = results[0].geometry.location;
    final coords = new LatLng(latlng.lat, latlng.lng);
    // Map
    final mapOptions = new MapOptions()
      ..zoom = 18
      ..center = coords
      ..mapTypeId = MapTypeId.ROADMAP;
    final map = new GMap(querySelector(container), mapOptions);
    // Marker
    final markerOptions = new MarkerOptions()
      ..position = coords
      ..map = map
      ..title = address;
    final marker = new Marker(markerOptions);
    // complete the future.
    c.complete(true);
  });
  return c.future;
  }
}
```

Let's see how to use this awesome class and how the future objects work here.

```dart
import 'package:chapter_23_sample/contacts.dart';

void main() {

  // Managing contacts on IndexedDb storage.
  var id;
  var idb = new IdbContacts();
```

```dart
      // Adding new contact.
      idb.add({'fname': 'Moises'}).then((k) {
        // new key created for this contact.
        id = k;
        print(id);
        // getting info for the given ID
        return idb.get(id);
      }).then((contact) {
        print(contact);
        return idb.update(id, {'fname': 'Moisés', 'lname': 'Belchín'});
      }).then((_) {
        print('updated');
        // showing changes after updating.
        return idb.get(id);
      }).then((contact) {
        print(contact);
        // After updating we gonna delete the contact.
        return idb.delete(id);
      }).then((_) {
        // getting a nonexistent key will return NULL
        return idb.get(id);
      }).then((contact) => print(contact));
    }
```

We've imported our idbContacts class located in the contacts.dart file. After we instantiate our IdbContacts class we've added a new contact to our browser database, when the add method finishes its job we'll get the new id for the contact added. With this id we can get its information using the get method.

We've updated the contact information by passing the id and a map with the information to update on our browser IndexedDb database. Finally we've deleted the contact using delete method. After running this code you will see these messages on your Output view window.

```
c_14180566623240908087689
{fname: Moises}
updated
{fname: Moisés, lname: Belchín}
null
```

Let's see now how to add multiple contacts, view it on our browser, and use the list and search methods to list all the contacts or to look for one of them.

```dart
import 'dart:async';
import 'package:chapter_23_sample/contacts.dart';
```

```dart
void main() {

  var idb = new IdbContacts();
  // Cleanup the database and add contacts to DB for list and search.
  Future.wait([
   idb.dropDB(),
   idb.add({
      'fname': 'Moises',
      'lname': 'Belchin',
      'address': 'paseo del prado, 28',
      'zip': '28014',
      'city': 'Madrid',
      'country': 'Spain'
   }),
   idb.add({
      'fname': 'Patricia',
      'lname': 'Juberias',
      'address': 'Paseo de la Castellana, 145',
      'zip': '28046',
      'city': 'Madrid',
      'country': 'Spain'
   }),
   idb.add({
      'fname': 'Peter',
      'lname': 'Smith',
      'address': 'Cyphress avenue',
      'zip': '11217',
      'city': 'Brooklyn',
      'country': 'EEUU'
   }),

  ]).then((_) {

    // List all records
    idb.list().then((results) {
      results.forEach((k, v) {
        print('$k :: ${v['fname']}');
      });
    });
  });
}
```

If you run this code you will get these messages on your Output view window.

```
c_14180569406757565057583 :: Moises
c_14180569406785295107053 :: Patricia
c_14180569406785694021442 :: Peter
```

Now we'll show you how to see these new contacts on your Chromium browser. Open the developer tools on Chromium and go to the **Resources** tab. On the right pane you can see the different storages that Chromium supports. Go to **IndexedDB ➤ idbContacts ➤ contacts**. Here you can see the new contacts we added to IndexedDb.

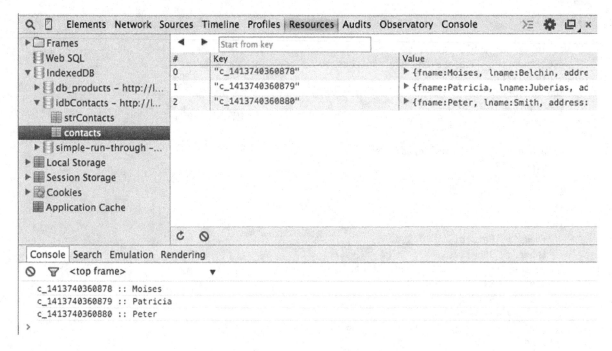

Figure 23-1. *Viewing our new contacts on IndexedDb through Chromium Developer Tools*

Let's see how to find a contact on our IndexedDb database using the `idbContacts search` method.

```dart
import 'dart:async';
import 'package:chapter_23_sample/contacts.dart';

void main() {

  var idb = new IdbContacts();

  // Cleanup the database and add contacts to DB for list and search.
  Future.wait([
    idb.dropDB(),
    idb.add({
      'fname': 'Moises',
      'lname': 'Belchin',
      'address': 'paseo del prado, 28',
      'zip': '28014',
      'city': 'Madrid',
      'country': 'Spain'
    }),
    idbC.add({
      'fname': 'Patricia',
      'lname': 'Juberias',
```

```dart
        'address': 'Paseo de la Castellana, 145',
        'zip': '28046',
        'city': 'Madrid',
        'country': 'Spain'
    }),
    idbC.add({
        'fname': 'Peter',
        'lname': 'Smith',
        'address': 'Cyphress avenue',
        'zip': '11217',
        'city': 'Brooklyn',
        'country': 'EEUU'
    }),
]).then((_) {

    // full search
    var term1 = 'cyphress';
    idb.search(term1).then((regs) {
     print('Searching for: $term1');
     if(regs.length <= 0) {
       print('No matches found');
     } else {
       print('Found ${regs.length} reg(s)'); // Found 1 reg(s)
       regs.forEach((k,v) {
         print('$k :: ${v['fname']}');
       });
     }
    });

    var term2 = 'Spain';
    idb.search(term2).then((regs) {
     print('Searching for: $term2');
     if(regs.length <= 0) {
       print('No matches found');
     } else {
       print('Found ${regs.length} reg(s)'); // Found 2 reg(s)
       regs.forEach((k,v) {
         print('$k :: ${v['fname']}');
       });
     }
    });
  });
}
```

You can see something like this after running this code sample on your Dart Editor.

```
Searching for: cyphress
Found 1 reg(s)
c_14180570189567842745959 :: Peter

Searching for: Spain
Found 2 reg(s)
c_14180570189524856050621 :: Moises
c_14180570189566459398852 :: Patricia
```

Finally we're going to show you how to use the map method to get the map from google maps using google_maps library and show it on our HTML web page. You must add a script tag to your chapter_23_sample.html file. Replace these tags located between <head> and </head>.

```
<script async type="application/dart" src="chapter_23_sample.dart"></script>
<script async src="packages/browser/dart.js"></script>
```

For these tags:

```
<script async type="application/dart" src="chapter_23_sample.dart"></script>
<script src="http://maps.googleapis.com/maps/api/js?sensor=false"></script>
<script async src="packages/browser/dart.js"></script>
```

Note that you'll need to select a key from those in your own indexdb.

```
import 'package:chapter_23_sample/contacts.dart';
void main() {

  var idb = new IdbContacts();
  idb.get('c_14180572994103464119734').then((contact) {
    var address = """${contact['address']}, ${contact['zip']},
  ${contact['city']}, ${contact['country']}""";
    idb.map(address, '#sample_container_id');
  });
}
```

If you run this code on Dart Editor you can see after few seconds the map for the contact location.

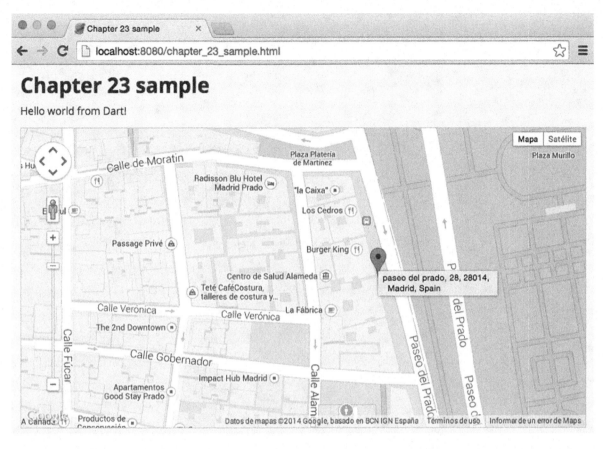

Figure 23-2. *Loading the google map for the given contact address location*

Summary

In this chapter we have learned:

- What asynchronous programming is

- What Future and Stream classes are

- How to work with Future objects

- How to work with Stream objects

- How you can create your own asynchronous functions in Dart using Future API constructors or Completers.

- How to combine abstract classes, libraries, packages, and your own asynchronous functions to develop an application for managing contact information stored in IndexedDb.

CHAPTER 24

■ ■ ■

An Advanced Syntax Summary

When you learn a new programming language, it is very useful to have a cheat sheet to check quickly the main instructions and the syntax. Here's the summary of syntax we have learned until now.

Exceptions and Errors

Table 24-1 lists the exception management cheat sheet and some examples of use. In Tables 24-2 and 24-3 you can see the Exception and Error types supported in Dart.

Table 24-1. *Exception Management Cheat Sheet*

EXCEPTION MANAGEMENT	
throw	To throw exceptions
try {}, on {}, catch {}	To catch exceptions
finally {}	To execute a code snippet always, occurs or not an exception

Table 24-2. *Exception Types Cheat Sheet*

EXCEPTION TYPES	
Exception	Abstract class that represents a system failure. You must inherit from this class to create your own exceptions.
FormatException	Format error when a string or other value is not formatted correctly.
IntegerDivisionByZeroException	Except for dividing a value by zero.

Table 24-3. *Error Types Cheat Sheet*

ERROR TYPES

AssertionError	Failure in an assert statement.
TypeError	Failure in a type assert statement.
CastError	Failed to convert a value from one type to another.
NullThrownError	When null value is thrown.
ArgumentError	An error occurs in function arguments.
RangeError	Try to access an index that is outside the object indexes range.
FallThroughError	Reached the end of a switch case.
AbstractClassInstantiationError	Try to instantiate an abstract class.
NoSuchMethodError	Try to access a nonexistent method on an object.
UnsupportedError	Operation is not allowed by the object.
UnimplementedError	The method is not implemented in the object.
StateError	Operation is not allowed by the current state of the object.
ConcurrentModificationError	Collections are modified during iteration.
OutOfMemoryError	Without enough memory.
StackOverflowError	Stack Overflow.
CyclicInitializationError	Lazily initialized variable cannot be initialized.

Let's see some examples of exception management. Below you can see how to throw exceptions or errors:

```
throw new Exception('The password is incorrect !!');

throw new TypeError();
```

Use try-on-catch to capture and handle exceptions.

```
try {
  login();
} on PasswordEmptyException { // Catchs a specific exception.
  reLogin();
} on Exception catch(e) {      // Catchs any type of exception.
  print('What happend here? ');
} catch(e) {                   // Catchs anything else than will happen.
  print(' Something has gone wrong. I have no idea what happened !');
}
```

Use finally to execute code at the end of the try-catch block.

```
var myresult;
try {
  // I try to to access to the system.
  myresult = login();
} on Exception catch(e) {
  // An error occurs in the system.
  myresult = ' You did not say the magic word !';
} finally {
  // Displays the answer to the user.
  print(myresult);
}
```

Classes

In Tables 24-4 and 24-5 you can see the basic syntax for classes and inheritance, interfaces, abstract classes, mixins, generics, and typedefs.

Table 24-4. *Classes Cheat Sheet*

CLASSES

`class ClassName {}`	Create a class.
`var obj = new classConstructor();`	Instantiates a class.
`.method()` `.instance_variable`	Access your instance or static variables or methods
`this.method()` `this.variable`	Self-reference
`const ClassName {}`	Constant class
`_variableName`	Private variable

`<    +    |    [ ]    >    /`
`[ ] =    <=    ~/    &    ~`
`>=    ^    *    <<    ==`
`-    %    >>`
	Operators you can override in your classes definition.
	
	`class GPS {`
	`  num latitude;`
	`  num longitude;`
	`  GPS(this.latitude, this.longitude);`
	`  GPS `**`operator`**` +(GPS g);`
	`  GPS `**`operator`**` -(GPS g);`
	
	`}`

Table 24-5. *Inheritance Cheat Sheet*

INHERITANCE	
class subClass extends parentClass	Create subclasses
super	Refer to Parent class
STATIC VARIABLES AND METHODS	
static method() {} static variable = value;	Create static methods or variables
INTERFACES	
class NewClass implements classA, classB, classC {}	Define a class that implements another class or classes.
ABSTRACT CLASSES	
abstract class myAbsClass {}	Abstract class defining
MIXINS	
abstract class myMixin {}	Class must extends from Object
	Class has no declared constructors
	Class has no calls to super
	You can add more functionalities into your classes using mixins without inheritance using with keyword.
	class MyClass extends Object with myMixin {}
GENERICS	
<..>	Indicate that the contents of a list, map, or your own classes is Generic. It would work with any generic value, num, string, etc.
TYPEDEFS	
typedef DataType FunctionName();	Indicates the data type result that this function should return.

Table 24-6 lists all the basic syntax to work with libraries.

Table 24-6. *Libraries Cheat Sheet*

LIBRARIES	
library LibName	Defines a Library
import 'LibName.dart'	Imports a Library
import 'dart:LibName'	Imports Dart native Library
import 'package:LibName.dart' import 'package:path/LibName.dart'	Imports a Package

(continued)

Table 24-6. (*continued*)

LIBRARIES

import 'LibName' as Prefix Ej. import 'dart:math' as Math	Imports a Library with prefix
import 'LibName' show partToShow	Imports only a part of the library
import 'LibName' hide partToHide	Imports all names except partToHide
library LibName; part 'file1.dart'; part 'file2.dart'; file1.dart: part of LibName; file2.dart: part of LibName;	Creates libraries with multiple files In file1.dart and file2.dart you must indicates that these files are part of the library LibName with part of keyword.
export LibName	Exports a Library
export LibName show partToExport	Exports only a part of the library

In Table 24-7 you can see basic methods to work with Future and Streams.

Table 24-7. *Future and Stream Cheat Sheet*

FUTURE	
Future fut = new Future(myFunction)	Creates a future containing the result of calling your function asynchronously with run.
Future.then()	Get result of the asynchronous function
Future.catchError()	Get error of asynchronous function
Future.whenComplete()	Get the value when the asynchronous function has completed
Future.timeout(Duration, onTiemout: () {})	Detects excessive time consumed by asynchronous function and execute a given function.
new Future.delayed(Duration duration, myFunction)	Creates a future that runs your function after a delay.
new Future.value("my_values")	A future whose value is available in the next event-loop iteration.
Future.wait([myFuture1, myFuture2]);	Wait for all the given futures to complete and collect their values.
STREAM	
Stream.listen(onData, onError, onDone, cancelOnError)	Subscribe to the Stream events

Dart and Other Web Technologies

CHAPTER 25

■ ■ ■

Integrating Dart and HTML5

In this chapter we'll cover what the Document Object Model (DOM) is and how you can manage it from Dart using the dart:html library. We'll see how HTML documents are structured in dart:html and how to retrieve elements with the querySelector and querySelectorAll methods. Later, we'll look at DOM events and how to create event handlers that are attached to DOM elements.

Throughout this book we have seen some similarities to and differences from JavaScript. Dart's goal is to solve some problems inherent in current web development, and therefore it allows us to develop in a more uniform and structured way and to debug and maintain large applications more effectively.

Dart is fully integrated with HTML5 and CSS3; they can work together perfectly. In this chapter we'll see how to work with HTML from within our Dart applications, we'll handle the DOM, and we'll introduce DOM events and how to manage them.

Working with HTML

The dart:html library contains the classes and methods you'll need to handle the DOM. Furthermore, if you want to take advantage of all the HTML5 APIs supported by modern browsers, you must use dart:html and some additional libraries such as dart:web_audio, dart:svg, dart:web_gl, dart:indexed_db, and dart:web_sql.

These libraries will let you work with processing and synthesizing audio in web applications, with scalable vector graphics on various browsers, with rendering interactive 3D and 2D graphics within any compatible browser, with managing storage on the client side through key-value pairs with IndexedDb, or with storing data in databases that can be queried using a variant of SQL. These libraries are located separately from dart:html core functionalities so as to optimize our Dart applications when we compile to JavaScript using dart2js.

WHAT IS THE DOM?

The DOM is the Document Object Model, which is the responsibility of the W3C, and could be defined as an API that provides you with the following:

- A standard set of objects for representing HTML and XML documents.
- A standard model of how to combine these objects.
- A standard interface for accessing and manipulating these objects.

When you work in an HTML document, the DOM is a tree where all the tags or nodes are placed to build the entire document. Each node can have other nodes, and so on. The root of this tree is the document object, which itself descends from a window object.

As you've seen in other examples, in order to work with the Dart HTML library you must import it into your applications in this way:

```
import 'dart:html';
```

Let's start with some examples in which we will see how Dart can work with HTML documents. From a web application created with Dart Editor and sample content we can start quickly working and testing the library:

```
import 'dart:html';

void main() {
  var text = document.querySelector('#sample_text_id');
  text
    ..text = 'Welcome to Dart !'
    ..lang = 'EN'
    ..attributes.forEach((k, v) => print('$k: $v'))
    ..style.backgroundColor = '#f87c45';}
```

We can use the querySelectorAll and querySelector methods, which indicate a selector, to find elements within the document:

```
var text = document.querySelector('#sample_text_id');
```

If you have previously worked with JavaScript, you'll see that this can greatly simplify and unify how to work with and retrieve elements from the DOM. In JavaScript we have the **getElementById**, **getElementByClassName**, **getElementByName**, and **getElementByTagName** methods. However, with these Dart methods the work is more similar to how you'll work with the jQuery framework and its query $(selector) method.

In the first versions of Dart, the querySelector and querySelectorAll methods were called **query** and **queryAll**, but then they changed to support the new proposed HTML5 standard. The **querySelector** and **querySelectorAll** methods are methods of the Document class. Besides these two methods, the Document class has the same methods as JavaScript to locate elements in the document. Let's see a few examples comparing querySelector and classic JavaScript methods in Dart.

You can select elements by their id attribute:

```
var element = document.querySelector('#sample_text_id');
var element = document.getElementById('sample_text_id');
```

You can select elements by their class attribute:

```
var element = document.querySelector('.class');
var element = document.getElementByClassName('class');
```

You can select elements by their type:

```
var element = document.querySelector('p');
var element = document.getElementsByTagName('p');
```

And you can select elements by their name attribute:

```
var element = document.querySelector('[name="myName"]');
var element = document.getElementsByName('myName');
```

As you can see, the **querySelector** and **querySelectorAll** methods always work in the same way; you only have to change the *selector string* depending on what you want to find. The **querySelectorAll** method returns a list of elements that match the specified selector. Each found element is an object and so has all the properties and methods defined in dart:html for DOM elements.

Another great advantage of using this method is that you'll get built-in Dart real-data collections; i.e., **querySelectorAll** will return a list of elements that match the specified selector, and therefore you will have all the methods that you have seen in dart:core at your disposal to work with the List data type. See the following:

```
var elements = document.querySelectorAll('p').toList(growable: true);
var divs = document.querySelectorAll('div');
elements.addAll(divs);
elements.forEach((el) => print(el.tagName));
```

No doubt, this is one of the biggest Dart advantages in this library, because all of the DOM is perfectly structured and all the elements are treated as native Dart objects with all of Dart's properties and methods. When you have located and retrieved a specific DOM element you can access its properties, events, and methods in the following way.

If your document contains a paragraph HTML element, like this:

```
<p id="sample_text_id" class="clase" name="myName"></p>
```

From your Dart application you can retrieve the element and change any of its properties, like this:

```
var text = document.querySelector('#sample_text_id');
text.text = 'Welcome to Dart !';
text.lang = 'EN';
```

You can display all the element attributes with the **.forEach** function because the attributes of the element are stored in a built-in Dart **Map**:

```
text.attributes.forEach((k, v) => print('$k: $v'));
```

When you're working with Dart Editor and using the dart:html library you can view and study all the classes, methods, properties, and events of an object easily thanks to the auto-complete system, as you can see in Figure 25-1.

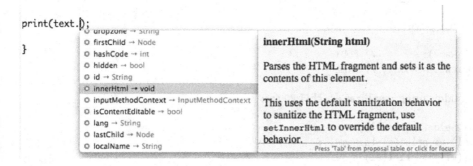

Figure 25-1. Auto-complete system for HTML objects

In dart:html everything is structured and classified using classes; all elements inherit directly from **HtmlElement**, which itself inherits from the base class **Element** that defines any HTML element of a document and contains the properties and methods common to all elements.

Later, the peculiarities of each element are defined in their own classes; for example, the checked property of an InputElement or the **addRow** method of a **TableElement** will be defined in their respective classes.

Thanks to this very detailed classification, creating elements when working in an HTML document is simple and structured. You can create a paragraph element in this way and use the cascade operator to easily assign value to multiple properties at once:

```
var myp = new ParagraphElement();
myp..id = 'sample_text_2'
  ..text = 'Welcome to Dart !!'
  ..title = ' Welcome to Dart !!'
  ..lang = 'EN';
```

Almost every DOM element has its own constructor. So, if you want to create a Div element you can use the new DivElement() constructor method; if you want to create an HTML table you'd use TableElement(), and so on.

■ **Note**   Many newer HTML5 elements (section, article, etc.) don't have their own constructors yet.

You've seen how to find elements in your document and create new elements. Let's see now how to add elements to the DOM. As we mentioned at the beginning of this chapter, the HTML document has a tree structure where each element is a node and can have more nodes.

The Element class in **dart:html** inherits from another, very important class called Node while simultaneously implementing two other classes: ChildNode and ParentNode. That means that **Element** has all the functionality to work with the nodes of a document, and as all HTML elements inherit directly or indirectly from Element, they all also have this functionality.

It does not matter if you create elements in the HTML file or you create them dynamically at runtime later. Any element can see which nodes have which others as children, and at the same time they can see who the node's parent is, so from an element you can navigate through the document up or down using parent or child nodes.

You can retrieve an element and access its parent in this simple way:

```
var p = document.querySelector('#sample_text_id');
print(p.parent.tagName); // DIV
print(p.parent.id);       // sample_container_id
```

You can move up as much as you need:

```
print(p.parent.parent.tagName);        // BODY
print(p.parent.parent.parent.tagName); // HTML
```

Or you can explore its children using **.children** or **.childNodes**:

```
var body = document.querySelector('body');
body.children.forEach((el) => print(el.tagName));
body.childNodes.forEach((el) => print(el));
```

The main difference between these options is that **.children** returns a list of Element objects and thus offers all properties and methods of these objects, while **.childNodes** returns a list of Node objects, representing each element of the document as a node.

Besides these two methods, each element of the document has the **.nodes** method, which returns a modifiable Iterable of all nodes of the element. Therefore, by using this method you can easily add elements to your document:

```
var myp = new ParagraphElement();
myp..id = 'sample_text_2'
  ..text = 'Welcome to Dart !!'
  ..title = 'Welcome to Dart !!'
  ..lang = 'EN';

document.body.nodes.add(myp);
```

If you want to remove an element from your HTML document, it is as simple as retrieving it and executing the **.remove()** method present in the **Node** class, and therefore present in all HTML elements. See here:

```
var p = document.querySelector ('# sample_text_id');
p.remove ();
```

If you prefer, you can also replace a node using **.replaceWith**, as follows:

```
var p = document.querySelector('#sample_text_id');
var div = new DivElement()
 ..id='sample_div_id'
 ..text = ' Replacement element';
p.replaceWith(div);
```

Event Management

We've already seen how to find and retrieve DOM elements, modify any of their properties, and delete or add new elements. Now we're going to look at how to manage events from these DOM elements when the user interacts with them. Let's see how to add event handlers to an element of your HTML document.

Create a new InputElement element and add it to your main container. Now you'll add events to this new text box. In this case, you're going to handle the onClick event. This event will be triggered whenever the user clicks on the text box. In addition, you'll add the onKeyUp event that will be triggered whenever the user types a key within the text box. See the following:

```
var input = new TextInputElement()
  ..id = 'sample_text_input'
  ..value = 'Insert value'
  ..placeholder = 'Insert value';

// onClick Event on input.
input.onClick.listen((event) {
  if (input.value.trim() != '') {
    print(input.value);
  }
});
```

```
// onKeyUp Event on input.
input.onKeyUp.listen((KeyboardEvent e) {
  print(e.keyCode);
});

var div = document.querySelector('#sample_container_id');
div.nodes.add(input);
```

In the example, each time the user types a key on the text box it will show the ASCII code of the pressed key. Each time the user clicks the input text box, if the text box has a value, you should see the value in the Output view. Let's play with this sample web application. Below you can see the basic HTML structure for the web application's sample content, which was created with Dart Editor:

```
<!DOCTYPE html>

<html>
  <head>
    <meta charset="utf-8">
    <meta name="viewport" content="width=device-width, initial-scale=1">
    <title>Chapter 25</title>

    <script async type="application/dart" src="chapter_25.dart"></script>
    <script async src="packages/browser/dart.js"></script>

    <link rel="stylesheet" href="chapter_25.css">
  </head>
  <body>
    <h1>Chapter 25</h1>

    <p>Hello world from Dart!</p>

    <div id="sample_container_id">
      <p id="sample_text_id">Click me!</p>
    </div>

  </body>
</html>
```

In this sample we've used an element.onEvent.listen form to create an event handler on that element, as you can see here:

```
// onKeyUp Event on input.
input.onKeyUp.listen((KeyboardEvent e) {
  print(e.keyCode);
});
```

While this is the preferred way to create event handlers, there is another way to do the same thing by using this form: element.on['event'].listen. See this example:

```
// onKeyUp Event on input.
input.on['keyup'].listen((KeyboardEvent e) {
  print(e.keyCode);
});
```

We're going to make some changes to the HTML elements and add different events to them. But first you have to add this code to your CSS file. In this chapter we are focusing on HTML and DOM elements; in Chapter 26 we'll see how to manage the element's style properties from Dart. Here is the required code:

```
.terminal {
  border:1px solid #cecece;
  font-family: Andale Mono, monospace; line-height: 1em;
  font-size:13px;
  float: left;
  width: 100%;
  max-height:210px;
  min-height:210px;
  background:#ddd;
  padding:10px;
  line-height:1.5em;
  color: #63de00!important;
  overflow-y:scroll;
}
```

This will be a little application to show you how to create new elements using their constructors, change some properties, add event handlers, and add these elements to the DOM. See the following:

```
import 'dart:html';
import 'dart:math' as Math;

void main() {
  // Different ways to use querySelector.
  var body = document.querySelector('body');
  print(body.innerHtml);
  var h1 = body.querySelector('h1');
  var p = body.querySelector('p');
  var sc = body.querySelector('#sample_container_id');
  var sp = sc.querySelector('#sample_text_id');

  // Change h1 text.
  h1.text = 'Integrating Dart and HTML';
  // Change p text.
  p.text = 'This is an example of using DOM elements from DART';
  // Cleanup p#sample_text_id text.
  sp.text = '';

  // Creating new Elements.
  var input = new InputElement()
    ..id = 'autocomplete'
    ..name = 'autocomplete'
    ..type = 'text'
    ..placeholder = 'Type to search'
    ..width = 40;
  var btnSearch = new ButtonElement()
    ..id = 'btn_search'
    ..name = 'btn_search'
    ..text = 'Search!';
```

```dart
  var btnClear = new ButtonElement()
      ..id = 'btn_clear'
      ..name = 'btn_clear'
      ..text = 'Clear';
  var br = new BRElement();
  var display = new DivElement()
    ..id = 'display'
    ..classes  = ['terminal'];

  // Setting event handlers.
  input.onKeyUp.listen((KeyboardEvent e) {
    var value = e.keyCode.toString();
    showText(display, 'Type: ${value}');
    if(e.keyCode == KeyCode.ENTER) {
      showText(display, 'Searching: ${input.value.toString()} ...');
    }
    if(e.keyCode == KeyCode.ESC) {
      input.value = '';
      display.nodes.clear();
    }
  });

  btnSearch.onClick.listen((e) {
    if(input.value.trim() == '') {
      showText(display, 'Nothing to search !');
    } else {
      showText(display, 'Searching: ${input.value.toString()} ...');
    }
  });

  btnClear.onClick.listen((e) {
    input.value = '';
    display.nodes.clear();
  });

  // Adding new elements to DOM
  sp.nodes.addAll([ input, btnSearch, btnClear, br, display]);
}

showText(display, value) {
  // adding new ParagraphElement with the value to the display DIV.
  display.nodes.add(new ParagraphElement()..text=value);
  // Autoscroll for the display DIV.
  var scrollHeight = Math.max(display.scrollHeight, window.innerHeight);
  display.scrollTop = scrollHeight - display.clientHeight;
}
```

The first time you run this application, you'll see the window shown in Figure 25-2. Notice the new text of the elements.

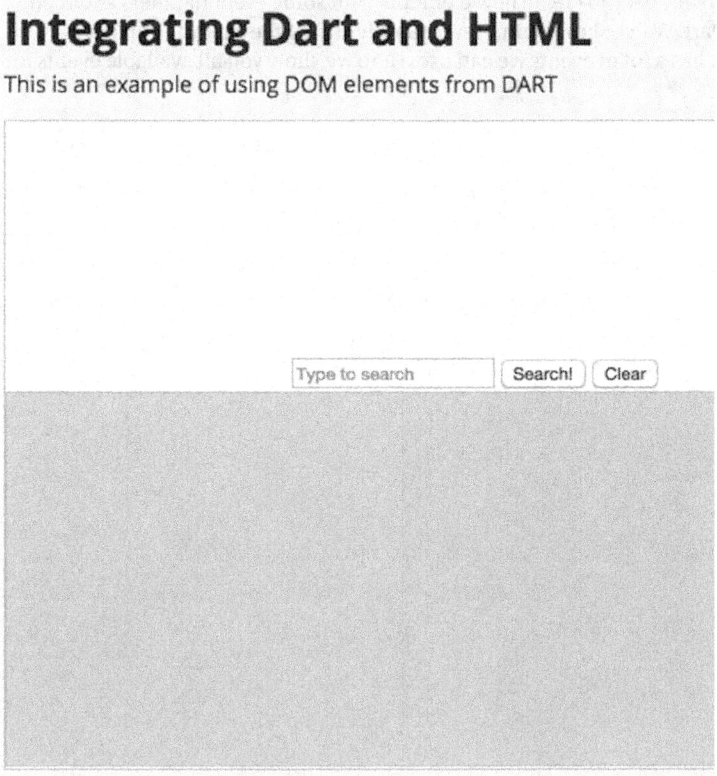

Integrating Dart and HTML

This is an example of using DOM elements from DART

Figure 25-2. *New elements on our sample Dart application*

Start typing within the text search input, and you will see in the grey bottom panel the character codes you're typing. If you hit Enter or click the Search! button you should see the Searching message, as you can see in Figure 25-3. The Clear button clears up the bottom panel.

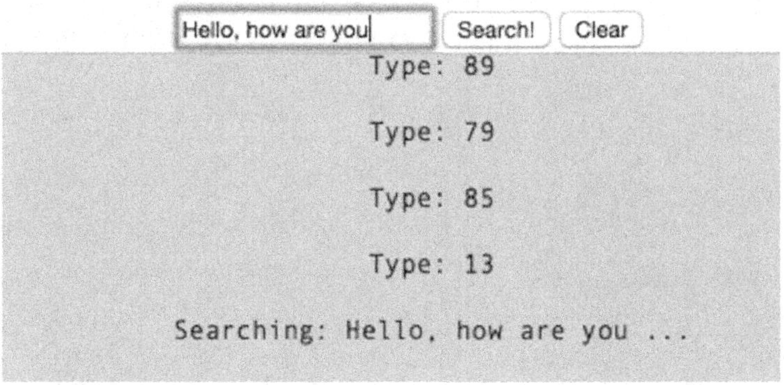

Figure 25-3. *Typing in the input box and viewing the results on the display on the bottom panel*

As you can see from these examples, it is really easy to create new elements with some event handlers and then add these elements into our document with Dart. We've shown you a few examples using the onKeyup and onClick event handlers; however, each HTML element has a lot of events we can use. Here we show you all available events for the HTML elements:

```
onAbort
onBeforeCopy
onBeforeCut
onBeforePaste
onBlur
onChange
onClick
onContextMenu
onCopy
onCut
onDoubleClick
onDrag
onDragEnd
onDragEnter
onDragLeave
onDragOver
onDragStart
onDrop
onError
onFocus
onInput
onInvalid
onKeyDown
onKeyPress
onKeyUp
onLoad
onMouseDown
onMouseEnter
onMouseLeave
onMouseMove
onMouseOut
onMouseOver
onMouseUp
onMouseWheel
onPaste
onReset
onScroll
onSearch
onSelect
onSelectStart
onSubmit
onTouchCancel
onTouchEnd
onTouchEnter
onTouchLeave
```

```
onTouchMove
onTouchStart
onTransitionEnd
onFullscreenChange
onFullscreenError
```

The listen() method returns the event subscription (**StreamSubscription**), and, working with the handler in your application, you can pause, resume, or cancel that subscription by using the pause(), resume(), or cancel() methods.

We're going to add a new button to our sample application. This new button will let us listen for characters being typed in the input search box or for a click of the Search or Clear buttons. We'll also be able to pause the listening with this button:

```dart
import 'dart:html';
import 'dart:math' as Math;

void main() {
  // Different ways to use querySelector.
  var body = document.querySelector('body');
  print(body.innerHtml);
  var h1 = body.querySelector('h1');
  var p = body.querySelector('p');
  var sc = body.querySelector('#sample_container_id');
  var sp = sc.querySelector('#sample_text_id');

  // Change h1 text.
  h1.text = 'Integrating Dart and HTML';
  // Change p text.
  p.text = 'This is an example of using DOM elements from DART';
  // Cleanup p#sample_text_id text.
  sp.text = '';

  // Creating new Elements.
  var input = new InputElement()
    ..id = 'autocomplete'
    ..name = 'autocomplete'
    ..type = 'text'
    ..placeholder = 'Type to search'
    ..width = 40;
  var btnSearch = new ButtonElement()
    ..id = 'btn_search'
    ..name = 'btn_search'
    ..text = 'Search!';
  var btnClear = new ButtonElement()
    ..id = 'btn_clear'
    ..name = 'btn_clear'
    ..text = 'Clear';
  var btnEvents = new ButtonElement()
    ..id = 'btnEvents'
    ..name = 'btnEvents'
    ..text = 'Events Off';
```

```dart
  var br = new BRElement();
  var display = new DivElement()
    ..id = 'display'
    ..classes  = ['terminal'];

  // Setting event handlers.
  var ss_keyup = input.onKeyUp.listen(((KeyboardEvent e) {
    var value = e.keyCode.toString();
    showText(display, 'Type: ${value}');
    if(e.keyCode == KeyCode.ENTER) {
      showText(display, 'Searching: ${input.value.toString()} ...');
    }
    if(e.keyCode == KeyCode.ESC) {
      input.value = '';
      display.nodes.clear();
    }
  });

  var ss_cs = btnSearch.onClick.listen((e) {
    if(input.value.trim() == '') {
      showText(display, 'Nothing to search !');
    } else {
      showText(display, 'Searching: ${input.value.toString()} ...');
    }
  });

  var ss_cc = btnClear.onClick.listen((e) {
    input.value = '';
    display.nodes.clear();
  });

  // On/Off events.
  btnEvents.onClick.listen((e) {
    if(btnEvents.text.toLowerCase().contains('off')) {
      btnEvents.text = 'Events On';
      ss_keyup.pause();
      ss_cs.pause();
      ss_cc.pause();
    } else {
      btnEvents.text = 'Events Off';
      ss_keyup.resume();
      ss_cs.resume();
      ss_cc.resume();
    }
  });

  // Adding new elements to DOM
  sp.nodes.addAll([ input, btnSearch, btnClear, btnEvents, br, display]);
}
```

```
showText(display, value) {
  // adding new ParagraphElement with the value to the display DIV.
  display.nodes.add(new ParagraphElement()..text=value);
  // Autoscroll for the display DIV.
  var scrollHeight = Math.max(display.scrollHeight, window.innerHeight);
  display.scrollTop = scrollHeight - display.clientHeight;
}
```

When you run the application, the input text and buttons have the event handlers activated, and by clicking on the new Events Off button, all the events will be paused and our button will change its label to Events On, as you can see in Figure 25-4. If you click the Events On button now, all the event handlers will resume.

Figure 25-4. *Pausing events on our application*

Summary

In this chapter we have learned:

- what the DOM is

- how you can manage the DOM from Dart with dart:html

- how HTML documents are structured in dart:html

- how to retrieve elements with the querySelector and querySelectorAll methods

- how to move up or down though your entire document using parent or children element methods, such as parent and children

- how to add elements to HTML documents

- how to manage and change element properties

- how to create event handlers attached to DOM elements

- how to pause, resume, and cancel event handlers attached to DOM elements

■ ■ ■

Integrating Dart and CSS

In this chapter we'll cover CSS and how you can work with CSS from Dart. We'll see how we can manipulate the style properties of an element and how we can add or remove CSS classes to an element. Later we'll see how to combine this with event handlers to change the appearance of an element when an event occurs. At the end of the chapter we'll show you how to create visual effects in your Dart applications, integrating CSS with Dart.

For a long time, development was limited to creating HTML documents composed with HTML tags and some JavaScript scripts and styles, often inside the HTML elements, to change their appearance, color, and format.

CSS (Cascading Style Sheets) was developed to better structure HTML documents and make the maintenance easier. These CSS style sheets let you separate the style of the elements that compose the document. Like HTML, CSS has evolved fast to support new and better features; all of these new features present in CSS3 are supported by Dart too. Now let's talk about Dart and CSS and how Dart can manage an element's style properties.

■ **Note**   Exploring the CSS syntax is beyond the scope of this book. We'll need an entire book to cover and talk about CSS syntax. If you want to improve your knowledge about CSS you can start with the W3C website http://www.w3.org/Style/CSS/.

Working with CSS

As you know Dart brings us very structured HTML documents and elements, so we can easily access an element's style properties, whether these properties have been defined directly in the document or defined in external CSS files. Let's see some examples of CSS manipulation and we'll see how Dart incorporates simple and well-defined mechanisms for working with these properties in a consistent and uniform way. You can access all the properties related to styles of HTML elements from Dart using the **style** property of an element and Dart Editor will show you all the available style properties as you can see in Figure 26-1.

```
var p = document.querySelector('#sample_text_id');
p.style.
```

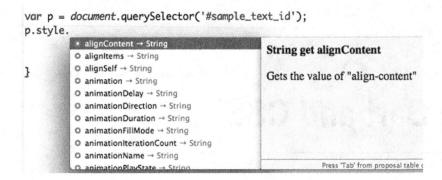

Figure 26-1. *Accessing the style properties of an HTML element*

Everything about CSS is structured in the **CSSStyleDeclaration** class inside **dart:html**, and all HTML elements have the **style** property to access the available style properties.

Starting with a new Web application created with Dart Editor with sample content, let's change the background color, font color, and font size of the **#sample_text_id** paragraph.

```
var p = document.querySelector('#sample_text_id');
p
 ..text = 'CSS BACKGROUND TEST';
 ..style.backgroundColor = '#459fc2';
 ..style.color = '#fff';
 ..style.fontSize = '10pt';
```

If you run this code snippet in Dartium, you'll see the result shown in Figure 26-2.

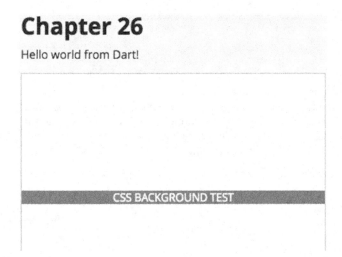

Figure 26-2. *Dartium running the Dart application that works with element styles*

As you might guess, from Dart you can work with any style properties of an HTML element, but if you want to structure everything perfectly and make it easily maintainable, you must separate HTML, CSS, and Dart code. In the same application we will edit the CSS file that Dart Editor has created when you create a new web application and we will create a CSS style class to subsequently apply to our items from Dart. For our paragraph element we will create different CSS classes with different styles. Below you can see the new CSS file for our sample application with the new success, error, and warning style classes.

```css
body {
  background-color: #F8F8F8;
  font-family: 'Open Sans', sans-serif;
  font-size: 14px;
  font-weight: normal;
  line-height: 1.2em;
  margin: 15px;
}

h1, p {
  color: #333;
}

#sample_container_id {
  width: 80%;
  height: 50px;
  position:relative;
}

#sample_text_id {
  font-size: 24pt;
  text-align: center;
  margin-top: 14px;
}

.success {
  background: #E6EFC2 5px 5px;
  padding: 1em;
  padding-left: 3.5em;
  border: 2px solid #C6D880;
  color: #529214;
}

.error {
  background: #FBE3E4 5px 5px;
  padding: 1em;
  padding-left: 3.5em;
  border: 2px solid #FBC2C4;
  color: #D12F19;
}
```

```css
.warning {
 background: #FFF6BF 5px 5px;
 padding: 1em;
 padding-left: 3.5em;
 border: 2px solid #FFD324;
 color: #817134;
}
```

The HTML code for this test application will look like this.

```html
<!DOCTYPE html>

<html>
  <head>
    <meta charset="utf-8">
    <meta name="viewport" content="width=device-width, initial-scale=1">
    <title>Chapter 26</title>

    <script async type="application/dart" src="chapter_26.dart"></script>
    <script async src="packages/browser/dart.js"></script>

    <link rel="stylesheet" href="chapter_26.css">
  </head>
  <body>
    <h1>Chapter 26</h1>

    <p>Hello world from Dart!</p>

    <div id="sample_container_id">
      <p id="sample_text_id">Click the buttons !</p>
    </div>

  </body>
</html>
```

Now in our sample Dart application we will add some buttons that change the style of our HTML document when we click on them.

```dart
import 'dart:html';

void main() {
// Get container and paragraph elements
var container = document.querySelector('#sample_container_id');
var p = document.querySelector('#sample_text_id');

// Create new buttons and attach onClick event handler
var btn1 = new ButtonElement()
 ..id = 'btn1'
 ..text = ' ERROR '
```

```
  ..onClick.listen((event){
    container.classes
      ..clear()
      ..add('error');
    p.text = 'This is an error message !';
  });

var btn2 = new ButtonElement()
 ..id = 'btn2'
 ..text = 'ALERT'
 ..onClick.listen((event) {
    container.classes
      ..clear()
      ..add('warning');
    p.text = 'This is an alert message !';
  });

var btn3 = new ButtonElement()
 ..id = 'btn3'
 ..text = 'OK'
 ..onClick.listen((event) {
    container.classes
      ..clear()
      ..add('success');
    p.text = 'This is an OK message';
  });

// Add new buttons to the document
document.body.nodes.addAll([btn1, btn2, btn3]);
}
```

If you run this application and click any of the buttons, you will see how the paragraph text changes and how we apply a new style class previously defined in the CSS, changing the appearance of the container element. You can see the result in Figures 26-3, 26-4, and 26-5.

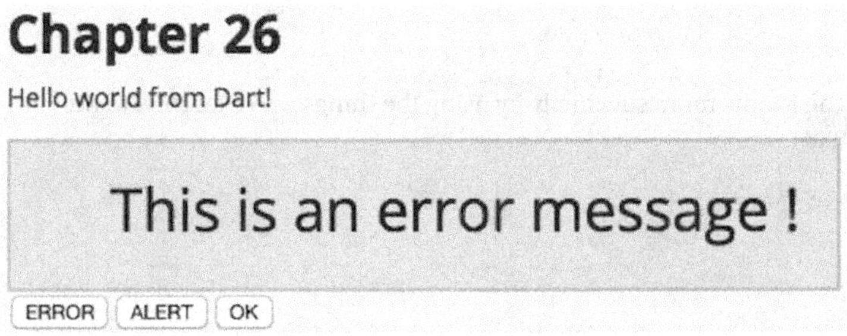

Figure 26-3. Clicking ERROR button

Chapter 26

Hello world from Dart!

This is an alert message !

| ERROR | ALERT | OK |

Figure 26-4. *Clicking ALERT button*

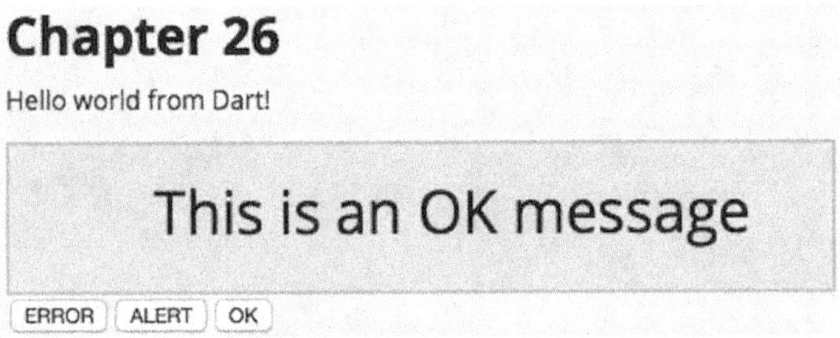

Chapter 26

Hello world from Dart!

This is an OK message

| ERROR | ALERT | OK |

Figure 26-5. *Clicking OK button*

The Dart code handles the click event on the button pressed and removes any class that the container had previously set, then adds the corresponding new class.

```
var btn2 = new ButtonElement()
 ..id = 'btn2'
 ..text = 'ALERT'
 ..onClick.listen((event) {
   container.classes
     ..clear()
     ..add('warning');
   p.text = 'This is an alert message !';
 });
```

We can rewrite the above code and make the events more succinctly by using the things we've learned in the functions chapter. So our btn1 could be written as:

```
var addClass = (String cls, String msg) => (event) {
  container.classes
    ..clear()
    ..add(cls);
  p.text = msg;
};

var btn1 = new ButtonElement()
 ..id = 'btn1'
 ..text = ' ERROR '
 ..onClick.listen(addClass('error','This is an error message !'));
```

We've created a new function called addClass which has cls and msg as parameters and then we use this function as an event handler. All HTML elements have the classes property. This method lets us apply the CSS classes to this element or we can use it to add new ones. This property represents a set of CSS classes of the element you can work with through these methods.

> toggle adds a class to an element if not present or removes it if the element has it already assigned.

> contains checks if a style class is assigned to that element.

> add adds a style class to the element.

> addAll adds multiple classes to the element.

> remove removes a class of an element.

> removeAll removes all classes of a given element.

In our previous example we use the clear() and add() methods on the container classes property. Let's see now how the **toggle()** method works adding a new button to our application. We add the new toggle class to the CSS file.

```
.toggle {
 background: #cbe0f4 5px 5px;
 padding: 1em;
 padding-left: 3.5em;
 border: 2px solid #96b6d3;
 color: #286eae;
}
```

In our Dart application we add a new button with the Toggle label. We attach the onClick event handler and finally add this new button to our document.

```
var btn4 = new ButtonElement()
 ..id = 'btn4'
 ..text = 'Toggle'
 ..onClick.listen((event) {
   container.classes.toggle('toggle');
   p.text = ' Toggle !';
 });
document.body.nodes.add(btn4);
```

This code snippet creates a new button displaying the "Toggle!" text and adds the toggle class to the container if it does not exist or removes it if it was already added (Figure 26-6). Click this new button repeatedly and combine with the other buttons to see how this property works.

Chapter 26

Hello world from Dart!

Figure 26-6. *Clicking the new Toggle button*

Visual Effects

It is increasingly common (especially since jQuery became more popular) to view web pages that use simple and elegant animations to make them more attractive to the user. If we combine the potential of HTML5, CSS3, and Dart, we can make very eye-catching visual effects quickly and easily. Let's see some examples.

FadeIn and FadeOut

We will add two buttons to our HTML document to display or hide a message to the user in a spectacular way using fade in or fade out effects.

We create a file called `fade.css` with these simple CSS classes.

```
body {
 background-color: #F8F8F8;
 font-family: 'Open Sans', sans-serif;
 font-size: 14px;
 font-weight: normal;
 line-height: 1.2em;
 margin: 15px;
}

.message {
 background: #cbe0f4 5px 5px;
 padding: 1em;
 padding-left: 3.5em;
 border: 2px solid #96b6d3;
 color: #286eae;
 opacity: 0;
}

.fade-in {
 opacity: 1;
 -webkit-transition: opacity 1s ease-in;
 -moz-transition: opacity 1s ease-in;
 -o-transition: opacity 1s ease-in;
 -ms-transition: opacity 1s ease-in;
 transition: opacity 1s ease-in;
}
```

```
.fade-out {
 opacity: 0;
-webkit-transition: opacity 1s ease-out;
 -moz-transition: opacity 1s ease-out;
 -o-transition: opacity 1s ease-out;
 -ms-transition: opacity 1s ease-out;
 transition: opacity 1s ease-out;
}
```

In this new fade.css file we've added a class that defines the style of the body of the document, one that defines the style of the message, and two others to make the effect *fade in* (appear) and *fade out* (disappear).

Create another file called fade.html with the content below. You'll see this is very similar to the example that allows Dart Editor to create a new web application.

```html
<!DOCTYPE html>

<html>
  <head>
    <meta charset="utf-8">
    <meta name="viewport" content="width=device-width, initial-scale=1">
    <title>Chapter 26 - FadeIn FadeOut</title>

    <script async type="application/dart" src="fade.dart"></script>
    <script async src="packages/browser/dart.js"></script>

    <link rel="stylesheet" href="fade.css">
  </head>
  <body>
    <div id="sample_container_id">
      <p id="sample_text_id"></p>
    </div>
  </body>
</html>
```

Last, below is our fade.dart file with the code to add functionality to our application.

```dart
import 'dart:html';

void main() {

  var p = document.querySelector('#sample_text_id')
      ..classes.add('message')
      ..text = 'Welcome to Dart !';

  var btn1 = new ButtonElement()
    ..id = 'show'
    ..text = 'Show'
    ..onClick.listen((e) {
      p.classes.retainWhere((c) => c=='message');
      p.classes.add('fade-in');
    });
```

```
var btn2 = new ButtonElement()
  ..id = 'hide'
  ..text = 'Hide'
  ..onClick.listen((e) {
    p.classes.retainWhere((c) => c=='message');
    p.classes.add('fade-out');
  });

document.body.nodes.addAll([btn1, btn2]);
}
```

First, and as usual, we must do the necessary imports. We're going to work with CSS styles and DOM elements so we'll need the dart:html library. Then we retrieve the paragraph element, add a message and set the CSS message class. Finally, we create two buttons, one to show the message and another to hide it. We've added the two buttons to our document.

If you run this example you will see how the message appears by clicking on Show, and disappears, clicking on Hide, thereby realizing a nice fade effect. You can see the fade in effect in Figure 26-7 and the fade out effect in Figure 26-8.

Figure 26-7. *Fade in Effect by clicking on Show*

Figure 26-8. *Fade out Effect by clicking on Hide*

Flashing Effect

We will now create a flashing message effect. We will create a red circle and we'll put into it the number of unread messages. We will do a small flashing effect to show the number to the users and get their attention.

This time we'll create a file called flash.css with the classes below.

```
body {
  background-color: #F8F8F8;
  font-family: 'Open Sans', sans-serif;
  font-size: 14px;
  font-weight: normal;
  line-height: 1.2em;
  margin: 15px;
}
```

```css
.inbox {
 width: 50px;
 height: 50px;
 background-color: red;
 border-radius: 100%;
 text-align: center;
}

.msg {
 position: relative;
 top: 15px;
 color: #ffffff;
 font-family: Verdana;
 font-size: 20pt;
 font-weight: bold;

 -webkit-transition: font-size 1s ease-in-out;
 -moz-transition: font-size 1s ease-in-out;
 -o-transition: font-size 1s ease-in-out;
 transition: font-size 1s ease-in-out;
}

.enlarge {
 font-size: 29pt;
}
```

Those classes define the style for the body document element. The inbox class defines the red circle that will contain the number of pending messages to read. The msg class defines the style for the number contained within inbox. Finally enlarge makes the font size of the number increase from 20pt to 29pt.

The flash.html file will display the div container of the previous examples inside it; we have the paragraph element that displays the number of messages. Your flash.html file will look like this.

```html
<!DOCTYPE html>

<html>
  <head>
    <meta charset="utf-8">
    <meta name="viewport" content="width=device-width, initial-scale=1">
    <title>Chapter 26 - Flash messagest</title>

    <script async type="application/dart" src="flash.dart"></script>
    <script async src="packages/browser/dart.js"></script>

    <link rel="stylesheet" href="flash.css">
  </head>
  <body>
    <div id="sample_container_id">
      <p id="sample_text_id" class="inbox">
        <span id="messages" class="msg">2</span>
      </p>
    </div>
  </body>
</html>
```

And our Dart code will be as simple as this.

```
import 'dart:html';
import 'dart:async';

void main() {
 var msg = document.querySelector('#messages');
 var timer = new Timer.periodic(new Duration(seconds: 1), (_){
   msg.classes.toggle('enlarge');
 });
}
```

We retrieve the item containing the number of pending messages to read and create a Timer object that repeats every 2 seconds. To use these objects we must import the dart:async library. Each time this process runs, it adds or removes the **enlarge** class to the element, causing the message number to enlarge or shrink its size to simulate a flashing effect.

The end result is that the number of messages has a very soft flashing effect to get the user's attention, as shown in Figure 26-9.

Figure 26-9. *Effect that flashes the number of pending unread messages*

Expand and Collapse Items

Another interesting and useful visual effect that you have seen in many websites is expanding or collapsing blocks of information. In documents with a lot of information it is really useful to give the user the possibility to show/hide blocks of information so they can read more information in some parts and leave the rest hidden. With this, we can load a lot of information in our documents without losing usability and navigability. Let's see how to develop such effects with Dart, HTML5, and CSS3.

First, create a block.html file with this content.

```
<!DOCTYPE html>

<html>
  <head>
    <meta charset="utf-8">
    <meta name="viewport" content="width=device-width, initial-scale=1">
    <title>Chapter 26 - Expand Collapse</title>

    <script async type="application/dart" src="block.dart"></script>
    <script async src="packages/browser/dart.js"></script>

    <link rel="stylesheet" href="block.css">
  </head>
```

```
<body>
  <div id="libraries" class="block">
    <h2><div class="arrow-right"></div>Dart SDK libraries</h2>
    <ul>
      <li>dart:async</li>
      <li>dart:collections</li>
      <li>dart:convert</li>
      <li>dart:core</li>
      <li>dart:html</li>
      <li>dart:indexed_db</li>
      <li>dart:io</li>
      <li>dart:isolate</li>
      <li>dart:js</li>
      <li>dart:math</li>
      <li>dart:mirrors</li>
      <li>dart:profiler</li>
      <li>dart:svg</li>
      <li>dart:typed_data</li>
      <li>dart:web_audio</li>
      <li>dart:web_gl</li>
      <li>dart:web_sql</li>
    </ul>
  </div>

  <div id="events" class="block">
   <h2><div class="arrow-right""></div>Dart DOM Events</h2>
   <ul>
      <li>onAbort</li>
      <li>onBeforeCopy</li>
      <li>onBeforeCut</li>
      <li>onBeforePaste</li>
      <li>onBlur</li>
      <li>onChange</li>
      <li>onClick</li>
      <li>onContextMenu</li>
      <li>onCopy</li>
      <li>onCut</li>
      <li>onDoubleClick</li>
      <li>onDrag</li>
      <li>onDragEnd</li>
      <li>onDragEnter</li>
      <li>onDragLeave</li>
      <li>onDragOver</li>
      <li>onDragStart</li>
      <li>onDrop</li>
      <li>onError</li>
      <li>onFocus</li>
      <li>onInput</li>
      <li>onInvalid</li>
      <li>onKeyDown</li>
```

```
            <li>onKeyPress</li>
            <li>onKeyUp</li>
            <li>onLoad</li>
            <li>onMouseDown</li>
            <li>onMouseEnter</li>
            <li>onMouseLeave</li>
            <li>onMouseMove</li>
            <li>onMouseOut</li>
            <li>onMouseOver</li>
            <li>onMouseUp</li>
            <li>onMouseWheel</li>
            <li>onPaste</li>
            <li>onReset</li>
            <li>onScroll</li>
            <li>onSearch</li>
            <li>onSelect</li>
            <li>onSelectStart</li>
            <li>onSubmit</li>
            <li>onTouchCancel</li>
            <li>onTouchEnd</li>
            <li>onTouchEnter</li>
            <li>onTouchLeave</li>
            <li>onTouchMove</li>
            <li>onTouchStart</li>
            <li>onTransitionEnd</li>
            <li>onFullscreenChange</li>
            <li>onFullscreenError</li>
        </ul>
    </div>
  </body>
</html>
```

We have created two div containers (libraries and events). Within it, we've created an h2 element (title) and then a list of the Dart SDK libraries and DOM events. Within the h2 element we added another div with the arrow-right class. This class will display an arrow pointing to the right. With CSS3 we can do this kind of thing and avoid using images.

Then create a block.css file with these classes.

```
body {
 background-color: #F8F8F8;
 font-family: 'Open Sans', sans-serif;
 font-size: 14px;
 font-weight: normal;
 line-height: 1.2em;
 margin: 15px;
}

.block {
  margin: 20px;
}
```

```css
.block h2 {
 font-size: 18px;
 display: block;
 padding-left: 30px;
 padding-left: 32px;
 margin: 0;
 color: #628066;
 text-decoration: none;
 font-weight: normal;
 border-bottom: 1px solid #628066;
}

.block ul {
 color: #628066;
 border: 1 px solid #628066;
 background-color: #B0E5B8;
 margin-top: 0px;
 margin-left: 25px;
}

.hide {
 display:none;
}

.arrow-down {
 width: 0;
 height: 0;
 border-left: 7px solid transparent;
 border-right: 7px solid transparent;
 border-top: 7px solid #000000;
 float:left;
 margin-right: 7px;
 cursor: pointer;
}

.arrow-right {
 width: 0;
 height: 0;
 border-top: 7px solid transparent;
 border-bottom: 7px solid transparent;
 border-left: 7px solid #000000;
 float:left;
 margin-right: 7px;
 cursor: pointer;
}
```

We set styles for body, h2, and ul elements and create three additional style classes: one to hide the lists, and two arrows classes (one pointing down and one to the right).

Finally, create a `block.dart` file and add the following code.

```dart
import 'dart:html';

void main() {
  var libs = document.querySelector('#libraries');
  var libs_list = libs.querySelector('ul');
  libs_list.classes.add('hide');
  libs.onClick.listen((e) {
    var arrow = libs.querySelector('h2 div');
    arrow.classes.toggleAll(['arrow-right', 'arrow-down']);
    libs_list.classes.toggle('hide');
  });

  var events = document.querySelector('#events');
  var events_list = events.querySelector('ul');
  events_list.classes.add('hide');
  events.onClick.listen((e) {
    var arrow = events.querySelector('h2 div');
    arrow.classes.toggleAll(['arrow-right', 'arrow-down']);
    events_list.classes.toggle('hide');
  });
}
```

This simple code block retrieves the main `libraries` or `events` div container element and the items list. It adds the `hide` class to the list so they are not visible when the web page is loaded the first time and adds an onClick event handler on the `div` container. As you can see, we repeat the code in the `libraries` container and `events` div container. As you can imagine, you can change that code using a function to do the same to the container element you pass as a parameter. When you click on the `div`, it will change the arrow pointing to the right to an arrow pointing down and display the events or libraries items list.

In the Figures 26-10, 26-11, and 26-12 you can see the effect.

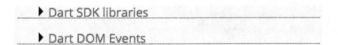

Figure 26-10. *Element that displays two folding lists of libraries and events*

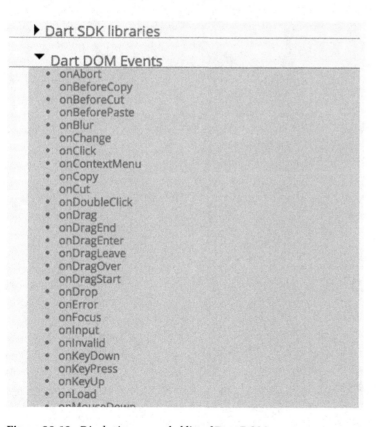

▼ Dart SDK libraries
- dart:async
- dart:collections
- dart:convert
- dart:core
- dart:html
- dart:indexed_db
- dart:io
- dart:isolate
- dart:js
- dart:math
- dart:mirrors
- dart:profiler
- dart:svg
- dart:typed_data
- dart:web_audio
- dart:web_gl
- dart:web_sql

▶ Dart DOM Events

Figure 26-11. *Displaying expanded list of Dart SDK libraries*

▶ Dart SDK libraries

▼ Dart DOM Events
- onAbort
- onBeforeCopy
- onBeforeCut
- onBeforePaste
- onBlur
- onChange
- onClick
- onContextMenu
- onCopy
- onCut
- onDoubleClick
- onDrag
- onDragEnd
- onDragEnter
- onDragLeave
- onDragOver
- onDragStart
- onDrop
- onError
- onFocus
- onInput
- onInvalid
- onKeyDown
- onKeyPress
- onKeyUp
- onLoad
- onMouseDown

Figure 26-12. *Displaying expanded list of Dart DOM events*

Summary

In this chapter we have learned:

- What CSS is

- How you can work with CSS from Dart

- How to manipulate the style properties of an element and how you can manage CSS classes for HTML elements

- How to combine CSS with event handlers to change the appearance of DOM elements when an event occurs

- How to create visual effects in your Dart applications by integrating CSS with Dart

Dart and the Web Server

■ ■ ■

Combining Web Services with Dart

In this chapter we'll see how to combine web services with Dart. We'll cover how to deal with HttpRequests from Dart, and through code examples we'll show you how to make requests to get information from a server as well as how to make requests to send data to the server using POST methods.

We have seen that by using Dart we can handle HTML documents and everything related to CSS. Currently websites download most functions on the client side using the power of the client's devices, thus reducing resource consumption on the server side.

One of the biggest advantages to increasing power on the client side is to be able to modify the DOM based on new data received from the server. With Dart we can develop the client side, and we will show you how to launch asynchronous HTTP requests to obtain data from the server and modify the DOM based on user actions.

In addition to asynchronous HTTP requests, we will use JSON (JavaScript Object Notation) as a model of light data exchange between our client and server applications. Dart includes support for JSON in its package dart:convert, and we will see how to use it to simplify the processing of message passing between client and server.

Asynchronous HTTP Requests with Dart

In Dart we can load or dynamically modify some parts of our HTML documents with the data obtained from the server using the HttpRequest class. In JavaScript, asynchronous requests are made using the **XMLHttpRequest** object.

With **HttpRequest** from Dart you can communicate bidirectionally with the server—i.e., to get data from the server or to make requests sending by data from the client side to the server.

The HttpRequest class has a security restriction related to the client browser. This restriction does not allow requests to be made from the client to a different domain outside the domain from which the resources were initially loaded. Let's see an example.

Suppose you initially load www.dart-awesome-app.com. This domain runs a Dart application inside your browser client, and this application uses the HttpRequest class to get data from the server. This application is forced to make requests to www.dart-awesome-app.com; it does not make requests to any other domain, such as www.google.com.

Obviously, if the server—in our example www.google.com—has enabled the CORS option (cross-origin resource sharing), then it is possible for our Dart application, loaded on the client from the www.dart-awesome-app.com domain, to make requests to the other domain.

In our coming examples, we will make requests on our own client to get JSON responses and to overcome the access problems from different origins. We will see some examples of requests to the server and the CORS security restriction just discussed. The first step will be creating a new web application in Dart Editor. Just click on the "Create a new Dart project" button to launch the window, which you can see in Figure 27-1.

New Project...

Create a sample web application with Pub support

Name and location

Project name: chapter_27

Parent directory: /Users/moisesbelchin/dart   Browse...

Sample content

Web application [mobile friendly]
Command-line application
Package Template
Sample web application using the polymer library [mobile friendly]
Chrome packaged application

Figure 27-1. *New Dart web application* HttpRequest

The **HttpRequest** class is located in the dart:html library and lets us make asynchronous requests. This class includes methods to simplify the job of receiving or sending data to the server. Using **HttpRequest.getString** we can make requests to a specific URL that will return the response in text format. With **HttpRequest.postFormData** we can make POST requests with the data encoded as a form, i.e., to send data to our server.

With **HttpRequest.request** we can make requests to the indicated URL. This method lets us create and configure all necessary parameters for the request. We can set the request method to GET, POST, PUT, DELETE, and so forth. We can also define the format of the data to be sent (as FormData, ByteBuffer, String, Blob, Document, etc.), the mime-type, the type of the server response, and the request headers.

We will use **HttpRequest.requestCrossOrigin** to make requests across domains if the domain supports CORS. The **HttpRequest** class includes the methods required to open, send, and close the HttpRequest objects and to manage responses from the server. These methods let you know the status of the response, the return code, or if it has timed out.

In our new project, we will change the default **chapter_27.css** file so as to include code that defines the styles of the elements that we will use. See the following:

```
body {
 background-color: #F8F8F8;
 font-family: 'Open Sans', sans-serif;
 font-size: 14px;
 font-weight: normal;
 line-height: 1.2em;
 margin: 15px;
}
```

```css
h1, p {
  color: #333;
}

#response {
  width: 100%;
  min-height: 200px;
  position: relative;
  border: 1px solid #ccc;
  background-color: #fff;
  text-align: left;
  padding-left: 5px;
  padding-top: 5px;
}
```

We will also change the file **chapter_27.html** so that it includes HTML elements that will build our base schema application, using the code below:

```html
<!DOCTYPE html>
<html>
  <head>
    <meta charset="utf-8">
    <meta name="viewport" content="width=device-width, initial-scale=1">
    <title>Chapter 27</title>

    <script async type="application/dart" src="chapter_27.dart"></script>
    <script async src="packages/browser/dart.js"></script>

    <link rel="stylesheet" href="chapter_27.css">
  </head>
  <body>
    <h1>Chapter 27 - Http request</h1>
    <div id="buttons"></div>
    <div id="response"></div>

  </body>
</html>
```

In addition, we will create another file called user_data.txt with content like this:

```html
<b>User:</b> Moises <br/>
<b>Email:</b> moisesbelchin@gmail.com <br/>
<b>Last Login:</b> Yesterday at 21:32 <br/>
```

This file will be used to simulate the response returned by the server. As is mentioned above, we can only make requests to the same domain that serves our application, so we will request data be sent to the same domain from which our Dart application is running.

And finally, our **chapter_27.dart** file will have the following code that will create the application. This application will use **HttpRequest** to request data and dynamically modify the contents of the document. You should be able to see how your webpage changes without having to refresh the page or navigate to another URL. See here:

```dart
import 'dart:html';

void request(String asset) {
  var response = document.querySelector('#response');
  var url = 'http://localhost:8080/${asset}';
  HttpRequest.getString(
    url,
    onProgress:(_) => response.text = 'Loading ...')
    .then((resp) => response.setInnerHtml('<pre>${resp}</pre>'))
    .catchError((error) => response.text = 'ERROR !!!: ${error.toString()}');
}

void main() {
  var buttons = document.querySelector('#buttons');

  var btn1 = new ButtonElement()
    ..id = 'btn1'
    ..text = 'Get CSS code'
    ..onClick.listen((_) => request('chapter_27.css'));

  var btn2 = new ButtonElement()
    ..id = 'btn2'
    ..text = 'Get Dart code'
    ..onClick.listen((_) => request('chapter_27.dart'));

  var btn3 = new ButtonElement()
    ..id = 'btn3'
    ..text = 'Get User info'
    ..onClick.listen((_) => request('user_data.txt'));

  buttons.nodes.addAll([btn1, btn2, btn3]);
}
```

The main method retrieves the container to which we will add buttons. We've created three different buttons: one to retrieve CSS code (file **chapter_27.css)**, another to retrieve the Dart app code (file **chapter_27.dart)**, and the last one to retrieve the content of the **user_data.txt** file. When you click these buttons, the **onClick** event associated will be dispatched and it'll run the **request** function.

The **request** function retrieves the container in which we'll display the response received from the server. This function also defines the URL, concatenating the server URL with the file to be requested. Then it uses the **HttpRequest** object and the **getString** method to make the request to our URL. It defines what to do during the request process. In our case, we show text that tells the user we are loading the requested information, seen in Figure 27-2.

Figure 27-2. *Running a request from the server*

HttpRequest.getString returns a Future object, and we'll use the **.then** and **.catchError** methods to handle the response or deal with any error that occurs. In the first case, when the response is correct, we'll display it in the response Div element. In the case of an error, we'll show an alert error and the error returned by the system, as shown in Figure 27-6.

By running this example, you can see the operation of this small application that dynamically modifies the content of our **response** Div element, displaying the message returned by the server when you click on the **Get CSS code**, **Get Dart code**, or **Get User info** buttons, shown in Figures 27-3 through 27-5, respectively.

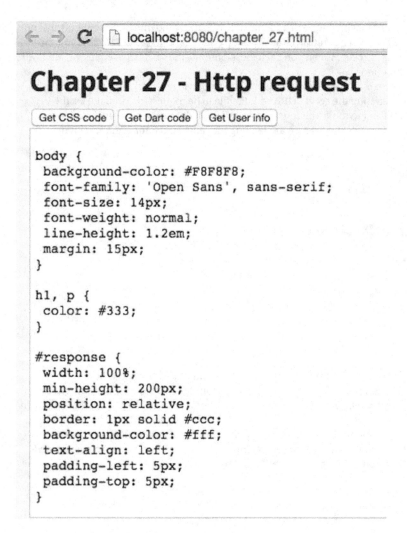

Figure 27-3. *Getting CSS code from the server*

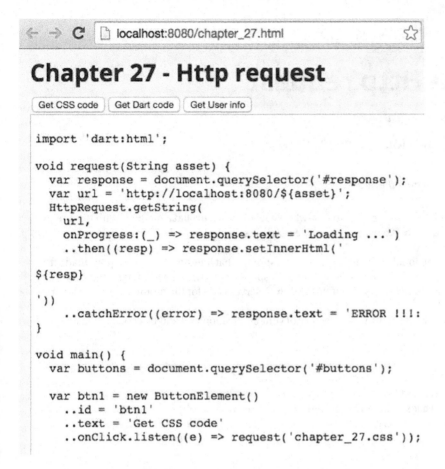

```
localhost:8080/chapter_27.html

Chapter 27 - Http request

Get CSS code    Get Dart code    Get User info

import 'dart:html';

void request(String asset) {
  var response = document.querySelector('#response');
  var url = 'http://localhost:8080/${asset}';
  HttpRequest.getString(
    url,
    onProgress:(_) => response.text = 'Loading ...')
    ..then((resp) => response.setInnerHtml('

${resp}

'))
    ..catchError((error) => response.text = 'ERROR !!!:
}

void main() {
  var buttons = document.querySelector('#buttons');

  var btn1 = new ButtonElement()
    ..id = 'btn1'
    ..text = 'Get CSS code'
    ..onClick.listen((e) => request('chapter_27.css'));
```

Figure 27-4. *Getting the Dart code from the server*

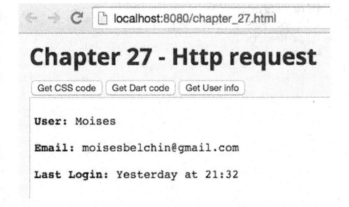

```
localhost:8080/chapter_27.html

Chapter 27 - Http request

Get CSS code    Get Dart code    Get User info

User: Moises

Email: moisesbelchin@gmail.com

Last Login: Yesterday at 21:32
```

Figure 27-5. *Getting the user information from the server*

Figure 27-6. *Error response received from the server*

Let's now look at how to send data to a server using the **HttpRequest.postFormData** method. With this method we can send data encoded as **Form Data**. We're going to create a simple sample where the user fills in a contact form and sends this information to our server.

For this example to be fully functional, we need a server environment that handles the POST request made from our Dart application. We will create a simple Dart web server that responds to us with the form parameters sent whenever we make a **POST** request. Do not worry about this Dart web server code for the moment, because we'll see how to handle it in the next chapter.

Create a file called **server.dart** within the web directory of your application and add this code to the file:

```dart
import 'dart:io';
import 'dart:convert';

void handlePost(HttpRequest request) {
  ContentType contentType = request.headers.contentType;
  BytesBuilder builder = new BytesBuilder();
  request.listen((buffer) {
    builder.add(buffer);
  }, onDone: () {
    String jsonString = UTF8.decode(builder.takeBytes());
    Map data = Uri.splitQueryString(jsonString);
    request.response.headers.add('Access-Control-Allow-Origin', '*');
    request.response.headers.add('Access-Control-Allow-Methods', 'POST, OPTIONS');
    request.response.headers.add('Access-Control-Allow-Headers',
        'Origin, X-Requested-With, Content-Type, Accept');
    request.response.statusCode = HttpStatus.OK;
    request.response.write(data);
    request.response.close();
  });
}

void handleGet(HttpRequest request) {
  switch (request.uri.path) {
    case '/':
      request.response.statusCode = HttpStatus.OK;
      request.response.headers.add(HttpHeaders.CONTENT_TYPE, 'text/html');
      request.response.write('<h1>Index of chapter_27/web/</h1><ul>');
```

```dart
      new Directory('.').listSync().forEach((FileSystemEntity entity) {
        var df = entity.path.split('./').last;
        request.response.write('<li><a href="./${df}">${df}</a></li>');
      });
      request.response.write('</ul>');
      request.response.close();
      break;

    default:
      final String path = request.uri.toFilePath();
      final File file = new File('./$path');
      file.exists().then((bool found) {
        if (found) {
          request.response.statusCode = HttpStatus.OK;
          request.response.write(file.readAsStringSync());
        } else {
          request.response.statusCode = HttpStatus.NOT_FOUND;
          request.response.write('not found');
        }
        request.response.close();
      });
      break;
  }
}

void main() {
  HttpServer.bind('127.0.0.1', 8088)
  .then((server) {
    print("Server running on http://127.0.0.1:8088/");
    server.listen((HttpRequest request) {
      switch(request.method) {
        case 'POST':
          handlePost(request);
          break;

        case 'GET':
        default:
          handleGet(request);
          break;
      }
    });
  })
  .catchError((e) => print('Error :: $e'));
}
```

In the code above we have the main() function, which starts our Dart web server, and then we have the functions handleGet() and handlePost(), which are in charge of handling GET or POST methods, respectively, when responding to the client.

Next, go to the web directory of the chapter_27 application and run this command:

```
dart/chapter_27/web$ dart server.dart
```

After executing the command you will see that the server responds and displays this message:

```
Server running on http://127.0.0.1:8088/
```

If you open your browser and navigate to this URL, you will see the files of our chapter_27 web directory, as shown in Figure 27-7.

Index of chapter_27/web/

- chapter_27.css
- chapter_27.dart
- chapter_27.html
- customers.json
- form.css
- form.dart
- form.html
- http_json.css
- http_json.dart
- http_json.html
- packages
- post.dart
- post.html
- server.dart
- user_data.txt

Figure 27-7. *Accessing our web server for the first time*

Let's see how our Dart application will handle making the POST requests to this new server. First, let's input the necessary styles into the file **form.css**:

```
body {
 background-color: #F8F8F8;
 font-family: 'Open Sans', sans-serif;
 font-size: 14px;
 font-weight: normal;
 line-height: 1.2em;
 margin: 15px;
}

h1, p {
 color: #333;
}

#response {
 width: 280px;
 height: 200px;
 position: relative;
```

```
  border: 1px solid #ccc;
  background-color: #fff;
  text-align: left;
  padding-left: 5px;
  padding-top: 5px;
  float:right;
}

#form {
  width: 200px;
  float:left;
}
```

We have created two parts: on the left side **#form** shows the data form and on the right side **#response** shows the server response, as you can see in Figure 27-8.

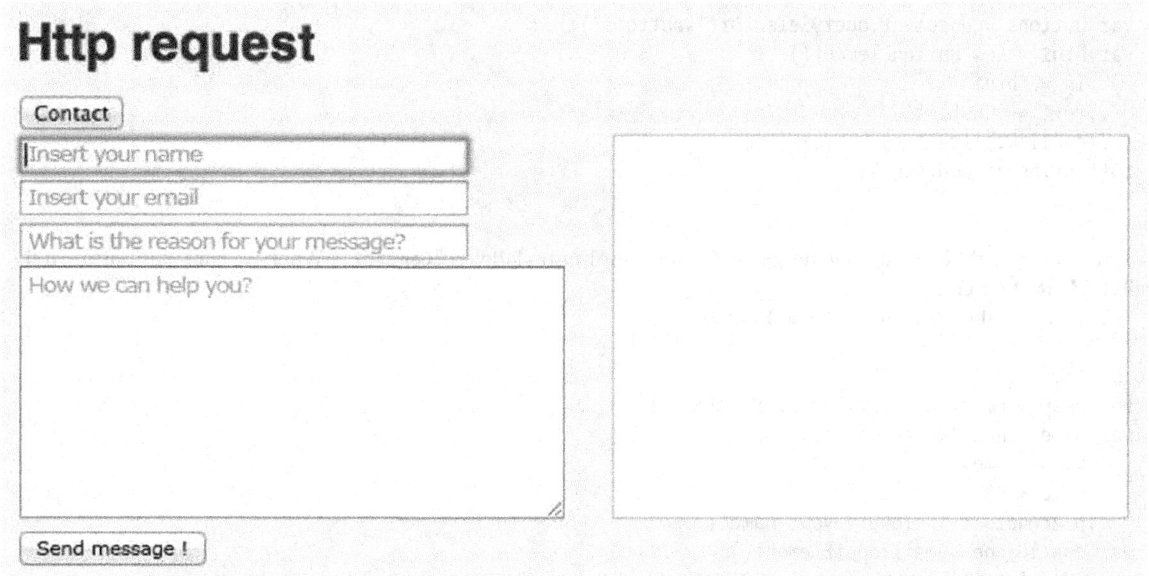

Figure 27-8. Application format

This will be the code for our **form.html** file, which includes the base schema container of our application:

```
<!DOCTYPE html>
<html>
  <head>
    <meta charset="utf-8">
    <meta name="viewport" content="width=device-width, initial-scale=1">
    <title>Http Request</title>

    <script async type="application/dart" src="form.dart"></script>
    <script async src="packages/browser/dart.js"></script>
```

```
      <link rel="stylesheet" href="form.css">
    </head>
    <body>
      <h1>Http request</h1>
      <div id="buttons"></div>
      <div id="form"></div>
      <div id="response"></div>
    </body>
</html>
```

You can see the three main divs: **#buttons, #form**, and **#response**. We will work with them within our Dart application.

Now let's look at the Dart code that will create our application. In the new file, **form.dart**, we have created different functions for each part of the application by structuring the code to make it easier to explain. In this example, we will use the **main()** method and then import **dart:html**.

```dart
void main() {
  var buttons = document.querySelector('#buttons');
  var btn1 = new ButtonElement()
    ..id = 'btn1'
    ..text = 'Contact'
    ..onClick.listen((e) => form());
  buttons.nodes.add(btn1);
}
```

Retrieve the **#buttons** div element and create a new button labeled **"Contact."** When we click this button, it'll call the **form()** function.

This will be the code for our **form()** function:

```dart
void form() {
  var resp = document.querySelector('#form');
  var name = new InputElement()
    ..id = 'name'
    ..size = 45
    ..placeholder = 'Insert your name';
  var email = new EmailInputElement()
    ..id = 'email'
    ..size = 45
    ..placeholder = 'Insert your email';
  var subject = new TextInputElement()
    ..id = 'subject'
    ..size = 45
    ..placeholder = 'What is the reason for your message?';
  var message = new TextAreaElement()
    ..id = 'message'
    ..cols = 40
    ..rows = 10
    ..placeholder = 'How we can help you?';
  var send = new ButtonElement()
    ..id = 'send'
    ..text = ' Send message ! '
    ..onClick.listen((e) => sendMessage());
```

```
      resp.nodes.clear();
      resp.nodes.addAll([name, new BRElement(),
                         email, new BRElement(),
                         subject, new BRElement(),
                         message, new BRElement(),
                         send]);
      name.focus();
}
```

This function retrieves the **#form** div element and adds **Input** and **TextArea HTML** fields to our contact form. In addition, it creates a button labeled "Send message !" that will launch the **sendMessage()** function when clicked. See here:

```
void sendMessage() {
  var resp = document.querySelector('#response');
  Map data = new Map();
  data['name'] = (document.querySelector('#name') as InputElement).value.trim();
  data['email'] = (document.querySelector('#email') as InputElement).value.trim();
  data['subject'] = (document.querySelector('#subject') as InputElement).value.trim();
  data['message'] = (document.querySelector('#message') as TextAreaElement).value.trim();

  var url = 'http://127.0.0.1:8088';
  var xhr = HttpRequest.postFormData(url, data,
    onProgress: (_) => resp.text = 'Sending ... ')
    .then((r) => response(r))
    .catchError((error) => resp.text = 'ERROR !: ${error.toString()}');
}
```

The **sendMessage()** function retrieves all the values of the form fields, makes a Map with the data, and uses the **HttpRequest.postFormData** method to send the data to the server. It sets a temporary text that reads "Sending ..." to be displayed in the div #response while the request is being processed.

This function also provides methods for managing the **Future<HttpRequest>** object returned by the **HttpRequest.postFormData** method. If an error occurs, it will show in the div #response the error returned by the system. It will execute the **response()** function when the correct response is returned by the server. See here:

```
void response(r) {
  var div_resp = document.querySelector('#response');
  var resp = r.responseText;
  resp = resp.replaceAll('{', '')
    .replaceAll('}', '')
    .replaceAll("['", "")
    .replaceAll("']", "")
    .replaceAll("'", "")
    .split(",")
    .join('<br/>');
  div_resp.setInnerHtml('<b>Status:</b> ${r.status} <br/>'
                                '<b>Response:</b> <br/> ${resp}');
}
```

This function receives as a parameter the response from the server and then gets the #response div, cleans up the response from the server by removing some characters and splitting it by using a comma, and finally displays it on the #response div element.

Here's all the code you must add to your **form.dart** file:

```dart
import 'dart:html';

void response(r) {
 var div_resp = document.querySelector('#response');
 var resp = r.responseText;
 resp = resp.replaceAll('{', '')
   .replaceAll('}', '')
   .replaceAll("['", "")
   .replaceAll("']", "")
   .replaceAll("'", "")
   .split(",")
   .join('<br/>');
 div_resp.setInnerHtml('<b>Status:</b> ${r.status} <br/>'
                       '<b>Response:</b> <br/> ${resp}');
}

void sendMessage() {
 var resp = document.querySelector('#response');
 Map data = new Map();
 data['name'] = (document.querySelector('#name') as InputElement).value.trim();
 data['email'] = (document.querySelector('#email') as InputElement).value.trim();
 data['subject'] = (document.querySelector('#subject') as InputElement).value.trim();
 data['message'] = (document.querySelector('#message') as TextAreaElement).value.trim();

 var url = 'http://127.0.0.1:8088';
 var xhr = HttpRequest.postFormData(url, data,
   onProgress: (_) => resp.text = 'Sending ... ')
   .then((r) => response(r))
   .catchError((error) => resp.text = 'ERROR !: ${error.toString()}');
}

void form() {
 var resp = document.querySelector('#form');
 var name = new InputElement()
   ..id = 'name'
   ..size = 45
   ..placeholder = 'Insert your name';
 var email = new EmailInputElement()
   ..id = 'email'
   ..size = 45
   ..placeholder = 'Insert your email';
 var subject = new TextInputElement()
   ..id = 'subject'
   ..size = 45
   ..placeholder = 'What is the reason for your message?';
```

```
  var message = new TextAreaElement()
    ..id = 'message'
    ..cols = 40
    ..rows = 10
    ..placeholder = 'How we can help you?';
  var send = new ButtonElement()
    ..id = 'send'
    ..text = ' Send message ! '
    ..onClick.listen((e) => sendMessage());

  resp.nodes.clear();
  resp.nodes.addAll([name, new BRElement(),
                    email, new BRElement(),
                    subject, new BRElement(),
                    message, new BRElement(),
                    send]);
  name.focus();
}

void main() {
 var buttons = document.querySelector('#buttons');
 var btn1 = new ButtonElement()
   ..id = 'btn1'
   ..text = 'Contact'
   ..onClick.listen((e) => form());
 buttons.nodes.add(btn1);
}
```

Run the form.html web application from Dart Editor. You can see Dartium running this URL http://localhost:8080/form.html as it loads the application, and we can test POST requests against the Dart server created, seen in Figure 27-9.

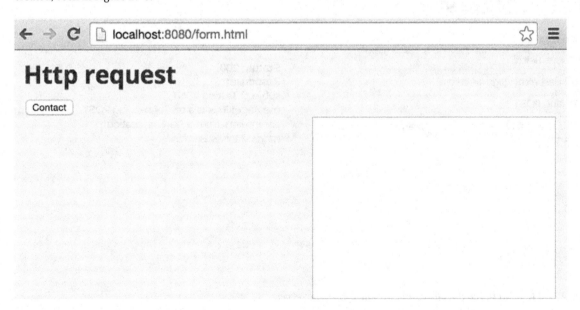

Figure 27-9. Initial loading of our application

Remember that the server must be running and that you need to load the new Dart form.html application into Dartium in order for it to run properly. Click on the **Contact** button to see the appearance of the form that we will fill in and send to the server, shown in Figure 27-10.

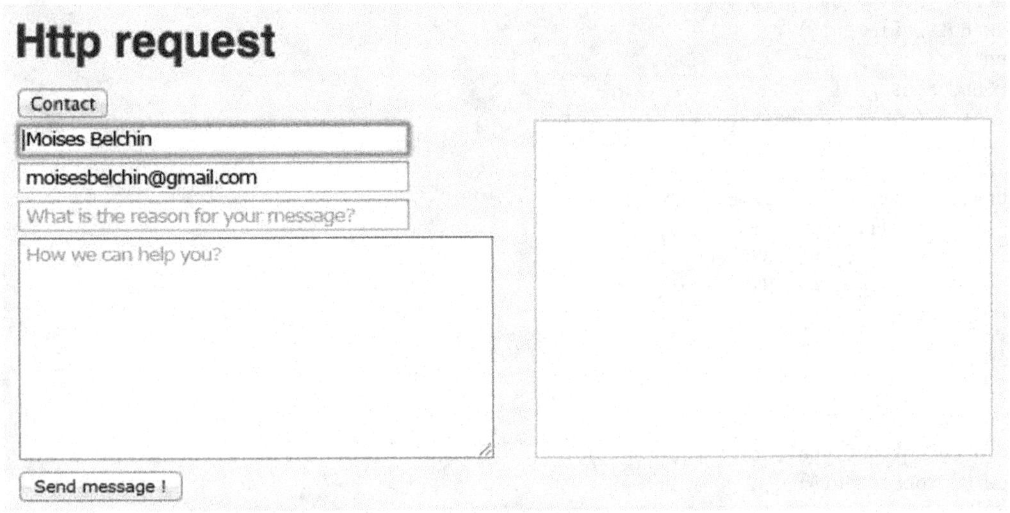

Figure 27-10. *Filling in the contact form to send to the server*

If you fill in the form fields and click on the Send Message! button, you can see how the server responds correctly and displays the response in the #response div element, shown in Figure 27-11.

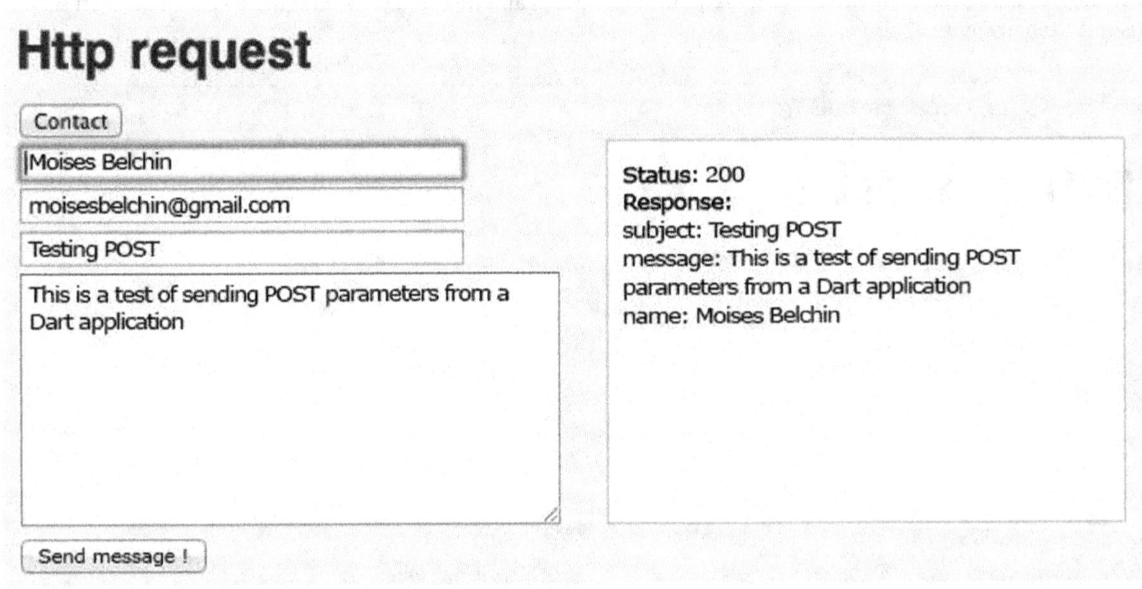

Figure 27-11. *Send the contact form and response from the server*

Until now we've seen how to make GET requests using HttpRequest.getString() and POST requests using the HttpRequest.postFormData() method. The HTTP GET method is useful for getting information from the server, and the HTTP POST method is used to send information to the server, but HTTP supports other methods as well, such as OPTIONS, HEAD, PUT, DELETE, TRACE and CONNECT.

Dart provides the HttpRequest.request() method to properly handle these other HTTP methods. Let's see an example of using the HttpRequest.request() method. We're going to create a new Dart web application called **get**. We'll have get.css, get.html, and get.dart files.

Our get.css file will have this content:

```css
body {
  background-color: #F8F8F8;
  font-family: 'Open Sans', sans-serif;
  font-size: 14px;
  font-weight: normal;
  line-height: 1.2em;
  margin: 15px;
}

h1, p {
  color: #333;
}

#response {
  width: 600px;
  height: 200px;
  position: relative;
  border: 1px solid #ccc;
  background-color: #fff;
  text-align: left;
  padding-left: 5px;
  padding-top: 5px;
  float:right;
}

TH {
  background: #cccccc;
  text-align: center;
}
```

The get.html file will look like this:

```html
<!DOCTYPE html>
<html>
  <head>
    <meta charset="utf-8">
    <meta name="viewport" content="width=device-width, initial-scale=1">
    <title>Chapter 27</title>

    <script async type="application/dart" src="get.dart"></script>
    <script async src="packages/browser/dart.js"></script>
```

```
      <link rel="stylesheet" href="get.css">
  </head>
  <body>
    <h1>Chapter 27 - HttpRequest.request</h1>
    <div id="response"></div>
  </body>
</html>
```

And finally the get.dart file will have this code:

```
import 'dart:html';

void main() {
  var url = 'http://localhost:8080/user_data.txt';
  HttpRequest.request(url, method: 'GET')
  .then((HttpRequest resp) {
    document.querySelector('#response').appendHtml(resp.responseText);
  })
  .catchError((error) => print(error));
}
```

The HttpRequest.request() method supports different named parameters, such as the following:

- **method** parameter allows you to run any HTTP method such as GET, POST, PUT, DELETE, etc.

- **withCredentials** parameter indicates that this request requires credentials. The credentials should be specified on authorization headers.

- **responseType** parameter tells the server the desired response format. Default is String. Other options are arraybuffer, blob, document, json, and text.

- **mimeType** parameter lets you specify a particular MIME type (such as text/xml) desired for the response.

- **requestHeaders** parameter is a Map with the request's headers.

Using JSON in Dart

In the previous section, we learned two methods that you'll often use to retrieve data from a server or to send data encoded as Form Data.

We talked at the beginning of this chapter about the dart:convert package used to work with JSON from Dart. We also discussed how to use it as a light data interchange format between client and server. Now let's see how to use this package. This time, for our examples, we'll use the HttpRequest class to set the asynchronous requests.

HttpRequest.request(), like the HttpRequest.getString() and HttpRequest.postFormData() methods viewed in our previous samples, are wrapper methods based on the HttpRequest class. This class is the base for handling asynchronous requests, and we will see a complete example of its use with JSON.

Let's create a simple application to make a request to the server and get data in JSON format, and then we'll work with this information in Dart.

The first thing we'll see is our **http_json.css** CSS style file:

```css
body {
 background-color: #F8F8F8;
 font-family: 'Open Sans', sans-serif;
 font-size: 14px;
 font-weight: normal;
 line-height: 1.2em;
 margin: 15px;
}

h1, p {
 color: #333;
}

#response {
 width: 600px;
 height: 200px;
 position: relative;
 border: 1px solid #ccc;
 background-color: #fff;
 text-align: left;
 padding-left: 5px;
 padding-top: 5px;
 float:right;
}

TH {
 background: #cccccc;
 text-align: center;
}
```

We next define the classes for the **#response** div element that will contain the request's result, and we also define the styles of the table headers so as to display results in a fancy way. Below you can find the basic HTML structure defined in our **http_json.html** file:

```html
<!DOCTYPE html>
<html>
  <head>
    <meta charset="utf-8">
    <meta name="viewport" content="width=device-width, initial-scale=1">
    <title>Chapter 27</title>

    <script async type="application/dart" src="http_json.dart"></script>
    <script async src="packages/browser/dart.js"></script>

    <link rel="stylesheet" href="http_json.css">
  </head>
  <body>
    <h1>Chapter 27 - JSON requests</h1>
    <div id="buttons"></div>
    <div id="response"></div>
  </body>
</html>
```

We have created two div elements, one for the application buttons and the other for the server response. We're next going to create a file using JSON format called **customers.json** that will contain a list of the customers in our system. See here:

```
{
"customers":
  [
    {"id": "0001",
     "name": "Patricia",
     "surname": "Juberias",
     "address": {
        "street": "Paseo de la castellana",
        "number": 145,
        "zip": 28046,
        "country": "Spain",
        "state": "Madrid"}
    },

    {"id": "0002",
     "name": "Moises",
     "surname": "Belchin",
     "address": {
        "street": "Pase del prado",
        "number": 28,
        "zip": 28014,
        "country": "Spain",
        "state": "Madrid"}
    },

    {"id": "0003",
     "name": "Peter",
     "surname": "Smith",
     "address": {
        "street": "Cyphress avenue",
        "number": 1,
        "zip": 11217,
        "country": "EEUU",
        "state": "Brooklyn"}
    },

    {"id": "0004",
     "name": "Lili",
     "surname": "Haydn",
     "address": {
        "street": "BOYLSTON ST",
        "number": 195,
        "zip": 98102,
        "country": "EEUU",
        "state": "Seattle"}
    }
  ]
}
```

We define a main object with the customer key, which is a list of customer objects. The objects define each client of our system by the attributes: id, name, surname, and address. The address is a new object and contains the attributes of street, number, zip, country, and state.

Finally, let's see how we designed our **http_json.dart** file and how we have structured our code. For this example we will use two libraries for handling HTML and JSON, and our main() method will create a button to make a request to the server when we clicked on it. See here:

```
import 'dart:html';
import 'dart:convert' show JSON;

void main() {
  var buttons = document.querySelector('#buttons');
  var btn1 = new ButtonElement()
    ..id = 'btn1'
    ..text = 'Get customers'
    ..onClick.listen((e) => getCustomers());
  buttons.nodes.add(btn1);
}
```

The getCustomers() function creates the HttpRequest object and makes the request to get the list of customers, as follows:

```
void getCustomers() {
  var url = 'http://localhost:8080/customers.json';
  var xhr = new HttpRequest();
  xhr
  ..onLoad.listen((e) {
    if ((xhr.status >= 200 && xhr.status < 300) ||
        xhr.status == 0 || xhr.status == 304) {
      listCustomers(xhr);
    } else {
      error(xhr.status);
    }
  })
  ..onError.listen((e) => error(e))
  ..onProgress.listen((_) => loading())
  ..open('GET', url)
  ..send();
}
```

It creates a new HttpRequest object with its constructor and then associates actions to different statuses. While the request is in progress, it executes the loading() method that displays the message "Loading ..." in the #response div element.

In the instance of an error, it will execute the error() method to display the error message returned by the system in the #response div element.

The onLoad event is called when the request is complete. The status of the request is validated, and if it is successfully completed then the listCustomers() function is executed. If it is completed, but has been done so inadequately, we'll launch the error() method again but now with the status returned by the system.

These are the methods for the events onProgress and onError:

```dart
void error(e) {
  var div_resp = document.querySelector('#response');
  div_resp.setInnerHtml('Error launching request: $e');
}

void loading() {
  var div_resp = document.querySelector('#response');
  div_resp.setInnerHtml('Loading...');
}
```

Now let's look at the listClustomers() function. When it gets the response from the server, it generates an HTML element table with the retrieved information. As the server returns data in JSON format, by using the JSON.decode() method we process the response and get a Map that we can use to generate our table.

Additionally, we've used the StringBuffer class to compose the HTML template with the table element that will display in our #response div element:

```dart
void listCustomers(HttpRequest xhr) {
  var div_resp = document.querySelector('#response');
  StringBuffer tpl = new StringBuffer('''<table border="1">
    <tr>
      <th colspan="3"></th>
      <th colspan="5"> Address </th>
    <tr>
      <th>ID</th>
      <th>Name</th>
      <th>Surname</th>
      <th>Street</th>
      <th>Number</th>
      <th>ZipCode</th>
      <th>State</th>
      <th>Country</th>
    </tr>''');
  Map d = JSON.decode(xhr.responseText);
  d['customers'].forEach((c) {
    tpl.write('''
    <tr>
      <td>${c['id']}</td>
      <td>${c['name']}</td>
      <td>${c['surname']}</td>
      <td>${c['address']['street']}</td>
      <td>${c['address']['number']}</td>
      <td>${c['address']['zip']}</td>
      <td>${c['address']['state']}</td>
      <td>${c['address']['country']}</td>
    </tr>''');
  });
  tpl.write('</table>');
  div_resp.setInnerHtml(tpl.toString());
}
```

This will be our full http_json.dart file:

```dart
import 'dart:html';
import 'dart:convert' show JSON;

void listCustomers(HttpRequest xhr) {
 var div_resp = document.querySelector('#response');
 StringBuffer tpl = new StringBuffer('''<table border="1">
   <tr>
     <th colspan="3"></th>
     <th colspan="5"> Address </th>
   <tr>
     <th>ID</th>
     <th>Name</th>
     <th>Surname</th>
     <th>Street</th>
     <th>Number</th>
     <th>ZipCode</th>
     <th>State</th>
     <th>Country</th>
   </tr>''');
 Map d = JSON.decode(xhr.responseText);
 d['customers'].forEach((c) {
   tpl.write('''
   <tr>
     <td>${c['id']}</td>
     <td>${c['name']}</td>
     <td>${c['surname']}</td>
     <td>${c['address']['street']}</td>
     <td>${c['address']['number']}</td>
     <td>${c['address']['zip']}</td>
     <td>${c['address']['state']}</td>
     <td>${c['address']['country']}</td>
   </tr>''');
 });
 tpl.write('</table>');
 div_resp.setInnerHtml(tpl.toString());
}

void error(e) {
 var div_resp = document.querySelector('#response');
 div_resp.setInnerHtml('Error launching request: $e');
}

void loading() {
 var div_resp = document.querySelector('#response');
 div_resp.setInnerHtml('Loading...');
}
```

```dart
void getCustomers() {
 var url = 'http://localhost:8080/customers.json';
 var xhr = new HttpRequest();
 xhr
 ..onLoad.listen((e) {
   if ((xhr.status >= 200 && xhr.status < 300) ||
       xhr.status == 0 || xhr.status == 304) {
     listCustomers(xhr);
   } else {
     error(xhr.status);
   }
 })
 ..onError.listen((e) => error(e))
 ..onProgress.listen((_) => loading())
 ..open('GET', url)
 ..send();
}

void main() {
  var buttons = document.querySelector('#buttons');
  var btn1 = new ButtonElement()
    ..id = 'btn1'
    ..text = 'Get customers'
    ..onClick.listen((e) => getCustomers());
  buttons.nodes.add(btn1);
}
```

If you run the application, you will see that after clicking the Get customers button, we obtained the data from the server in JSON format and processed it on the client side. It is then shown properly formatted as a table in the div #response, seen in Figure 27-12.

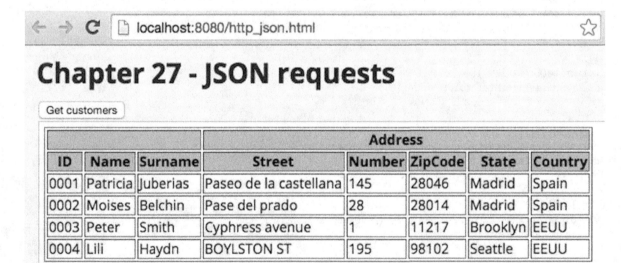

Figure 27-12. Response received from the server in JSON format and processed as HTML table

The JSON class of dart:convert also allows you to encode Dart objects as JSON to be sent and processed by the server. Imagine that we have a Map object with the user system information and the last system login of this user; we can encode this data as JSON and sent it to the server as follows:

```dart
void main() {

  Map data = {
    'user': 'moisesbelchin@gmail.com',
    'name': 'Moises Belchin',
    'access': '2014-10-29 17:22'
  };

  var url = 'http://localhost:8080';
  var xhr = new HttpRequest();
  xhr
  ..open('POST', url)
  ..setRequestHeader('Content-Type', 'application/json')
  ..send(JSON.encode(data));

}
```

We create a new HttpRequest object and call its open() method, indicating that we will make a POST and the destination URL. Then we add the Content-Type application/json header to tell the server that it will receive a JSON-valid message. Finally, we call the send() method of HttpRequest to send our Map object with the data encoded in JSON format using JSON.encode().

We wanted to show you how to make requests by instantiating the HttpRequest class directly, but generally only very complex or fine-grained cases require that. This sample could easily be completed using HttpRequest. request(), as you can see below:

```dart
void main() {

  Map data = {
    'user': 'moisesbelchin@gmail.com',
    'name': 'Moises Belchin',
    'access': '2014-10-29 17:22'
  };

  var url = 'http://localhost:8080';
  HttpRequest.request(url,
    method:'POST',
    requestHeaders:{
      'Content-Type': 'application/json'
    },
    sendData: JSON.encode(data)
  )
  .then((v) => print(v))
  .catchError((error) => print(error));
}
```

As you have seen, the JSON class allows you to easily manage the messages passing between client and server using JSON with the decode() and encode() methods.

Summary

In this chapter we have learned:

- how we can make asynchronous HTTP requests in Dart
- what the CORS is
- how to use `HttpRequest.getString` to get data from servers
- how to send information to a server encoded as `Form Data` using `HttpRequest.postFormData`
- what `dart:convert` is and how to use the `JSON` class
- how to use JSON as a light data interchange format to pass messages between client and servers
- how to get data from servers as JSON
- how to send data to servers as JSON

CHAPTER 28

■ ■ ■

Dart on the Server Side

Throughout this book we have seen how Dart works and the tools it lets us work with, and we have compared it to client-side languages like JavaScript and jQuery framework. However, development on the client side is not the only thing that you can do with this fantastic language. Dart also includes a complete library to work with on the server side.

In this chapter we will see the most interesting methods found in the dart:io library to use when building a web server with Dart. In the second part of the chapter we will add more functionality to our web server; we will also work with processes and see how to run external applications on our server. Finally, we'll see how to work with sockets in Dart.

The I/O Dart Library

The I/O Dart library is designed to develop server-side applications running in the Dart virtual machine. Thanks to this library you can use the same language to develop the backend and the frontend.

■ **Note**   This library does not work in applications that run within the browser.

This library, called dart:io, lets us work with files, directories, sockets, processes, and HTTP servers. If you want to start using this library in your projects, you need only import the corresponding SDK package, as follows:

```
import 'dart:io';
```

The following list includes all the source files that you'll find inside the dart:io package. We'll describe the most interesting of them later.

- bytes_builder.dart
- common.dart
- crypto.dart
- data_transformer.dart
- directory.dart
- directory_impl.dart
- eventhandler.dart
- file.dart
- file_impl.dart

- file_system_entity.dart
- http.dart
- http_date.dart
- http_headers.dart
- http_impl.dart
- http_parser.dart
- http_session.dart
- io_sink.dart
- io_service.dart
- link.dart
- platform.dart
- platform_impl.dart
- process.dart
- secure_server_socket.dart
- secure_socket.dart
- service_object.dart
- socket.dart
- stdio.dart
- string_transformer.dart
- timer_impl.dart
- websocket.dart
- websocket_impl.dart

Within the `http.dart` file are the necessary classes to create HTTP servers and clients. The file `directory.dart` contains the Directory class for handling and creating directories. `file.dart` contains the necessary classes to manage files in the system. **link.dart** has the functionality to manage symbolic links. Inside platform.dart you'll find the **Platform** class, used to access the machine and operating system features.

`process.dart` contains all classes and methods needed to work with processes in the system. If you need mechanisms for secure communication mode via TCP sockets using TLS and SSL, all the required classes are in the `secure_server_socket.dart` and `secure_server.dart` files.

In the `socket.dart` file are all the classes needed for managing sockets and communication over TCP sockets. Finally, `stdio.dart` allows you to read from the standard system input (`stdin`) and write both the standard output (`stdout`) and the standard error (`stderr`).

Creating a Server Application

Now we'll see how to use this library to create applications on the server side using some of the packages and classes we mentioned previously. We'll begin with a very simple web server that will display a welcome message when the users request a resource.

Create a new application in Dart Editor, select the command-line application option, and put a name for this new application. We'll use *server* as the name here. Here is the code for our `server.dart` file:

```
import 'dart:io';

void main() {
 HttpServer.bind('127.0.0.1', 8080)
 .then((server) {
   server.listen((HttpRequest request) {
     // Handle requests from the server.
     request.response.write('This is Dart on the server side !');
     request.response.close();
   });
 })
 .catchError((e) => print('Error :: $e'));
}
```

Once you've added this code to your project, click the Run button to execute your application. Now you can point your web browser to the address, in this case `http://127.0.0.1:8080`, to get a response message from your new web server, as seen in Figure 28-1.

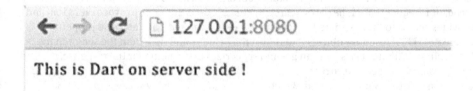

Figure 28-1. *First welcome message from your new web server written in Dart*

Not bad—only 13 lines of code and you have a web server with management errors fully operative. In this example we've used the `HttpServer`, `HttpRequest`, and `HttpResponse` classes. The `HttpServer` class is in charge of creating the web server that delivers content, such as webpages, using the HTTP protocol. The `HttpServer` is a `Stream` that provides `HttpRequest` objects. Each `HttpRequest` has an associated `HttpResponse` object. The server responds to a request by writing to that `HttpResponse` object.

In the example above, you can see how we listen to each request the server will receive and then use the `HttpResponse` object associated with that `HttpRequest` to show a message to the user.

The `HttpServer` class has different getters, setters, and methods, and we're going to detail the most interesting of them here:

- `serverHeader` gets and sets the default value of the server header for all the responses.

- `defaultResponseHeaders` is a set of default headers for the server responses. By default the following headers are in this set:

  ```
  Content-Type: text/plain; charset=utf-8
  X-Frame-Options: SAMEORIGIN
  X-Content-Type-Options: nosniff
  X-XSS-Protection: 1; mode=block
  ```

- autoCompress defines whether the server should compress the content. The default value is false.

- bind starts listening for HTTP requests on the specified address and port.

- bindSecure is similar to bind but is used for secure connections. In both methods, the address can be a String or an InternetAddress object. This class is located in the socket.dart file in the dart:io library and lets you create and manage Internet addresses.

- HttpServer.listenOn is a factory constructor that attaches the HTTP server to an existing ServerSocket.

- close permanently stops the server from listening new connections.

- port returns the port that the server is listening on.

- address returns the InternetAddress object with the address that the server is listening on.

- sessionTimeout sets the timeout, in seconds, for sessions of the server.

- connectionsInfo is a method that returns the HttpConnectionsInfo object with summary statistics about a server's current socket connections, such as total number of socket connections, active connections, idle connections, and the number of connections that are preparing to close.

The HttpRequest class creates server-side objects with the content of and information about an HTTP request, such as contentLength, method, uri, requestedUri, headers, cookies, certificate, session, protocolVersion, and connectionInfo and also provides access to the associated HttpResponse object through the response property.

The HttpResponse class creates HTTP response objects that return the headers and data from the server to the client in response to an HTTP request. With this class you can get and set certain information for the response, such as contentLength, statusCode, reasonPhrase, persistentConnection, deadline, bufferOutput, headers, cookies, and connectionInfo. This class also has a detachSocket method, which detaches the underlying socket from the HTTP server, and the redirect method, which responds to the client with a redirect to a new location.

In addition, this class implements IOSink, and for that reason we can do things like this:

```
request.response.write('This is Dart on the server side !');
request.response.close();
```

After the headers have been set up we can use methods from IOSink, such as write() or writeln(), to write the body of the HTTP response. When the response body is finished you can use the close() method to close the response and send it to the client.

Now that we've seen our first Dart web server sample and we've covered the main classes involved, we're going to add more functionality to our server to make it more interesting. Create a directory named web in this new project and make this the root directory on your new Dart web server.

Since we are simplifying things, we do not want to have a web directory as a sub-directory of bin, but rather we want to have our server navigate up out of the bin and into a web directory (e.g. ../web/..). Create the main file of the new server and name it index.html. We can also add additional directories in which to store images and CSS, as shown in Figure 28-2.

Figure 28-2. New web directory with files and directories on your server

Now let's change the code for our web server by adding paths and directory management, as you can see here:

```dart
import 'dart:io';

void main() {
 HttpServer.bind('127.0.0.1', 8080)
 .then((server) {
   server.listen((HttpRequest request) {
     // Handle server requests.
     switch (request.uri.path) {
       case '/':
       default:
         request.response.headers.add(HttpHeaders.CONTENT_TYPE, 'text/html');
         request.response.write('<h1>Index of /web/</h1><ul>');
         new Directory('web/').listSync().forEach((FileSystemEntity entity) {
           var df = entity.path.split('web/').last;
           request.response.write('<li><a href="web/${df}">${df}</a></li>');
         });
         request.response.write('</ul>');
         request.response.close();
     }
   });
 })
 .catchError((e) => print('Error :: $e'));
}
```

Now if you point your browser to the http://127.0.0.1:8080 address, the web server will list the directories and files from the web directory that we have defined as the root of our web server, shown in Figure 28-3.

Index of /web/

- css
- images
- index.html

Figure 28-3. *Listing the root server directory*

In this example we've used two new classes, `Directory` and `FileSystemEntity`. The `Directory` class is a reference to a directory and lets you manage directories on the file system. You can create, rename, or list directories.

This class has both asynchronous and synchronous version of these methods. For example, if you want to create a new directory you can use `create()`, which is the asynchronous version for this operation and returns a `Future` object, or you can use the `createSync()` method, which is the synchronous version.

In our example, we've used `listSync()` to list the sub-directories and files of the given directory. This method returns a `Stream` of `FileSystemEntity` objects. The `FileSystemEntity` class includes all the properties and methods to work with directories, files, or links on the file system. You can work with file system entities either asynchronously or synchronously. This class allows you to check whether the object exists using either the `exists()` or `existsSync()` methods, as well as allows you to rename or delete the object using `rename()`, `renameSync()`, `delete()`, and `deleteSync()`, respectively.

With this class you also can find out the file system entity permissions, size, mode, or when this object was changed, accessed, or modified using the `stat()` or `statSync()` methods. `FileSystemEntity` also lets you get file system entity parent information or find out whether that object is a link, directory, or file by using the `isLink()`, `isLinkSync()`, `isFile()`, `isFileSync()`, `isDirectory()`, and `isDirectorySync()` methods.

As you saw, `dart:io`, like many parts of the SDK, is designed to operate in a completely asynchronous mode, and all methods return a `Future` or `Stream` object. But many classes within `dart:io` have methods that perform certain tasks in synchronous mode, such as `listSync()`, which we have just seen for the `Directory` class. We'll go a step forward now and use our web server to navigate the directories and view their contents. In the CSS directory we've added an empty file called `main.css` in order to show a result when we browse through this web directory. See the following:

```dart
import 'dart:io';

void main() {
 HttpServer.bind('127.0.0.1', 8080)
 .then((server) {
   server.listen((HttpRequest request) {
   // Handle server requests.
     switch (request.uri.path) {
       default:
         var path = 'web${request.uri.path}';
         request.response.headers.add(HttpHeaders.CONTENT_TYPE, 'text/html');
         request.response.write('<h1>Index of /$path</h1><ul>');
```

```
    if(FileStat.statSync(path).type == FileSystemEntityType.DIRECTORY) {

      var dir = new Directory(path);

      if (request.uri.path != '/') {
        request.response.write('<li><a href="/">..</a></li>');
      }

      dir.listSync().forEach((FileSystemEntity entity) {
        var df = entity.path.split(path).last;
        request.response.write('<li><a href="${df}">${df}</a></li>');
      });
    }

    request.response.write('</ul>');
    request.response.close();
    }
  });
})
.catchError((e) => print('Error :: $e'));
}
```

With this simple code, we can now display the contents of our root directory. We can also browse directories within the root directory and display the contents for each one, as you can see in Figure 28-4. This time, we used the classes FileStat and FileSystemEntityType to open a directory with the statSync() method and list its contents.

Index of /web/

- css
- images
- index.html

Figure 28-4. *Listing the root directory contents*

We've added a link back to the parent directory for easy navigation, shown in Figure 28-5.

Index of /web/css

- ..
- /main.css

Figure 28-5. *Browsing the web server directories*

Our web server is getting into better shape, so let's allow the user to visualize the contents of the files it hosts. Add content to the main.css file and to the index.html file to open them from the web server and view their contents.

For the main.css file we have created this simple content:

```
/**
 * Main CSS
 */
BODY {
  background-color: #f4f4f4;
  color: #5a5656;
  font-family: 'Open Sans', Arial, Helvetica, sans-serif;
  font-size: 16px;
  line-height: 1.5em;
}
```

In the index.html file you can add something like this:

```
<!DOCTYPE html>
<html>
  <head>
    <meta charset="utf-8">
    <title>Index</title>
    <link rel="stylesheet" href="css/main.css">
  </head>
  <body>
    <h1>Welcome to Dart on server side !!</h1>
  </body>
</html>
```

Add the following code to the web server to allow users to navigate through the different directories and files and view file contents:

```
import 'dart:io';

void handleDir(String path, HttpRequest request) {
  request.response.headers.add(HttpHeaders.CONTENT_TYPE, 'text/html');
  request.response.write('<h1>Index of /$path</h1><ul>');
  var dir = new Directory(path);
```

```dart
  if (request.uri.path != '/') {
    request.response.write('<li><a href="/">..</a></li>');
  }
  dir.listSync().forEach((FileSystemEntity entity) {
    var df = entity.path.split(path).last;
    request.response.write('''<li><a href="${request.uri.path}${df}">
                        ${df}</a></li>''');
  });
  request.response.write('</ul>');
  request.response.close();
}

void handleFile(String path, HttpRequest request) {
  var fich = new File(path);
  request.response.write(fich.readAsStringSync());
  request.response.close();
}

void main() {
 HttpServer.bind('127.0.0.1', 8080)
 .then((server) {
   server.listen((HttpRequest request) {
     // Handle server requests.
     var path = 'web${request.uri.path}';
     switch(FileStat.statSync(path).type) {

       case FileSystemEntityType.DIRECTORY:
         handleDir(path, request);
         break;

       case FileSystemEntityType.FILE:
         handleFile(path, request);
         break;
     }
   });
 })
 .catchError((e) => print('Error :: $e'));
}
```

Now users can navigate through different web server directories, and they can also pick a file and show its contents in their browser, as seen in Figures 28-6 and 28-7.

```
←  →  C   🗋 127.0.0.1:8080/css/main.css

/**
 * Main CSS
 */
BODY {
  background-color: #f4f4f4;
  color: #5a5656;
  font-family: 'Open Sans', Arial, Helvetica, sans-serif;
  font-size: 16px;
  line-height: 1.5em;
}
```

Figure 28-6. *Viewing the contents of the main.css file*

```
←  →  C   🗋 127.0.0.1:8080/index.html

<!DOCTYPE html>
<html>
  <head>
    <meta charset="utf-8">
    <title>Index</title>
    <link rel="stylesheet" href="css/main.css">
  </head>
  <body>
    <h1>Welcome to Dart on server side !!</h1>
  </body>
</html>
```

Figure 28-7. *Viewing the contents of the index.html file on our server*

In this case we've used the FileStat.statSync() method to get the type of the file system entity. If it's a directory we call the handleDir() function, or we call the handleFile() function if it's a file.

The handleDir() function opens the directory using the Directory class and lists its contents with the listSync() method, giving the user the response in a text/html format. The handleFile() function creates a new File object and reads its contents using the readAsStringSync() method.

The File class has all the methods required to work with files on the file system. As we've seen with other dart:io classes, this class also supports asynchronous and synchronous operations such as create, rename, copy, get length, open, read, and write. The read method allows you to read a String as either Bytes or Lines with its corresponding methods. Write operations allow you to write content into the file as either Bytes or a String.

As you can see when you view the index.html file, the web server shows you the content as plain text; if you want to see it as an HTML file you have to add the corresponding header to the server response object before you write and close the response server.

Our code will look like the following:

```dart
import 'dart:io';

void handleDir(String path, HttpRequest request) {
  request.response.headers.add(HttpHeaders.CONTENT_TYPE, 'text/html');
  request.response.write('<h1>Index of /$path</h1><ul>');
  var dir = new Directory(path);
  if (request.uri.path != '/') {
    request.response.write('<li><a href="/">..</a></li>');
  }
  dir.listSync().forEach((FileSystemEntity entity) {
    var df = entity.path.split(path).last;
    request.response.write('''<li><a href="${request.uri.path}${df}">
                    ${df}</a></li>''');
  });
  request.response.write('</ul>');
  request.response.close();
}

void handleFile(String path, HttpRequest request) {
  var fich = new File(path);
  if(request.uri.path.endsWith('html')) {
    request.response.headers.add(HttpHeaders.CONTENT_TYPE, 'text/html');
  }
  request.response.write(fich.readAsStringSync());
  request.response.close();
}

void main() {
 HttpServer.bind('127.0.0.1', 8080)
 .then((server) {
   server.listen((HttpRequest request) {
     // Handle server requests.
     var path = 'web${request.uri.path}';
     switch(FileStat.statSync(path).type) {

       case FileSystemEntityType.DIRECTORY:
         handleDir(path, request);
         break;

       case FileSystemEntityType.FILE:
         handleFile(path, request);
         break;
     }
   });
 })
 .catchError((e) => print('Error :: $e'));
}
```

If you now run the web server and browse to the index.html file, you can see the file content, but it is interpreted as an HTML file, as you can see in Figure 28-8.

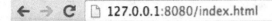

Welcome to Dart on server side !!

Figure 28-8. *Viewing the index.html file contents as text/html in the web server*

Handling Requests

In the previous chapter we saw how to use Dart with web services and how to make GET or POST requests. We also added a sample Dart web server in order to make POST requests and get a response from the server. Now we're going to see this example in detail and learn how to manage GET or POST requests in Dart web servers. We're going to combine that example with everything we've learned thus far in this chapter.

Our main() function will look like this:

```
import 'dart:io';
import 'dart:convert';

void main() {
 HttpServer.bind(InternetAddress.LOOPBACK_IP_V4, 8080)
 .then((server) {
   print("Server running on http://${InternetAddress.LOOPBACK_IP_V4.address}:8080/");
   server.listen((HttpRequest request) {
     switch(request.method) {
       case 'POST':
         handlePost(request);
         break;

       case 'GET':
         handleGet(request);
         break;

       default:
         request.response
         ..statusCode = HttpStatus.NOT_IMPLEMENTED
         ..write('Unsupported method')
         ..close();
         break;      }
   });
 })
 .catchError((e) => print('Error :: $e'));
}
```

As you can see, in this case we're using the InternetAddress class and its LOOPBACK_IP_V4 getter to bind our Dart web server to the 127.0.0.1 address. Our server will be listening to that address and port and will analyze the HttpRequest method so as to properly handle POST methods and GET methods for the rest of the supported HTTP methods for which we're displaying a message to the user.

The following is our handleGet() function. In this case we're using the same methods we've seen throughout this chapter to manage files and directories. See here:

```dart
void handleGet(HttpRequest request) {
  var path = 'web${request.uri.path}';
  switch(FileStat.statSync(path).type) {

    case FileSystemEntityType.DIRECTORY:
      handleDir(path, request);
      break;

    case FileSystemEntityType.FILE:
    default:
      handleFile(path, request);
      break;
  }
}

void handleDir(String path, HttpRequest request) {
  request.response.statusCode = HttpStatus.OK;
  request.response.headers.add(HttpHeaders.CONTENT_TYPE, 'text/html');
  request.response.write('<h1>Index of /$path</h1><ul>');
  var dir = new Directory(path);
  if (request.uri.path != '/') {
    request.response.write('<li><a href="/">..</a></li>');
  }
  dir.listSync().forEach((FileSystemEntity entity) {
    var df = entity.path.split(path).last;
    request.response.write('''<li><a href="${request.uri.path}${df}">
                        ${df}</a></li>''');
  });
  request.response.write('</ul>');
  request.response.close();
}

void handleFile(String path, HttpRequest request) {
  request.response.statusCode = HttpStatus.OK;
  if(request.uri.path.endsWith('html')) {
    request.response.headers.add(HttpHeaders.CONTENT_TYPE, 'text/html');
  }
  var file = new File(path);
  file.exists().then((bool found) {
    if (found) {
      request.response.statusCode = HttpStatus.OK;
      request.response.write(file.readAsStringSync());
    } else {
      request.response.statusCode = HttpStatus.NOT_FOUND;
      request.response.write('not found');
    }
    request.response.close();
  });
}
```

We've used the `statusCode` setter on the `HttpResponse` object to set the status code for each response. `HttpStatus` class contains all the supported HTTP status code, which you can use to make your code more readable.

In the `handleFile()` function, we've used the asynchronous version of the `File.exists()` method to discover whether the file requested exists or not and to display either its contents or a message informing the user that the requested file doesn't exist. If you browse to this URL— `http://127.0.0.1:8080/file.html`—you'll see the "not found" message on your browser.

Finally this will be our `handlePost()` method:

```
void handlePost(HttpRequest request) {
  ContentType contentType = request.headers.contentType;
  BytesBuilder builder = new BytesBuilder();
  request.listen((buffer) {
    builder.add(buffer);
  }, onDone: () {
   String bodyString = UTF8.decode(builder.takeBytes());
   Map data = Uri.splitQueryString(bodyString);
   request.response.headers.add('Access-Control-Allow-Origin', '*');
   request.response.headers.add('Access-Control-Allow-Methods', 'POST, OPTIONS');
   request.response.headers.add('Access-Control-Allow-Headers',
        'Origin, X-Requested-With, Content-Type, Accept');
   request.response.statusCode = HttpStatus.OK;
   request.response.write(data);
   request.response.close();
  });
}
```

In this case we're listening for all the information the client is sending on the request body; remember that the `HttpRequest` class implements the `Stream` class. When the `listen` method has finished, the onDone method is invoked and the request body is processed.

This code decodes the bytes from the `BytesBuilder` to a UTF8 string and then splits it into a `Map` using the `Uri.splitQueryString` method. After adding the corresponding header to make the Dart web server support CORS, we send the data to the client as a `Map` converted to a `String`.

Working with Processes

Let's see how to run processes from our Dart applications on the server side. Continuing with our web server example, we're going to create a specific handler to execute certain function systems by running a particular process using the `Process` class. The handler that we will create is /ps, so when the user puts and address into the browser's address bar, such as `http://127.0.0.1:8080/ps`, the result will show the processes running on our system.

■ **Note** On Windows you must have installed `ps` command to properly run this example.

This will be our new web server:

```dart
import 'dart:io';

void main() {
  HttpServer.bind('127.0.0.1', 8080)
  .then((server) {
  server.listen((HttpRequest request) {
    // Handle server requests.
    switch(request.uri.path) {
      case '/ps':
        request.response.headers.add(HttpHeaders.CONTENT_TYPE, 'text/html');
        request.response.write('''
         <html>
           <head><title>System processes</title></head>
           <body>
           <h2>System processes</h2>
         ''');
        var proc = Process.runSync('ps', [], runInShell:true);
        request.response.write('<pre>');
        if(proc.exitCode == 0) {
          request.response.write(proc.stdout);
        } else {
          request.response.write(proc.stderr);
        }
        request.response.write('</pre>');
        request.response.write('</body></hmtl>');
        request.response.close();
        break;

      default:
        var path = 'web${request.uri.path}';
        switch(FileStat.statSync(path).type) {
          case FileSystemEntityType.DIRECTORY:
            request.response.headers.add(HttpHeaders.CONTENT_TYPE, 'text/html');
            request.response.write('<h1>Index of /web${request.uri.path}</h1><ul>');
            var dir = new Directory(path);
            if (request.uri.path != '/') {
              request.response.write('<li><a href="/">..</a></li>');
            }
            dir.listSync().forEach((FileSystemEntity entity) {
              var df = entity.path.split(path).last;
              request.response.write('''
                <li><a href="${request.uri.path}${df}">${df}</a></li>
              ''');
            });
            request.response.write('</ul>');
            request.response.close();
            break;
```

```
      case FileSystemEntityType.FILE:
        var fich = new File(path);
        if(request.uri.path.endsWith('html')) {
          request.response.headers.add(HttpHeaders.CONTENT_TYPE, 'text/html');
        }
        request.response.write(fich.readAsStringSync());
        request.response.close();
        break;

      case FileSystemEntityType.NOT_FOUND:
        request.response.write('Not found');
        request.response.close();
        break;
      }
    }
  });
})
.catchError((e) => print('Error :: $e'));
}
```

We've added a new code block to control specific handlers, so if we get one of these new handlers, then we'll execute the specific function. Otherwise, we will continue working with files and directories. Within this particular handler, we'll execute a process with the runSync() method of the Process class and monitor if the process terminates successfully so that we know whether to display the standard output (stdout) or the error output (stderr). See here:

```
var process = Process.runSync('ps', [], runInShell:true);
if(process.exitCode == 0) {
 request.response.write(process.stdout);
} else {
 request.response.write(process.stderr);
}
```

In addition, we've added the runInShell optional named parameter to this method, which allows the process to be spawned through a system shell. On Linux and Mac OS, /bin/sh is used, while %WINDIR%\system32\cmd.exe is used on Windows.

When you want to run processes, you can also pass parameters to the .run() method or to .runSync() as a list. In the above example we have not added any parameters for the ps process, seen in Figure 28-9.

← → C ⬚ 127.0.0.1:8080/ps

System processes

PID	PPID	PGID	WINPID	TTY	UID	STIME	COMMAND
4476	1	4476	4476	con	500	11:42:10	/usr/bin/ps

Figure 28-9. *Running ps on our web server*

We will improve our web server somewhat so as to allow us to pass parameters to our handler /ps. We will pass query string parameters in the URL like this:

```
http://127.0.0.1:8080/ps?p=aW
```

The web server will retrieve the parameters entered by the user and pass them to the ps command in order to run the process with the selected parameters.

Replace this line:

```
var proc = Process.runSync('ps', [], runInShell:true);
```

With this block of code the web server can manage query parameters and pass them to Process.runSync(), as follows:

```
var myParameters = [];
if (request.uri.queryParameters.keys.length > 0) {
 if (request.uri.queryParameters.containsKey('p')) {
   myParameters.add('-${request.uri.queryParameters['p']}');
 }
}
var proc = Process.runSync('ps', myParameters, runInShell:true);
```

Now we can view all system processes, as you can see in Figure 28-10.

127.0.0.1:8080/ps?p=axcj

System processes

USER	PID	PPID	PGID	SESS	JOBC	STAT	TT	TIME	COMMAND
root	1	0	1	0	0	Ss	??	0:22.23	launchd
root	16	1	16	0	0	Ss	??	0:03.04	UserEventAgent
root	17	1	17	0	0	Ss	??	0:03.38	syslogd
root	19	1	19	0	0	Ss	??	0:01.09	kextd
root	20	1	20	0	0	Ss	??	0:04.41	fseventsd
root	22	1	22	0	0	Ss	??	0:00.04	thermald
root	23	1	23	0	0	Ss	??	0:18.14	mtmd
_appleevents	25	1	25	0	0	Ss	??	0:00.61	appleeventsd
root	26	1	26	0	0	Ss	??	0:03.12	configd
root	27	1	27	0	0	Ss	??	0:01.58	powerd
root	30	1	30	0	0	Us	??	0:05.68	airportd
root	32	1	32	0	0	SNs	??	0:00.28	warmd
root	33	1	33	0	0	Ss	??	0:15.98	mds
_iconservices	37	1	37	0	0	Ss	??	0:00.06	iconservicesd
root	38	1	38	0	0	Ss	??	0:00.02	iconservicesagent
root	39	1	39	0	0	Ss	??	0:00.30	diskarbitrationd
root	40	1	40	0	0	Ss	??	0:01.13	PocketCloudService
root	43	1	43	0	0	Ss	??	0:07.05	coreduetd
root	44	1	44	0	0	Ss	??	0:00.25	backupd-helper
root	45	1	45	0	0	Ss	??	0:00.03	wdhelper
root	47	1	47	0	0	Us	??	0:03.45	mtmfs
root	48	1	48	0	0	Ss	??	0:00.09	awdd

Figure 28-10. All processes running in our system by passing parameters to /ps handler

Sockets

In addition to all the things we have seen so far, dart:io will also let us work with sockets in command-line applications and websockets in browser applications so as to communicate between client and server via TCP. A socket is a method for communication between a client program and a server program in a network and is defined as the endpoint in a connection. Let's see a simple example of a server and a client using sockets to communicate to better understand how they work.

We've created two files, server_socket.dart and client_socket.dart, to show you a simple way to communicate between client and server. The server_socket.dart file will be responsible for creating the server socket and for listening to the messages from clients. See the following:

```dart
import 'dart:io';
import 'dart:convert';

void main() {
  ServerSocket.bind('127.0.0.1', 4041)
  .then((serverSocket) {
    serverSocket.listen((socket) {
      socket.transform(UTF8.decoder).listen(print);
    });
  });
  stdout.writeln('Waiting for messages from clients...');
}
```

The client_socket.dart file is the client that connects to the server at the specified address and port and sends a message to the server. See here:

```dart
import 'dart:io';

void main() {
  Socket.connect('127.0.0.1', 4041).then((socket) {
    socket.write('Hello server socket !');
  });
}
```

First, start both server_socket.dart and client_socket.dart. The client connects to the server's socket and sends it a message. The server receives the message and displays it on screen, shown in Figure 28-11.

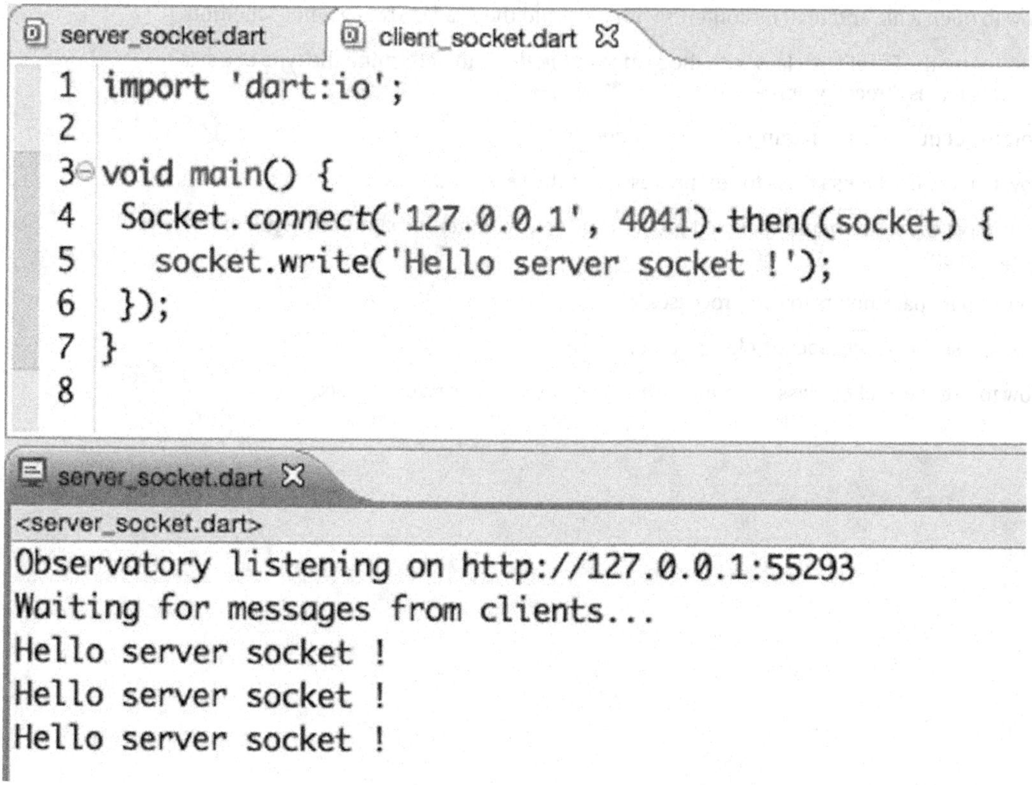

```
server_socket.dart          client_socket.dart  ⊠

1  import 'dart:io';
2
3⊖ void main() {
4    Socket.connect('127.0.0.1', 4041).then((socket) {
5      socket.write('Hello server socket !');
6    });
7  }
8
```

```
server_socket.dart  ⊠

<server_socket.dart>
Observatory listening on http://127.0.0.1:55293
Waiting for messages from clients...
Hello server socket !
Hello server socket !
Hello server socket !
```

Figure 28-11. Client and server communication using sockets in Dart

Summary

In this chapter we have learned:

- what the I/O library is and all the files it contains

- how to use dart:io to build web server applications

- how to build a web server, starting from the most basic and step by step adding functionality

- how to use the HttpServer class to build a web server and then manage requests and responses

- how to add additional headers to our responses

- how to generate responses from our server to the clients with the response.write() and response.close() methods

- how to open directories and read their contents with the Directory class and listSync() method

- how to open a file and read its contents with `File` and the `readAsStringSync()` method
- how to use the `FileStat` class with the `statSync()` method to determine the type of a system entity, such as directory or file
- how to get query string parameters from requests
- how to use the `Process` class to run processes on the server side
- how to get the status of the executed process and return either the standard result or standard error
- how to pass parameters to run processes
- how to use the `ServerSocket` class to create servers
- how to use the `Socket` class to create clients that connect to server sockets

PART VII

Dart's Future

■ ■ ■

Implementing Design Patterns and Creating Web Components

Web components are the latest trend, and they are a very interesting resource because they bring web development "to the next level." They allow us to use the MVC pattern (Model-View-Controller) in a more natural and coherent way and allow us to encapsulate and reuse functionality.

In this chapter we will see what web components are, what the Shadow DOM is, and how the Shadow DOM can be used to create web components. Later we will see how to use these functionalities in Dart thanks to the `Polymer.dart` library. We will also develop a full example to show you the power of web components and how use them with Dart.

Web Components

If you have previously developed with .NET or Java, then you know it's very easy to take some parts or specific components of an application and reuse them in another application or even create a new component by borrowing from an existing one. With web components you can do exactly the same thing in web development. You can create a component with its styles and its particular behavior, then everything is packaged and you can easily use this component with your application. This is possible thanks to the new possibilities offered by HTML in its latest version, including:

- **DOM mutation observers.** Observers that indicate changes in DOM elements.

- **Pointer events.** Handle the mouse and touch devices in the same way on all existing platforms.

- **Shadow DOM.** Encapsulate structure and style within elements.

- **Custom Elements.** Define your own HTML5 elements. A hyphen is used for the names of those custom elements, as a way to do namespacing and to differentiate them from standard HTML elements. The hyphen in the name is required for names according to the W3C specification.

- **HTML Imports.** One way of packaging elements. These packages can contain HTML, CSS, and JavaScript.

- **Model-Driven Views (MDV).** Enables bind interface, logic, and data binding directly into HTML.

- **Web Animations.** An API to unify the different animation web techniques.

We can use all of these new features right now in Dart thanks to the **Polymer.dart** library. Below we will show you an example of creating and using **Polymer.dart**, the framework to work with web components from Dart.

Polymer.dart

`Polymer.dart` includes the **Polymer** library (http://www.polymer-project.org/) so you can use all these latest web technologies to create your own HTML components from Dart. You can create new web components for use in your web applications like standard HTML tags. Below you can see an example of a custom web component.

`<user-login></user-login>`

With this simple tag you're displaying the user login web component with its custom styles, HTML structure, and behavior. This tag will contain HTML, CSS, and Dart code in a package. If you have worked in complex web projects and you've needed to include any framework, JavaScript library content, or even any styles sheets from another project, a big problem arises: **name collision**. For instance, your project CSS could have definitions with the same name as the CSS of any library you have added to your project. There's a solution: We have web components to solve this problem and let us enjoy more benefits, including:

- Encapsulating
- Reusing
- Data binding

You can encapsulate the structure, style, and behavior of a particular item. Also, you can reuse this element in other HTML documents, and can separate the graphic element representation from the business logic, but with data perfectly linked to flow from one side to another. That means, one change made in the interface is reflected in a data model and vice versa.

Polymer uses many of the web technologies we discussed earlier in this chapter: DOM mutation observers, HTML imports, Model-Driven Views, custom elements, and especially the Shadow DOM to let you create new web components easily from Dart. This technology allows you to isolate the components from other components to avoid name collisions and encapsulate its structure, style, and behavior.

What is the Shadow DOM?

Previously we mentioned that the Shadow DOM is one of the new HTML technologies used to create web components, but what does the Shadow DOM mean? The Shadow DOM refers to the ability of the web browser to create and include a new DOM tree node within the rendering document, not in the main DOM tree, but as a kind of sub-tree. A new element created with the Shadow DOM is called the Shadow Host and this new element's main node to host the rest is known as the Shadow Root.

Enough theory, let's see the Shadow DOM in action, in Google Chrome for example. If you point your web browser to http://jsfiddle.net/ you can see how your screen is divided into four areas where you can create HTML, CSS, JavaScript, and get the result of all this. It is a good tool for small test scripts or CSS styles, and we'll use it for the next example.

Create an HTML5 calendar input element with `type="date"` (as shown in Figure 29-1) and then click the Run button located in the top-left corner.

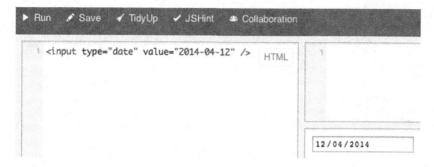

Figure 29-1. *Input date element running in jsfiddle.net*

In our example we've added a date as the default value, so an input box with the date set appears in the result panel. If you click on the input, a calendar appears to change the date. In the calendar (as you can see in Figure 29-2) you can navigate between days, weeks, months, and years. That makes the date selection easier for users.

Figure 29-2. *Calendar View*

We have created a standard HTML input element, but Google Chrome shows this great calendar when you need to pick a date. This "magic" is the Shadow DOM in action. The browser detects when we create a date input element and automatically loads the calendar.

■ **Note** We're using Google Chrome in our example because not all browsers currently offer this functionality.

Mouse over the item created in jsfiddle.net, right click, and select *Inspect element*, as shown in Figure 29-3.

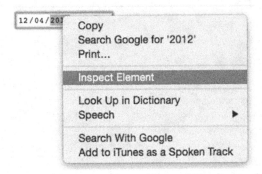

Figure 29-3. *Inspecting the element using Google Chrome DevTools*

Special panels will appear in Google Chrome showing the rendered document and the calendar element information (Figure 29-4).

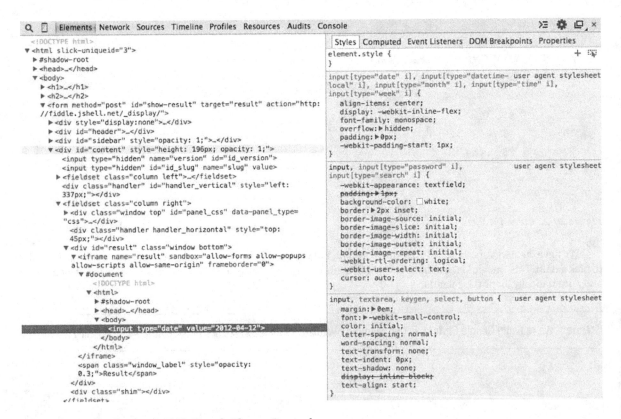

Figure 29-4. *The Shadow DOM in Google Chrome Dev tools*

Select the gear in the top-right corner. A new window will show up. Check the *Elements* ➤ *Show Shadow DOM* checkbox (Figure 29-5).

Figure 29-5. Checking Show Shadow DOM in the Google Chrome Dev tools

Once you've activated this option in the Google Chrome development tools, you'll see new options when you inspect our date input element (Figure 29-6).

```
▼<input type="date" value="2014-04-12">
  ▼#shadow-root (user-agent)
  │ ▶<div pseudo="-webkit-datetime-edit" id="date-time-edit">…</div>
  │  <div pseudo="-webkit-clear-button" id="clear"></div>
  │  <div pseudo="-webkit-inner-spin-button" id="spin"></div>
  │  <div pseudo="-webkit-calendar-picker-indicator" id="picker"></div>
  </input>
```

Figure 29-6. Inspecting our date input element with the Shadow DOM enabled

As you can see, before enabling the Shadow DOM it was just an HTML input element. Now you can see its content, and the different div elements that compose the great calendar date picker. You'll get exactly the same result when working with Polymer and Dart. A simple HTML tag and inside of that tag would be the HTML structure, CSS styles, and its behavior. Let's see how you can work with Dart and Polymer with an example of how to create custom web components.

Working with Polymer.dart

We have seen the "magic" of the Shadow DOM and we've discussed what we can do with the new HTML5 technologies. In this section we'll see an example of how to create our first element using Polymer and Dart. We have commented that Polymer.dart lets you create your own web components and use them in your HTML documents easily from Dart. So let's do a full example to see this in action and we'll see the structure and HTML tags that compose the component. This structure will be separated from the style (the CSS definitions for styling our component) and from the Dart code. The Dart code will provide functionality, event management, and data binding between interface and logic.

Before creating our custom elements, let's see how simple it is to begin with Dart and Polymer using Dart Editor. We're going to create a new Dart application as usual by clicking *Create a new Dart project* icon or selecting *File ➤ New project...* In the window, type the name of your new Polymer project and select *Sample web application using the polymer library [mobile friendly]* and click *Finish* (Figure 29-7).

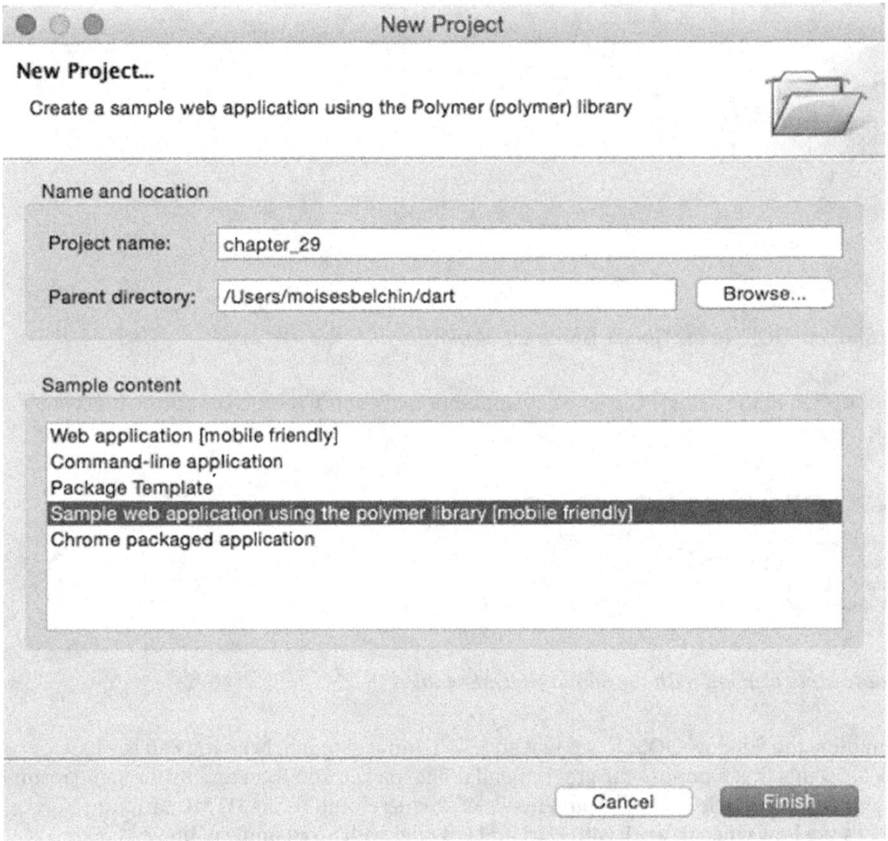

Figure 29-7. Creating our first sample polymer dart application

You can see in Figure 29-8 how Dart Editor creates all the directory structure for the new project and Pub begins to download all the necessary packages.

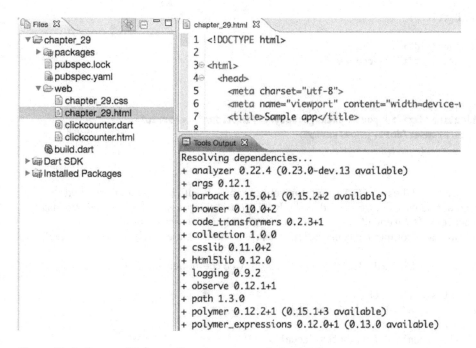

Figure 29-8. *Dart and Polymer directory structure in Dart Editor*

As you can see the directory structure is very similar to any simple web application. Dart web applications with Polymer only need more packages to run properly. Now let's see the generated code to understand a Dart Polymer application. The main file is **chapter_29.html**. As you can see below we've marked as bold the most important parts of this code.

```
<!DOCTYPE html>

<html>
  <head>
    <meta charset="utf-8">
    <meta name="viewport" content="width=device-width, initial-scale=1.0">
    <title>Sample app</title>

    <!-- include the web_components polyfills with support for Dart. -->
    <script src="packages/web_components/platform.js"></script>
    <script src="packages/web_components/dart_support.js"></script>

    <!-- import the click-counter -->
    <link rel="import" href="clickcounter.html">

    <link rel="stylesheet" href="chapter_29.css">
  </head>
```

```
<body>
  <h1>Chapter 29</h1>

  <p>Hello world from Dart!</p>

  <div id="sample_container_id">
    <click-counter count="5"></click-counter>
  </div>

  <!-- bootstrap polymer -->
  <script type="application/dart">export 'package:polymer/init.dart';</script>
  <script src="packages/browser/dart.js"></script>
</body>
</html>
```

In the header of the file we added the necessary scripts for web components with support for Dart. Then we imported our custom web components. Later we created the body HTML and structured and referenced our custom web component <click-counter>. At the end of the file you can see the scripts in charge of starting Polymer. Dart Editor has created a custom web component called <click-counter>. Let's see the clickcounter.html and clickcounter.dart files.

In the clickcounter.html file, we have the HTML structure for our web component.

```
<!-- import polymer-element's definition -->
<link rel="import" href="packages/polymer/polymer.html">

<polymer-element name="click-counter" attributes="count">
  <template>
    <style>
      div {
        font-size: 24pt;
        text-align: center;
        margin-top: 140px;
      }
      button {
        font-size: 24pt;
        margin-bottom: 20px;
      }
    </style>
    <div>
      <button on-click="{{increment}}">Click me</button><br>
      <span>(click count: {{count}})</span>
    </div>
  </template>
  <script type="application/dart" src="clickcounter.dart"></script>
</polymer-element>
```

The first part imports the required polymer package. Then we create our custom web component with the **<polymer-element>** tag with the name of our web component. Inside this tag we can find two important parts. The first one is the **<template>**. This tag will contain all the CSS styles and the HTML structure for our web component. The second one is the Dart code script tied to our web component.

In this web component we've marked as bold two important things: {{increment}} and {{count}}. The {{increment}} element is a method and it will be executed every time the user clicks the button. The {{count}} element is a variable defined alongside the {{increment}} method in the clickcounter.dart file.

The important thing here is, with those simple tags, Polymer will do data binding automatically for us. So you do not need to retrieve the button element with document.querySelector method and attach a new event handler for the onClick event. The clickcounter.dart file contains the Dart code to bring functionality to our web component.

```dart
import 'package:polymer/polymer.dart';

/**
 * A Polymer click counter element.
 */
@CustomTag('click-counter')
class ClickCounter extends PolymerElement {
  @published int count = 0;

  ClickCounter.created() : super.created() {
  }

  void increment() {
    count++;
  }
}
```

We'll import the polymer package and then we'll create our custom click-counter element with this simple code. We've created the ClickCounter class annotated as @CustomTag with the custom tag name. Every web component you define must extend from the PolymerElement class.

In our ClickCounter class we have the count variable annotated as @published, that lets Polymer data bind with the previous HTML code we've seen. We also have the default created() constructor. Finally, we can see the increment() method, which we've referenced in the clickcounter.html file. It's time to enjoy, so let's run this Polymer application to see how it works. Click on the *Run* button and you'll see how Dartium starts and shows your first Dart and Polymer application as you can see in Figure 29-9.

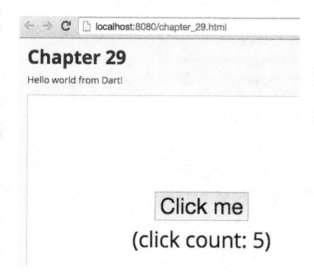

Figure 29-9. Running a Dart and Polymer application in Dartium

Click multiple times on the *Click me* button and you'll see how the text below is updated. Now that you know how to create a Dart web application with sample content using the Polymer library, we're going to create a custom web component to manage the user's access. This component will be composed of an HTML file, which will define the component's structure, as we've seen in the previous example, and CSS definitions, for styling the login system. It will look like Figure 29-10.

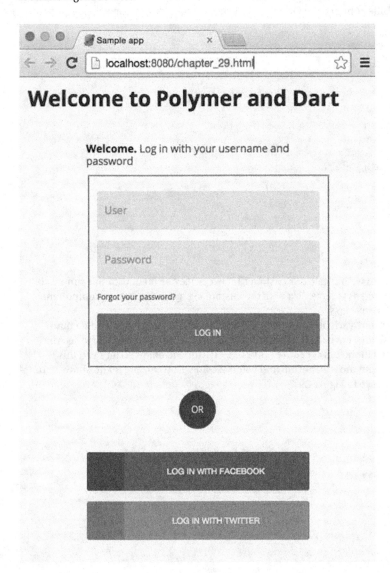

Figure 29-10. *Example of our Polymer element to manage user access*

Below you can see the code for the main HTML file for our application, the chapter_29.html file.

```
<!DOCTYPE html>

<html>
  <head>
    <meta charset="utf-8">
    <meta name="viewport" content="width=device-width, initial-scale=1.0">
    <title>Sample app</title>

    <!-- include the web_components polyfills with support for Dart. -->
    <script src="packages/web_components/platform.js"></script>
    <script src="packages/web_components/dart_support.js"></script>

    <!-- import the login-user component -->
    <link rel="import" href="login.html">

    <link rel="stylesheet" href="chapter_29.css">
  </head>
  <body>
    <h1>Welcome to Polymer and Dart</h1>

    <login-user></login-user>

    <!-- bootstrap polymer -->
    <script type="application/dart">export 'package:polymer/init.dart';</script>
    <script src="packages/browser/dart.js"></script>
  </body>
</html>
```

We've imported the login.html file that contains the HTML structure and style for our <login-user> web component. In the body of the document we've added an h1 element and our <login-user> custom element.

Let's see now how our <login-user> element is defined.

```
<!-- import polymer-element's definition -->
<link rel="import" href="packages/polymer/polymer.html">

<polymer-element name="login-user">
  <template>
    <!-- import the login-user css styles -->
    <link rel="stylesheet" href="login.css">

    <div id="login">
     <h1><strong>Welcome.</strong> <span>Log in with your username and password</span></h1>

      <template if="{{error == true}}">
       <div id="login_msg">{{login_error}}</div>
      </template>
```

```
      <fieldset>
       <p><input type="text" required id="user" name="user" placeholder="User"></p>
       <p><input type="password" required id="password" name="password" placeHolder="Password"></p>
       <p><a href="#" on-click="{{rememberPassword}}"> Forgot your password?</a></p>
       <p><button on-click="{{login}}">Log in</button></p>
      </fieldset>

      <p><span class="btn-round">or</span></p>
      <p>
       <a class="facebook-before"><span class="fontawesome-facebook"></span></a>
       <button class="facebook" on-click="{{facebookLogin}}">Log In with Facebook</button>
      </p>

      <p>
       <a class="twitter-before"><span class="fontawesome-twitter"></span></a>
       <button class="twitter" on-click="{{twitterLogin}}">Log In with Twitter</button>
      </p>
     </div>
   </template>
   <script type="application/dart" src="login.dart"></script>
 </polymer-element>
```

As you can see the first step is to import the polymer package then we define our custom element using the `<polymer-element>` special tags with the custom element name. We use the `<template>` tag to define the basis of our element template. Here we define all the necessary HTML elements that will shape our element. In this case we first place the reference to the style sheet. This will add color and style to our element. At the end of our definition we've added the link to the Dart code file script that will provide functionality to our custom element. In our element we can reference variables of our Dart application using the notation `{{variable}}`. We can also set actions attaching events in the interface with our code Dart methods using the same nomenclature and indicating the event that will execute the method.

```
<button on-click = "{{login}}"> Log in</ button>
```

When you click the *Log in* button, the `login` method of our Dart application will be executed, as discussed below. The Polymer template system allows us to iterate over our HTML structure and establish conditions, as you can see in this code block.

```
<template if="{{error}} == true">
  <div id="login_msg"> {{login_error}} </ div>
</ template>
```

In case there is an error, we'll define an error variable set to true. With the template system, we can set a condition to display a message describing the login error. Once we've defined the structure of our component and designed the actions, then we must set the style for the access system. This is the CSS code of your component.

```
/* CSS Document */
a { text-decoration: none; }

h1 { font-size: 1em; }

h1, p {
margin-bottom: 10px;
}
```

```css
span {
 color: #5a5656;
 font-weight: lighter;
}

strong {
font-weight: bold;
}

.uppercase { text-transform: uppercase; }

/* ---------- LOGIN ---------- */

#login {
margin: 50px auto;
width: 300px;
}

#login_msg {
 background: url('error.png') no-repeat #FBE3E4 5px 5px;
 padding: 1em;
 padding-left: 3.5em;
 border: 2px solid #FBC2C4;
 color: #D12F19;
}

fieldset input[type="text"], input[type="password"] {
background-color: #e5e5e5;
border: none;
border-radius: 3px;
-moz-border-radius: 3px;
-webkit-border-radius: 3px;
color: #5a5656;
font-family: 'Open Sans', Arial, Helvetica, sans-serif;
font-size: 14px;
height: 50px;
outline: none;
padding: 0px 10px;
width: 280px;
-webkit-appearance:none;
}

fieldset button {
background-color: #008dde;
border: none;
border-radius: 3px;
-moz-border-radius: 3px;
-webkit-border-radius: 3px;
color: #f4f4f4;
cursor: pointer;
font-family: 'Open Sans', Arial, Helvetica, sans-serif;
```

```
height: 50px;
text-transform: uppercase;
width: 300px;
-webkit-appearance:none;
}

fieldset a {
color: #5a5656;
font-size: 10px;
}

fieldset a:hover { text-decoration: underline; }

.btn-round {
background-color: #5a5656;
border-radius: 50%;
-moz-border-radius: 50%;
-webkit-border-radius: 50%;
color: #f4f4f4;
display: block;
font-size: 12px;
height: 50px;
line-height: 50px;
margin: 30px 125px;
text-align: center;
text-transform: uppercase;
width: 50px;
}

.facebook-before {
background-color: #0064ab;
border-radius: 3px 0px 0px 3px;
-moz-border-radius: 3px 0px 0px 3px;
-webkit-border-radius: 3px 0px 0px 3px;
color: #f4f4f4;
display: block;
float: left;
height: 50px;
line-height: 50px;
text-align: center;
width: 50px;
}

.facebook {
background-color: #0079ce;
border: none;
border-radius: 0px 3px 3px 0px;
-moz-border-radius: 0px 3px 3px 0px;
-webkit-border-radius: 0px 3px 3px 0px;
color: #f4f4f4;
cursor: pointer;
```

```
height: 50px;
text-transform: uppercase;
width: 250px;
}

.twitter-before {
background-color: #189bcb;
border-radius: 3px 0px 0px 3px;
-moz-border-radius: 3px 0px 0px 3px;
-webkit-border-radius: 3px 0px 0px 3px;
color: #f4f4f4;
display: block;
float: left;
height: 50px;
line-height: 50px;
text-align: center;
width: 50px;
}

.twitter {
background-color: #1bb2e9;
border: none;
border-radius: 0px 3px 3px 0px;
-moz-border-radius: 0px 3px 3px 0px;
-webkit-border-radius: 0px 3px 3px 0px;
color: #f4f4f4;
cursor: pointer;
height: 50px;
text-transform: uppercase;
width: 250px;
}
```

Once we've defined the structure and style of our element, we will create the controller that will handle the events and will provide functionality to our Polymer component.

This is the code of our login.dart file. We have not detailed the implementation of the methods because in this example we focus on the data binding between the variables and methods defined in the controller and interface.

```
import 'package:polymer/polymer.dart';

/**
 * A Polymer login user system.
 */
@CustomTag('login-user')
class LoginUser extends PolymerElement {
  @observable String user;
  @observable String password;
  @observable bool error = false;
  @observable String login_error = '';

  LoginUser.created() : super.created();
```

```dart
  /// Validates user name and password.
  void login() {
    if(user == null || user.trim() == '' ||
        password == null || password.trim() == '') {
      error = true;
      login_error = 'Please type user and password.';
      return;
    }
  }

  /// To remember the forgotten password.
  void rememberPassword() {}

  /// To login with Facebook.
  void facebookLogin() {}

  /// To login with Twitter.
  void twitterLogin() {}

}
```

The first thing to do is import the polymer package to create your own components.

```dart
import 'package:polymer/polymer.dart';
```

Later you must create the component name and create a class that extends from `PolymerElement`.

```dart
@CustomTag('login-user')
class LoginUser extends PolymerElement { ... }
```

All elements that inherit from `PolymerElement` have the `created()` constructor, which creates the element in our main document.

```dart
LoginUser.created() : super.created();
```

Now let's look at the instance variables and methods and how we indicate that we want them associated with the interface.

```dart
@observable String user;
@observable String password;
@observable bool error = false;
@observable String login_error = '';

  /// Validates user name and password.
  void login() {
    if(user == null || user.trim() == '' ||
        password == null || password.trim() == '') {
      error = true;
      login_error = 'Please type user and password.';
      return;
    }
  }
```

```
/// To remember the forgotten password.
void rememberPassword() {}

/// To login with Facebook.
void facebookLogin() {}

/// To login with Twitter.
void twitterLogin() {}
```

For methods we should not do anything special. You only need to create the different methods that our element will have. To use the instance variables, we must use the @observable annotation to indicate that this variable is visible and referenceable from the element. Therefore, in the HTML element definition we can use the notation {{user}}.

The real power is the *data binding*. Polymer records any change in our variables and updates bidirectionally. If the user enters the username in the box, we receive this data automatically in real time in our @observable String user; variable. Similarly if we change the value of the @observable String login_error = ''; variable this change is automatically reflected in the interface. That is possible because of the @observable annotation. That's the difference with the @published annotation, which we saw in the previous sample. With the first one data goes from Dart code to HTML element and vice versa, with the second one the data only goes from Dart to HTML.

The @published annotation means that a variable can be referenced as an attribute on the custom HTML tag we've created, such as:

```
<user-login username="xxx"></user-login>
```

We have already defined the structure of our first element; we have defined the desired design and added functionality managing actions associated with certain events of the interface. Now if you want to use this component in action, as we've done in our previous example, click on the *Run* button to see how Dartium runs our application with the <login-user> custom element. Play with this element; click the *Log in* button without the username and password as you can see in Figure 29-11.

Figure 29-11. Our login user component displaying an error message

Summary

In this chapter we have learned:

- What web components are
- What new HTML technologies they use
- What is the Shadow DOM
- How to enable the Shadow DOM in Google Chrome developer tools to see the content of web components
- How to use Dart Editor to create a sample Dart web application with the Polymer library
- How to create custom web components
- How to create the HTML structure for web components
- How to style your components both inline and in referenced CSS files
- How to create controllers for your custom elements

■ ■ ■

CHAPTER 30

Developing a Dart App

We're at the final chapter of the book and it's time to roll up our sleeves and develop a complete application with Dart using everything we've learned. In this chapter we're going to develop a Dart web application using the Polymer library, Google Maps, and IndexedDb. With these tools we're going to develop an application to manage your contacts. We're going to use some classes we developed in previous chapters such as the idbContacts class developed in Chapter 23. In this final chapter we want you to use everything you know about Dart so we're going to use asynchronous programming, Future objects, abstract classes, maps, polymer, and other pub packages. Now, let's merge all this knowledge and see how we can create a practical Dart web application.

Designing the Application

Your new applications let you manage your contacts with their information. So you can add new contacts, and edit or delete existing contacts. Your contacts will be stored in IndexedDb inside the browser using the lawndart pub package.

You can view their locations with Google Maps using google_maps pub package. You'll use HTML and CSS to create the interface of the application. You'll use the Polymer library to create the web components required in this application and you're going to use the Bootstrap HTML, CSS, and JavaScript framework (http://getbootstrap.com) to style your web components.

Although this amazing framework lets us use a lot of components and JavaScript, we're only interested in the HTML and CSS part. In Figure 30-1 we show you a brief schema of your new application. The application will query the database to get a list of the existing contacts. It lets you add new contacts to the IndexedDb browser database, and delete or modify any of them. It also will use the database to search for contacts and with their address will retrieve the exact map using Google Maps.

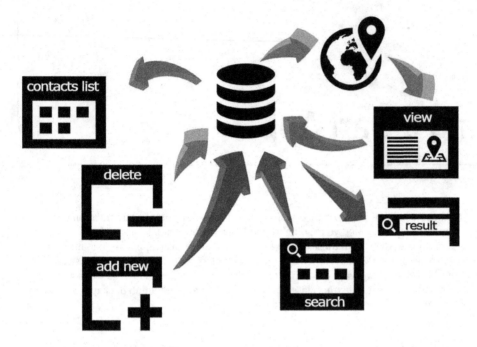

Figure 30-1. *Brief application schema*

Creating the Application

The first step will be to open Dart Editor and create a new Dart web application using the Polymer library as you can see in Figure 30-2.

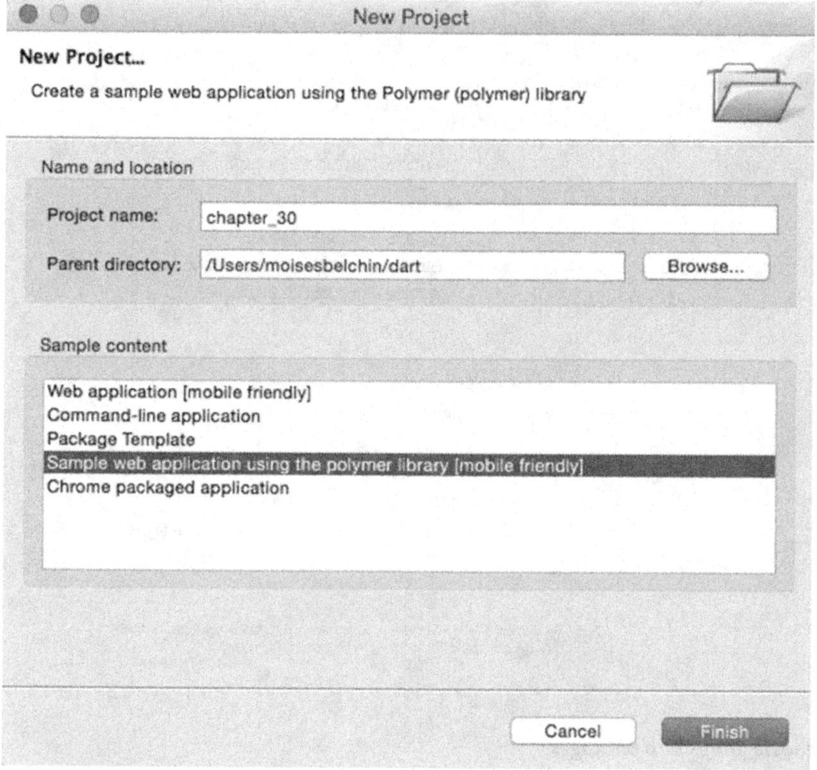

Figure 30-2. *Creating the project*

We've decided to call it chapter_30 but you can change the name if you wish. By default Dart Editor has created the chapter_30.html, chapter_30.css, clickcounter.html, and clickcounter.css files. You can delete chapter_30.css, clickcounter.html, and clickcounter.css because we won't use them. As we mentioned above we're going to use the Bootstrap CSS framework to style our application and we'll create our own web components.

Next we will add the necessary pub packages for this application. So you must add lawndart and google_maps as you can see in Figure 30-3. The Polymer library is already added by default because you used the Polymer library when you created the project.

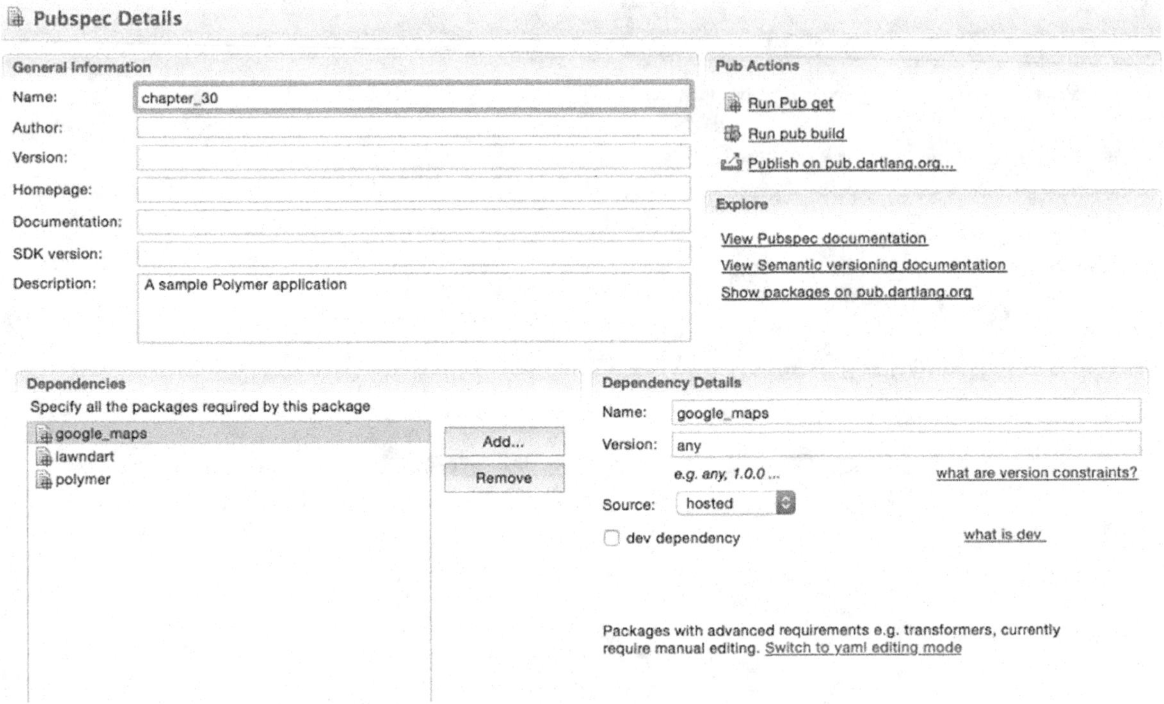

Pubspec Details

General Information

Name:	chapter_30
Author:	
Version:	
Homepage:	
Documentation:	
SDK version:	
Description:	A sample Polymer application

Pub Actions

- Run Pub get
- Run pub build
- Publish on pub.dartlang.org...

Explore

- View Pubspec documentation
- View Semantic versioning documentation
- Show packages on pub.dartlang.org

Dependencies

Specify all the packages required by this package

- google_maps
- lawndart
- polymer

Add...
Remove

Dependency Details

Name:	google_maps
Version:	any
	e.g. any, 1.0.0 ... what are version constraints?
Source:	hosted
	☐ dev dependency what is dev

Packages with advanced requirements e.g. transformers, currently require manual editing. Switch to yaml editing mode

Figure 30-3. Adding lawndart and google_maps pub packages

Coding the Application

This will be our chapter_30.html main file application.

```
<!DOCTYPE html>
<html>
  <head>
    <meta charset="utf-8">
    <meta name="viewport" content="width=device-width, initial-scale=1.0">
    <link rel="stylesheet" href="https://maxcdn.bootstrapcdn.com/bootstrap/3.2.0/css/bootstrap.min.css">
    <title>My Contacts!</title>

    <!-- include the web_components polyfills with support for Dart. -->
    <script src="packages/web_components/platform.js"></script>
    <script src="packages/web_components/dart_support.js"></script>

    <!-- import the web components -->
    <link rel="import" href="my_contacts.html">
  </head>
```

```
  <body>
    <my-contacts></my-contacts>

    <!-- bootstrap polymer -->
    <script type="application/dart">export 'package:polymer/init.dart';</script>
    <script src="http://maps.googleapis.com/maps/api/js?sensor=false"></script>
    <script src="packages/browser/dart.js"></script>
  </body>
</html>
```

In the header of this file we've added the Bootstrap CSS style link and we've imported our my_contacts.html web component to use it in the HTML body. At the end of the file we've added the link for the Google Maps API. Let's see how our my_contacts.html file looks. This is the main Polymer element, which will build the application interface. This Polymer element will use other web components, for example, to add or edit contacts. In Figure 30-4 you can see how our application will look.

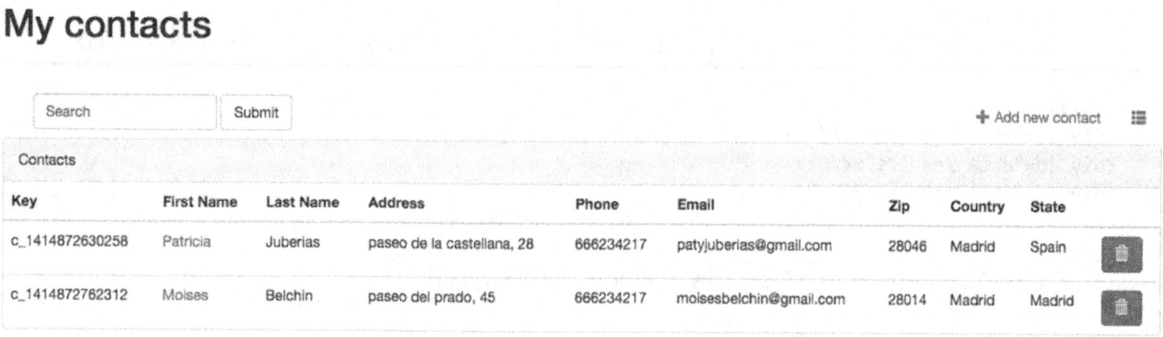

My contacts

Key	First Name	Last Name	Address	Phone	Email	Zip	Country	State	
c_1414872630258	Patricia	Juberias	paseo de la castellana, 28	666234217	patyjuberias@gmail.com	28046	Madrid	Spain	
c_1414872762312	Moises	Belchin	paseo del prado, 45	666234217	moisesbelchin@gmail.com	28014	Madrid	Madrid	

Figure 30-4. *Application interface*

Below we'll show you the my_contacts.html file, which will contain the HTML and CSS structure for our main web component.

```
<!-- import polymer-element's definition -->
<link rel="import" href="packages/polymer/polymer.html">

<!-- import web components -->
<link rel="import" href="grid.html">
<link rel="import" href="add.html">

<polymer-element name="my-contacts">
  <template>
    <link rel="stylesheet" href="https://maxcdn.bootstrapcdn.com/bootstrap/3.2.0/css/bootstrap.min.css">

    <div class="container"><br/>
      <button type="button" class="navbar-toggle collapsed" data-toggle="collapse"
      data-target="#bs-example-navbar-collapse-1">
      <span class="sr-only">Toggle navigation</span>
        <span class="icon-bar"></span>
        <span class="icon-bar"></span>
        <span class="icon-bar"></span>
      </button>
```

```
      <div class="page-header">
        <h1>My contacts</h1>
      </div>
    </div>

    <div class="container">
    <div class="collapse navbar-collapse" id="bs-example-navbar-collapse-1">
      <div class="navbar-form navbar-left" role="search">
        <div class="form-group">
          <input type="text" class="form-control" placeholder="Search"
            on-keyup="{{handle_search_input}}" value="{{search_term}}">
        </div>
        <button class="btn btn-default" on-click="{{search}}">Submit</button>
      </div>
      <ul class="nav navbar-nav navbar-right">
        <li><a on-click="{{add}}"><span class="glyphicon glyphicon-plus"></span> Add new
          contact</a></li>
        <li><a on-click="{{list}}"><span class="glyphicon glyphicon-th-list"></span> </a></li>
      </ul>
    </div>
    <div id="info_results"></div>
    <div id="data_results"></div>
    <div id="data_form"></div>
    </div>
  </template>
  <script type="application/dart" src="my_contacts.dart"></script>
</polymer-element>
```

We've imported the polymer package and two additional web components: we're going to show the grid with the contacts information using grid.html and add new contacts or edit the existing contacts in the database using add.html.

We've created the structure for this component and added the variables or methods using the {{variable_or_method}} template notation. At the end of the file we've added the Dart file script for this component, my_contacts.dart.

We're going to show you the different parts of the my_contacts.dart file. The first part is all the required packages, classes, and additional web components.

```
import 'dart:html';
import 'package:polymer/polymer.dart';
import 'contacts.dart';
import 'grid.dart';
import 'add.dart';
```

Once we've imported everything we will use we're going to create the Polymer element with its instance variables, constructor method, and the special method **attached**. The Polymer library executes this method once the web component is inserted in the DOM.

Every custom element in Polymer has a constructor and three life-cycle methods that can be overridden:

- CustomElement.created(). The constructor used when creating an instance of a custom element.

- attached(). Called when an instance of a custom element is inserted into the DOM.

- detached(). Called when an instance of a custom element is removed from the DOM.

- attributeChanged(). Called when an attribute, such as class, of an instance of the custom element is added, changed, or removed.

```dart
/**
 * Contacts application.
 */
@CustomTag('my-contacts')
class MyContacts extends PolymerElement {

  /// IndexedDb idbContacts object.
  idbContacts idbC;
  /// search term.
  @observable String search_term = '';
  /// contacts in database
  Map contacts;
  /// results div container.
  DivElement data_results;
  DivElement info_results;
  DivElement data_form;

  /// constructor
  MyContacts.created() : super.created();

  /// void attached
  void attached() {
    super.attached();
    data_results = shadowRoot.querySelector('#data_results');
    info_results = shadowRoot.querySelector('#info_results');
    data_form = shadowRoot.querySelector('#data_form');
    idbC = new idbContacts();
    list();
  }
}
```

In the attached method we retrieve some HTML elements we'll use later. To accomplish this task we must use shadowRoot.querySelector instead of document.querySelector because we're located inside a Shadow DOM element. After that we create the idbContacts object we'll use in this component and execute the list method.

```dart
/// list existing contacts in database
  void list() {
    idbC.list().then((results) {
      contacts = results;
      grid();
    });
  }
```

413

The list method is in charge of querying the IndexedDb to get all the existing contacts and then calling the grid method to show the grid web component. Now we've created the methods necessary for the search functions. handle_search_input is executed whenever the user types a character in the search input text box. The search method is executed to query the browser database to look for contacts with the typed term.

```dart
/// Handles onKeyUp events in search input text.
  void handle_search_input(KeyboardEvent e) {
    if(e.keyCode == KeyCode.ENTER) {
      search();
    }
    if(search_term.trim().isEmpty) {
      info_results
        ..nodes.clear()
        ..classes.clear();
      list();
    }
  }


  /// Perform the search.
  void search() {
    if(search_term.trim().isNotEmpty) {
      idbC.search(search_term.trim().toLowerCase()).then((results) {
        if(results.length <= 0) {
          data_results.nodes.clear();
          contacts.clear();
          _show_info_results();
        } else {
          data_results.nodes.clear();
          contacts = results;
          _show_info_results();
          grid();
        }
      });
    }
  }
```

At the end of this file you can find the grid, add, and _show_info_results methods.

```dart
/// Display data as grid
  void grid() {
    ShowGrid grid = new Element.tag('show-grid');
    grid.contacts = contacts;
    data_form.style.display = 'none';
    data_results
      ..style.display = 'block'
      ..nodes.clear()
      ..nodes.add(grid);
  }
```

The grid method is used to instantiate the show-grid Polymer element with the contacts found in the browser database and to show the grid.

```
/// Display the add new contacts form.
void add() {
  AddContact add = new Element.tag('add-contact');
  data_results.style.display = 'none';
  data_form
    ..style.display = 'block'
    ..nodes.clear()
    ..nodes.add(add);
}
```

The add method is used to instantiate the add-contact Polymer element, which it displays to add new contacts to the IndexedDb database.

```
/// Show info results
void _show_info_results() {
  if(contacts.length <=0) {
    info_results
      ..nodes.clear()
      ..classes = ['alert', 'alert-warning']
      ..setInnerHtml('No matches found');
  } else {
    info_results
      ..nodes.clear()
      ..classes = ['alert', 'alert-info']
      ..setInnerHtml('Found ${contacts.length} reg(s)');
  }
}
```

The helper method _show_info_results is used to display a message informing the user if results were found or not, as you can see in Figures 30-5 and 30-6.

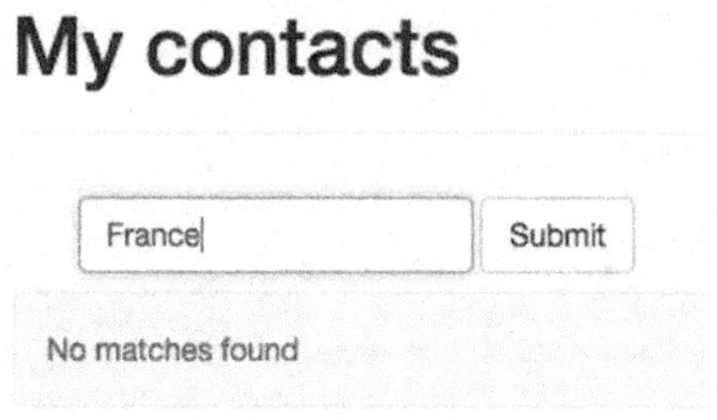

My contacts

| France| | Submit |

No matches found

Figure 30-5. *Information message after failed search*

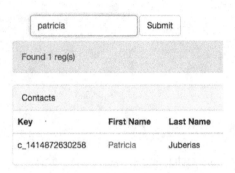

Figure 30-6. *Information message after successful search*

This is the entire my_contacts.dart file.

```dart
import 'dart:html';
import 'package:polymer/polymer.dart';
import 'contacts.dart';
import 'grid.dart';
import 'add.dart';

/**
 * Contacts application.
 */
@CustomTag('my-contacts')
class MyContacts extends PolymerElement {

  /// IndexedDb idbContacts object.
  idbContacts idbC;
  /// search term.
  @observable String search_term = '';
  /// contacts in database
  Map contacts;
  /// results div container.
  DivElement data_results;
  DivElement info_results;
  DivElement data_form;

  /// constructor
  MyContacts.created() : super.created();

  /// void attached
  void attached() {
    super.attached();
    data_results = shadowRoot.querySelector('#data_results');
    info_results = shadowRoot.querySelector('#info_results');
```

```
    data_form = shadowRoot.querySelector('#data_form');
    idbC = new idbContacts();
    list();
  }

  /// list existing contacts in database
  void list() {
    idbC.list().then((results) {
      contacts = results;
      grid();
    });
  }

  /// Handles onKeyUp events in search input text.
  void handle_search_input(KeyboardEvent e) {
    if(e.keyCode == KeyCode.ENTER) {
      search();
    }
    if(search_term.trim().isEmpty) {
      info_results
        ..nodes.clear()
        ..classes.clear();
      list();
    }
  }

  /// Perform the search.
  void search() {
    if(search_term.trim().isNotEmpty) {
      idbC.search(search_term.trim().toLowerCase()).then((results) {
        if(results.length <= 0) {
          data_results.nodes.clear();
          contacts.clear();
          _show_info_results();
        } else {
          data_results.nodes.clear();
          contacts = results;
          _show_info_results();
          grid();
        }
      });
    }
  }

  /// Display data as grid
  void grid() {
    ShowGrid grid = new Element.tag('show-grid');
    grid.contacts = contacts;
    data_form.style.display = 'none';
```

```
      data_results
        ..style.display = 'block'
        ..nodes.clear()
        ..nodes.add(grid);
   }

  /// Display the add new contacts form.
  void add() {
    AddContact add = new Element.tag('add-contact');
    data_results.style.display = 'none';
    data_form
      ..style.display = 'block'
      ..nodes.clear()
      ..nodes.add(add);
  }

  /// Show info results
  void _show_info_results() {
    if(contacts.length <=0) {
      info_results
        ..nodes.clear()
        ..classes = ['alert', 'alert-warning']
        ..setInnerHtml('No matches found');
    } else {
      info_results
        ..nodes.clear()
        ..classes = ['alert', 'alert-info']
        ..setInnerHtml('Found ${contacts.length} reg(s)');
    }
  }
 }
}
```

Before we show the rest of our web components we're going to show you the contacts.dart file. This file is very familiar to you because it's almost the same as the one we developed in Chapter 23. This file contains the abstract class and the concrete class to manage contacts in the IndexedDb database and to get the Google Map associated with the contact's addresses.

```
library idb_contacts;
import 'dart:async';
import 'dart:html';
import 'dart:math';
import 'package:lawndart/lawndart.dart';
import 'package:google_maps/google_maps.dart';

/// Abstract class to manage contacts.
abstract class Contacts {
  /// Creates a new contact.
  /// It'll return the new contact ID.
  Future add(Map data);
```

```dart
  /// Updates an existing contact.
  Future update(var id, Map data);

  /// Deletes an existing contact.
  Future delete(var id);

  /// Gets data for a given contact id.
  Future get(var id);

  /// Lists the existing contacts.
  Future list();

  /// Search for contacts,
  Future search(String query);

  /// Gets map from contact location.
  Future map(String address, String container);
}

/// Concrete class to manage contacts stored in browser using IndexedDb.
/// This class requires lawndart package.
/// https://pub.dartlang.org/packages/lawndart
class idbContacts extends Contacts {

  /// IndexedDb database object.
  IndexedDbStore _db;
  /// Database name.
  String _dbName;
  /// Database table name.
  String _tableName;

  /// Constructor.
  idbContacts([String dbName='idbContacts', String tableName='contacts']) {
    _dbName = dbName;
    _tableName = tableName;
    _db = new IndexedDbStore(_dbName, _tableName);
  }

  /// Delete all the information in the DB
  Future dropDB() {
    return _db.open().then((_) => _db.nuke());
  }

  /// Creates a new contact.
  Future add(Map data) {
    var now = new DateTime.now().millisecondsSinceEpoch;
    var rand = new Random().nextDouble().toString().split('.')[1].substring(0, 10);
    var id = 'c_$now$rand';
    return _db.open().then((_) => _db.save(data, id));
  }
```

```dart
/// Updates an existing contact.
Future update(String id, Map data) {
  return _db.open().then((_) => _db.save(data, id));
}

/// Deletes an existing contact.
Future delete(String id) {
  return _db.open().then((_) => _db.removeByKey(id));
}

/// Gets data for a given contact.
Future get(String id) {
  return _db.open().then((_) => _db.getByKey(id));
}

/// Lists the existing contacts.
Future<Map> list() {
  var results = {};
  var c = new Completer();
  _db.open().then((_) {
    _db.keys().listen((key) {
      results[key] = _db.getByKey(key);
    }, onDone: () => Future.wait(results.values).then((vals) {
      var i = 0;
      results.forEach((k, v) {
        results[k] = vals[i];
        i++;
      });
      c.complete(results);
    }));
  });
  return c.future;
}

/// Search for contacts.
Future<Map> search(String query) {
  var matches = {};
  var c = new Completer();
  list().then((results) {
    results.forEach((k, v) {
      v.values.forEach((f) {
        if(f.toString().toLowerCase().contains(query.toLowerCase())) {
          matches[k] = v;
        }
      });
    });
    c.complete(matches);
  });
  return c.future;
}
```

```dart
Future map(String address, var element) {
  var c = new Completer();
  var req = new GeocoderRequest();
  req.address = address;
  new Geocoder().geocode(req, (results, status) {
    // Get lat,long for the address geocoder
    var latlng = results[0].geometry.location;
    final coords = new LatLng(latlng.lat, latlng.lng);
    // Map
    final mapOptions = new MapOptions()
      ..zoom = 18
      ..center = coords
      ..mapTypeId = MapTypeId.ROADMAP;
    final map = new GMap(element, mapOptions);
    // Marker
    final markerOptions = new MarkerOptions()
      ..position = coords
      ..map = map
      ..title = address;
    final marker = new Marker(markerOptions);
    // complete the future.
    c.complete(true);
  });
  return c.future;
}
}
```

We're going to show you the show-grid Polymer element we mentioned above in the my_contacts.dart file. In common with every Polymer element, show-grid has two files: grid.html for the component's structure and grid.dart for its functionality.

```html
<!-- import polymer-element's definition -->
<link rel="import" href="packages/polymer/polymer.html">

<!-- import web components -->
<link rel="import" href="add.html">

<polymer-element name="show-grid">
  <template>
    <link rel="stylesheet" href="https://maxcdn.bootstrapcdn.com/bootstrap/3.2.0/css/bootstrap.min.css">

    <div id="grid_result" style="display:none;" class="alert alert-success">Contact deleted
    successfully</div>

    <div id="del_alert" class="alert alert-danger alert-dismissible fade in" role="alert"
    style="display:none">
      <button type="button" on-click="{{alert_close}}" class="close" data-dismiss="alert">
       <span aria-hidden="true">×</span><span class="sr-only">Close</span></button>
      <h4>You're going to delete this item</h4>
      <p>Are you sure you want to delete this item ?</p>
```

```html
      <p>
        <button type="button" on-click="{{alert_accept}}" class="btn btn-danger">Yes,
          delete it!</button>
        <button type="button" on-click="{{alert_cancel}}" class="btn btn-default">Nope</button>
      </p>
  </div>

  <template if="{{contacts.keys.length <= 0}}">
    <h2>No contacts found</h2>
    <p> User + Add new contact button to create new contacts in your database </p>
  </template>

  <template if="{{contacts.keys.length > 0}}">
  <div class="panel panel-default">
    <div class="panel-heading">Contacts</div>
    <table class="table">
      <thead>
        <tr>
          <th>Key</th>
          <th>First Name </th>
          <th>Last Name</th>
          <th>Address</th>
          <th>Phone</th>
          <th>Email</th>
          <th>Zip</th>
          <th>Country</th>
          <th>State</th>
          <th></th>
        </tr>
      </thead>
      <tbody>
        <tr template repeat="{{k in contacts.keys}}" id="tr_{{k}}">
          <td>{{k}}</td>
          <td><a on-click="{{edit}}" id="edi_{{k}}">{{contacts[k]['fname']}}</a></td>
          <td>{{contacts[k]['lname']}}</td>
          <td>{{contacts[k]['address']}}</td>
          <td>{{contacts[k]['phone']}}</td>
          <td>{{contacts[k]['email']}}</td>
          <td>{{contacts[k]['zip']}}</td>
          <td>{{contacts[k]['city']}}</td>
          <td>{{contacts[k]['country']}}</td>
          <td><button class="btn btn-primary" id="del_{{k}}" on-click="{{delete}}">
            <span class="glyphicon glyphicon-trash"></span></button></td>
        </tr>
      </tbody>
    </table>
  </div>
  </template>

</template>
<script type="application/dart" src="grid.dart"></script>
</polymer-element>
```

In grid.html, we've imported the required polymer package and the other web components we'll use inside it. Then we've added the necessary CSS and created the HTML structure. At the end we've added the Dart code script. The most important part of this file is the use of <template if> tags to add conditions and the <template repeat> tag to create the grid. With these blocks of code we'll show a message if it's the first time the application has run.

```
<template if="{{contacts.keys.length <= 0}}">
  <h2>No contacts found</h2>
  <p> User + Add new contact button to create new contacts in your database </p>
</template>
```

With these, we build the table element with the results found. In this case the **template repeat** part is inside the tr element. This is a special behavior of the Polymer library to repeat tr elements for each element in our contact results map.

```
<table class="table">
  <thead>
    <tr>
      <th>Key</th>
      <th>First Name </th>
      <th>Last Name</th>
      <th>Address</th>
      <th>Phone</th>
      <th>Email</th>
      <th>Zip</th>
      <th>Country</th>
      <th>State</th>
      <th></th>
    </tr>
  </thead>
  <tbody>
    <tr template repeat="{{k in contacts.keys}}" id="tr_{{k}}">
      <td>{{k}}</td>
      <td><a on-click="{{edit}}" id="edi_{{k}}">{{contacts[k]['fname']}}</a></td>
      <td>{{contacts[k]['lname']}}</td>
      <td>{{contacts[k]['address']}}</td>
      <td>{{contacts[k]['phone']}}</td>
      <td>{{contacts[k]['email']}}</td>
      <td>{{contacts[k]['zip']}}</td>
      <td>{{contacts[k]['city']}}</td>
      <td>{{contacts[k]['country']}}</td>
      <td><button class="btn btn-primary" id="del_{{k}}" on-click="{{delete}}">
        <span class="glyphicon glyphicon-trash"></span></button></td>
    </tr>
  </tbody>
</table>
```

Now, we'll see the grid.dart file. As you know the first step will be to import the required packages and components and create the custom web component with its instance variables and methods.

```dart
library show_grid;
import 'package:polymer/polymer.dart';
import 'dart:html';
import 'contacts.dart';
import 'add.dart';

/**
 * Display contacts as grid.
 */
@CustomTag('show-grid')
class ShowGrid extends PolymerElement {

  /// list of contacts
  @observable Map contacts;
  /// selected item.
  var item;
  /// alert div element
  DivElement alert;
  DivElement grid_result;
  /// IndexedDb contacts object
  idbContacts idbC;

  /// constructor
  ShowGrid.created() : super.created();

  void attached() {
    super.attached();
    idbC = new idbContacts();
    alert = shadowRoot.querySelector('#del_alert');
    grid_result = shadowRoot.querySelector('#grid_result');
  }

  /// Edit contacts
  void edit(Event event, var detail, var target) {
    item = target.id.replaceAll('edi_', '');
    AddContact edit = new Element.tag('add-contact');
    edit.edit = true;
    edit.item = item;
    this.parent.parent.querySelector('#data_form')
      ..style.display = 'block'
      ..nodes.clear()
      ..nodes.add(edit);
    this.parent.style.display = 'none';
  }

  /// Delete a contact
  void delete(Event event, var detail, var target) {
    item = target.id.replaceAll('del_', '');
    alert.style.display = 'block';
  }
```

```
/// alert close
void alert_close() => alert_cancel();

/// alert cancel action
void alert_cancel() {
  item = null;
  alert.style.display = 'none';
}

/// alert accept action and delete item
void alert_accept() {
  idbC.delete(item).then((_) {
    contacts.remove(item);
    shadowRoot.querySelector('#tr_${item}').remove();
    grid_result.style.display = 'block';
    alert.style.display = 'none';
  });
}

}
```

After that, we used the attached method to initialize some variables and objects and retrieve the alert div element, which is an additional div element to confirm when a contact is going to be deleted. For this reason we've created **alert_close**, **alert_cancel**, and **alert_accept** methods.

The alert_close and alert_cancel methods make the alert div element disappear. alert_accept is executed when the user clicks on accept to permanently delete the selected item. This method will execute the idbContacts.delete method and after the delete operation will display a success message as you can see in Figures 30-7 and 30-8.

My contacts

Contacts									
Key	First Name	Last Name	Address	Phone	Email	Zip	Country	State	
c_1414872630258	Patricia	Juberias	paseo de la castellana, 28	666234217	patyjuberias@gmail.com	28046	Madrid	Spain	🗑
c_1414872762312	Moises	Belchin	paseo del prado, 45	666234217	moisesbelchin@gmail.com	28014	Madrid	Madrid	🗑
c_1414936137734	Peter	Smith							🗑

Figure 30-7. Clicking the delete button on one item and displaying the confirm element

My contacts

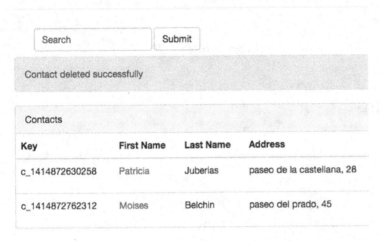

Figure 30-8. *Displaying the success message after item deletion*

As you can see below, the edit method on the show-grid Polymer element is executed when the user clicks on the contact's name. This method retrieves the item key, instantiates the AddContact Polymer element, and shows it in the corresponding HTML element.

```
/// Edit contacts
  void edit(Event event, var detail, var target) {
    item = target.id.replaceAll('edi_', '');
    AddContact edit = new Element.tag('add-contact');
    edit.edit = true;
    edit.item = item;
    this.parent.parent.querySelector('#data_form')
      ..style.display = 'block'
      ..nodes.clear()
      ..nodes.add(edit);
    this.parent.style.display = 'none';
  }
```

Let's see the final custom web component **add-contact** developed to create new contacts in the database, as you can see in Figure 30-9.

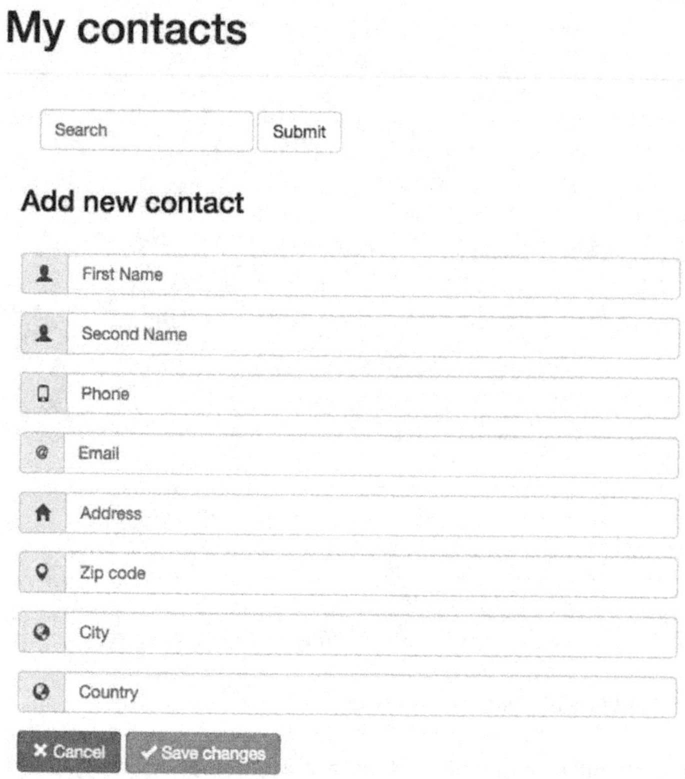

My contacts

Search   Submit

Add new contact

First Name

Second Name

Phone

Email

Address

Zip code

City

Country

✗ Cancel   ✓ Save changes

Figure 30-9. Component to add new contacts to the browser database

This component is also used to edit an existing contact in the database and to show the Google Map of the contact's address (Figure 30-10).

My contacts

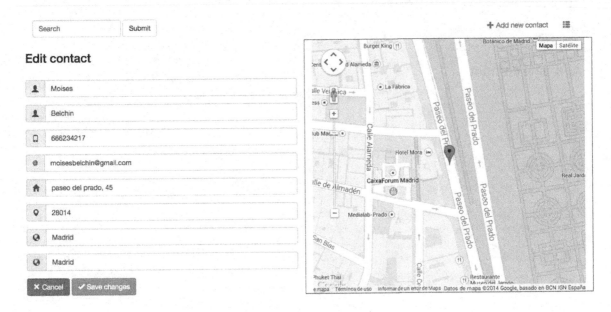

Figure 30-10. *Displaying contact's information and address location*

The `add.html` file will contain the HTML structure and two conditions, `<template if="{{edit==false}}">` to display some parts depending on whether we're adding a new contact or `<template if="{{edit==true}}">` if we are editing an existing one:

```
<!-- import polymer-element's definition -->
<link rel="import" href="packages/polymer/polymer.html">

<polymer-element name="add-contact">
  <template>
    <link rel="stylesheet" href="https://maxcdn.bootstrapcdn.com/bootstrap/3.2.0/css/bootstrap.min.css">

    <div class="container">
      <div class="row">

        <div class="col-xs-12 col-sm-6 col-md-6 col-lg-6">
          <template if="{{edit==false}}">
          <h3>Add new contact</h3><br/>
          </template>

          <template if="{{edit==true}}">
          <h3>Edit contact</h3><br/>
          </template>
```

```
<div id="info" class="alert" style="display:none;"></div>

<form role="form" action="#">
  <div class="form-group">
    <div class="input-group">
      <div class="input-group-addon"><span class="glyphicon glyphicon-user"></span> </div>
      <input class="form-control" name="fname" id="fname" value="{{fname}}" type="text"
      placeholder="First Name" required autofocus>
    </div>
  </div>
  <div class="form-group">
    <div class="input-group">
      <div class="input-group-addon"><span class="glyphicon glyphicon-user"></span> </div>
      <input class="form-control" name="lname" id="lname" value="{{lname}}" type="text"
      placeholder="Second Name">
    </div>
  </div>
  <div class="form-group">
    <div class="input-group">
      <div class="input-group-addon"><span class="glyphicon glyphicon-phone"></span> </div>
      <input class="form-control" name="phone" id="phone" value="{{phone}}" type="text"
      placeholder="Phone">
    </div>
  </div>
  <div class="form-group">
    <div class="input-group">
      <div class="input-group-addon">@</div>
      <input class="form-control" name="contact-email" id="email" value="{{email}}"
      type="email" placeholder="Email">
    </div>
  </div>
   <div class="form-group">
    <div class="input-group">
      <div class="input-group-addon"><span class="glyphicon glyphicon-home"></span> </div>
      <input class="form-control" name="address" id="address" value="{{address}}"
      type="text" placeholder="Address">
    </div>
  </div>
  <div class="form-group">
    <div class="input-group">
      <div class="input-group-addon"><span class="glyphicon glyphicon-map-marker"></span> </div>
      <input class="form-control" name="zip" id="zip" value="{{zip}}" type="text"
      placeholder="Zip code">
    </div>
  </div>
  <div class="form-group">
    <div class="input-group">
      <div class="input-group-addon"><span class="glyphicon glyphicon-globe"></span> </div>
      <input class="form-control" name="city" id="city" value="{{city}}" type="text"
      placeholder="City">
    </div>
  </div>
```

```
                <div class="form-group">
                  <div class="input-group">
                    <div class="input-group-addon"><span class="glyphicon glyphicon-globe"></span> </div>
                    <input class="form-control" name="country" id="country" value="{{country}}"
                      type="text" placeholder="Country">
                  </div>
                </div>

                  <a type="button" class="btn btn-danger" on-click="{{cancel}}"><span class="glyphicon
                    glyphicon-remove"></span> Cancel</a>
                  <a class="btn btn-success" on-click="{{save}}"><span class="glyphicon glyphicon-ok">
                    </span> Save changes</a>
              </form>
            </div>

            <template if="{{edit==true}}">
            <div class="col-xs-12 col-sm-6 col-md-6 col-lg-6" style="min-height:500px; border:1px solid #000;">
              <div id="contact_map" style="height:500px;"></div>
            </div>
            </template>

          </div>
        </div>

      </template>
      <script type="application/dart" src="add.dart"></script>
</polymer-element>
```

In this file we've defined the HTML structure of the form fields used to add or edit contacts. If we're editing a contact we also show the Google Maps result of the address location. At the end we've added the Dart code file script.

The add.dart file provides functionality to the add-contact Polymer element. As usual in the first part we define the imports and the AddContact class for this Polymer element with its instance variables, constructor method, and the rest of the methods. Below you can find the code for the add.dart file.

```
library add_contact;
import 'package:polymer/polymer.dart';
import 'dart:html';
import 'contacts.dart';
import 'dart:async';

/**
 * Display contacts as block.
 */
@CustomTag('add-contact')
class AddContact extends PolymerElement {

  /// Define if we're adding or editing a contact.
  @observable bool edit = false;

  /// Item to be edited.
  @observable var item;
```

```dart
/// observable fields
@observable String fname = '';
@observable String lname = '';
@observable String phone = '';
@observable String email = '';
@observable String address = '';
@observable String zip = '';
@observable String city = '';
@observable String country = '';

/// info result div element
DivElement info;
/// IndexedDb contacts object
idbContacts idbC;

/// constructor
AddContact.created() : super.created();

void attached() {
  super.attached();
  idbC = new idbContacts();
  info = shadowRoot.querySelector('#info');
  if(edit == true && item != null) {
    idbC.get(item).then((c) {
      fname = c['fname'];
      lname = c['lname'];
      phone = c['phone'];
      email = c['email'];
      address = c['address'];
      zip = c['zip'];
      city = c['city'];
      country = c['country'];

      var full_address = '$address, $zip, $city, $country';
      if(full_address.trim().isNotEmpty) {
        idbC.map(full_address, shadowRoot.querySelector('#contact_map'));
      }

    });
  }
}

/// saves changes
void save() {

  if(fname.isEmpty) {
    info
      ..classes = ['alert', 'alert-danger']
      ..style.display = 'block'
      ..setInnerHtml('Please, type First name for the contact');
    _hide_info();
    return;
  }
```

```dart
    var data = {
      'fname': fname,
      'lname': lname,
      'phone': phone,
      'email': email,
      'address': address,
      'zip': zip,
      'city': city,
      'country': country
    };
    if(edit == false) {
      idbC.add(data).then((id) {
        info
        ..classes = ['alert', 'alert-success']
        ..style.display = 'block'
        ..setInnerHtml('Contact saved successfully!');
        _cleanup();
        _hide_info();
      });
    } else {
      idbC.update(item, data).then((_) {
        info
          ..classes = ['alert', 'alert-success']
          ..style.display = 'block'
          ..setInnerHtml('Contact saved successfully!');
          _hide_info();
      });
    }
  }

  /// cancel adding new contact
  void cancel() {
    (this.parentNode as Element)
      ..style.display = 'none'
      ..previousElementSibling.style.display = 'block';
  }

  /// cleanup form
  void _cleanup() {
    fname = '';
    lname = '';
    phone = '';
    email = '';
    address = '';
    zip = '';
    city = '';
    country = '';
  }
```

```
/// hide info after 4 seconds
void _hide_info({int seconds: 4}) {
  new Timer.periodic(new Duration(seconds:seconds), (t) {
    info.style.display = 'none';
    t.cancel();
  });
}
```
}

The following method is executed when the Polymer element is loaded into the DOM and we take advantage of it to make the declarations and first actions.

```
void attached() {
    super.attached();
    idbC = new idbContacts();
    info = shadowRoot.querySelector('#info');
    if(edit == true && item != null) {
      idbC.get(item).then((c) {
        fname = c['fname'];
        lname = c['lname'];
        phone = c['phone'];
        email = c['email'];
        address = c['address'];
        zip = c['zip'];
        city = c['city'];
        country = c['country'];

        var full_address = '$address, $zip, $city, $country';
        if(full_address.trim().isNotEmpty) {
          idbC.map(full_address, shadowRoot.querySelector('#contact_map'));
        }

      });
    }
  }
```

If we're editing an existing contact we retrieve its information from the database to show in the form fields. In addition we execute the idbContacts.map function to get the Google Map of its address. In our add or edit contact form we have two buttons: one used to cancel the action and another one to save the information in the database. The cancel method is attached to the onClick event and it shows the previously loaded grid system and hides the add-contact component.

```
/// cancel adding new contact
void cancel() {
  (this.parentNode as Element).style.display = 'none';
  (this.parentNode as Element).previousElementSibling.style.display = 'block';
}
```

The save method makes a validation to force the user to at least type a name for the contact they are adding or editing. This method also builds a map with all the contact information from the form fields and determines if we're adding or editing to execute the idbContacts.add method or the idbContacts.update one, respectively.

```
/// saves changes
  void save() {

    if(fname.isEmpty) {
      info
        ..classes = ['alert', 'alert-danger']
        ..style.display = 'block'
        ..setInnerHtml('Please, type First name for the contact');
      _hide_info();
      return;
    }

    var data = {
      'fname': fname,
      'lname': lname,
      'phone': phone,
      'email': email,
      'address': address,
      'zip': zip,
      'city': city,
      'country': country
    };
    if(edit == false) {
      idbC.add(data).then((id) {
        info
        ..classes = ['alert', 'alert-success']
        ..style.display = 'block'
        ..setInnerHtml('Contact saved successfully!');
        _cleanup();
        _hide_info();
      });
    } else {
      idbC.update(item, data).then((_) {
        info
          ..classes = ['alert', 'alert-success']
          ..style.display = 'block'
          ..setInnerHtml('Contact saved successfully!');
          _hide_info();
      });
    }
  }
}
```

This file also contains two helper methods, _cleanup and _hide_info. The first one is executed after adding a new contact and it cleans the form fields, so you can add another contact easily. The second one is used to automatically hide the information message shown to the user with the result of their operation, as you can see in the Figure 30-11.

```
/// cleanup form
  void _cleanup() {
    fname = '';
    lname = '';
    phone = '';
    email = '';
    address = '';
    zip = '';
    city = '';
    country = '';
  }

  /// hide info after 4 seconds
  void _hide_info({int seconds: 4}) {
    new Timer.periodic(new Duration(seconds:seconds), (t) {
      info.style.display = 'none';
      t.cancel();
    });
  }
}
```

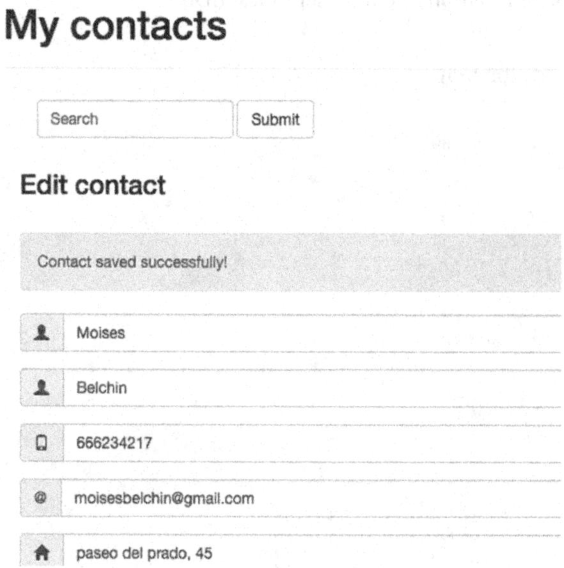

My contacts

Search		Submit

Edit contact

Contact saved successfully!

👤	Moises
👤	Belchin
☐	656234217
@	moisesbelchin@gmail.com
🏠	paseo del prado, 45

Figure 30-11. *Message displayed after saving changes to a contact*

As you can see with only three web components, none of them with more than 150 lines of code, and a simple and powerful class to perform the backend operations we've built a very strong and structured web application using modern libraries and the latest HTML technologies in a very simple way.

Summary

In this chapter we learned how to:

- Integrate different Dart functions to build a complete application

- Use the Polymer library from Dart to build all the application's interfaces

- Interoperate between different web components

- Create the HTML structure for your custom web components

- Style your components using external CSS files and the Bootstrap CSS framework

- Create controllers for your custom elements

- Use the `attached` polymer library method to perform actions after the web components are loaded into the DOM

- Use `shadowRoot` to query for the HTML element located in a shadow DOM element

- Use the power of the asynchronous programming to build the backend of our application in conjunction with other libraries

- Use lawndart pub package to store all the contact's information into browser IndexedDb database

- Use google_maps pub package to get the address location map

Index

Get the eBook for only $10!

Now you can take the weightless companion with you anywhere, anytime. Your purchase of this book entitles you to 3 electronic versions for only $10.

This Apress title will prove so indispensible that you'll want to carry it with you everywhere, which is why we are offering the eBook in 3 formats for only $10 if you have already purchased the print book.

Convenient and fully searchable, the PDF version enables you to easily find and copy code—or perform examples by quickly toggling between instructions and applications. The MOBI format is ideal for your Kindle, while the ePUB can be utilized on a variety of mobile devices.

Go to www.apress.com/promo/tendollars to purchase your companion eBook.

Printed in the United States
By Bookmasters